THE DARKNESS AND THE LIGHT

THE DARKNESS AND THE LIGHT

A Philosopher Reflects Upon His Fortunate Career and Those Who Made It Possible

Charles Hartshorne

State University of New York Press

Published by
State University of New York Press, Albany

For information, address State University of New York
Press, State University Plaza, Albany, NY 12246

Library of Congress Cataloging in Publication Data

Hartshorne, Charles, 1897-
    The darkness and the light : a philosopher reflects upon his
fortunate career and those who made it possible / Charles
Hartshorne.
        p.   cm.
    ISBN 0-7914-0337-8. — ISBN 0-7914-0338-6 (pbk.)
    1. Hartshorne, Charles, 1897-   . 2. Philosophers—United States-
-Biography.   I. Title.
B945.H354A3   1990
191—dc20   89-29354
[B]   CIP

10   9   8   7   6   5   4   3   2   1

Dedication

To those teachers of my infancy, childhood, or youth who, though they cannot read this book, helped to make it possible: Francis Cope and Marguerite Hartshorne, affectionate and wise parents; Aunt Amy Hartshorne, substitute mother in my second year; Grandfather Charles Hartshorne, substitute father in the same period; Frederic Gardiner, founder of and science teacher in Yeates, a short-lived but superb precollege boarding school; Rufus Jones, Haverford scholar in mysticism and the first professional philosopher the already philosophizing young Charles encountered; several nurses who were his ranking superiors in an army base hospital and whose character and disciplined minds helped him to escape the superstition of innate male superiority; Harvard teachers in philosophy or psychology, James Haughton Woods, W. E. Hocking, C. I. Lewis, H. M. Sheffer, R. B. Perry, and Leonard Troland, who together prepared him to deal critically with Husserl and Heidegger in Germany and with Peirce and Whitehead when he encountered them on returning to Harvard (even Peirce was almost physically present in a vivid dream). To all of these, any readers who like this book have reason to be grateful. If I do not name any public school teachers through the eighth grade, it is because no such names survive in my memory. My present feelings about them are positive but vague and do not clearly individualize any. There was one of several mother's helpers our family had whose name, Miss Shedlock, has been retained, and when, long afterward, I visited her in her home in Brooklyn I saw that from her I would have learned little or nothing stupid, ignorant, or vicious. There too, young Charles was fortunate.

CONTENTS

LIST OF FIGURES

Preface

This is both less and more than an autobiography. It is only very roughly chronological and chiefly a mixture of memories of people with reflections on these memories. Or, it is an exercise in philosophical reliving of some personal relationships or encounters in my past. The title, I think, does describe the book—provided one stresses the words *philosopher* and *reflects*.

The first five words of the title are from a sublime but rather neglected short, unrhymed, mystical poem of Wordsworth's. It is one of the few poems of his in which the scenery is neither British nor French. Any lover of Wordsworth who does not know which poem it is has missed something in reading that poet. (See Chapter 13, 8th Section.) I might have missed it, too, had not Lascelles Abercrombie called attention to it in a lecture at the University of Chicago. It is not found in general anthologies and is in only one of the two chief selected editions (Douden's) of Wordsworth's poems. It begins "Brook and road ..."

The word *reflects* is important. Although I have written many books and a great many essays, there are topics, nevertheless, about which I wish to go on record here in a manner not appropriate to these other writings. Or, if I have discussed the topics elsewhere, it will have been in writings that very likely will not have been read by some who might be interested in the present book, which is more concrete than my other works. There is also some advantage in associating philosophical beliefs with specific life situations. Some novelists—Fielding and Tolstoy, to take two illustrious examples— have done this in their novels. The present book is not intended as fiction, but it has some of the characteristics of fiction.

The reader will find, here and there in this book, suggestions for a philosophy of life and a philosophy of religion. The religion will not be identifiable as simply one or another of the competing orthodoxies or classical religious views; but it will have recognizable relations to several of them, including Judaism, Buddhism, and some forms of Hinduism. No doubt my Episcopalian upbringing will have left its impress. The philosophy will also not be identifiable with any historical philosophical system, but will have analogies to beliefs of the American mathematician, logician, scientist, and philosopher Charles S. Peirce, the French philosopher Henri Bergson, and the Anglo-American mathematician, logician, theoretical physicist, and philosopher Alfred North Whitehead. Also, so far as my incompetence in mathematics can judge, it will be somewhat in harmony with views of the great biophysicist Prigogine, and the distinguished geneticist Sewall Wright. To this extent it is more than merely my personal whim.

Another theme of the book hints toward a theory of the selectiveness of conscious recollection: why we forget so much, and what determines the degree of completeness and accuracy of the little we can definitely recall of our past.

My former colleague, no longer alive, Thomas Vernor ("T. V.") Smith once was sitting at luncheon with me and another professor; the conversation at first took the form of a dialogue between myself and this other professor about what we found open to criticism in Smith's way of thinking. T. V. listened for a time and then said, "Anything you please, gentlemen, so long as you talk about me." The reader will not be surprised to be told (if he or she does not already know) that Smith was a successful politician as well as a popular professor. But the quoted remark without doubt expresses one of the reasons for autobiographical writing. However, I wish to write and induce talk about a number of people other than myself.

One problem in writing memoirs is to judge how far one's interest in the people one has known (including oneself) means that they will be interesting to others. Many patches of autobiographical writing seem rather dull reading; partly, I think, because the writer refers to various persons as though they were interesting but does not show you definitely and specifically what made them so. From this point of view, writing autobiographically has something in common with novel or short-story writing. It is a poor novelist who merely tells but does not show what sorts of persons his characters are. I would have liked to be a writer of fiction, as I would also have liked to be a poet;

and in this volume I make my one effort to give something of the flavor of various individuals who seemed, when I encountered them, interesting, amusing, or even inspiring. I do not hope to rival a good novelist; but I do hope to do better than some autobiographers.

One way to think of this book is as a celebration of life. In my view, life is sheer gift. Had my life been much less good than it has been, I should still, I like to think, not have regarded the universe, society, or God, as in debt to me. (Recall Stephen Crane's poem, "A man said to the universe ...") And no one, whatever he or she may *say*, is compelled to exist. Living is voluntary, the will to live is a wish to live, however little conscious as such. It is not the universe, (nor is it God) that is in debt to me because of my life; it is I who am in debt, a debt that could not be overpaid.

This book may interest not only those concerned with philosophy or religion, but also historians and others who would like to see how this century appears to one whose nature was formed before World War I, when the human future seemed to most people both secure and promising. Or, as I hope, it may appeal to some simply because they enjoy witty remarks, humorous incidents, and oddities of character, including its author's character. Or persons (perhaps sociologists) interested in the history of the institution of the family. I have tried to be candid, to avoid prettifying events or people, even myself. Therefore, this book could be called by the old-fashioned title, "Confessions." However, I spare the reader some of the least admirable of my recollected actions.

The reader should bear in mind that, except for the Epilogue, nearly all of this book was written when I was eleven or more years younger than when the book (I trust) will have been published. I have sometimes made slight changes to bring it more nearly up to date. All of the book represents maturity, (except the few poems and early letters of mine) as reflecting upon life as a whole. It seems doubtful if there has ever been a philosopher as chronologically old who had engaged in written and spoken dialogue with as many other philosophers of as many countries and cultures. I attribute this to modern medicine and hygiene, and modern means of communication and travel.

Acknowledgments

I thank *The Southern Journal of Philosopy* for permission to republish (as Chapter 13) "Recollections of Famous Philosophers and Other Important Persons" [8, no. 1 (1970); 67-82].

I also thank Rita Brock for reading much of the manuscript and making helpful suggestions. As usual, I thank my wife, Dorothy, who, in difficult circumstances, gave me the benefit of her editorial skill.

Prologue

A man said to the universe,
   Sir, I exist.
However, replied the universe,
The fact has not created in me
   A sense of obligation.

—STEPHEN CRANE

All thoughts, all passions, all delights,
   Whatever stirs this mortal frame,
All are but ministers of love,
   And feed his sacred flame . . .

He prayeth best who loveth best
   All things both great and small;
For the dear Lord who loveth us,
   He made and loveth all.

—S. T. COLERIDGE

Tumult and peace, the darkness and the light—
Were all like workings of one mind, the features
Of the same face, blossoms upon one tree,
Characters of the great Apocalypse,
The types and symbols of Eternity,
Of first, and last, and midst, and without end.

—WORDSWORTH

CHAPTER ONE

The Author
Introduces Himself

Thoughts on Memory

Concerning the bits of conversation reported from memory in most of the following chapters, usually conversations that took place several or many decades ago, I wish to affirm my confidence that they are largely faithful to what actually happened. This requires some explanation.

T. V. Smith, referred to in the Preface, called his autobiography *The Nonexistent Man*, on the ground that memory of one's past self is unreliable. Yet I, who was among his colleagues through a considerable portion of the life he chronicles, found no significant discrepancy between his recollections and mine, wherever mine were definite on the same matters. This illustrates a general point. In my experience, it is not the inaccuracy of memory (which so impresses some philosophers) that is its most notable limitation, rather it is the sheer gaps, the blank pages. Here is an example. Between the ages of perhaps six and twelve, my playmates were chiefly my four brothers and two boys living a block away, sons of a Presbyterian minister. With these two, named Henry and Joseph, I must have associated scores of times, but what do I recall? That they were reasonably acceptable playmates, that the younger, Joseph, was a bit more to my liking than the older (who I think was closer to my age); but as to what I did not completely like in Henry I have scarcely the vaguest idea. Was it that he did not treat his younger brother as well as I thought he should? I simply am not sure. And not one sentence or phrase either of the two boys ever uttered remains with me. The yard, apple tree, and barn belonging to that family I recall better than those two boys. Yet, of another playmate that I surely saw less often (he was older and lived farther away) I recall precisely a sentence (I could not have invented it) he uttered and several other rather definite things about him, including that there were no qualifications to my liking for him. We shall come to that. Are some people just more memorable than others?

The reasons for, and nature of, errors of memory are often misunderstood. Immediately after any experience (within a few seconds, or even fractions of a second) one is still rather vividly, distinctly, and correctly aware of some features of the experience. This is immediate memory. Before long this awareness fades and one may never distinctly recall it. If, however, for some reason one wishes to recall it, one is likely to *fill in the gaps,* or clarify the vaguenesses, by *imaginings* of what may have been. Later still one remembers not simply the original experience but that experience *fused with the subsequent imaginings.* The imaginings were in the past as was the original experience, but in a later portion of the past. I flatly deny that there is such a thing as remembering whose entire content is created in the present. *Memory is always experience of the real past,* never a mere present imagining. But the past is a very complex business; and much of it is remembered very vaguely indeed. Hence if, as we often do, we need or desire definiteness, we are likely to eke out each reremembering of an incident with definiteness created in a later past than the one we wish to recover.

In memorizing poetry this obviously happens. I have sometimes misquoted a line from Robinson Jeffers' poetry: "The mountain ahead of the world is not forming but fixed." My version changed *fixed* to *formed.* I had preserved the idea (Jeffers was a causal determinist, as were Mark Twain, Ambrose Bierce, and Thomas Hardy) but had *amended* a too vague intuition of the final word by substituting a nearly synonymous and phonetically somewhat similar one. When I made the substitution the first time, I may even have known it to be a guess. Later, that it was a guess had been forgotten. All this does happen. It may be, too, that the poet *manqué* in me had tried to improve the line. The logic is made sharper by my change, though a phonetic contrast is lost.

There are, however, cases in which the amending process does not happen because sufficient definiteness had already come into our possession. Suppose the thing to be remembered is very striking and appealing, or shocking. One may then start to think back over it before immediate memory has faded. This dwelling on a not yet faded memory (I surmise) forms connections in the brain that make its later correct recall possible. (After writing the previous sentence I came across the same idea in a writing by Karl Popper.) The immediate storing away of memories by going over them with interest cannot take place if one interesting event after another occurs in quick succession. Thus, in attending professional meetings, one hears a succession of papers, many of them read rapidly. By the third paper one has largely forgotten the first, having been too busy with following sentences, paragraphs, or papers to do much arranging of contexts by which to recover previous sentences, paragraphs, or papers.

In sum, the accuracy of memory has little to do with how many years have elapsed since the remembered events. Rather, what happened soon afterward, how strong the interest in the event was then, and how persistent has been the interest and consequent habit of reremembering the event, largely determine the recoverability and accuracy of the recollection.

It is my conviction that philosophers in general have not dealt very well with this topic of memory. (The chief exceptions are Peirce, Bergson, and Whitehead. This alone would go far toward explaining my admiration for these three writers.) On the one hand, philosophers in general have tended to take memory for granted without wondering how it is possible and what its real structure is. Thus, Hume has a hasty paragraph on memory as knowledge of the past, but spends many pages on how we anticipate the future on the basis of knowing the past. The prior question concerns how we know the past. Kant talks much about perception, sensation, imagination, reason, and understanding, but again has very little about the wondrous capacity we have to know what has been going on in our own minds; how we have been feeling, thinking and planning, or deciding, to act.

On the other hand, philosophers have stressed the distortions of memory, its unreliability, to such an extent that it often seems we can scarcely be sure of anything at all about the past. Bertrand Russell went so far as to say that, for all we can know for certain, the world process may have had an absolute beginning five seconds ago. Between taking memory for granted and excessive distrust in its deliverances, the philosophical profession (even including Wittgenstein) is, it seems to me, in a sad muddle about one of the two obviously fundamental avenues to truth, which are perception and memory (or intuition of our own previous experiencing).

If we do not know the past through memory, what do we know at all? Even to follow a mathematical deduction, we have to be aware of what we have thought in the premises when we draw the conclusion. To make use of an observation, we have to remember what it was. Suppose we have written it down; we shall find that, to use written testimony, we have to remember the first part of a sentence as we read the last part. Unless there is a basic reliability in memory, there is no knowledge; and unless we understand this reliability, we do not understand how knowledge is possible. The three philosophers just mentioned (other than Hume or Russell) had some understanding of how we intuit the past itself (not a mere present image supposed to be evidence of the past); most philosophers by comparison seem to be in the dark about this.

Aside from any inaccuracies of memory, the incomparably greater limitation is its incompleteness. For one page or one day of my past with a clear recollectable item or two, there are scores or hundreds of blank pages; for one minute that is at all clear, there are millions that are not. I suspect that some persons have much less incomplete recall, but they, too, forget more than they remember.

The Freudian thesis that our forgetting is partly flight from troublesome aspects of the past, those we cannot recall because we have disliked them so much, doubtless has some truth, especially for some persons; but I do not find it very illuminating in my own case. I had no mean childhood playmates or cruel nurses or relatives. I do remember feeling some rebellion against my father; but it was mild, and the reasons are not hopelessly obscure. They involved some siding with Mother against Father, but I never have had a real mother fixation, having lived much away from Mother both in early childhood and in my teens. Besides, Father treated both me and

Mother reasonably well and gave me a lot of freedom to develop in my own way.

In denying a mother fixation I have in mind partly this: that when I hear or read of a man with such a fixation (e.g., as in D. H. Lawrence's *Sons and Lovers*), or of one who postpones marriage for years until his mother has died, or remains a bachelor because of his emotional attachment to his mother, or who marries an older woman so that she can be to him like his mother, I have a feeling of wonder that such things can be, no feeling of understanding them from my own inner life.

I will admit, as Darwin did, that I have a tendency to forget counterexamples and objections to beliefs I hold; and I agree with him that we need to struggle against this weakness. But most of the blanks in my past as remembered seem to come not from repression of something unpleasant but either from lack of keen enough interest in the events at the time or from lack of immediately following leisure to "store them away" in recoverable fashion.

The I and the Me

This chiefly is a book of recollections of people I have encountered. Among these people is a person called Charles Hartshorne. Does one encounter oneself? Quite so. Relations to oneself are not so different from relations to others as many suppose. Indeed, perhaps the greatest illusion of all is not to see this. Buddha and his followers saw it. The Hindus, generally, almost saw it. Unfortunately, most Western philosophers have not been able to see it. But Peirce and Whitehead saw it; and I began to see it before I knew about them or the Buddhists.

The philosophers called *linguistic analysts* seem to miss many things about language. One of them is that, whereas one can say, "I love me" or "I love myself" or "I am aware of myself," one cannot say "I am aware of I" or "I love I." Is this a merely grammatical point, or is it one of those ways in which grammar is more than merely that? If self-love is sheer identity, then "I love I" cannot be wrong simply because it treats an "object" as a "subject." For, if the referent in both cases of "I" is identical, the first referent, the subject, must be the same as the second referent, and then neither can be object *in con-*

trast to subject. And in any case myself as a child cannot be without qualification identical with myself as an adult. Two entities so different cannot be simply one entity. And if I think about myself, surely the thinker and the thing thought about cannot be simply the same. *Self-awareness* is an easy word to form, but what it says is less easy to grasp.

My teacher W. E. Hocking had an argument against strict causal determinism that I take to be cogent. In order to think "I am fully determined by past conditions," one has to make the self that is said to be determined an object thought about, and then the I doing this thinking cannot be included. To do that would require another subject to think the determined subject. Each act of thinking is a creation, and the subject possessing it is as new as the act. For if it were not, then that subject must have been there before the act. But, as before the act, the subject lacked that particular thought, which has just been thought for the first time in all history.

These arguments will probably not convince those who do not, on still other grounds, see the point. There are such other grounds.

Because, while one is alive and conscious, there is always one self that is not yet object, to have oneself as object is either to remember one's past self or selves, and thereby objectify them, or to make the abstraction: what all one's experiences, each with its own selfhood, have in common. In either case the actual self doing the thinking is neither those past selves nor the abstraction. What in the West is often meant by *self-identity*, taken as though it were sheer identity, is nothing but the confusion just set forth. Few releases from a 'mental cramp' are more joyful and liberating than to see through this confusion. (See Chapter 6.)

To be objective about oneself is partly possible and partly impossible. It is possible because one's past selves are indeed all objects for the latest or present self. It is also impossible (for one reason) because only for a still later self can the erstwhile latest self be an object. Other people also are fully objective only when their lives have reached their terminus. Every time we think that we have taken the measure of another still living person, there is in that person a slightly new self whose measure we have not taken. Part of the truth in the saying that God cannot be objectified is that the imperishable God can never be wholly in the past, in the sense in which deceased persons are.

The foregoing analysis is one of many ways in which self-relation and relation to others are analogous. This would be unintelligible if the one relation were sheer identity and the other sheer nonidentity.

Why is it that physics has come to say what Buddhists said long ago and Whitehead said more than fifty years ago, namely, that the cosmos consists of "events not things?" Self-relation for a physicist is one sort of relation of events to *other* events. In the last analysis all relation is other-relation. Only by abstraction, treating many events as one thing or person, disregarding their differences and plurality, can one view the matter otherwise. The physicists did not come to their insight by studying Buddhism; and the Buddhists had a very primitive version of physics. In both cases what happened was that careful thinking about well-defined problems cleared away the confusions I have been criticizing.

There is one clear difference between self-knowledge and knowledge of others. To know one's own past selves after infancy and early childhood one has two basic resources *only one* of which is available in knowledge of the past selves of other persons. Myself as infant or very small child can be definitely known to me now only through the testimony of others, or by photographs, written records, and the like. Such objective evidence can be had equally of the infant selves of other persons. In contrast, my past self as child of five (or possibly three or four), still more as a child of eight, ten, or twelve, can be known both by objective evidence and also (in increasing degree) by direct memory. We do not in the same sense remember the past selves of other persons. What we remember is our past seeing of their bodies or hearing their voices. We can, similarly remember our past hearing of our own voices or seeing of our own hands or legs. But we cannot recall the past of another "from the inside" as it were; rather, we recall the others only as objects seen or heard from outside. We remember the visible or audible expressions of the feelings of others, not their very feelings themselves. The memory is via our past perceptions. Thus, a portion of self-knowledge is one degree *more direct* than other-knowledge. But this direct knowledge would be extremely inadequate and precarious if not checked and extended by testimony of others and still existing perceptible evidences (including echoes, tape recordings, phonograph records, or videotapes).

An example of the awareness of past selfhood is the following. Across the river from my childhood home in Kittanning, Pennsylvania, is or was a steep wooded hillside with a road winding up it. Somewhere partly up this hill and accessible but not conspicuous from the road or any nearby house was a long rope swing hung from a tree. A child discovered this swing and on at least one enjoyable occasion swung on it for quite a while. From the swing one looked out over the river. Who had made the swing, and for what child to swing on, the child did not know. But he enjoyed the swing as his own secret. I remember *being* that child. I do not remember being the swing or any other child. This memory of *being* something is what is unique in self-knowledge.

There is a further distinction. My memory of that swinging is "recollection," which means, remembering after intervening forgetting. But suppose one pronounces a long word like *onomatopoetic*. In pronouncing the final syllable one has not yet totally forgotten the first syllable. This is simple memory. Recollection is vastly more complicated. The remembering of the same incident may have occurred many times, each time separated from the next by forgetting, by total lapse of conscious recall.

Remembering *before* forgetting has had time to occur is what is sometimes called *introspection,* as though this were a third something over and above both memory and perception (in the ordinary 'five senses' meaning). Introspection differs from simple memory only in this, that we say we introspect only when we are deliberately seeking knowledge of ourselves. As Ryle correctly says, introspection is a certain way of *using* memory, especially in its relatively simple short-run form. Much mystification about introspection is avoidable only by assimilating this concept to that of memory.

Geographical

The Pennsylvania town of Kittanning where I spent my first twelve years (1897-1909) is on the East bank of the Allegheny River some 45 miles North of Pittsburgh and is still a small town. On my bicycle I could ride out into the country to the west by crossing the river on a bridge a short block from our house (which looked out over the river) and climbing the hill on the other side. The nearest town in that direction was Walk-chalk, a mere village a few miles away. The roads were mostly simple narrow dirt roads, and cars were few. Traffic dangers were so slight that I was allowed to ride at will where I wished. We were sternly forbidden, however, to play in or close to the river (at least until we learned to swim), for fear of our drowning. We could coast with sleds in winter down either two steep, short slopes in a yard at some distance from our house or a long slope on the other side of the river. Also across the river and downstream a bit was a little valley ominously called Whiskey Hollow by most people and more descriptively and constructively "Pleasant Hollow" by Mother. Here we might go to find wild flowers or to fish feebly with bent pins for tiny swimmers in the stream. Somewhere not far from town there were chestnut trees (the blight had then not yet struck), where the small, sweet nuts could be found.

Downstream on the Kittanning side was the smaller Ford City where (perhaps) toilets are still made and bricks were made then. But we seem never to have gone there. As to the direction upstream from the town, I recall nothing whatever. Father had a folding canvas boat he used when the river flooded parts of the town.

Those were the days (before 1909, when we moved to the East) of the horse and buggy in summer, sleighs and sledges in winter. The sleigh bells deserved their fame. One can always "hear" them in memory.

After I had learned to swim, I could bicycle with other boys some miles to a lovely natural swimming pool on a rocky stream. Not that this happened often! The country was hilly: farms and woodlots.

The town was a county seat and I remember the stone courthouse. There was a story (told by my father in later years) about the building of the courthouse. The man in charge of letting the contract for the town was so fond of driving a sharp bargain that he did so even when the town, rather than he, reaped the benefit. He had the contract worded: so much to be paid "for each foot of wall *actually laid*." Normally one reckoned the footage by multiplying height and length of walls, so that windows counted too. But the contractor was told that because windows are not "actually laid," their area must be subtracted from the total. When the case came to court the contractor lost. This was said to have eliminated his profit. The joke was on the contractor; but he cannot have enjoyed it.

Another instance of sharp practice may have involved the same character. A certain man owned a foundry upon which the taxes were said to be ridiculously low because of the absurd valuation put upon it by the assessor. The owner disputed this. He was told that his property was worth at least $5000, much more than the assessed value. "Why," said he, "if you can find anyone who will offer me $5000 for this property I'll give you $1000." This was said in the presence of witnesses. So these others got together, agreed upon a promising young man in the community, asked him if he'd like to own the foundry. When he said yes, but that he had no money with which to buy it, he was told that that was no problem. They got a banker to lend the money to the young man, who came to the foundry owner and offered him $5000 for it. "Oh," said he scornfully, "don't you know that agreements to buy or sell real estate have to be in writing to be binding." "Yes," said they, "but you said in the presence of witnesses that if anyone offered you $5000 for the property you'd give him $1000. And that sort of agreement does not have to be in writing." Despite legal appeals the $1000 had to be paid.

There was another story about some "city slickers" from Pittsburgh coming to town to outsmart the yokels and getting the worst of the deal, but I forget the specifics.

In Kittanning we had telephones and electric lights, also street cars, but of course, no radio or television. We heated by gas or coal fires in every room (perhaps only on the ground floor). I was given the job of keeping the parlor stove supplied with coal from the basement. There were electric lights in the basement; but I disciplined myself to go there in the dark, I suppose to prove that I was not afraid. I was also given a job of growing vegetables (after Father showed me how to plant and nurture them) for the family. I was paid so much for the products, and this supplied me with pocket money. (I believe it was somewhat later, in our second town, that Father gave us money for good grades in school besides regular monthly allowances.) I sold some of the vegetables to neighbors also.

At first we had no automobile. But almost as far back as I can recall very much, Father had a car. There was one other car in town, owned by a good friend of Father's, and for all I know that was all. A smelly, livery stable near our house (and others less near) supplied those who needed and could afford them with horses. Most things were within walking distance; there were bicycles, and some street-cars. Father had a bicycle. He once rode it 300 miles to visit his relatives in Merion. He also rode it in Kittanning to a friend's house where there was a suitable place to park his car. I early had a bicycle. I grew up less sedentarily—I am tempted to say less lazily—than many do now. The automobile was not the primary means of getting around.

Quite an event in my life at Kittanning was encountering, who could say how, the magazine *Popular Electricity*, which later merged with *Popular Mechanics*. It had an article explaining the elementary concepts of electrical engineering: volts, watts, ohms, amperes; wiring in parallel and wiring in series. I bought a tiny motor and tried to make it run by sticking wires into an electric light socket. This blew a fuse and I was about to try again in another socket when Father caught me and, instead of scolding me as I feared, said cheerfully, "The first thing I'm going to show you is how to fix fuses." I was soon to come as close (?) to being an electrical engineer as I was ever to get. I still understand how to introduce resistance into an electrical circuit and for some years used this knowledge in my detached study to slow down an electric fan that ran faster, making more breeze and noise than desirable, and taking more energy than needed. I used one, or in parallel two, bulbs of varying wattage to determine the amount of resistance. The speed of the fan could be nicely controlled. The light bulbs giving the resistance were put outside a window so as not to add any heat to the study. From the energy point of view the scheme was near to perfection. The study was so well insulated that no further air conditioning in summer was needed.

Early in adult life I became fascinated by energy and insulation problems, not after, but long before, the oil boycott. I once made a mildly solar outdoor study, using two pieces of canvas, one black and the other white (with aluminum on the underside to reflect rather than absorb the sun's heat). It worked rather well. I also toyed with the idea of living partly underground, another idea now beginning to

Fig. 1. Grandfather Charles Hartshorne

attract the attention it deserves, as well as other ways to save energy. I can imagine myself as an inventor. I put together an electric egg boiler using less than a cup of water, hence very efficient. It is natural for me to look for new ways of dealing with old problems. If I am not doing this in philosophy, I tend to try to do it in other contexts. Mere routine is the hard way for me to live. Although I have used fairly extensive notes in class work I have scarcely bothered with the notes of previous years, if I could even find them. Probably, I would have been a better teacher had I routinized my course work somewhat more than I did.

Kittanning was not an industrial town, and wealthy inhabitants were scarce, nor was I aware of any there. The population was described as Scotch-Irish, Stephen Leacock, the humorous writer makes the Canadian town in which he grew up seem a good deal like Kittanning. Perhaps the people were Scotch-Irish! Father's first arrival from his parish in eastern Pennsylvania was spectacular, and his western Pennsylvanian congregation is said to have taken a long time to fully recover from it, if they ever did. Grandfather Charles Hartshorne did not believe in giving his grown-up sons very much money while he was still alive; but he was willing to use his high position in two railroads to help his son Francis move to his second parish.

Thus, it came about that Father, with his wife, daughter, considerable furniture and the like, arrived at the Kittanning station in a private R. R. car. The effect on the reception committee can be imagined. Yet this new and apparently rich minister was to live, until his father died, on a small ministerial salary plus inherited income of perhaps $15,000. I have almost no recollection of the economies in living this made necessary (there were ten persons in the house), beyond this; I was once rebuked for eating too much butter, and was told that it was expensive. This is perhaps the nearest I ever came to the endurance of poverty. We had a full-time cook and a mother's helper for the six children. *Poor*, we were not.

In 1909, when I was barely twelve, we moved nearly the length of Pennsylvania to Phoenixville, 28 miles from Philadelphia on the Schuylkill River. This time we lived out of sight of the river and 2-3 blocks from the bridge. Again, too, we were in rolling country, now east of the Appalachian Mountains instead of west of them. Again, there was a swimming pool in the country; but this time within easy riding or even walking distance, and we used this pool a good deal. It was a dam rather than a natural hole in a stream bed. A covered bridge was just below the dam. The population of the town was two-and-one-half times as large as that of my birthplace; and the nearest big city was now a good deal nearer.

Until I was twelve I did not really know what a city was. We had not been in the habit of going to Pittsburgh to shop. Rather, there was a professional shopper who came to our house, took down a list of things we wanted him to buy for us in the city stores, and—doubtless for a consideration—did so. I remember how, at the end of the consultation, he rattled off the list of errands he was to do, using initials for the various stores.

The boarding-school I attended in 1911-1915 was 40 miles west of Phoenixville, near Lancaster, in the very rich farming country owned chiefly by Mennonites, Amish, or Pennsylvania Dutch. On holidays, I usually went home by train, having to change once. Eagles Mere, our beautiful summer resort, was in Sullivan County, Northeastern

Pennsylvania. It was a two-day car ride in those days. There was then a narrow gauge R. R. from Sonestown and part of the family went that way. Our maternal and paternal relatives mostly lived nearer Philadelphia than Phoenixville was— in Merion, Haverford, Bryn Mawr, or Paoli— all within easy bicycling distance from Phoenixville.

The class structure of Phoenixville, then with 10,000 people, is of some interest. The one big industry, a steel mill that had been there since the eighteenth century, was owned by a family named Reeves. Its president was David Reeves, but the vice-president, William Reeves, was the one we had dealings with because of his interest in our church. The estate of these brothers was a hundred yards from our rectory, but across a wide street and with the several houses largely hidden in trees. It was a little community apart, with its own private bridge across the Reading Railroad so that members of the Reeves family could take a train to Philadelphia without mixing with the proletariat. They had their own grass tennis court, vegetable and flower garden, and much else besides. At the opposite end of town was another branch of the Reeves family with a less luxurious estate.

Altogether, I grew up definitely a Pennsylvanian (including a partly Quaker background) with a somewhat comprehensive experience of the state. The only state I know better is one I have lived in only for short (though numerous) periods of time—California. I have driven, been driven, or ridden a bicycle, over nearly all chief parts of that spectacular Western state, from north to South and from east to west.

In maturity I have been in almost every state of my own country and most major parts of the world except the Soviet Union and the People's Republic of China. In contrast to most traveled persons, I know the birds of the regions visited better than the people (do). (The ambiguity is largely true both ways.)

My German is pretty good, my French is not too bad; I know a little Italian and Spanish, and some words of Japanese. As was said of Shakespeare, I have "a little Latin and less Greek." Nearly 10 percent of my life since childhod has been lived outside my own country, mostly in France, Germany, Belgium, Australia, India, Japan, and Latin America. Two years of this were in the army in France, two (mostly in Germany) as a postdoctoral student; the rest involved three

Fulbright grants to lecture abroad, two other paid lectureships abroad (Germany and Belgium) or were personally financed trips. Usually, but not always, there was a professional reason – or excuse – for the travel, such as an international philosophical (or ornithological) meeting.

More Personal than Modest

Modesty is one virtue about which boasting is logically contradictory. (Peirce speaks of himself when young as having an attitude to be partly expressed as follows: "Above all I yield to no one in my ineffable modesty!") But I may perhaps state as a fact that in the company of mathematicians, physicists, high-powered geneticists, and symbolic logicians I feel abashed by my failure to get far in the use of advanced mathematics to express and understand ideas. It is not from prejudice, or even innate disability, but from a sort of laziness, or failure to set aside time and make the effort. What mathematics I did study was never difficult for me. There is another group of people in whose company I feel abashed: musicians. The western musical scale seems to me as obscure as advanced mathematics. A "stupid musician" is to me a contradiction in terms. But I married a well-trained musician; so here, too, my limitation is not a matter of prejudice.

A third form of modesty in my case is that I hesitate to criticize administrators and politicians; for I know that what they do I could not do. Their problems are to me insoluble: so I hesitate to condemn their solutions. If it were not a civic duty, I would scarcely try to judge political issues. Most metaphysical puzzles seem to me easy by comparison. Apart from the foregoing qualifications, I may be a sufficiently conceited – and opinionated – fellow.

A clever colleague says that everyone is either (more or less) paranoid or schizoid. As paranoia clearly is not my trouble, the dichotomy leaves me scant choice as to my classification. And in fact the only official psychiatric verdict that I have been the subject of (after only a single consultation) and which my sister Frances told me about many years later, was as follows: "I'm not sure. He's either schizophrenic or a genius." The reader does not need to be told which horn of this dilemma I have preferred to embrace. The fact is that from early youth I took for granted that I was marked out for something special. For some years I was to be a great poet. When I entered the army medical corps, in which I was exposed to far less than the normal soldierly danger (once we had crossed the submarine-infested Atlantic), I thought of the possibility of being killed, not as my own dreadful loss (I think I had probably already accepted Shaw's "it doesn't hurt a man to kill him") but as the world's loss. What the world would lose was not wholly clear, as the poetic ambition, though still there, was growing less firm. A sophisticated fellow soldier, whom I first knew as an older student at Haverford College, said something like the following: "You are clearly preparing for something important. I don't know what it is, but I find your sense of mission appealing." Some of my Harvard teachers, and also Edmund Husserl, later expressed somewhat similar impressions.

A maternal Aunt Augustine, a rather opinionated lady, sensing some presumption on my part, once informed me, "You are not a genius." I don't recall that the *word genius* had become any favorite of mine in this application—for one thing it has always seemed to me a word with only a vague meaning, or one admitting of many gradations—but I was not impressed with Aunt Augustine's equipment for judging the matter at that early stage.

Another aunt, Father's sister Nanna, surprised me by saying, while I was still a student, "I suppose you all agree that your (two-years younger) brother Richard is the most promising of you five boys, isn't that so?" I do not recall my reply but am sure that it implied no acceptance of the, at best, second place I was asked to allot to myself. I had a high opinion of Richard, now a famous geographer, and no doubt of his future success. But it would not have occurred to me then to set mediocre limits to my own future achievements. My aunt was right in this, however, that prediction of Richard's kind of fame was easier than prediction of mine (such as it is).

Aunt Nanna told me about an instance in which she had been the one to be put down. She married in succession two early Ethical Culture Society preachers, Walter Sheldon (who, shortly after, died) and Percival Chubb. Another leader in that society, named Newman, was, as she thought, a friend. Once he asked her to do something or other for the society which did not strike her as a flattering proposal.

"I will put my pride in my pocket and do it," she told him. "I hope you have a large pocket" was his to her rather crushing reply.

A delightful former Haverford classmate, Evan Phillips, some years after our college days, invited me to go sailing with him (which I did), saying that when we were together at Haverford, "I almost despaired of your ever having enough common sense. But then you had so much uncommon sense."

One result of special ability is the tendency of some in one's environment to illustrate the saying of the wise psychiatrist Harry Stack Sullivan: "There are people whose attitude seems to be, 'If I cannot be great, by God there shall be no greatness!' " A minor example of this: in my Haverford class was an irritating man, with surely no great special ability at all (he was a budding chemist and doubtless made a good living), whose only contribution to my existence was a vein of petty teasing. After an interval of many years I encountered him at a class reunion. Immediately he began his same procedure of reducing me to size—his size or smaller, showing how little life had taught him. How could it teach him, when the only excellence he was willing or able to recognize was that little to which he could himself lay claim?

Fortunately, many are delighted that there is greatness to which they make no claim at all. And *we are all in a position to share this delight*. For none of us is great save in some quite limited respects. There always are abilities and excellences we grievously lack. Therefore, what Rebecca West spoke of (in writing to the superb Danish writer Isak Dinesen about her book *Out of Africa*) as the "peace of knowing my superior" can come to all of us.

Persons of exceptional ability are bound to be tempted to overestimate themselves and underestimate their fellows. Charles Peirce, who was accused of conceit himself, said that he had seen many clever young men ruined by conceit. Such persons can best save themselves by opening their minds to the vastness of human potentialities, and the immensity of the universe. As Newton had it, at best we learn about only a few shells we have picked up on the cosmic beach. A. J. Ayer, author of *Logic, Truth, and Language*, is reported to have said, "My greatest misfortune was that my first book was such a success." A wise saying. And I leave it at that, except to add that I have been saved any similar misfortune. My first book got perhaps less notice at the time than David Hume's, which, according to him, was a catastrophic failure. And I believe that, as Hume's first book deserved more notice than it got, so did mine. But I was stimulated by the lack of much acclaim to try harder and explore other fields of thought.

By contrast with that Haverford classmate who annoyed me (I withhold his name) was a young woman, Dorothy Demos (later Dorothy Lee) who has since become an admirable writer in anthropology, but who, when I first met her, teased me as somehow naïve in personal relations (I forget just what her point was). Yet when I came to know her as a married woman, she judged her former behavior to me more severely than I had done. Indeed I didn't mind it at all. She was a person whom life had taught much. Her husband, an able philosopher, died prematurely.

I will now relate an instance in which I was the one who needed to learn. It is also an example of the reliability that memory is capable of after many years. At the age of twenty-seven or -eight, when traveling with my Aunt Amy and her lady companion (more of them later), I partly amused and partly shocked the two ladies by vehemently accusing them of inconsistency because they enjoyed the music of Beethoven and other German composers and yet expressed contempt for Germans because of their behavior in the First World War. (I had spent many months in Germany of the mid-twenties, exposed to plenty of German propaganda.) Many years later, the three of us were together again, and we fell to talking about the incident. It turned out that we agreed perfectly as to my behavior on this occasion, including the approximate sentence in which I had expressed my point. We also agreed as to the absurdity of that behavior. I had outgrown a certain immaturity and temporary lack of balance. The reason we three all remembered the incident so well was that it was the kind of thing one dwells on after it happens and thus fixes in the permanent accessible memory; also we were sufficiently at leisure in the following moments to do this, nothing else of importance having quickly followed.

Still another instance of accurate memory, as shown by agreement with others, is the following. I roomed for seven months at

Haverford College with William Henry Chamberlin, later a distinguished journalist. After our seven months as roommates, I did not see Chamberlin for many years. When I did, we reminisced about events at Haverford, especially some dramatic ones involving a man named Dunn (Zeke). We had no disagreement as to what had occurred. Here again, it was the sort of affair each stage of which one would want to go over and over right after it occurred, if there was time to do so. And there was. Perhaps there are people who seldom store things away in memory without mixing them with imagined elaborations and distortions. If so, I doubt that I am one of them. Rather, I have a sea of dense fog, out of which a few and (I claim) fairly accurately defined isolated peaks lift their heads. To return to the question of special ability and how it is responded to by others. Professors, who presumably have some of such ability, are proverbially termed *absentminded*. My relatives gave me this reputation in my youth. I suspect that I have somewhat more of it than most of my colleagues, but not as much more as one would think from the stories about me. In the fifty-three years in which I taught classes I forgot to show up for class four times. Four too many, still only once per thirteen years. In hundreds of lectures as a visitor in other institutions in forty-five states and a good many countries, I once turned up a day late. But this was because I had misunderstood a voice at the other end of an inefficient telephone line in India as to the scheduled date. I also never failed to show up with the appropriate manuscript, when I had, as I nearly always did, written the speech. Once I did start with the wrong one of two manuscripts, but I had the other with me and shifted quickly on being told the mistake.

Do not tell me that I have forgotten how many such mistakes have occurred. These are not the kind of things I could forget. My most-often recurrent nightmare, near the end of a vacation as school time approached, has been that I was wandering about the campus a few minutes before the first meeting of a class with no idea where the class was to meet. In waking life this never happened.

A few of the stories that came back to me did happen. I did dismiss a two-hour seminar once at the end of the first hour but returned on remembering, at the bottom of the stairs, what the situation was and found the students still in the room discussing the matter. Once I accepted a cigarette from a certain physicist, put it into my mouth, then snatched it out again and said, "But, I don't smoke." The explanation, however, makes sense. I did for some twenty years smoke slightly, off and on, never a lot, but some months prior to the incident in question, I had decided once for all to give up smoking. I had had no appreciable addiction and felt no special trouble carrying out this decision. Momentarily, I had forgotten it, and anyway, talking with a physicist of competence I had my mind on something more interesting than my relation to tobacco. It seems possible that this story caused someone to invent the absurd, and for me not possible aberation, of forgetting that I had a daughter, my relation to whom was anything but a minor fact of my life. As someone has said, "Getting married is an adventure, having a child is a revolution." In our case it was doubly, trebly so. It followed a tragic miscarriage, giving up any idea of having a child, and then, after many anxious, careful months of a doctor-encouraged pregnancy, having a child who from birth was admired as few children, comparatively speaking, have been, and particularly by the father in the case.

The reader will understand me if I now say that I feel quite safe in viewing, as a classic example of how untrue legends arise, the story, as it reached me, that I forgot I had a daughter. In fact, I was, and still am, far closer to my daughter, more aware of her, than most fathers are of their children. I take such vagaries as indirect compliments.

Oddly enough, I have been accused repeatedly of "liking everyone." The reader will already have learned, and will learn more fully later, that this is not true. What is true is that those I have disliked are a small minority.

I have disliked a few, a very few, of the philosophers I have met. Nicolai Hartman was one—vain, pompous, humorless, cold, was my impression of him. (I heard many of his lectures, and not all that creative either.) Heidegger I did not exactly dislike; but for me he had no great appeal. I am speaking of a time long before his ghastly Nazi period.

His scorn for other philosophers, unless they lived long ago, and his lack of any convincing ethics bothered me. I respect mystics— and Heidegger has recognized his affinity for Zen—but not if the mystics lack what most mystics have had, a long discipline in, and commitment to a profound ethical tradition. I met and liked Harold Joachim (whose philosophy, however, was for me perverse); also Samuel Alexander, perhaps somewhat more congenial philosophically; but I did not much like G. E. Moore, after seeing him in action twice. I do not claim to have really known him. On the basis of one encounter I rather disliked Pritchard, but, again, did not know him. I definitely disliked Joad; but he was simply unimportant. John Dewey struck me as noble and in many ways wise, though his responses to critics in the Schilpp volume seem somewhat peevish. By contrast, my former teacher C. I. Lewis's responses in the same series are models of generosity and humor. I did indeed like him.

Husserl was acceptable as a person, but with rather obvious defects. Ryle told me that he found Husserl simply "without *any*" sense of humor. In a fair number of encounters with the founder of phenomenology, I recall no humor to speak of. I do not think this a superficial complaint. I think it went with a grim determination to exaggerate the importance of his special way of philosophy. There was something of this in the positivist Carnap, though a bit less — not, however, in Neurath or Feigl. Husserl said to me, "What we need is young men with the courage to take themselves seriously." That courage he had. He also liked to speak of his "honest work." Yes, he did a lot of it (as I have done). But I never felt in him such a wealth of creative insight as I feel in reading Peirce, Bergson, or Whitehead, or in talking to the last-mentioned. I did find Husserl's writing eloquent in its earnest way, but it shed for me no great light.

I did like well enough all my teachers at Harvard in various subjects, including psychology, English literature, and biology. Nor did I really dislike any, and I admired several, of my teachers at Haverford during my two years of study there. At the boarding-school I attended for four years, I disliked one pupil, and actually had a fist fight with him (the only one in my life) but I liked all the teachers, save perhaps for one dour, colorless German. Also, though without, therefore, disliking him, I resented the petty tyranny of the French teacher, an Englishman, who prevented me from eating the legs of the frog I had caught and the chef had cooked for me, by saying to the waiter, "Take that horrid thing away!" But this was just an English provincial being himself. I submit that this happens also in philosophy, though usually with greater subtlety. I am thinking of Moore and Pritchard, among others.

I could perhaps be said to have a love-hate relation to the English tradition. On the one hand, I can scarcely imagine life without the background furnished by the stretch of English literature, at least from Shakespeare to Trollope. Two examples: Thomas Love Peacock and Bernard Shaw (Irish, to be sure). The civilized, grammatical language of British radio and television announcers is a welcome contrast to the language we otherwise often hear in this country (*fortuitous* when *fortunate* is meant, *lay* when *lie* is meant)—but why go on? Yet, on the other hand, British philosophy, from Occam and Hume to Moore, Russell, and Wittgenstein seems to me a pitifully one-sided and limited affair. Ortega-y-Gassett said of British empiricism: "not a philosophy, but a series of very astute objections to all philosophy." Yet, British culture and academic life produced the greatest speculative mind of this century, Whitehead—produced him, then largely ignored him. Ah, well.

Why are English philosophical writers so influential? In considerable degree it is because they are so much at home in the English language. Whatever they have to say (and it often is not a great deal) is said so deftly, with such serene confidence, and with such a sense of team play with other English writers, that many Americans feel it must be true. This—or so I fancy—is the old British secret that once helped give England such political power. It lingers on in philosophy.

A German refugee professor said of Ryle, "He bullies his reader." True enough! But how skillfully and neatly he does it. So all the world, at least the English-speaking world, took him seriously right away. Yet my one-time colleague Arthur Murphy, who was not so easily bullied, said of *The Concept of Mind*, "It leaves the problem of mind and body about where it was." Naturally, this too, was not the whole truth. But it was, I think, nearer to true than the notion that, thanks to Ryle, we now know how a mind is related to its body.

Among the persons I had the chance, when they were alive, to like or dislike in direct encounter was Bertrand Russell. Did I like him? I cannot give a simple answer. He was witty, of course a great logician, and an almost unbelievably gifted and versatile person. Moreover, there was a noble passion for justice and freedom. And yet, at least in his last years, this passion was tarnished, it seems to me, by an element of personal resentment for the way certain Americans in official positions had treated him. As for his love life, there are various feelings one may have about that. Among them I would not find admiration the most suitable. Nor did I sense much warmth in the man. Or much humor, as distinct from wit. A young woman I thought well of had lunch, together with her husband, with Russell. Her impression: "I felt that he was an evil old man." This, of course, was one-sided. I add one thing: Russell in his first marriage acquired a mother-in-law I should not like to have had to deal with. This was an immense piece of bad luck for which I would not hold Russell to blame. But I suspect it had important effects in all his later life. His first wife, by her own declaration, never ceased to love him. But that mother-in-law! (I am trusting Russell's account of her. But he could not have invented so objectionable a character.) And she was a Quaker to boot, as were some of my own paternal relatives. I had not known such a combination was possible.

A. N. Whitehead was liked by almost everyone who encountered him, so that I acquire no distinction by saying that I shared in this feeling. He combined greatness and beauty of character in rare degree. As his wife once said with quiet satisfaction, his abilities never seemed to take the form of vanity. After giving a lecture he would come home and say to Mrs. Whitehead, "It came off well. Wasn't that lucky?"

True enough, Whitehead was no orator, and doubtless knew this. But in general he was as objective about his truly extraordinary abilities as so gifted a person could well be. He was also warm and humorous, and not without a touch of wit, as shown in his numerous neat epigrams; for example, "Seek simplicity—and distrust it."

Because I was harsh earlier about Russell, let me recall an incident in which he appeared favorably enough. A notoriously obscure graduate student at Harvard was present in a group with which Russell met for informal discussion. The said student began one of his unintelligible perorations. Russell listened a bit, then asked him to start over again as he, Russell, had not understood the question. The student tried again. Still none of us knew what he intended. It was embarassing. Said Russell, "I can't get the hang of it." So we all relaxed and someone else had a chance to query the great man.

Although a few German professors I have met seemed to me pompous and pretentious, I met one who gave as vivid an impression of really angelic character as any person whatever. This was Heinrich Scholz. I visited him in Münster 1949. He knew that I was editor of the works of Peirce, which he proudly showed me on his shelves, and which as a logician he had some need to have. I suppose he knew something, but not much I think, about my writings. He greeted me as though I were the prodigal son. Such warmth and goodness as streamed from that man! He had been a theologian before turning to logic, a change which, he told me, was for the sake of theology. "I saw that we could make no further progress in theology until we had a better logic." Scholz also told me that he had virtually no stomach, because of an operation (an ulcer I suppose) and that he had to eat a very special diet which his wife, whom he described as an angel (and I could see he had reason to do so), prepared for him at every meal.

It was a delight to encounter in the writings of Karl Barth, who ought to know, the statement that, whereas certain theologians, when they wrote about Christian love ("agape"), did not make one feel what they were writing about, Scholz did make one feel this. Here is a good example of the possibility of intuitive knowledge. I knew two of the persons Barth was writing about, and we had exactly the same impressions of them.

Another German professor always seemed to me not far from an angel. The Nazi bullies drove him from his classes. This was Richard Kroner, a refugee first from Germany, then from Italy. I first knew him in 1924 in Germany. He heard me give a talk in Austin, Texas, in 1961, and after it was over, he was the first to put a question, remarking "I asked you the same question twenty years ago." I had no recollection of this other occasion and now have none of the question, but I answered it as best I could, whereupon he said, in his gentle sweet voice, "That's a better answer than you gave twenty years ago." "That's very encouraging," I replied.

If "you like everybody," addressed to me, means, "you don't bitterly hate anyone" then I may be guilty of the charge, provided *anyone* means any person I have personally known. But then I have led a sheltered life. Mussolini's one-time mistress said of him, "he was the most despicable man I have ever known." I trust her to have known what she was talking about. But then Mussolini, like Hitler and Stalin, were not among my acquaintances.

In the first town in which my life was spent I recall no one I definitely disliked, simply no one, except—an odd thing—that there is in me an extremely vague sense that in that town was a boy who seemed to me a bully and about whom I felt in something of a moral dilemma. Would I have to fight him, ought I to fight him? But nothing whatever about the boy is definite for me now, not his looks, not a single circumstance in which I encountered him, except that I feel fairly sure it was in the public school we attended. About one definite bully (at boarding school) the reader has already learned. What an inestimable blessing, to go all through childhood (to the age of fourteen) without encountering a single person memorable as hateful, or even egregiously unpleasant or annoying. I do recall a distant relative who went about in shabby neglected clothes and looked unhappy. He was said to be troubled by the conviction that he had committed "the unforgivable sin"—whatever that meant in his case. But the relationship was so distant that I don't even know the precise measure of it.

This reminds me of a delightful remark by a man whose *stepmother* was my father's sister Nanna (already mentioned). I called on this man with my daughter Emily, a child of ten. After a while Emily whispered to me, loud enough for the man (Walston Chubb) to hear: "What relation am I to this man?" Walston: "Emily, I'll tell you something very comforting: We're no relation at all."

A Frustrating but Constructive Philosophical Dream

I've had a few philosophical dreams in which, as I found on awakening, I talked rather nonsensically. I've had rather more dreams in which I philosophized, in discussing with another (sometimes identified, sometimes not), and made little or no worse or better sense than I do when awake. In two cases a dream having to do with philosophy produced, as I was waking up, some useful results. The dream I am about to relate was the more significant one of these two.

In the dream, I was attending a philosophical conference. First a speaker gave a speech about philosophy and somehow illustrated a point or two by distributing to his listeners some attractive samples of food; one, I recall, of cheesecake. Then we were all confronted with a horizontally long blackboard at which, side by side, some of us were to write down some brief but centrally important thoughts about philosophy. I picked up a piece of chalk to write my epoch-making philosophy-in-a-nutshell but—alas—no thought whatever came to me. I simply *could not think philosophically* and stood there vainly trying to force my mind or brain to deliver. Worse, I had a sense that those to the right and left of me were starting to write things; I did not see what. I was afraid that my inability was unique. In any case, it was so radically unusual for me as to constitute a crisis. But finally (and I think this was not quite while I was still dreaming but occurred as I began to waken but had not yet recognized that the crisis was not a real but only a dreamt situation), I at last hit upon a pertinent thought: "To know is to value." This was not a new idea for me. I learned, probably first from Emerson and Wordsworth, then from Plato, that concern for the Good, for value, is involved in all thought, whether we realize this or not. The idea was reconfirmed by reading J. E. Creighton, the Cornell idealist, whose essays I read (while studying or beginning to teach at Harvard) on the advice of Rufus Jones, my Haverford teacher (on the history of Christian doctrine) with whom I had kept in touch. For Creighton the notion of mere knowing, simply apart from feeling or appreciating, is a mythical abstraction. Concretely, knowing is always appreciative. From this thought (now more awake and aware that my frustrating experience was only a dream) I went on through some quick steps to summarize my form of metaphysics. In all thinking (or perceiving) we are aware of reality as more or less good. And what is a reality that one is aware of as good? The proper word for this is *beautiful*. Aesthetic value is that the mere contemplation of which is a good in itself. "So shines a good deed in a naughty world" (Shakespeare) shows that even ethical value, as directly given to experience, is aesthetically pleasing. Novelists and poets know this well.

What then is philosophy? (At this point I was certainly well out of the dream state.) Philosophy is the attempt to achieve forms of valuation, or principles of valuing, that are as little as possible *arbitrary, self-serving*, individually or collectively, and as little *merely regional or provincial.* They should not unduly exalt even our own animal species rather than the other forms of life on high levels; that is, mammals, especially primates and whales or dolphins. Our view should be at least planetary and admit some intrinsic value, despite Kant but with virtually all Asiatic philosophers, also with Schweitzer and a fair number of Western philosophers of recent times, in all animals, and even in animal and plant cells. And the evidence *against* the idea of other inhabited planets, perhaps multitudes of them, need not be taken as anything like conclusive.

If the ideal is to transcend regional as well as individual prejudices, where can we stop the enlarging of our perspective? I say, "Not short of the cosmos itself." It is cosmic life we must, in principle, favor.

But here opens a parting of the ways. *Either* all definite concrete life and experience is localized, on the highest level merely animal, subject to birth and death, *or* there is an at least cosmic, unborn, and undying form of life and experience. Plato, the uniquely great Western philosopher, said it first: the cosmos as one is either besouled or not besouled; it either is or is not aware of itself and its members. To Plato it was obvious that a soulless cosmos is at best a poor product of superhuman creativity. All soul is self-moved; which I take to mean self-creative in that it gives the individual new qualities, not merely new locomotions. And soul is the source of all motion. Plato is explicit in denying that there is any perfection that is entirely unmoved. Here he transcends his former self (or Socrates) as in the *Republic*, Book 2. Even the perfect can change, though only in a certain supremely excellent way.

I now put a question: do we not all take for granted that our bodily cells are there primarily for our sakes and not simply for theirs? Do we not have to live by this conviction? Well, is the entire cosmos merely there for your sake and mine, or even merely for our animal species? How conceited can we be? If our multitudinous lives add up to something important, in what concrete reality does this addition occur? You cannot, I cannot, embrace in our own enjoyment all human enjoyment. The sum of human enjoyments is not an enjoyment of any of us. In us is only the feeblest faint surmise of this sum. Coming back to our bodily cells, what is their relation to us like?

Why not say, as a disciple of Freud I once talked to in Germany said, that we are to God somewhat as our cells are to us. Francis Bacon said that he would rather believe in all the superstitions he knew about than that "this universal frame is without a mind." And if reality is to be self-explanatory, the cosmic soul must be unborn and undying.

If we don't know what mind is, we don't *know that we know* anything. And the scientific structures science attributes to matter have yet to be proved incompatible with the Leibnizian-Whiteheadian, also Peircean and Bergsonian, conception that physical phenomena as we have them are simpiy our way of experiencing the most widely distributed low-level forms of mind. They are sentient but not much more. They feel but cannot think or know that and how or what they feel. An infant is between normal adults and single cells; a normal child of two or three is between infant and adult. In the reverse direction, from cells to molecules or atoms, is another large step toward the least forms of life or sentience, or what Whitehead calls trivial "puffs" of feeling. Whitehead speaks of nature as an "ocean of feelings." I have yet to be told how anyone knows that this psychicalist theory is false. It has the intellectual advantage of enabling us to avoid the monstrosities of a mere dualism or of a reductive materialism.

The strength of materialism is the weakness of a mere dualism; but that weakness also is the strength of psychical monism, together with the extreme weakness of reductive materialism. The trouble with the emergence of mind from mindless matter is not simply that it cannot then give a reasonable account of the togetherness of mind and the body. It is further that there is no non-question-begging criterion of mindlessness. There is indeed a valid criterion for the application of the proposition that some physical objects do not feel. It is inertness. Trees do not feel; for they do not move themselves. Their active constituents do move themselves, in growth and other processes. Stones do not move themselves; but their molecules do. The cells or molecules act, and that *is* the growth, or other processes, in the tree or the stone. What does not act as one does not feel as one. The fact that in animals the entire animal moves as one is to be viewed in combination with the introspective fact that the human animal feels as one. And we know the physiological explanation of this second fact: that the nervous system by its subtle interconnections can, except in dreamless sleep, so unify neurone activities as to furnish the human type of awareness with its appropriate field of data. A blow on the head may destroy the required unity, which explains our loss of consciousness. Similarly with epilepsy.

On the psychical view, when we feel pain, it is because there is something like pain in injured cells, and our essential mind-body relation is that we feel the radically subhuman feelings in the neurones, feel these feelings, with the *indistinctness* that distinguishes all direct intuitions (or Whiteheadian prehensions) other than those attributed to God. The mind-body relation is one of the innate forms of *sympathy* by which the world hangs together. If this is not the truth, then what is? I see only reductive materialism, which, as Peirce said, "leaves the world as unintelligible as it finds it." It cannot tell us what *positive* character makes matter mind*less* in cases in which it is said to be mindless; whereas psychicalism can tell us very well why the mind has spatial and temporal relationships, including those discovered by science. Compared to us, atoms are *relatively* mindless. And, as for stones, clouds, or trees, they are groups, aggregates, or colonies of self-active and minded singulars. Groups whose members feel need not as groups feel, except as shorthand for their members' similarities in feeling. And groups that act as unitary agents and so feel may have parts that do not. One's hand does not act or feel as single agent, except as shorthand for what the neurones and muscle cells bring about. "Fallacies of composition" and "distribution" are easy for even great minds to fall into here; but I think Peirce and Whitehead avoided them.

Relative to the subject of this section the just mentioned fallacies are the following. From the apparent inertness and unfreedom of a whole, such as a stone or a tree, one cannot (fallacy of division) deduce the inertness or unfreedom of its single parts or constituents, including invisibly small ones. This fallacy was committed by Plato and Aristotle, but not by Epicurus, who, however, should have seen that, because activity and freedom are the signs of soul or mind, the everactive and partly free atoms should not have been taken as merely material or insentient. Conversely, one cannot (fallacy of composition) from the lack of free activity in many of the apparent parts of a whole deduce the unfreedom or mindlessness of the whole — except where the whole itself is essentially a group of agents of action rather than a single agent, as in a galaxy or solar system, or even a sun or planet.

Plato, seeing that animals are single agents, in spite of their many parts, interpreted a city of many persons by a rather farfetched analogy with a single besouled animal, and then, with an immense leap of imaginative intuition, interpreted the inclusive whole, the cosmos, by a similar (and to some of us better-based) analogy raised to a higher or the highest level. What prevented him from having much success with this analogy was the complete absence of anything like a cell theory of the animal organism, or any really viable form of atomic and molecular theory. The World Soul's relation to the all-inclusive body could only be analogous to the relation of a human or animal soul to its body if the latter consisted of something like self-active cells, and these in turn were composed of self-active molecules or atoms. Only in this way could the scheme have the power Plato thought it should have. In contrast, the view of a city as a single besouled agent weakens the argument. The "group mind" in this form is a dubious metaphor.

In such ways, we at least partly explain the fact that Aristotle and the neo-Platonists either rejected or badly distorted Plato's scheme and were followed in this by all too many Middle Age and Reformation theologians. They missed the life and freedom of mind or soul as such and instead attributed becoming and change to the partial dependence of soul on matter. Plato assumed matter, but only because of his ignorance of the dynamic microstructure of nature (which the atomists assumed, though in a reductive materialistic form). What Plato and Epicurus had together, neither had by and for himself. This is where we come in.

Influenced early in my career by Emerson, Wordsworth, and Shelley, who were all more or less Platonists, I have never been able to understand how either materialism or dualism (or atheism) can make sense out of the whole of reality. My doctoral dissertation was on this subject. If no human enjoyment can sum up the totality of human and animal enjoyments, and thus constitute the public or impartial reality of this totality, neither could an unbesouled cosmos or a mediocrely besouled cosmos do so. Only a cosmic soul with unsurpassable scope and sensitiveness could suffice. Now Plato, unlike Aristotle, held that the World Soul does know the lesser souls. And he definitely does *not*, in the late dialogues, say or imply that any soul is "unmoved." Soul as such is at least "self-moved." Nor is the cosmic soul exclusively eternal or without becoming. Not Plato but neo-Platonists worshipped these negative abstractions. Much of the time "platonism" in modern talk refers to a corruption of Plato's message by Philo, Plotinus, or ...

Another principle, already implicitly involved, is what may be called the *true positivism: all truths, adequately stated, are primarily positive.* The earth is not flat, but the more complete truth is that it is approximately spherical. That I feel pain, say, is not good; however, the pain shows that I am alive, and being alive is good. Being dead is neither good nor bad for what is dead. Only dying, or being almost dead, can be an actual state of an individual. Even for others we cannot *be* dead; only our corpses can be that. Shakespeare, as often, had it right: "for no man, and for no woman, but for one that *was* a woman" had the grave been dug.

One of Popper's many excellences is that he tells us explicity that we falsify an empirical assertion, not by observing a negative fact, but only by observing a positive one. There are no *merely* negative truths (though there are some merely positive ones, the very abstract truths obtained, if we are successful, in metaphysics). We falsify "the temperature is 70 degrees" by observing some thermometer reading, or other indication, showing that the temperature is greater or less than 70. Always while awake, except when just awakened from a dreamless sleep, we have a sense of feeling our just past experiences. We also have a sense, however indistinct, of bodily processes. Occurrences, not nonoccurrences, are the data of experiences. "Something has just happened" is never false. The more definitely we try to describe what happened, the greater (other things being equal) is the likelihood of error.

To the standard fallacies of the textbooks, I add the "zero fallacy." "Zero elephants in the immediate vicinity" can be a safe assertion. In contrast, "zero life or mind" (other than one's own) is unobservable. Such an observation would have to exclude God, by definition ubiquitous, also deal with the pervasiveness of microorganisms, and in addition take into consideration that molecules and atoms are organized wholes, acting as one, and insofar like animals.

The reader now knows something of my way of thinking. What follows will to some extent explain how such a way of thinking could come to be, and what interesting other "forms of life" were encountered in the process.

CHAPTER TWO

A Sheltered Childhood

(1897-1911)

Earliest Recollections

An early memory is of being sick, and waking from a doze to see our current "mother's helper," as we called them, sitting by my bedside. Probably I had begun to convalesce because my feeling was of comfort and security. I was being looked after by a friendly presence; all was well!

Another memory is possibly ambiguous. (One hears others telling what has happened to one and later may have trouble distinguishing between remembering images produced by these tales and remembering the actual events told about.) A painter's two-wheeled hand cart was parked outside our house. One end of the cart rested on the ground, the other was up in the air. I climbed into the cart and on toward the upper end until it abruptly changed from upper to lower, spilling me head first upon the brick pavement. I think some sewing of the head wound was required. How much of this I know from direct memory of the events and how much from remembering what I was told later, I cannot say. Either way, it is the real past I am recalling (philosophers, please note), whether past perceptions of the accident, or past perceptions of hearing about the accident, is a secondary question. In one of the two ways, or in both, it is real past experiences of mine that I now vaguely recall.

I also fell, but probably I know this only or chiefly through accounts of others, out of a second-story window, landing on my head this time, too, upon a wooden cellar door, one of the, now rare, sloping

Fig. 2. Charles Hartshorne at 22 months, Holmhurst, Merion, Pennsylvania

semihorizontal kind. The slight flexibility or give of the door saved my life, as a brick or concrete sidewalk would not have. I suppose it could have been either of the two accidents just related, but most likely the second, that caused the kink in my neck bones about which I learned only decades later through X rays. It has not caused any symptoms other than, or since, the mild one that led to its discovery. What might have killed me did no significant harm.

Another early memory (of the event or only of hearing others tell about it?) is of setting fire to a dress of my sister's and throwing it out through the bathroom window. Why I did this I've no idea, unless it was merely my fascination with fire. (There was another rather horrifying instance of this.) Altogether, one may infer that my life might easily have ended not long after it began. Only a superstitious disbelief in chance, I am convinced, can prevent one from seeing that this is true of any life. So far from its being the case that "chance is only a word for our ignorance," the supposition that there is always a precise reason for what happens is itself only ignorance posing as knowledge. The closer science comes to the realities of nature, the more the exact order many have sought in nature recedes from our grasp, the more indications we uncover that there is a pervasive element of randomness in the universe. Precise laws still can be formulated and confirmed, but they are statistical, applying not to single events but to large classes of events. Taking events one by one, a reasonable view is that "disorder is as real [and pervasive] as order" (Whitehead). Until about 1878 (Cournot, Maxwell, Peirce), scarcely a single important modern philosopher or scientist suspected this. Since then, many philosophers and scientists, more from decade to decade, have become convinced of it.

The childhood diseases I definitely recall are mumps and scarlet fever. For the latter we were given calomel. Remarkably enough, neither that nor the disease killed any of us! I think, on second thought, some of us had whooping cough and measles, but this memory is less clear. Brother Richard says we all had chicken pox. The mumps I remember because mine was discovered the morning of the day for the Sunday School picnic on the river steamboat. I stayed home. The calomel no one could forget—a ghastly poison. Presumably, the bacteria didn't like it either.

I remember nothing of what was said in Sunday School classes in Kittanning, though we undoubtedly attended, and I can picture the building. But it appears that I began to listen with interest to Father's sermons in church. My twin brothers would drop off to sleep at such times; and Mother reported, years later, that my comment was, "That's what I would expect of those twins!" Years later in the army Jacques Leclerc told me I was an "academic snob." That could have been said much earlier.

A Noble Friend

When I was about eleven years old, I had a friend, somewhat older than I was, named Dick Bowers. He was a strong, thoroughly sound chap with whom I recall making one day-long bicycle trip and otherwise amusing myself. I recall teasing him to make him chase me; because, though he was stronger and faster, I prided myself on my dodging ability. When he caught me in spite of my artful dodges, he merely laughed. With even a trace of sadism, he would have been less good-natured. What he was like will be manifest from the following incident. We were walking up a long hilly road (already mentioned) pulling sleds with which we planned to coast down. A young fellow from the country—the road we used for coasting being near the edge of West Kittanning—approached us and said in a surly, threatening tone: "City slickers!" "Well," said Dick mildly, "I wouldn't be a mean one." Just that and no more. By seven syllables, with no sign of irritation or fear, my noble friend had disposed of the situation. The boorish stranger had been given no counter insult to resent, he had no reason to take Dick as less strong than himself, and had just been shown good evidence of Dick's intelligence and moral resourcefulness. There was nothing more to say.

I would like to be able to recall (but I cannot do so) having ever met an abrupt and menacing challenge in so ideal a manner as Dick Bowers did more than eighty years ago. I know nothing of his later life; but if it has not been a good and happy one this must have come from very bad luck. In him there seemed no false note, no moral weakness.

In a far easier predicament I once, decades later, did make an ideal reply to a sudden challenge. In Australia I was introduced to a

man (about whom I recall only what I am about to relate) who immediately, with a smile, said, "You know we Australians work harder
than you Americans." Why he wanted to open a conversation in that
manner I cannot say. Inspiration came to me: "You mean you *play*
harder." He laughed. We both knew to whom that round had gone.
Australian tennis was a wonder of the world, and much more could
be said to justify my remark and invalidate his.

(I have been told of a Northerner who scolded a Southern lady for
not speaking the language properly. "Then," said the lady, "I propose
that you teach me language while I teach you manners." Again the
perfect put-down, one not likely to lead to new aggression. Life would
be so much better if more of us had this art!)

Marguerite Haughton Hartshorne

A superb example of saying the right thing in difficult circumstances
was once furnished by my Mother. She had an Afro-American laundress whom she called Mrs. Smith. When she recommended the
woman to a female parishioner of our church, the other lady replied:
"Mrs. Smith? I don't know a laundress called that. Oh, you must
mean Lizzy. You know, we don't say Mr. or Mrs. with negroes. Just
first names are enough." Said Mother, in her gentle, serene voice: "I
am accustomed to calling her Mrs. Smith. I think I will continue to
call her Mrs. Smith." Here, too, the incident was closed. (Note, this
was not in the old South.) Mother was exquisitely conscientious, but
also sane, sound, and quietly self-assured—an example of "lady" in
the fullest, best, if somewhat old-fashioned, sense. She normally did
not expect to be instructed concerning her customary relationships.
On the other hand, it was not her way to defend her dignity by aggression against that of others. She also knew the ethical implications of
racism, and that the 'neighbor' whom her religion (like several others) enjoins us to love "as ourselves" is not to be identified by skin
color or anything of the sort. All these values were adequately embodied in the eighteen words that came to her. (I only know of this incident from Richard; but it is entirely in character, and I have no doubt
that it happened about as he related it.)

I confess that when confronted with racism I have sometimes
come off far less well than Mother did. I tend to turn aggressive and

intolerant against the aggressive and intolerant. This of course, is worse than futile. (I throw in here a perfect example of how *not* to meet aggression. When an armed robber—in an incident reported in the press—began taking purses from a group of seven women, one of these, according to the robber's account, spat in his face. He had not intended, he said, to shoot the women; but the utter contempt shown to him by one of them moved him to kill them all. We need not take this self-serving account at face value. But it remains valid that it is sheer folly, and ethically questionable besides, to treat one in whose power one has fallen as less than human.)

I am also reminded of an incident in a book by a missionary to China. He was captured by some bandits, and heard them discussing (in a language he understood) what to do with him. Some wanted to kill him. He began to feel afraid and decided to pray. His prayer was a classic specimen of the best kind of petitionary prayer. It asked for no miracle. And it was answered. It ran, "Oh God, if I must die let me die like a man." (The hint of male chauvinism can, I trust, be forgiven.) Immediately he felt relief from panic, and began to talk cheerfully and humorously to his captors, who soon dismissed any idea of killing him.

One may argue that this was mere autosuggestion. It was indeed autosuggestion, but—merely that? Rather, it was autosuggestion *made with a sense of the presence of divine love*, and that is not mere anything as without that sense. Prayer at its best is self-reflection of a creature aware of its supreme creative Origin and its supreme everpresent social Other. The missionary gave a perfect example of how to meet one kind of threatened aggression.

Another instance of Mother's way of meeting life's challenges is the following. My youngest brother, Alfred, brought home (to Phoenixville) from his college town, though not from his college campus, a girl in whom he thought he was seriously interested. A sorry specimen was this young person! (Her name is utterly lost.) Not that she lacked good intentions, but this was her only manifest merit. She was frightfully thin, as though starved from infancy, and seemed lacking in physical stamina. As my brother Henry remarked (out of Alfred's hearing): "If you're going to marry into the proletariat, at least you ought to get good health." There was no special charm, high degree of intelligence, or anything above mediocrity in Alfred's friend. She was a shopgirl, not outstanding as such. But she had been nice to Alfred when he patronized the shop she worked for.

What did Mother do in this somewhat threatening situation.? Was she cold or unkind to the girl? She was not that to anyone. Did she scold Alfred for his folly or wrongheadedness? Mother was not a scold. Besides, she knew well it would probably be counterproductive (without benefit from this now fashionable expression). What she did do she took me aside to relate: "I told him that marriage is a serious matter, and that it is not enough for a man to know that he is in love with the girl. He needs to know that he can remain in love with her through the years. *It's not fair to the girl,* if this is not the case." At that time (c. 1921) casual love affairs of the young were not taken as lightly as many take them now. So Alfred could make no objection to these statements. But here was a mother thinking seriously, not of what people would say, or simply of her stake in her son's marriage, or even simply of her son's stake in it; she thought also of the girl's stake. Nor is this all. "Alfred could easily," she said to me, "do something worse than marry this girl." In short, Mother had a grasp of the wide range of possibilities we face in life's decisions. Alfred married a different girl. There were troubles; but it was probably a better choice.

Once when I was fussing about a situation with a girl with whom I did not take myself to be in love and whom I did not wish to marry, but who had annoyed me or wounded my vanity, while also charming me considerably, Mother said, "Charles, life is big!" In short, don't blow up this temporary trouble beyond its proper magnitude.

I have not mentioned Mother's humor. She loved, and sometimes sang, songs of Gilbert and Sullivan, though she rarely had a chance to experience their production. A favorite quotation of hers was, "Though on pleasure she was bent, she had a frugal mind." It was she, more than her husband, who could be counted on to see the funny side of situations. An item in her diary ran, "Henry is such a comical baby." She once spoke to me in a serious vein about the importance of humor, an importance about which I have felt moved to write here and there in my books and articles.

Though Marguerite Haughton Hartshorne was an old-fashioned wife and mother of the best quality, she would not have argued against women's emancipation. She was tolerant of the mistakes of a very bright sister-in-law of her husband's, Aunt Clementine, whose behavior was not always wise, remarking, "It was a great pity that C. was not allowed by her parents to go to college." (Indeed it was.) Mother knew that she herself had made substantial sacrifices to be what she had become. She made this clear to me once in a few seconds. And she would never have wanted all women to be forced to fit the same mold.

A favorite word of Mother's was *developed*—"so and so has developed" was high praise from her. She would have seen the point of Dewey's moral imperative: (something like) choose and act so that your capacity to choose and act is increased! As T. V. Smith succinctly put it, "Be always on the grow!"

Being without college training or wide reading, Marguerite was not an intellectual. But she knew the scores in life's games. And if she ever acted notably selfishly in relation to husband, children, other relatives, or neighbors, I know nothing of it. She made friends with a Chinese laundryman in our town; and I remember some exquisite gifts from China (or San Francisco?) that he gave her. Probably to most in the town he was just a Chinaman, or what not; but to Mother no one was "just" anything. He or she was another human being toward whom one had religious duties, and whose qualities could be interesting and perhaps delightful. She drew the line at grossly selfish or rude behavior, but social status or wealth were not the point. This is my idea of the true aristocrat in the best sense. No one's status intimidated her, and no one's was beneath notice.

It should not be inferred from the preceding that I fully appreciated Mother in my youth. We had some difficulties. At times she was upset by my argumentativeness. "None of the other children ever act in this way," she once despairingly said. And she disapproved of me neglecting some college course I did not care much about and getting a low grade in it. She feared that I was becoming a lazy fellow. There were other causes of mild conflict. But I doubt that I ever thought she was essentially selfish about any issue. And I gradually came to see the remarkable wisdom she had acquired from a rather

saintly minister father, an intelligent mother, a decent basic education, a bright and loving husband, and her own struggles with difficulties and not a little suffering. She had six children in less than six
years (one pair of twins), and lost one in his early manhood.

If Mother had a fault it was in a kind of stubbornness. She would
get an idea of what should be done, and in a quiet but persistent way
keep coming back to it. I recall only one instance of this that concerned me as a youngster. She thought it important that upon arising one should throw back the bedclothes to air the bed. If I did not
do this, I heard about it. To me this seemed too trivial to merit so
much attention.

The ones of us that found this trait in Mother really troublesome
were those that remained at home, or within easy driving distance of
Mother, much later in their lives than Richard or I did. Especially
James and Alfred felt this. Richard tells a story about James and
Mother that perfectly illustrates the matter. Richard was visiting the
parental home and heard Mother asking James if he would do (I
forget what) and James said, "No." "But," began Mother, "you ought,"
etc. To Richard the thing at issue seemed so trifling that he wondered
James would persist in opposing it, considering how much it seemed
to matter to Mother. "It's all very well," said James to Richard, "for
you, who only stay here for a few days at a time, to say, 'Why not do as
Mother says, since it is such a slight concession?' But for me who
lives here it's different. I have to make a stand on something and it's
better that it be something unimportant." Richard saw the point.

Mother did once say to my wife, Dorothy, "When my children
marry and go away to live, I lose all responsibility for them." But
apparently the principle did not apply while they were still single and
living under the same roof, nor even altogether, if, as married Alfred
did, they lived within a few miles.

My one recollection of James's problem here was when as visitor
I heard Mother ask James, "Will you [I forget what] today?" "Yes" said
James to Mother. Then to me, *sotto voce* (Mother was getting deaf), "I
always do."

Another trait in Mother that somewhat troubled me was her
weakness for a form of medical faddism propagated by a certain doctor. It was a rigid diet, protein-only one meal and carbohydrates-only

another meal. This is all I remember of the regimen. Mother had absolute faith in the scheme and regarded it as scientifically authoritative. When I questioned this she replied, "Charles, you're not very scientific." So far as I could see her only claim to being scientific was that she believed what Dr. Hay told her. While following this diet, Mother developed an ulcer. She kept right on eating the salads the diet prescribed until the ulcer burst. She survived and gave the credit for her survival to Dr. Hay! Father said once that the members of Mother's family were all "the natural prey of quacks." Some of them followed Dr. Hay, and one maternal aunt followed another questionable medic. There is something pathetic and to me irritating about the dogmatic faith scientifically untrained people may acquire in some one professed authority they happen to like and find persuasive. But all this was a minor matter so far as Mother's relations to her children were concerned. It happened when they were nearly grown up; and she did get over it, I think.

Some years before her death at a great age, Mother went to a doctor about some possibly serious symptoms, remarking to me beforehand with a smile, "If it's serious, I won't have to live much longer." She of course believed in the continuation of one's personal life after death. Her education would scarcely have prepared her to grasp the meaning of "objective immortality" in the Whiteheadian sense with which I happen to be quite satisfied. If she ever had doubts about her Christian faith, she probably told them to no one. Probably they were extremely minimal or lacking—in spite of Browning's poem about the universality of doubt. If her faith was realistic, she now knows or will know its truth; if it was an illusion she will never know its falsity. By contrast, if I am wrong, I will come to know this, and if I am right, then I already know all that I ever can on the question. This is the situation in which we all stand. Belief in personal survival in the usual sense could (or so it seems) be verified; but it could not be falsified, by experience after death. Conversely, disbelief could be falsified but not verified.

I do not find a reason for the traditional belief in this situation. True, my Mother cannot suffer after death (whereas, it may seem, I could) from having been mistaken. But then I, as an intellectual, would not be willing to miss the chance to understand my nature as a mortal, finite being, in contrast to the immortal deity, just because, from the, to me, doubtfully coherent hypothesis of survival (with no body or with a new body) it apparently follows that only the truth of this hypothesis, not its falsity, could ever be known by posthumous experience. I have too much intuition that the falsity is *known now* from the very nature of life and the universe. But by virtue of objective immortality, my Mother, for example, is an everlasting reality, not because she goes on to a posthumous career, but for two reasons: she goes on in the memory of those who knew her (so long as they are alive) and she goes on in divine memory forevermore, where there is no forgetting or failure to cherish all that is good, beautiful, or otherwise valuable. I think that Mother, education and early religious conditioning apart, had the intuition and courage to accept this view. So I do not think my religious difference from her a very deep one. I, too, can readily smile at the thought of death. It has no horrors for me. Not death but some ways of dying are horrible. Mortality simply as such is no evil at all; rather it is in principle good. I am happy to let the Immortal be the Immortal, and the mortal be mortal. And, according to my theory, God, not the human animal, is deathless, and God's career continues forevermore, carrying with it all our earthly experiences.

Mother's diary tells us of one incident that must have made a considerable though not easily traceable difference to this writer. "It almost breaks my heart that dear [she also called me "merry"] Charles [then in my second year] must be sent away [to Aunt Amy who was ideal for this temporary charge, lasting a year]; but it seems necessary." The worst blow, probably, in Mother's entire life, the only time I saw her deeply sad, was when her son Henry died in his twenties.

Mother liked to tell long afterward about an incident arising from my having (in my teens) made an unfavorable comment on an item of food put before me at mealtime. That I should have done so is to me the only surprising aspect of the story because, without her memory to the contrary, I would have said that the family menus, invariably cooked, according to my recollections, by our faithful cook Anne, were of gourmet quality and greatly to my satisfaction. However, this is apparently what took place:

Charles: (objects to the food set before him)
Mother: *Charles, you shouldn't criticize the food.*
Charles: (thinking no doubt he had a trump card to play)
Father does!
Mother: *When you are grown up and have a family of your own, you can do as Father does.*
Charles: *I can hardly wait until that time.*

It was a long wait, perhaps fifteen years. And when I was actually a husband, my wife and not a hired servant usually cooked the food. Besides, Dorothy was (and is) an artist at preparing food, one of her not easily counted accomplishments. Above all, she was the dearest friend I could ever have. So the few items of food I did not especially like have seldom evoked any negative remark from me, other than protests against the amount — my eating capacity being that of 125 pounds of normal weight.

If modesty is, as Galbraith says, "an overrated virtue," it follows that it is a virtue. Mother had this virtue totally. Boasting, calling attention to a merit of hers, is something one does not recall her doing. One does recall her saying, with genuine disgust and almost with indignation, "So *stupid* of me!" (In what contexts she said this is lost in the foggy sea previously mentioned.) Mother, married to a mentally energetic and highly educated man, had many opportunities to feel her limitations. But we are all stupid — at times and in some matters; that being the human condition. It needs considerable maturity to learn in how many ways one can exhibit stupidity. I only began to realize this in middle age. If Mother felt that one of us was parading his or her cleverness a bit too much, her reproof came in one word, "Smarty!" Or perhaps, "Smarty cat!"

When Mother was getting too old and feeble to look after herself, her one daughter, Frances, my (older) sister, found a very small old peoples' house run by a retired nurse where Mother could stay within easy driving distance of her daughter. It was a farm in Connecticut, quite in the country, with animals to watch, a family type of situation. Mother agreed to this place, though it took her away from a good house and garden where she had been living for many years. An acquaintance, told about all this, tried to persuade Mother that her children were being cruel to her, taking her away from her home, and so on. Mother thought about it overnight and then informed her partisan friend that the project represented her own convictions, as well as her children's, and that it really would be best for her, because she could not manage by herself and there was no one near enough to help. No complaint was ever heard from her about this change in her life, drastic as it was.

My brother James remarked, after Mother's death, that sometimes Mrs. _____ would speak severely to Mother. No doubt this occurred. But only someone who has dealt with nearly helpless, confused, more or less deaf, slow-moving, and at times a bit stubborn and opinionated persons, could judge such a situation.

I have never, to my recollection, harshly condemned societies in which old, no longer functional, people were exposed to die, or in which infants were so treated. It is too easy to claim moral superiority because of such customs. In some situations not everybody *can* be taken good care of. It is then a tragic necessity to make choices. We claim today to take care of the old and the young, and we do— sometimes, and more or less! Do we also provide properly for those in the prime of life? Many of these die who could easily be saved. There are *always* scarcities (e.g., of skilled doctors or advanced medical machines). Moral problems can be extremely difficult, and a certain modesty about our own ethical goodness becomes most of us. This applies to "pro-life" people and antihomosexual crusaders also. As to the latter, have they ever thought seriously about the way our prisons, by isolating the sexes, increase the likelihood of homosexual or lesbian behavior, even if these persons are lucky enough to be naturally averse to it?

I am old enough to have some empathy for other old people. But, if my society exposed hopelessly nonfunctional persons, I can imagine accepting this fate in my own case. It is an unhappy thought, that of no longer being "worth one's salt"—contributed to but not contributing.

Francis Cope Hartshorne

Father was a man of vigorous and highly trained intelligence. He studied law, was admitted to the bar, and perhaps practiced law for a

Fig. 3 Marguerite Haughton Hartshorne
and the Reverend Francis Cope Hartshorne

short time; but then decided to leave the law for the ministry. He
attended the General Episcopal Seminary in New York City and also
the Episcopal Seminary in Philadelphia. While he was a law student
at the University of Pennsylvania, he wrote a standard monograph
on the Interstate Commerce Clause of the Constitution. He also wrote
and published some essays on biblical topics. He was, he told me, "a
Jack of all trades and master of none." His sister Amy thought he
should have been an engineer; and there is evidence he could have
succeeded in that. He had also at one time thought of a medical
career and, so far as I see, could have done well in it.

His father, however, preferred that he be a lawyer. His own difficulty with that was that his father, a high official in two railroads,
wanted him to represent the railroad, whereas he would rather have
defended the victims of railroad accidents. His mother was first a
Quaker, like her husband, but then converted to Episcopalianism

shortly before Father's birth. And the woman Father wanted to marry was a very pious daughter of a beloved and saintly Episcopalian minister, James Haughton, in the wealthy parish of Bryn Mawr. The net result of these influences upon Father was the choice of the Episcopal ministry. He fitted this career somewhat imperfectly. He was not quite a natural orator on religious subjects. Arguing in court would have been more natural for him. He was decidedly argumentative and had a clear head for legal disputes. His sermons tended to be somewhat like lawyer's briefs. I early learned to reason partly by listening to them.

By good luck he was given a job, some time after a rather early retirement from the ministry, as manager of the pension fund of the Episcopal diocese of Philadelphia. This suited him perfectly. He understood financial matters rather well, he knew both civil and canon law, and he loved writing letters to ministers whose parishes failed to send in the annual premiums. One minister who received such a letter wrote back, "Your acrid letter received. You should write with something closer to Christian charity." "However," said Father with satisfaction, "he sent the premium!"

Once Father wrote to me apologizing for a previous letter in which he had scolded me about not repaying a debt to him promptly. "It was a fault of long standing, overarguing a good case. And I did not do you justice." At an earlier time, when I wrote him about my plan to be a philosopher, he typed a long letter pointing out the indecisiveness of philosophical reasoning. I replied with a long letter defending philosophy. His next letter began, "An excellent *apologia* for philosophy." And he accepted my decision as settling the matter.

When my brother Richard decided to change from a student in mathematics to a candidate for a degree in geography, he told Father about this with misgivings, fearing that he would be accused of having wasted a year. Instead Father said he was pleased, that he preferred geography to mathematics. Richard has become famous in his finally chosen subject. I trust the reader gets the impression that Father was open to rational argument. He was, fortunately, not one of those who meet an attempt to present a reasoned case with a refusal to listen.

Father preached a religion of love (not of absolute yet specific rules) and tried to get the church to relax the marriage and divorce

canon laws. (Changes at last were made, but after his death.) He did
not stress sexual rectitude in considering ethical questions nearly
as much as justice and unselfishness. If a "victorian" (Tennyson
suited him well as poet and he liked Arnold, as well as Coleridge's
"Ancient Mariner"), he was not an illiberal or stupid one. He understood the workers' side in industrial disputes and objected strongly
to the 12-hour day then in effect in the steel mill in our town. Yet
his father had been a rich man.

Did Father live his religion of love? I should say that he did, with
remarkably few inconsistencies or lapses. He was capable of occasionally allowing righteous indignation to blend with personal dis-
likes. Thus he found a certain relative by marriage (doubly so, the
husband of a sister of his wife) hard to bear (for one thing both men
were better talkers than listeners) and rather crassly scolded him (by
mail) for having been intoxicated at a family party. It was a wedding
party and Uncle Duncan tended to be sentimental at such a time and
to celebrate with liberal amounts of wine. He "slobbered" on the
blouse of the bride's mother, who told Mother, who unwisely (but it
was not her habit to keep things from Father) told him. As Aunt
Augustine said, the chief agents in this affair acted "predictably."
Since the party was not in my parents' house it was not clear what
business it was of Father's how Uncle Duncan behaved at it. Nevertheless, Father wrote the distinguished professor and well-meaning
person a letter accusing him of intoxication. The accused wrote
(Richard told me) several furious, long letters and wisely put them
into the waste basket. Then he produced a short literary masterpiece
and mailed it to Father. It began, "Your epistolary intemperance ..." I
think Father was not without appreciation of the literary skill of this
rebuttal. But he still didn't want to have to see the man. As he told
me, "I don't have to associate with all my wife's relatives if I don't
want to," or something like that. In view of his wife's liking for the
person in question this was lacking in consideration of her. So this
counts as a blemish. Still, it was a very good life in the main and did
express the religion he professed.

F. C. Hartshorne was genuinely pious, and he had a liberal English theological teacher (named Wolcott, father of the novelist) at the
General Seminary thanks to whom he had escaped the worst trap

into which traditional or classical theology had fallen. This was the to me the blasphemous identification of God with the philosophical Absolute, or with all-determining Omnipotence. Father believed in human freedom in the creative sense according to which it is simply contradictory to say that what happens in the world is fully determined by divine fiat. If a human person, say Smith, suffers injury at the hands of another person, say Jones, it is not God who has decided that this shall occur. Jones, and only Jones, has made exactly that decision. A human action is decided humanly, not divinely. Hence, for the injured to ask, "Why has God done this to me?" is a misunderstanding. God has not done it. Of course, God could have made decisions about the world such that Jones could not have harmed Smith, indeed, such that neither Jones nor Smith could have existed. But no matter what God decides about the world, creatures still must make decisions that God has not made. *Creatures are lesser creators.* To have a world is for God to run the risks of fallible decision makers determining details of that world. God *must* "throw dice," in spite of Einstein. Providence *could not* be an all-determining action upon the world.

Just how clear Father was about all this I cannot now know, but he certainly did reject a very common idea of the divine power. He said, all-powerful means, "with power *over all.*" In other words, *every* creature is significantly influenced, and in origin made possible, by divine action, but exactly what happens to creatures or is done by them depends partly on creaturely rather than exclusively on divine decisions or volitions. Thus, in the face of the famous problem of evil, and of the relations between divine and creaturely power, Father and I have had much the same basic idea. This is why *that* problem has never caused me any agony or serious religious skepticism. I have no recollection of having *ever* believed in what some mean by "omnipotence."

I am sure that Father did not think, any more than I do, that to deny this fearful concept of an all-determining deity is to "limit" divine power. Rather it is to make sense instead of nonsense out of the phrase *divine power.* To be able to elicit freedom, genuine initiative, in creatures is greater and nobler than to be able to make or predetermine their decisions, if this even makes sense.

Did Father definitely generalize, as I do (and some others before me did) the idea of creaturely freedom so that it applies in some degree to all creatures (even atoms), not simply to human beings? From the fact that he had an English translation of Boutroux's *The Contingency of the Laws of Nature* I incline to infer that he might have made this generalization. But I cannot be certain. If his theological teacher had any knowledge of the then available writings of Charles S. Peirce he could have gotten the idea from him as well. But there is no evidence that any of this happened.

I do know that Father was suspicious of traditional ways of defining God. He wrote me that the Scholastic theologians posited certain premises from which they deduced various conclusions, all of which, said Father, was acceptable procedure *provided* the reasoner stands ready to *reconsider the premises* should the conclusions be unacceptable. But, according to him, the Schoolmen refused to do this. The idea that all happenings, no matter how horrible, are divinely decided, seemed unacceptable to him, as it has to so many; yet the definition of divine power that implies it was adhered to for centuries. I am confident also that it was not merely the problem of evil that led Father to form a somewhat nontraditional idea of the power of God. It was even more fundamentally the absurdity of denying human creative decision making while attributing Eminent, or ideally great and wise, decision making to God. F. C. Hartshorne had no trust in the method of exalting God by demeaning human capacities.

I think it comes to this: Father worshipped supreme love, and supreme power only as an aspect of supreme love. For him God Is Love was the key, not God Is Power. Love wishes the other to be partly self-determined. That Father was not himself a very tyrannical person harmonizes with this.

After looking through my book *Man's Vision of God*, especially its first half, Father remarked, "Charles, I don't object to what you say in this book. But there is one thing: you don't say anything about sin." To my reply, "I have a paragraph on sin," he responded only by slowly repeating the third and fourth of my six words. Too late I encountered or remembered Kierkegaard's wonderful passage: "If you tell a systematic philosopher [presumably thinking of Hegel] that he has left out the most important thing, what does he do? He writes another paragraph." How Father would have enjoyed that!

My difficulties with orthodox Christianity might have begun when I read Emerson (the *Essays* was in Father's library) at the age of 15 or 16. But in fact I recall no stresses of that kind until, a year or two later, I read Matthew Arnold's *Literature and Dogma*. (Was this, too, in Father's library? I'm not sure.) This did indeed create a turmoil in my mind. I did not keep my thoughts on the matter entirely from my parents. Mother was distressed, but sadly—indeed, tearfully—decided that she could not argue the question with me. With Father I kept up a certain amount of religious discussion for several years, almost entirely by correspondence. We finally reached a tacit agreement not to argue further about our beliefs. I really have no complaint against either parent for their behavior in regard to this for them rather serious matter. At the outset of the discussion Father remarked, "I have not tried to mold you." He expected his children to become really adult and find their own way in life. He made clear what reasons he had for his own belief—centered on the acceptance of a miraculous resurrection of Jesus as the best explanation of the emergence of a church dedicated to the memory of a crucified man. (This was Doctor Samuel Johnson's argument. And I know a wonderful, learned, scholarly lady, Jeremy Ingalls, who also believes on this basis.) But after he had stated his position it was not in Father's nature to allow my response or lack of response to his argument to poison our relationship. In this too he lived by his professed values.

Did I have an Oedipus complex? Yes, but a mild one. At one stage I thought Father was not as kind as he ought to be to Mother. And I argued rather fiercely with him about political matters, for instance about war—during a short period when I was a convinced Tolstoyan pacifist. Also about causes of World War I. But Father's gentleness in personal relations (except sometimes when writing letters about a matter concerning which he had strong convictions of righteousness), his willingness to respect the freedom of others, and real affection for his children made a severe case improbable. There is also the fact that I disputed a good deal with Mother, though not about religion, and only in maturity came to fully appreciate her rare merits. Then, too, I was taken away from both parents for many months at the age

Fig. 4. The six siblings at Kittanning, 1909 (Left to right: Frances, Charles, James, Henry, Richard, and Alfred)

of less than two (to reduce the burden on Mother, who had four children under four years old and was pregnant with a fifth): and later I went to boarding-school many miles from home for four school years.

Perhaps it should be said that Mother had a wholesome attitude toward sex. There is a startlingly explicit letter that proves it. She and her husband undoubtedly knew happiness in love. Their principal trouble about that came, we have gathered, from the difficulty, in those days, of controlling conception. Mother told Richard about that after his marriage. I recall Mother once asking me to leave her dressing-room so that she could change her clothes. "Otherwise," said she with a charming smile, "I might embarrass you."

As was usually true of parents then (and is very often true now), my parents did not manage to give much helpful information or advice about sex. But they gave no wrong information. There were no insinuations that sex was nasty, or enjoyable only for men and the like.

Our parents were not musical performers, though they could sing nicely. Mother's French-Swiss (Huguenot) mother, my only non-Anglo-Saxon ancestor, had taught her some French songs that Mother taught us to sing. In this way I was introduced in some small degree to the sound of French words.

Father liked music and in Phoenixville he bought a pianola, worked by a foot pump. I liked to operate this machine. Father preferred classical pieces, and Chopin's funeral march—for me still the most penetrating of all musical reflections upon death—became a favorite of mine. Though the ingenious system of perforations in paper doubtless did not absolutely reproduce the skill of the original performer who made the "score" (or whatever it is called), it must have come reasonably close to that. Chopin's eloquence was very apparent. And operating this machine was at least doing something, not merely having something done to you.

Our parents moved from Phoenixville when Father retired. His retirement was not because of age, but because the man who dominated the church made certain difficulties for him. William Reeves was a pious man whose family inherited a steel mill in Phoenixville. William was vice-president of the mill and his brother David was president. David did not attend our church but William was constant "warden" (treasurer) of it. He was a bachelor—it was said that he had lost a fiancée through a fatal accident. He seemed to me as a youngster a joyless man, but apparently he was deeply concerned about religion and about the church in which Father preached. Perhaps it was his primary chance to exert influence.

Father saw Reeves as a person of limited intelligence, but with power to get his own way. The natural leaders in the church worked in the mill, and could not lightly go against their employer's wishes. (Besides, Reeves had an imposing manner.) Father understood their position perfectly and felt that it would be cruel as well as probably vain to force issues. Frequently, he found, Mr. Reeves would see after a year or more what to Father had been apparent all along. For a person of vigorous intelligence, it was a trying situation. The things that Reeves did not easily grasp were not, so far as I ever heard, theological points. They were practical, even financial ones. This may have been partly because Reeves had all his life been a rich man, whereas Father had for some years lived on a moderate income and for still more years had associated much with persons of moderate or small incomes.

After his retirement, Father lived near Philadelphia. Mother had a nice flower garden there. Once when Dorothy was visiting, Father called out to Mother, "Come here, Marguerite, I want to consult you." To Dorothy, Mother confided, "He never consulted me in his life." Returning to Dorothy, Mother said, "He wanted to show me where he intended to plant a bush."

After Father's death, we found about the house various indications of his peculiarities. Here was a minister of the gospel who left, by Alfred's recollection, twenty-seven (or was it only seventeen?) screwdrivers scattered about the house. They were of many sizes and shapes, for many purposes. His motto had been, Alfred said, "Always have a screwdriver within reach." (Father could fix anything, including his car, unless a whole machine shop was required.) A very different relic was a copy of a letter to the town newspaper that we were proud to find. There had been a movement in the town to introduce the Ku Klux Klan, and this was more than Father could stand. His letter was a masterly satire on the project. It ended, "Gentlemen of the darkness, the floor is yours. Will someone tell us what the meeting is about?" The project died.

Another amusing relic was a letter from an officer of the company that made Father's typewriter and to which he had evidently written complaining about something that had or had not been done to his machine. Knowing how much vigor and zest Father could put into that kind of letter, we took the good humor and disarming nature of the official's reply to show that the man appreciated these qualities and admired them, though with some amusement. Father, in front of a person he was addressing, was a remarkably gentle man, but in front of a typewriter he could be rather fierce. I have known one philosopher, and I think one ornithologist, with this combination of traits.

A funny thing happened to the philosopher. He is known as kind to his colleagues; but he is also known to write rather harsh reviews of books. A lady, wife of another philosopher, read one such review and was aghast. She told me about it: "How could he write such an unkind review? I know he is a kind person." The more she thought about it, the more puzzled and upset she became. In bed that night she could not dismiss the matter from her mind sufficiently to go to

Fig. 5. Boy scouts (Left to right: James, Richard, Charles, and Henry)

sleep. At 2 A.M., she called the reviewer long distance and put the question to him. "Do you have to waken me at 2 A.M.," he wanted to know, "to ask me about this?" "Yes," she said, "I can't sleep for thinking about it." "Don't you understand," he explained, "that the reason I can be so kind is that I write such reviews?" I imagine that my father would have understood this.

It was like Father to have seen to it that Phoenixville had either the first or the second Boy Scout troop in the United States. It had an admirable leader. He showed me a book by Gifford Pinchot on forestry that made me for a while think favorably of a career in forestry. My previous idea had been to be a farmer, but I gave that up as soon as I realized that keeping cows, chickens, and so on meant one could not go away even for a day without neglecting these creatures. I still think I could have stood the forest service far better than any "business" in cities. However, once I had begun to write poetry, there could be no question of a career that did not make writing primary.

Fig. 6. Alfred, James, Richard, and Henry

My Four Brothers

I was the oldest son; the brothers nearest to me in age were identical twins, James and Henry. They were strikingly different in personalities but easily confused otherwise.

This leads me to discuss the question often debated nowadays under the rather fatuous heading, "When does life begin?" Life began some billions of years ago on this planet; no one knows when it began in the cosmos, if indeed it did begin. I think not. Here I get some support from Fred Hoyle, the astronomer and science-fiction writer. As for human life, it began some millions of years ago. "Stop," I hear someone object, "The question is, When does an *individual* life begin?" I reply that the question is still hopelessly vague or ambiguous. It might be answered, "When the egg cell that later, through self-multiplication, produced so-and-so was first formed, just then so-and-so's life began. For the cell was alive, not dead."

"No," the objector protests, "the cell must be fertilized before it becomes so-and-so." (I ask the reader to take me seriously, I am not joking in this discussion. I am deeply indignant at the way this topic is often handled.)

So let us consider the fertilized egg; in what sense is it so-and-so? So-and-so is a person; a single cell does not seem much like a person.

"Ah, but it could become a person."
So could an unfertilized cell.
"Only if it were fertilized."

Yes, but is there no "if" about the fertilized cell becoming a person? Is this merely automatic? The mother has to act in certain ways and avoid acting in other ways if there is to be any very good chance of the child ever being born alive and growing into full personhood. For even being physically born does not of itself guarantee eventual personhood, if the dictionary meaning of fully actualized personhood is to apply: "conscious, able to reason and distinguish between right and wrong." There is no single known case of an infant becoming a person in the full sense without a lot of care and effort on the part of the mother or other true person or persons.

In what sense is a fertilized cell an individual human being? We know the answer today: the fertilized cell determines the special chemical gene structure—the DNA—of the person it may develop into. But note; with identical twins even this does not distinguish that person from all others. For the chemistry in that case is shared with at least one other person (four, in the case of identical quadruplets). But waive that difficulty. What crude thinking it is that identifies individuality with mere genetic chemistry! What made my twin brothers, now no longer living, physically individual was something more than the chemistry of their cells. This something more was the structure of their nervous systems. And that is just not there in the fertilized cell. Nor could it be predetermined by the cell, for then my brothers Henry and James would have been mere duplicates. They were far from that.

The chemistry of the genes has an important influence on neural development; but so do several other factors, including without doubt environmental *stimuli* (first of all in the womb environment), which are never entirely the same for two individuals. Also influencing neural development, I do not in the least doubt, though some (but not all) neuropsychologists would disagree with this, are the partly free *decisions* (which could not be duplicated exactly in another individual) made by the nascent person. We ourselves, as well as parents, nurses, teachers, brothers and sisters, and so forth have a hand in molding our neural development and making us the persons we become. To dismiss all this from consideration and identify the egg cell with a person in the full sense really "blows the mind." If these two things are identical, then how refute the Hindu mystics who say that all things are the identical Brahman?

To say that a cell *shall become* a person is to issue a command to quite a number of creatures that *already are* persons. Indeed, it is to decide for society at large some important questions. The fact that those who freely issue such decisions may be ready to quote some religious text in support of their behavior does not impress me very much, in spite of or because of my own religious beliefs. And we do not have a state church, to Jefferson's lasting credit.

"Do you deny that an infant is a person." Yes, I deny it, if by person you mean, in the full value sense of actually having what makes human beings superior to the nonhuman animals. As the infant is *actually* it shows no more "rationality," rather much less than a grown up chimpanzee.

"So there is nothing against infanticide?" Oh yes, there is something against it. But what is against it is not that it is murder in the full proper sense. (Even Bill Buckley admits that *murder* as used by pro-lifers is "metaphorical.") An infant is sufficiently far along toward personhood to be treated with a good deal more respect than a cell, or a three-month-old embryo. Pearl Buck in her *My Two Worlds* tells of five Chinese mothers talking together about their having each allowed a female infant to die. They all wept! It is no slight thing to stop the ascent toward personhood at that somewhat advanced stage. And, as with other legal questions, lines have to be drawn. When is a youth legally adult? There is no absolute answer grounded in the nature of things. Will human rationality ever transcend the childish level of trying to reduce important relative distinctions to absolute ones? *Relative*, or matter of degree, is not at all the same as *unimportant*. Importance, too, is a matter of degree.

One of the best comments on the abortion question was made by blunt-spoken Margaret Mead: "Abortion is a nasty thing; but our society deserves it." Why? Because that society does everything needed to make unwanted pregnancy in multitudes of cases overwhelmingly likely, and then (when it acts as pro-lifers would have it) tries to use police power and economic factors to make it improbable that the poor can, with minimal risk to persons, use what is, for those of means, the effective remedy. Many primitive societies, as Mead well knew, treat their young with more wisdom, kindness, and good sense in sex matters than our society does.

As the level-headed column writer Raspberry says, there is not going to be universal agreement on this issue. Argument seems to fall largely on deaf ears. But I have long felt a duty to present the case for a qualified acceptance of the right of women to decide in their own case about this matter. It is not just the embryo that is the potentiality of a person. That potentiality is the embryo *and* the mother *and* still other persons. *By itself* the embryo is not even potentially a person. And still less is it by itself the potentiality of a good person. It could turn into a viciously destructive individual, and this is the answer to Pearl Buck's argument: that the fertilized egg or the embryo may be a potential genius. It may be a potential murderer of a genius. And, I repeat, even an *un*fertilized egg is also a potential genius — or criminal. Where do we stop with this sort of thinking? Potentialities have their importance but this importance is in many gradations, and there have to be priorities. Trying to see to it that the proportion of wanted to unwanted children be kept high is an eminently reasonable priority. Anyway I shall be on record about a matter that I feel deeply about. My sympathy for actual persons, including pregnant mothers, is far stronger than my sympathy for fertilized eggs.

My twin brothers were fine playmates through all my childhood and youth. (As adults we were almost always in different places and different activities.) *Not once* did I ever quarrel with either of them, or so it seems from my memory. Jim, who lived until a few years ago, was a person almost no one quarreled with, so far as I know, and many regarded as a benefactor. Henry, who died prematurely, was more absorbed in his own thoughts and affairs, but he, too, was not quarrelsome. Neither had any mean streak. Henry was more cynical, and also more the artist. He studied art for years, but died before he had shown much fulfillment as an artist. I incline to think that lack of achievement is what killed him. But if Henry or James ever did anything seriously unkind I do not recall it.

The brother I had most to do with after childhood was Richard, 2½ years my junior. With him I roomed for nine months at boarding school. It was a trouble free relationship. As children we had but a single brief quarrel, which even involved some violence on my part. I am not proud of this. Many decades later we discovered that each of us had felt guilty rather than resentful through the years about this incident. This was because Richard remembered, more definitely than I did, that he had deliberately teased me before I lost my temper. With the youngest brother Alfred I also had a brief, physically slightly

Fig. 7. Camping near Loyalsock Creek, Pennsylvania

Fig. 8. Henry, James, Mother, Alfred

violent, quarrel that we both remembered through the years, but in this case the point of disagreement was totally beyond recall for us both. I have not a clue as to the reason for my annoyance with him. Otherwise, I do not recollect quarreling with a brother—and only once very briefly with my one (older) sister. In our group of six siblings quarreling was limited and led to no permanent estrangement.

For some years Alfred (by Father's will) invested money for all of us. We felt no uneasiness about this, and it turned out advantageously for us. We knew he was practical, bright, level-headed, and perfectly honest. When Father died, leaving considerable money to Mother, Alfred was entirely in charge of her finances, which involved considerable amounts of money. Richard was worried about this because Mother had had only small amounts of money to spend through the years, Father attending to all the major expenditures. I told Richard not to worry, that Mother was not the kind of person that confidence men prey upon (their victims being usually greedy people, longing to get something for nothing). (Actually Richard was afraid Mother might be extravagant in giving to causes she believed in, church-related causes.) Besides, there was Alfred whose judgment Mother would respect. I recalled, too, what Father had said when a man in our town died leaving to his daughter all his money and to his wife the kitchen utensils! Father thought this atrocious, remarking: "A mother will look after her children, but children will often not look after a mother." So he counted on Mother to make such use of the inheritance as would be for the good of all of us. How right he was! Mother asked Alfred whether she needed to keep all the money for her own use or could manage to live on a part of it. He told her that she could spare such and such a portion, and she immediately turned over that amount to divide among us.

Male Chauvinism

Richard and I agree that Father was not a male chauvinist. He did narrowly limit his wife's financial responsibilities, but when it came to making a will he demonstrated complete confidence in her. I found this rather moving. Father backed my intelligent sister (though some-times she had to argue a bit with him about specifics) for all the education and whatever career—really careers—she desired. He greatly admired a sister of Mother's, Augustine Haughton. "Oh, she's bright!" he said enthusiastically. He had three strong-minded sisters, and a brilliant though sometimes unwise sister-in-law (his brother's wife Clementine).

If I have been a feminist for over sixty years this is not particu-larly surprising. I had admirable, educated female cousins, aunts, mother's helpers, and so on. Women as I knew them were manifestly capable. When, during World War I, I read in a British newspaper (*Daily Mail*, continental edition) letters to the editor expressing doubt or surprise about the ability of women to drive trucks while the men were in the army I smiled and recalled how I had learned to drive at the hands of my sister, who had many years earlier also taught me to ride a bicycle. "What's all the fuss about?" I asked myself.

How often since I have wondered at the need so many of my sex seem to feel to exalt their half of the species by underestimating the other half. And I cannot forgive Aristotle, or Confucious, for their atrocious degrees of this weakness. It is no credit to their intelligence, for one can see with half an eye and half a brain the disadvantages (other than hypothetical inborn limitations) under which women generally have had to labor whenever they attempted to compete in cultural activities. Modern hygiene, making a far lower birth rate desirable or even necessary, opens up new possibilities — at long last.

In principle this was predictable centuries ago, but what man had enough concern for and grasp of women's situation to make the prediction? It follows from truths that have long been obvious enough. (Science was going to decrease the death rate, "conquer diseases," therefore . . .) In many ways men were too little able to put themselves in the place of women to see the implications of this prospect for sex

Fig. 9. Five members of the Hartshorne baseball team: Walt McCallum (top), Malcolm Deans (2nd row, left), The twins (2nd row, right, and 1st row, left), and Charles Thompson (1st row, right)

roles. Many don't see it even now. Over and over again it has been necessary for a woman to see the truths about women that men (and some women, too) had the intelligence and the factual information but not the will to grasp. What a light on human nature this throws!

Kant, the great rationalist, held that women should not vote. He had a sensible reason, their lack of economic independence. But why, oh why, did he assume that this was bound always to be so? He knew that science, pure and applied, makes many changes. He knew that women were "rational animals" in the same basic sense as men (only rather irrational animals can deny this). He argued that being a rational animal implied participating in the governing of one's society. Why then not say: so long as women have no economic independence let them not vote, *but* because this is incongruous with their humanity as thinking creatures, let means be found to increase the economic independence of women. Some women by Kant's time had seen the incongruity (e g., John Adams's wife). Why didn't Kant? Was it his sex that blinded him? Even Plato came closer to seeing the point, and Socrates (here I trust Gregory Vlastos) closer still. But not Aristotle and not Confucious. They were blind in this respect with the blindest of their time. So, according to some psychiatrists, was Sigmund Freud.

Public School

My primary education was entirely in the public schools of two Pennsylvania towns. I recall nothing particularly bad about these schools and their teachers. In the smaller town, my birthplace, there was some physical punishment, and oddly enough, perhaps, one article that was made in the "manual training" class I remember taking part in was a stout wooden paddle to be used in disciplining difficult pupils. I only saw (so my skimpy memory says) the use of this instrument once, and this was by a principal, not a teacher. It was a single blow on the back of a boy in the playground. I had one teacher with a reputation of free use of physical punishment but the year I had with her there was little or none of it. I reached the conclusion that her reputation for doing it was almost enough. I did once tempt her by stealing to the waste basket (contrary to the rule) without permis-

Fig. 10. Diving into the swimming hole near the
covered bridge.

sion. If she struck me I have forgotten, so it could not have been very
painful. But I rather think she did catch me in the act.

Learning to read is something I am unable to recall. I do not
remember being very bored in school, though I recall throwing spit-
balls using a ruler as instrument and this suggests some lack of
scholarly concentration. On the other hand, I never minded when
the long summer holiday began, just as I never have minded this
since I became a teacher. Either way, at school or not at school, life
was all right. In the eighth grade, in the second of the two towns, the
teacher was particularly interesting. We were seated according to
grades, and sometimes I, sometimes a certain girl, were in the first
seat. But wait, there was a boy who also came into this rivalry—or
was this in seventh grade?

There was another girl who fixed herself in my memory by being
without doubt the first one who ever took a fancy to me. She showed

her fondness quite obviously by the way she commented on my recitations in class. We were encouraged to criticize one another, and she persisted in pointing out inadequacies in my performance. Of itself, this might not seem to show fondness, but the tones of voice and manner were unmistakable expressions of it. We were to directly address one another in such comments and I can still hear the loving voice in which she would begin, "Charles, you said ... " What came thereafter has dropped out of the picture. It was not the *what* but the *how* that struck me. I was only mildly concerned to be the object of such attentions, but did go so far as (after consulting Mother) to send her a valentine. She was presumably Irish, Margaret Murphy. Years later, in the army, I came to know a chap who had been a friend, in some degree, of the same girl. But the friendship struck a bad snag, he told me, in the following way. He was driving out from Philadelphia where he lived (30 miles away) to see Margaret, and before he got to Phoenixville two girls, strangers to him, hitched a ride with him. Margaret never, it seems, forgave him for picking up these girls with whom he was seen driving into the town. Nothing further can be narrated by this author about Margaret Murphy. I hope her life has been a happy one. She deserves no ill from me.

CHAPTER THREE

A Boarding School in the Country: Religion, Nature, Becoming A Writer

(1911-1915)

Dr. Gardiner

The founder and headmaster of the boarding-school I attended for the four years corresponding to High School was an Episcopal minister. This no doubt was one reason my father sent me there. He did well to do so. The school eventually failed financially. Probably it was too small to pay for itself, but it was a great success so far as I and my brother Richard were concerned. Richard came to the school in my second year there and stayed a year after I left. Dr. Frederic Gardiner was an admirable person. Back then, before World War I, he taught physics and biology without any suggestion that I or Richard recall of a conflict between either of these sciences and religion. He must have presented evolution to us in a favorable light, because that is the only way we have the faintest recollection of ever having regarded it. Details of his teaching in class are lost for me; but I have a sense of a pervasive enthusiasm for science.

Gardiner of Yeates School was certainly a believing Christian; for he conducted a confirmation class that I attended in which his piety was unmistakable. But this piety was a very positive thing. He didn't hate science or fear it. He had been athletic at Yale, I seem to recall; and he prided himself on his physical condition (in late middle age). Indeed, this led him into a bit of trouble; for once after dinner in the school dining-room he undertook to show his strength by lifting one of the biggest of the boys and strained his back. Ever since then, I have felt a touch of caution when tempted to show how strong I am, particularly since reaching a similar age.

A few remarks of Gardiner's are still with me. One was that "Overeating has broken up more families than overdrinking." Mrs. Gardiner was obese, so the remark was scarcely a purely objective and unprejudiced one. Exaggeration or not, who today would deny that overeating can and doubtless often does break up families — and

Fig. 11. Yeates School Dormitory and classrooms

destroy many lives? When Gardiner talked to Father about sending me to school, he said among other things that a mother is "no good to her son after the age (I think it was) of seven." We did have a boy or two not so very far above that age in the school. Concerning the teaching of English, Gardiner said that the odd thing about teaching English grammar was "there's no such thing" — or something of the sort. Possibly it was, "there's so little of it."

The school gave a prize for the best essay on any subject we wanted to write about, and a prize for the best piece of nature study. To win both prizes, as I did, was a moderate achievement in that the school had a total of only forty-eight pupils, so that competition was slight. I have no doubt that the idea to have the two prizes was Gardiner's. There also were book prizes for high grades. I got a book on Egyptian birds. It was many years before I had any interest in Egyptian birds or Egyptian anything; but in time I did have a use for it.

Concerning the nature study, I have one more of Gardiner's sayings to reproduce. He said to me, about the time of my graduation, that my interest in nature was a valuable thing and that I should take care not to lose it in the future. When I replied confidently, "Oh, I will never lose that," he mildly rebuked me: "Don't flatter yourself. It is very easily lost." Eventually, I had reason to see the wisdom of this. During the next dozen years or so I did very little of the bird watching I had done so much of at school. That I then began to resume and gradually increase my ornithological studies was not, I would now grant to Gardiner, inevitable. It might not have happened that way. For instance, not every wife would have done even a part of what D. C. Hartshorne did to encourage me in this pursuit.

From the little that I definitely recall, it stands out that the founder of Yeates was a man of unusual opinions, who did not speak in clichés and who was really concerned about the youths in his care. It is a bit shameful to recall that some of the pupils affected to see only the oddity in this man and crassly referred to him as "Crap." I felt as much in common with Gardiner as with my age peers and (I believe) did not join in the disparagement implied by the use of the customary nickname. All my life I have been less a member of a gang than many of those I have known, not that I am extreme in this matter. As Mrs. A. N. Whitehead, a wonderfully perceptive person, said: "You are fundamentally social." But still I rather expect to be in a minority, as my father so often was.

I seem always to have been something of an elitist with a sense of noblesse oblige, even though our family home was an ordinary church rectory, and I attended public school until the age of fourteen. Being one of six children of an Episcopal minister was a shelter from the world of democratic leveling downward in taste that is a danger of our American version of the Anglo-Saxon heritage. Going to an Episcopal school continued and intensified this sheltered existence. And there was no radio or T.V. to break into it.

I have no recollection whatever of homosexuality or autosexuality at that school, and I recall extremely little talk about sex. When Dr. Gardiner, in confirmation class, spoke about sexual morality, he was direct and convincingly sincere in referring to the desirability of a young man "when he comes to offer himself to a pure girl" being no less pure himself. This probably had more influence upon my behavior later than I was explicitly conscious of.

Some Other Boarding School Teachers

James Carey Thomas, or Jame Scarey Thomas, or simply "Scarey," was perhaps the most interesting, after Gardiner, of the Yeates teachers, though they were all interesting (more or less). Thomas taught English literature and taught it well. He also coached soccer. He had vivid red hair, which I felt was harmonious with his nickname. He was interested in my experiments in writing poetry. When in my last year, I wrote the class poem, he said it was a good poem. Probably, it was about the peak of my achievement in that activity. I recall only the line, "filtering through the softening veil of time." But when I read him an unfinished poem about the "spirit of solitude" or something of the sort and came to the line, "while dark plots he weaves," he could not resist the crushing comment: "the nasty thing!" This was too much for me, and that poem never got finished.

Thomas was a thinking man. I kept track of him long after leaving school. He finally thought through the ultimate philosophical question to the (for him) definitive solution: "nothing is absolute— except relativity." It is unlikely that he meant anything much like my concept of "divine relativity," but I take pleasure in relating the two expressions.

Thomas for a time was in love with a girl from my home town of Phoenixville, but he became disillusioned with her before much happened beyond his writing some sonnets in her honor. Being a punster Scarey liked to speak of "fun-nix-ville" as the place Richard and I, and the only girl I knew of his caring about, came from. One day in each week the school had corned beef and cabbage, which for him was "scorned beef and garbage." I believe it was he who quoted someone as describing Whitman's verse as "dactylic hexameters bubbling through sewage." He must have said things more worthy of memory than my strange flair for preserving foibles and witticisms has retained. I am sure that he had real feelings for literature. As I said at the outset of this book, it is the blank pages rather than the inaccuracies of memory that cause me to wonder.

Now for some foibles. Thomas was mostly rather solemn, and his sense of humor was not always apparent. In my (and his) first year at Yeates he had some difficulty with discipline and was known to lose his temper to the extent of losing his head. The peak of this was when he met a period of loud confusion in class with the following: "What's the matter with you fellows? Every time I open my mouth, some fool begins to speak!" Alas, that class hour, for all practical purposes, was at an end. Result: three of us, including the youthful version of this writer, were hauled up before the assistant headmaster, Mr. Schwacke, and threatened with expulsion. "I have every confidence in that man [Mr. Thomas], and if you [pointing to Truxton Brodhead] don't stop making trouble in his class, you'll go to Parksburg; and you'll [pointing to me] go to Phoenixville, and you'll [the third name and place are lost] go to _____." The threat had its effect. Things quieted down. What my special contribution to the disturbance had been, beyond just laughing, I can't now say.

Here is another example of Scarey's tendency to fall into a trap of his own making. At his dinner table, Richmond ("Nap") Rucker, my roommate of the year, spoke about the danger of sleeping in moonlight. "Why Nap," said Scarey, "there's no harm in that. I slept in the moonlight all summer." Nap's reply is easily guessed: "*now* we understand," or something of the sort.

Mr. Schwacke taught government and history. I recall only one item from his teaching. He was a realist about politics, and he told us about a case of an idealistic young politician who was informed by a powerful individual in his area that he must make a speech supporting a policy flatly inconsistent with the young man's declared principles; he would make such a speech — or else! And, said Schwacke with grim earnestness, "he made the speech." So the idea of frightful pressures on politicians has been nothing new to me since school days. Schwacke eventually, when Yeates ceased to be, gave up teaching and became an Episcopal minister. (Perhaps the pressures would be less in that vocation than in politics; but I should think they would be worse than in teaching.)

Like nearly all those teachers, except Gardiner and one other, these men were young and unmarried. (Schwacke, perhaps, was early middle aged.) The other exception was Sammy, Mr. Sampson, who taught Latin. His wife had headaches much of the time; and one fears she had a dull life at best. Her husband I recall as a dry man. He taught well enough, to the best of my recollection. Perhaps I am prejudiced in not remembering him more favorably by the fact that he didn't especially like me, it seemed, and felt that I talked too much or too irrelevantly, or something. "Charles is thinking out loud," he would say at dinner, when I was at his table. Often since then, I find myself saying things (in my wife's presence, perhaps) that might as well be left unsaid and I then may apologize by saying, "I was merely thinking out loud." I know what Sampson meant, but why is it so nearly all that I can remember of his conversation?

I do recall one other bit. Sammy was from Maine, and he told a story supposed to illustrate something about his state. A character from the backwoods was telling how he survived during a hard winter with short supplies while camping near a frozen lake. For some reason connected with his line of work he had with him a one-inch augur. So his tale runs:

Backwoodsman: *"I took the augur and bored a hole through the ice and put a baited fish hook and line down and pretty soon caught a five pound lake trout."*

Listener objects: *"How could you pull a five pound fish through a one inch augur hole?"*

Backwoodsman: *"Why, I never thought of that!"*

Somehow this did not seem of first quality as humor. But it's the best Sammy did, so far as my memory preserves him. (In fact, by boring enough holes close together, the feat probably could be done.)

Thanks to Richard's offering me some of his recollections, I can now draw a better portrait of Sammy and some of the others. Sampson was a man who perhaps had bad luck in his second marriage, but who was more colorful than I remembered him as being. He was an efficient disciplinarian who had in a fashion thought out the problems of discipline. He told stories about how things are in country public schools, where, as he held, unless you beat up one of the bigger boys at the outset, you were lost.

At Yeates he was known for only two instances of violence, both involving the same boy, none other than the notorious Spencer. The first time, Sammy picked him up by the scruff of the neck and threw him on the floor. The second time was when Sammy observed Spencer stick a pen into the wrist of the boy behind him. With a few quick steps he reached Spencer's seat and with one swing of his arm knocked him off his seat and onto the floor. As the culprit began to rise, Sammy stopped him with a stern, "Stay there!" So Spencer spent the rest of the class period on the floor. Of course, Spencer was a sick soul, and probably needed a psychiatrist rather than violence in response to his violence. But the school was not equipped to furnish what nowadays might possibly be available.

Once Richard thought Sammy was mistranslating a passage in Vergil. He explained his idea of the correct translation; whereupon his teacher, after considering a moment, said, "You are right." Then to the class, "You see, I have been teaching Vergil now for forty years and every year I learn something new." When Scarey was told about this, he could not resist making the comment, "Isn't that wonderful. Sammy now knows forty things about Vergil!"

Once Sammy told a faculty group, "My greatest regret in life is that my _____ (male organ) is so small." Richard recalls Sammy at dinner losing patience and saying to his wife, "Mrs. S., you make me tired!" (I had forgotten his use of this locution but it comes back to me.) One winter Sammy was sick a good deal, and his wife took care of him. That year, it was said, she had no headaches. The poor woman had no role in that little community and was not up to the task of inventing one. The difficulty was transparent; but no one could find the remedy.

The mathematics teacher, named Reiter, who was also the football coach, was a manly fellow; and I liked him well enough. From him I recall just two sentences. One was his saying about me, as I approached a group of boys with whom he had been talking, "here comes a fellow who is strong." The other was his saying, apropos of dear knows what, "Charlie, be a man first and a student afterwards." The advice was acceptable; why it seemed needed just then is one more secret of the past.

Mr. Reiter was both a good teacher and a good disciplinarian. His methods were different from Sampson's. He told my brother once, after Richard had spoken, as Reiter judged, inappropriately, "Think twice before you speak—and then don't say anything."

Once, when there was pie for dinner, Reiter had just finished dividing the pie for his table into the required number of pieces, when the head table (where Dr. Gardiner and the senior boys ate) sent word via the waiter that the head table was short one piece of pie. Reiter, who (says my brother) took pains about the mathematically precise dividing of the pie's circle, was not willing to revise his solution of that problem, so he simply did without a piece himself. On another occasion, when there was rice pudding, a boy said, "I don't eat rice pudding," whereupon Richard exclaimed, "Good, then there'll be more for the rest of us. Give me a lot." Reiter said nothing but, as he sent helpings of pudding around the table he passed over Richard, who wondered if this was punishment for his brash remark. But no, his punishment was to be the opposite. What Reiter did was to fill two dishes very full of pudding and hand them to Richard saying, "Eat that." Richard did as he was bade, but was somewhat afraid his stomach would burst afterwards. Evidently Reiter was, in his way, something of a Solomon.

School Life

Youthful sophistication was expressed at Yeates by, "It's a funny world," or "It's a great life if you don't weaken." The first of these is surely connected with Yeates by my memory; the second possibly came later. No doubt both of them have been or are current in many other communities.

There were a few somewhat rough practical jokes in the school. A German teacher, unpopular because of his sullenness and his refusal to attend the school football games, had a dead frog put into his bed and also a live lamb put into his room to greet him with a "*baaa*" as he entered. The one vicious such joke was putting a set muskrat trap into someone's bed. This must have been done by the boy—already mentioned—whose first name was Spencer, an obnoxious character. Luckily, no damage was done.

I have heard Wilhelm Pauck, the distinguished church historian, and another professor relate tales of life in Lutheran schools, one in Germany and one in the United States, that they attended as boys. Discipline was rather repressive and the boys schemed to get the better of the teachers. They did three rather mean things. A teacher used to bang the door on going out when he was in a bad temper. So the boys secretly loosened the glass transom above the door, which fell with a crash the next time the door was slammed. They also put a sponge soaked with ink on the teacher's chair, but he saw it before sitting down. "Ha," said the teacher, "you thought you could fool me." So the boys set the trap again, and this time the teacher did sit on the sponge.

The third trick was to plan a campaign to fool the Latin teacher. They noticed that the latter followed a fixed order in calling on boys to translate; so they divided up the text among themselves to insure that everyone would be prepared to translate his particular portion of the text. The teacher congratulated his seemingly most studious and adept class. Alas, years afterwards, the teacher was told what had happened. It soured his memory of a class he had long felt proud of.

Yeates School was on the whole a gentle and civilized institution, for which I shall always be thankful to Dr. Gardiner, its creator.

One chap at school whom I can still picture vaguely to myself persists in my memory only as having objected to or made fun of my habit of prefacing remarks with "probably." He did not appreciate, it seems, my precocity in having at that early age (say sixteen) discovered the truth expressed by Bishop Butler: "probability is the guide of life." Much later I came to see that it, rather than the classical deterministic conception of causality, is the guide of science also.

Out of four school years at Yeates, in my fourteenth to eighteenth years, only a tiny handful of sentences uttered by anyone are still recoverable. One of them was close to the beginning of the first year. I had thought I was a fast runner; but in a game of tag with several boys I discovered that one of them (Hal Denkla) was faster than I was. To my expression of surprise, he responded, "Wait till you see Johnnie Mitchell run; he's faster than I am." When I did see Mitchell run, the correctness of this assertion was obvious. He was a beautiful runner. I gave up any dreams of shining in that line. Mitchell later married a second cousin of mine; but I was never in touch with the couple.

I had one satisfaction as a runner, nevertheless. In athletics the school was divided into two groups, Blues and Browns; and each of these groups was again divided into Juniors and Seniors. I began as a Junior Brown, and, as I was older than most of the Juniors, I had a chance to shine that season. In football I played end. I recall almost no plays except one. Hal Denkla, star fullback for the Blues, ran around the other end of our team, and had a clear field for a touchdown. The score was tied. I ran after Hal, even though I knew he was a better runner than I was. Was it the ball he carried that slowed him down, or did he not know I was coming after him? Or was he tired from so much running in the game already? However that was, I caught up to him and brought him down some 10 yards or so from the goal line. The Blues never got that touchdown. The game ended a tie. As I picked myself up, a member of our team, I know not who it was, ecstatically said into my ear, "You'll get the prize." This was an annual prize for the best player in the Juniors, whether Blues or Browns. I did get it. The following year I was no longer a Junior, and consequently lost interest in football. If I was big, and of some significance as a junior athlete, it was obvious that as a senior football player I was negligible. Soccer was different; and I did play that, though without distinction.

Our genes and early development set limits to our prowess in athletics, as in other things, and in every sport I soon reached a low plateau, from which further progress seemed difficult. Reaction time is one of the factors setting such limits. As soon as I had seen the great tennis players (Big Bill Tilden and Little Bill Johnstone, for example) and therefore knew how beautiful tennis can be, I began to lose enthusiasm for my own possible skill at it, and finally gave up playing in my early thirties. Since then I have dreamed of taking up the game again, perhaps five times, but even in dreams I do not do it well. Since having a good T.V. set, so that I can see the balls in their flight, I have watched some of the great recent matches. It is my most frivolous hobby.

In a class ahead of me at Yeates was a vigorous, hard-driving young man who could be counted on to do all the standard things well. I recall him only from the athletic field and from his reading, upon graduating, in a somewhat coarse voice, Kipling's poem that ends:

> And he tackled the thing that couldn't be done
> And he did it.

No doubt this man made something of his life. However, in spite of the real admiration, indeed gratitude, I feel in thinking of Kipling (chiefly for his *Jungle Books*), to the poem just mentioned I prefer the slogan of the U.S. Army engineers:

> The difficult we do immediately,
> The impossible takes longer.

This unrhymed little poem has the humor that Kipling, in that one of his moods, and perhaps the Yeates student in nearly all of his, was without.

Another Yeates boy nearer my own age seemed a classic specimen of school "grind." He too seemed rather humorless and without charm, but—no question about it—he was and would always be an A student. Probably, he became a paradigm of the organization man in some business.

One of the older boys on the periphery of my existence, even in that small school, was named Edward Gernant. I have a faint picture of him in my mind, but recall no word passing between us. However, I could never forget the following little incident. An aunt of his came to the school to visit her nephew and see how he was getting on. At lunchtime, outside the dining room, a group of the boys sang in chorus, obviously prepared and coached by Mr. Stansfield, the Englishman who taught French: "Eddie Gernantie was the pride of his aunty," etc. (I still have the tune but no more words.)

Comparing notes with Richard, I again confirm my view that memory, at least with persons of disciplined minds, is far less inaccurate than it is incomplete. Wherever I have had to correct what I had written about Yeates, it was because I had tried to fill in blanks in my memory with inferences as to what must probably have been the case, rather than because I had a definite recollection, and Richard had an equally definite but incompatible one. I also confirm my theory about the causation of the blanks in question. Richard was more a member of the gang than I, less solitary, and so had talked more with others about his teachers, and chatted more, also, with the teachers. So he had stored away more items about the school life, though fewer items about animals in the surrounding country.

Richard has always been in the best possible sense an organization man as well as an original scholar. The history of the University of Wisconsin would be more incomplete with him left out than the history of any university I have functioned in with me left out of account. For Richard always took his full share of responsibility for institutional policies, and I have rather shirked my share by comparison. This difference between us was apparent when we were roommates at school in 1912-1913. I predicted that he would be a college president and that I would not. He escaped that fate; but he was chairman of his department for six years and also he did everything one could do to save his university from mistakes of policy without being dean or president. In early middle age he ran an office in wartime Washington under the OSS with seventy-five researchers in geography working in it.

In thinking about Yeates, I tend to recall what I have read about the so-called public schools in England and the way a sensitive, gifted boy was sometimes treated, both by other pupils and also by masters. Perhaps I am confusing nineteenth-century customs with those of the early twentieth century, but it seems to me that by comparison Yeates was remarkably free from brutality of any kind. There was almost no physical punishment. Mr. Stansfield had a reputation for temper; but all I ever saw him do was hurl a small book at a boy many feet away, which did him no hurt. There was no hazing of new pupils.

The pupils did not seriously mistreat one another. There was the school bad boy, already referred to, but he was too stupid and uncharismatic to set a fashion. When I unwisely told him that the roots of a wild plant (the Jack-in-the-Pulpit) *if* carefully parboiled for hours, could be safely eaten like potatoes and was so eaten by Indians, he got one of these roots and offered it, *not* parboiled, to another boy who tried eating it and soon found his mouth in bad shape. The other boy was bigger, and retaliated by pushing his malicious enemy into the creek with all his clothes on. No, there was little need to fear that bad boy. He was simply a nuisance. He took a fancy to me, and for some time I could hardly escape his unwelcome company. Finally, I had the one fist fight of my life with him. It was quickly stopped by a teacher and did not reach a definitive ending. Thereafter, Spencer was still a nuisance, though somewhat less so.

That fight was probably the last time that I ever even wanted to strike another human being. People who go through life banging, knifing, or shooting other people (men, or especially, women), I have to make an effort to even begin to understand. I certainly never once so much as *wanted* to strike a woman. Not that I like any better to see a woman strike a man (on television).

It was important that the school was only for nine months of the year, so that there were the long summer vacations, besides Christmas and Easter holidays, with the family to look forward to. In summer we went to Eagles Mere, an idyllically beautiful mountain lake resort in northeastern Pennsylvania where I could continue observing birds. This, too, meant an unusual environment. Our hotel, The Lakeside, was owned by a Quaker family and was between the cheapest and the most expensive of the hotels. It had a tennis court. I played tennis with my twin brothers, whom I could almost always beat, though by a comfortably small margin, and with the son of the hotel owner. How well he played I can't now recall, oddly enough. The hotel also had table shuffle board, the only game in which I ever came near to real prowess. I have never seen waxed tables of that kind since, except once on television.

A tragic and for me somewhat shameful memory of life at Eagles Mere is of a drowning. That summer we were living in a house close to the hotel and getting only meals at the hotel. Early in the morning, while still in bed, I heard a hoarse voice calling "help, help, help." The shame is that I did not instantly jump out of bed and rush toward the lake whence the sounds came. Instead I debated with myself about the meaning of the cries and what my response should be for perhaps half a minute or more, and then heard footsteps of two men rushing down to the lake. Two hotel employes had gone swimming before their daily work started. One was drowning and the other trying to save him. He was not successful, and help came too late.

At school, as later in the army and later still in my teaching career, I seem to have been found somewhat odd by some of those around me. At school the bird-watching, shared by no one else there, was perhaps the chief reason for this. But another circumstance, in substance totally irrelevant, seems to have played a role.

This circumstance was that our rectory in Phoenixville was across the street from an alley leading into a section of the town entirely owned by the town's iron works and occupied by its workers, who had been imported from central Europe. Another boy from Phoenixville who came to the school, Charles Vanderslice (not meaning any harm, Richard thinks) spread the word around that Richard and I lived next to a part of Phoenixville called Hunkey Row; and this led—by what logic, you tell me—to my being called the Big Guinea and Richard, the Little Guinea. I suspect, too, that big meant worst and little less bad. None of this made any special difference to Richard or to me. I was not lonely, though often quite solitary, at Yeates, and surely Richard was not.

In general, feeling lonely has not been an outstanding feature of life for me. One reason is a somewhat Wordsworthian feeling for nature, a feeling that came to me not only, though partly, from reading Wordsworth. But it came directly from nature itself. Yeates was an ideal setting for such experiences. They could be quite intense.

There was at school one lovely chap, Hayward Smith (brother of H.P. or "Horse power" Smith, the school's football hero), who shared the fondness for poetry that burst upon me as a new discovery while at Yeates. (I also had one competitor in the nature study, Paul Denkla, who studied rabbits, while I studied a family of woodpeckers of the kind called flickers conspicuously nesting in a hole on the side of an apple tree in the center of the school grounds.) The poetic youth, as I learned later, has had a career in his father's business. He was a second Dick Bowers, good right through. I still can "see" his candid face.

Among various rules devised by Dr. Gardiner, one was that each boy would either attain a certain average grade or else spend 1¼ hours each weekday morning after breakfast studying in a long room assigned to that purpose. If, as my brother and I did, one made the required grade, then what one did with that period was one's own affair. In spring, with bird migration going on, I often spent it bird watching, and this was one reason that I made such rapid progress in bird identification. As all bird watchers know, mornings are the time for bird watching, and spring is much easier than fall for identifying species.

Another ingenious rule concerned Sunday afternoons. We were not allowed then to be in any school building except the gymnasium. In wet weather that was where we usually went. Otherwise we often went walking in the countryside. There wasn't much else to do. In those days, there were, near the school, no commercial stores, taverns, and, of course, no service stations, radio, or T.V. The surrounding country was just farmland and woodlots, except for one town several miles away. The city of Lancaster, as I have said, was forbidden. At some neighboring farms, they would sell us pies. But at one farm we were told that selling on Sunday was contrary to their religion (they were Mennonites); but we could take the pie and bring the money on a weekday.

There was a dammed-up creek with an electric generating plant for the school, and we could canoe on the stream for some distance in the piled-up deep water. At flood times one also could canoe downstream below the dam. I had my own canoe.

There were two fraternities in the school, but they were not national and were rather mild in their effects. I recall playing billiards on the table that my fraternity had assigned to it. I played with Charles Perot, whom I recall almost exclusively as a billiards opponent. Which of us usually won I have no idea, but probably it was not I, or I would recall better how it was. Besides, I tended to be mediocre in physical skills. Charles had an older brother (not at the school) who was an oddity. He had the largest private coin collection I have ever seen. I met him only once. He told me that it was his regret that he "could not even be sure that death is the end." It was the uncertainty that bothered him, not the idea that death was final. That he did not object to. I have come to sympathize with him in this, having myself a firm belief that our careers are bounded by birth and death, and that this is as it should be and not in principle objectionable. (See Chapter 2, 3rd Section.) When and how we die is another matter, and one that calls for wisdom and hope.

Two other boys and I built a tree house by the stream near the school. One of the other two boys was named Zimmermann, and a nice boy he was. He had lived for a time in Cuba and could read Spanish. The third boy (oddly) I cannot identify in any way at present. I guess the worldly-wise Zimmermann had planned the construction and ordered the lumber and other materials. It was nicely designed with two stories, the lower one narrow and sleeping only one boy, the other wider and sleeping two. I slept alone on the narrower lower floor. I cannot recall which night of the week we were allowed to sleep there but it seems slightly remarkable that this was allowed at all. However, this was not a repressive school. I presume that the growth of the trees has destroyed the structure long before now. It was in a small piece of woods and very close to the stream, a pretty spot indeed, not far from the athletic field. It seems ridiculous that I recall how this tree house looked, inside and out, better than I recall either of the boys who built and used it with me, particularly that third one. *Zimmermann* means "carpenter" in German, but that hardly seems a likely explanation of how one of us was able to design, and see to its full construction, so neat a little building as I know it turned out to be. It also seems unlikely that I designed it and forgot so completely having done so. Perhaps we worked it out together.

Richard says that, the year after I left Yeates, Zimmerman associated much with Spencer, the school rascal; thus, one of the nicest with the least nice of the boys. The only explanation apparent for this is that Spencer needed no invitation to haunt a person he had decided upon, and the question always was how to get rid of him. Is there a possibility of his having corrupted Zimmerman in some way? It seems to me unlikely. I recall thinking Z. was nice, but no very definite evidences of his niceness. However, no counter-indications could have been apparent to me; for they would have caused my sense of the niceness to be vaguely or sharply qualified. It is possible Z. was sorry for Spencer and tried to help him.

In retrospect (and even at the time) I have had some sympathy for Spencer. His father (or was it an uncle?) came to see him once, and he looked no more attractive than Spencer, who was clearly a disadvantaged youngster reacting not well to unfavorable home circumstances.

A quite undisadvantaged youngster was Truxton Brodhead. I knew because I visited him at his home in Parkesburg. He was an amiable youth, remarkably slender but healthy; and he somehow seemed not only slender but physically pliable. At least, my most distinct recollection of him is of several of us stuffing him, as it were, down into a large clothes basket and shutting the lid (or was it, vainly attempting to do this?), Truxton giggling all the while. He went down into that basket, it seemed, like a structure of macaroni.

Some of the Yeates pupils were boarders and some were day pupils from Lancaster. My recollections do not very clearly sort them into the two classes. Lancaster was 4 miles away, an easy trip by electric trolley. The city was out of bounds except on Sunday mornings when we all took the trolley there to attend the Episcopal Church, where several pews up front were consigned to us. After church we were allowed to go to a drug store for an ice cream sundae to fill the time before the next trolley departed. Before taking the trolley for church, each boy had to present a closed envelope addressed to his family. One of the teachers told how at some schools the master would insist on seeing that there was a written letter inside it, whereas at Yeates it was, sensibly enough, left to parents or other guardians to police the contents of the envelope.

The Rev. Mr. Twombly, who preached to us in the Lancaster Church, I recall as a grimly earnest soul, with less than usual of the Episcopal urbanity. He was an activist and locally famous for his attacks on houses of prostitution. If he had anything of philosophic depth or originality, it failed to register in my mind. But his sincerity seemed indubitable. Some years ago I noticed that a colleague here in the University of Texas was named Twombly. We were both delighted to discover that my Lancaster rector was his grandfather. The grandson has the geniality I at least did not detect in the grandfather.

Mixed society at Yeates was restricted. Mrs. Sampson was almost negligible, and Mrs. Gardiner came into our lives little except when, and if, we went to hear her read aloud Sunday evenings. One year there was a woman who taught drawing and painting. She came out from Lancaster one day each week. I remember little of her. That there was no teaching of music was, I think, a misfortune, for me at least. (I ought to have had instruction in music and never did after an early year in public school where we did start to learn to sing from notes.)

The school arranged to have some dancing with selected girls in Lancaster, but my feeling now is that this was a very few times a year. Just one girl comes to mind vaguely, and the most definite thing about her is that she was little more to me than a possible dance partner and a harmless, unexciting person. The school had daily evening chapel. I recall chiefly the dismal tune of "Abide with me/Fast falls the eventide."

Appendicitis and Poetry

During the autumn of my second year at Yeates I suffered from appendicitis without knowing it. The gnawing dull abdominal pain at times meant I knew not what. During Christmas vacation at home it returned more acutely. I gathered from what Father told me afterwards, more than clearly recall it directly, that when a doctor diagnosed it as appendicitis and advised an operation Father urged waiting to see if the trouble wouldn't pass away without an operation. He said later that this had been a mistake on his part. In fact my death was the most likely result, for I had peritonitis (or so a doctor diagnosed the symptoms I recall) and this, before antibiotics, usually was fatal. This was one of several times when my death was a reasonable prediction.

The operation finally took place and I spent some time in the local hospital, though the surgeon came out from Philadelphia. I had no idea in the world that I was in danger while this was going on. I merely knew that I went without eating several days before the operation, was given ether, and at no time after the operation suffered pain that I recall from that part of myself. But something else happened that changed my life from then on. Very likely it was partly a result of the ether and partly of not eating for several days. One remembers how the Amerindians used to fast to see visions, have spiritual experiences. Regaining consciousness from the ether, I found myself in a remarkable and pleasant enough state. Lying there peacefully, I had only to close my eyes to have vivid and changing visual experiences. Nice green landscapes would flow horizontally in front of me, for instance.

Perhaps a day or two later I found myself wanting to write poetry, for the first time in my life. For eight years thereafter, I continued to try my hand frequently at this new occupation, at the end of which time it had become clear to me that my interest in prose discussion of philosophical questions was stronger and intruded too much into the poetry for the good of the latter. But my reading of classical English poetry, later also German, was enormously stimulated by this experience of trying really hard to write poetry myself. This interest is still with me. Alas, Robert Frost and Robinson Jeffers were the last of the recent poets I could respond well to. Wallace Stevens, in spite of considerable effort, I cannot assimilate or much enjoy. This makes me feel an old fogey. Carl Sandburg I do somewhat appreciate.

The fasting-and-ether binge that got me started in poetry was not the stimulus that led me to study birds. That must have started earlier; for the first poem I wrote was about "The Song of the Hermit Thrush," and when I went to Yeates I scarcely knew one bird from another—or so it seems to me now. What started my bird study was a quite definite event. At Christmastime, in 1913, while on vacation from Yeates School, and in Philadelphia to buy some Christmas presents for relatives, I saw in the book division of a department store a pocket-sized bird guide, probably the best ever prepared in this country, perhaps in the world, up to that time. It was so good that not very many years ago, it was reprinted. The author was Chester A. Reed. His book was as though designed for me, because it was limited almost entirely to songbirds, so that I began to specialize from the outset in what was for me the most congenial aspect of bird study, listening to, analyzing, and trying to understand the significance of bird song. For a nonprofessional ornithologist to attempt to identify the species of hawks, owls, ducks, gulls, shore birds, and so on, as well as all the songbirds, would be too much, especially if he wanted to know about songbirds around the world, and the phenomenon of song as such, which is what I eventually realized I did want to do.

The Evening Hymn of the Hermit Thrush

'Tis the quiet of twilight 'neath lofty trees,
    And the leaves are unrustled by passing breeze;
In the west o'er the hill glows a dying fire,
    Now are silent the birds, nature's winged choir.

In the shady ravine pale shadows grow dark,
    Silence broods o'er the woods like a dove, but hark!
Steal melodious sounds through the forest hush,
    "Tis the evening hymn of the hermit thrush.

How serene, clear, and pure is the song he sings,
    And how solemn the peace and joy it brings
To a heart that is yearning the music to hear
    That murmurs through all things inaudibly near.

Oh whence that etherial melody sweet —
    Like the rising of fountains so rythmically fleet?
Would that mine were the fountain from whence it springs,
    Then my verses were sweet as the song he sings.

For the soul of the beautiful breathes through the tones —
    Neither gladness nor sadness nor nightingale's moans
The spirit of nature, the breath of the spring,
    The voice of the autumn — the leaves whispering;

The sternness of winter, the softness of snow;
    The mildness of summer when warm breezes blow.
The soul of the universe dwells in my soul
    Where unseen clear streams of loveliness roll.

Birds may not have souls, but it seems to me
    Divine the real source of their music must be.
Would that mine were the fountain from whence it springs,
    Then my verses were sweet as the song he sings.

There's a foretaste of heaven in this lofty strain
  To deserve which from sin may I ever refrain.
Need I further assurance that heaven is bliss
  When I find such delight in a world like this?

On and on sings the minstrel disdaining applause,
  Hymning with only a rhythmical pause.
Little matters it him if his song's unheard,
  A true artist he, though only a bird.

The first damp breath of night now is stirring the leaves
  While a web of dark shadows the moonlight weaves:
When at last the bird ceases, the forest o'er
  The strange silence of solitude settles once more.

—JANUARY 1915

Except for a verse of four lines, this is the only poem I know of
about the song of this species. If the bird occurred in England or
Europe this would be inconceivable. A Hermit Thrush song, like
many bird songs, has a theme and a number of variations, following
each other in unpredictable or free order. In such cases the pauses
between any two variations are rather brief (hence, the "rhythmical"),
meaning in my later developed theory, that the bird has not forgotten
the preceding utterance and is enjoying the contrast between the
two. The proof is that no variation is sung twice in direct succession.
By contrast, with singers that have but a single pattern and can
only repeat themselves, pauses tend to be much longer. This, I hold,
shows a primitive aesthetic sense, a tendency to avoid monotony.

Each variation begins with a prolonged flutelike tone, followed
by a rapid (hence, the "fleet") series of higher pitched but also mu-
sically pure tones. If a recording of the singing is played at half or
quarter speed, lowering the pitch, the tones are still wonderfully
flutelike. This is not true of a nightingale's singing. The Hermit
Thrush's song is not a riotously happy sounding song like the Bobo-
link's, nor does it, like a Mourning Dove's and even more a certain Afri-
can dove's, seem to express sadness. (The "moans" in the poem refers
to a part of the nightingale's singing that to some seems to express
grief.) If a poem by a subhuman animal could express reverence, reli-

gious exaltation, this would be it. Bach in human music comes to mind. The American Wood Thrush's singing, lower pitched and more leisurely in tempo, but also flutelike, is like Handel in feeling. Peter Szöke, of Hungary, world authority on bird song as music, furnished with a recording of the Hermit Thrush's song, found it more musical, by his criteria, than any European song, with the wood lark the closest competitor. This confirmed my impressions formed before reading Szöke, or talking to him.

When the poem was being written, five or six months had passed since I last had heard the song. Also it was my first serious attempt to write poetry, and I was only seventeen. I had probably read what two musicians had said about the song of this thrush, using the terms *spiritual, sublime, more of the joy of heaven than the passions of earth, sweet, silvery,* and *grand climax of all bird music.* No other bird's song in the world, it seems, has produced quite this effect on human listeners, and especially not any song heard in Europe. Shelley's marvellous poem about the European skylark is certainly a far greater piece of verbal artistry, but in both cases the poem fits the species remarkably closely—as Keat's nightingale, for instance, does not, wonderful poem though it is.

Memory, Youth, and Age (not quite a sonnet)

> *Memory is a magic forest glade*
> *of time-mysterious, zephyr-tuned trees,*
> *From whence arising from the gloomy shade*
> *the soul of youth, enticed by phantasies,*
> *Looks longing to the sky where luring float*
> *ambition tinted visionary clouds;*
> *But age with lowered eye alone doth note*
> *the withered leaves like swiftly falling shrouds.*
> *In youth the streams of life flow onward fast*
> *from labyrinthine vales of memoried past;*
> *In age the backing waves the rivers climb,*
> *till turns in death the surging tide of time,*
> *Then flow they down, of time forever free.*

> —JUNE, 1915

I wrote a few complete sonnets but have mislaid them.
About fifty years after the poems just cited were written, I began
a poem whose final version is as follows.

Of Geographical Names

Oh how I like to hear
  Of Semipalatinsk;
How up it makes me cheer
  When there is talk of Minsk,
Nor does it turn me off
  To learn a town's named Pskoff.

What luck if one could rambla
  As far as Cochabambla
See Tacna in Peru,
  Or British Borneo
And Mount Kinabalu.

And Oh the liquid sounds
  That come from Indonesia:
Palambang, Pankalan,
  Samarang, Cheribon —
I swear that these must please ya.

How lovely are Nairobi,
  N'gasa or N'gong,
Riobamba or Manabe,
  Amarillo or Penang.

There's San Luis Obispo
  And the misnamed San Francisco,
The improbable Pango Pango
  And beautious de Janeiro.

There's the nearly unpronounceable
  Hajduszobörmeny
And the not easily announceable
  St. Brieue in Brittany.

Let's not forget the loved ones,
Or were they named in malice?
Virginia and Victoria
   And the lonely Springs of Alice.

Louise, Lucile, and Lucy,
   Florenceville and Fay,
Opal, Elsa, Elnora,
   Evangeline and May,
Martha and Marietta,
   Mary'svile and Kay.

With apologies to all geographers, including my brother Richard, for the intercontinental, interhemispheric scrambling, also to Ogden Nash whose influence I think I detect, and to whom I owe some good hours that might have been not so good. Dorothy read him to me soon after a serious operation.

I see in this poem some confirmation of an idea expressed here and there in this book, that a person's actual career is in no way programmed in advance or eternally (that least of all) but depends on chance intersections of free decisions of countless agents or active singulars. I could have been, and actually thought of being, a teacher of English literature, and then I would very likely have continued to write poetry, and perhaps fiction as well, as my primary contribution, along no doubt with some non-technically philosophical essays.

CHAPTER FOUR

Some Playmates and Relatives

Small Town Society

During the times when I was at home in Phoenixville (and not at boarding-school, Haverford College, the army, or Harvard) I experienced some bits of social life with a very small number of boys and girls considered as on our social level. There was one "queen," clearly the prettiest one. Her father was rather well-to-do. She married the man I shall mention presently who became a naval officer. He died of cancer; and she refused to see him after the disease was rather advanced. It was a miserable ending to a human life. I know not what happened to the widow afterwards. She and I never meant much to each other.

In Phoenixville, as I have said, there were two branches of the wealthy Reeves family. William Reeves, who lived near us, had largely financed our church. Miss May Reeves, of that branch, was a vigorous middle-aged (or so she seemed to me) spinster who played tennis and once invited me to play with her. I don't know now who played better; but this perhaps means that I did not. (We did not see much of either Reeves family socially.) I recall a big Christmas party given by William, a semipublic affair.

One scion of the other, or Alfred, Reeves family occasionally came to visit his relatives in Phoenixville for a while, and we got to know and like him. He was in every sense a young gentleman, but does not stand out very distinctively beyond that characterization. He brought with him a splendid collie dog when we went to our swimming-hole

Fig. 12. The complete family and Aunt Amy at Phoenixville (Front row, left
to right: Henry, Charles, Mother, Father, James; (Second row, left to
right: Alfred, Aunt Amy, Frances, and Richard)

in the creek that ran not far from the Alfred Reeves estate. I remember that he found out somehow that I had an inaccurate idea of the sex organs of females, and he called his dog to him in order to show me my mistake. I recall his doing this without any air of superiority, but simply to make clear what he was talking about. I found nothing wrong with this boy.

Our regular playmates in the town were less aristocratic, definitely middle-class. They were not all in the Episcopal Church; I think one or two were Presbyterian. (Anyone who changed from another church to the Episcopal was accused of social climbing; however, this rarely happened.) There was Walt McCallum, who may have saved my life on one occasion. I say *may* because I find it hard to believe that I would have been so incompetent (I was then definitely a swimmer) as to have drowned in the small pool in a stream in which he saw me choking from having swallowed water; but he instantly dived in and pulled me out. If it is not certain that I would otherwise have drowned, it is not certain that I would not have. I shall tell later of an occasion when without reasonable doubt my life was saved by a companion; and when the chances of there being present a companion capable of saving it at the precise moment when he was needed were rather slight.

Walt was a good youthful companion, but not a lifelong associate for an intellectual person. When I saw him in maturity, I discovered with some shock that he had not become a reader of books. He explained his low level of literacy by saying that he was "saving his eyes." What he was saving them for was left obscure. It was not, I gathered, a question of abnormal eyes. He evidently wanted a reason for not reading.

Another youthful companion, a pleasant enough chap, later became a naval officer. He once told me how he and some fellow officers, when on land in China, would force natives out of their way as they swaggered through Chinese streets. When I reported this to Father, he commented, with his usual vigorous realism, "They're storing up trouble for us all." (Remember the question, "Why did we lose China?" Did we ever "have" China? And how did we treat Chinese and Japanese when they came, or wanted to come to this country?) Youthful companions are one thing; companions in maturity are

Fig. 13. The Weston Cousins at Holmhurst: Carl (left) and Harold (right)

somewhat different. The longer we live the more we may diverge in interest, values, and skills.

Two other youthful companions were less far apart from us in values; but circumstances intervened to prevent us from seeing much of them in maturity. So with all six of us children our mature associates were not our childish and youthful ones. This of course is in part simply the mobility of the population of this restless country. But it seems also (unluckily) in the nature of highly civilized, highly differentiated cultures.

The closest to exceptions to the foregoing were the family relatives of our generation, especially siblings and first cousins on the paternal side. I always enjoyed seeing Harold, "Carl" (Charles), and Esther Weston; Emily Hartshorne Mudd, Clementine ("Tina") Hartshorne Jenney, and Ted (Edward Yarnall) Hartshorne (alas, mysteriously murdered in his prime in Germany by two German soldiers after the Second World War). These relatives all had somewhat similar backgrounds, values, and common memories with the children of F. C. Hartshorne. Every one was of superior quality and a benefit to society. Several became famous; and though Tina did not, she is one of those nearly faultless personalities that are a blessing to as many people as come to know them.

Harold was a fine artist, and at times a statesman of sorts as well. He founded Foods for Freedom, an organization that probably had some effect in bringing about a constructive policy toward Europe after the war (Marshall Plan and the like), dropping his painting for several years to accomplish this. He went to Washington, found a way to see Eleanor Roosevelt. through whom he met several key people, including Secretary Acheson. The latter told him, "We're taking care of these matters, why don't you go back home?" to which Harold (as he told me) replied, "This is my country as much as it is yours. I'm

Fig. 14. Harold Weston, my distinguished
cousin (deceased)

going to stay here and see this thing through." Which he did. Carl became a lawyer in the Justice Department. Aunt Amy told a story about him at the age of five. He was taught a well-known prayer to say before going to bed. Once he reedited the prayer as follows: "Now I lay me down to sleep / I pray the Lord my soul to keep / All this day thy care hath led me / *Nevertheless, the bee stung me* / And I thank thee for thy care.

I have no knowledge of Carl's mature thinking about the age-old theological problem of evil thus hinted at by himself when five years old. I do know that it points to an ambiguity in the idea of Providence that theologians for nearly twenty centuries lacked the clarity or the courage to face and overcome. Did God deliberately design that bee sting as wise punishment, stimulus to moral development, or what not? I think the truth is simple: God did not design it at all. Carl and the bee between them, though unwittingly, designed it. The details of what happens in the world are *unintended, even by God*. Of few things am I more confident than this negative statement. And my father would have agreed with me, clergyman though he was. If this surprises some readers, then so much the worse for a dominant strand in the theological tradition of the West.

Another boy from Phoenixville who went to Yeates when Richard did was Charles Thompson. (See figure 9) He was the son of a judge and became a lawyer himself. In Phoenixville he was the pitcher of the baseball team formed by the four older Hartshorne boys (all except Alfred) and five other boys. I was president of the club and, as I recall it, secretary and treasurer as well. Richard, because of being cross-eyed (and having to wear glasses from even an earlier age than I did) did not shine, and Alfred was too young then to be considered. There was a boy we always hoped would hit a home run because he once did; but usually he swung hard and struck out. The ball field was beside our house, an empty lot on which the parish was supposed some day to build something. It is now a parking lot. The field was not full baseball size, and we played nearer to the right side of the field so that a hit over the first base would not have to be struck very hard to go over the right fence, which counted for a two-base hit, whereas a hit sharply to the left, with somewhat greater range, could make the fence on that side for a "threebagger," and a hit straight down the field could, once in a long while, go over the back fence for a home run. I seem to recall doing (or was it almost doing?) it once. Those two years before going to Yeates I read the professional baseball news and took the game quite seriously. At Yeates and at Haverford I cannot recall baseball.

Later, at Harvard, I actually played baseball against Yale—but these were Phi Beta Kappa teams, and extremely mediocre players, all except one good pitcher on the Yale team that, therefore, naturally won the game. It has been a satisfaction to me ever since that I *did* catch the only fly that came to me in the outfield. At bat I either struck out or failed to reach first base. After Harvard I played only once. That was when my daughter was at summer camp, and there was some affair involving parents and their children. I failed to shine. At Haverford, I suppose I could have learned to play cricket but did not avail myself of the opportunity; so that the language of that game still is meaningless to me. Golf I tried; but it seemed a stupid game, lacking in drama. The whole transaction is between oneself and that inanimate sitting ball; whereas in tennis, baseball, or soccer, one mostly deals with the ball as propelled or carried by another. Always one has to anticipate the other's (or others') actions and try to outwit as well as outnerve and outskill the others. As for basketball, it does not seem to have existed in my vicinity when I was young.

Tennis was the only game that has interested me in maturity, although I did see one baseball game of the major league "Phillies" and saw an outfielder named Strunk make one of the most nearly impossible catches of all time. The fly was short and he dove forward along the ground with outstretched glove and got up with the ball still in the glove. Who won? No idea, but who could forget that catch?

Paul Weiss, to whose help in editing Charles Peirce I shall always feel indebted, as I also shall to his founding of the Metaphysical Society and *The Review of Metaphysics*, has written a *Philosophy of Sport*, which I found interesting. He considers various theories as to the value of sport and decides that the best one (as I recall it) is that it gives many young people a definite chance to achieve fame for a definite and measurable kind of excellence. All human skills are interesting. Although many kinds of animals play, they do not play with objects made for the purpose and according to conscious rules.

Charles Thompson's father, a judge, was humorous, and his mother seemed by comparison solemn; but there was a vein of sly humor in her, too. She came to Yeates to visit Charles and invited him, Richard, and me to a dinner at a hotel in Lancaster. She told us beforehand what we were going to have—I think, corned beef and cabbage, which was no delicacy in our eyes if in anyone's—but when the time came, the meal turned out to be a splendid feast. She meantime was amused to see our unenthusiastic faces while listening to her oral menu. Mother delighted in this story told to her by Mrs. Thompson.

Charles was the Phoenixville playmate who stands out for ability and character, but, alas, not one word that he uttered is still with me. (Wrong! A phrase or two does come.) He was younger than I. Older than I was the third Charles ("Chug"), son of a druggist. (I was then called "Chick.") We went canoeing on the canal or the river. They were close to each other. He had a twenty-two rifle and I took a bow and arrow; we shot frogs with these weapons. I remember Chug's speech better than Thompson's. He was a safe playmate, but rather prosaic. We were both in the same army medical unit in the war. I recall a few remarks he made there, also, but again they were not very notable. One was why (in the army) after one trial, he stopped having sex with the available women. "It's not as much fun as you think it will be." He was a fellow who lived carefully and unadventuresomely; except that he returned from the war with an Italian bride who seemed much more colorful than he. Alas, she apparently came to that conclusion and finally left him.

A relative of Chug's actually died of scurvy without ever setting foot on a ship and without being poor or underprivileged. Simply he decided, as a matter of taste, to live exclusively on cooked meat, and perhaps some bread and potatoes, and so had far too little vitamin C. One guesses that the doctors in that town were not used to seeing scurvy and may have been slow to diagnose the disease. Moral: if you think to live differently from everybody else you had better know something about the item you add to, or drop from, the universal practice and its effects on human body and mind. If everybody who can do so eats some fruits and green vegetables there may be a reason other than mere taste.

Sister Frances, Cousin Emily, Some Aunts

My sister, a year older, did not move in the same social circles as her brothers. The society of Phoenixville was not very satisfying to her. She had one rather naive young man who seemed to like her, and he came to dinner once. We often afterwards recalled his suddenly saying, "You know, I'm not at all noticeable; I never saw that _____" (something or other visible in or from our dining room).

In my teens, almost no female, unless my mother, was as vivid to me as my female cousins. My cousin Emily, later famous as an expert on marriage counseling, early in our acquaintanceship informed me that because we are first cousins we could never marry. Perhaps the warning was not necessary; but she was always interesting, and so was her mother, a person with whom (though she had not gone to college) a college student could discuss Meredith's novel, *The Egoist*, for instance (and elicit relevant comments), as surely he could not (then or now) with most women—or men. She was the relative who had given me books, and suitable good books, as a boy. She was also one who, besides sharing my intellectual interests to some extent, could deftly take me down a peg when it was desirable. Once in the company of Aunt Clementine and another lady, I made a remark about humor that seemed a bit too pretentious to her, so she said, "Give us a résumé of the philosophy of humor, Charles." Then, turning to the other lady, "He's perfectly capable of it, you know." This is not the only instance of the kind I could relate. Always her criticism was perceptive. This was not the case with another Aunt (a sister of Mother) who once told me I would "all through life miss the subtleties of conversation," but only because I had not physically *heard* a word or phrase she had just uttered. I did not misunderstand the word or phrase, it simply did not reach my auditory cortex. This was the aunt who also informed me that I was not a genius. Aunt Clementine would have known, I think, that I was not hopelessly devoid of subtlety or talent. It is a pleasure to add that both I and the aunt who set limits to my abilities (and with whom I had other difficulties) mellowed with age so that a tête-à-tête could be a pleasure to us. I took her to dinner not long before she died at about ninety, and we had a splendid time.

She was the relative my father called "bright" with enthusiasm. She lived her last years in Santa Fe and drove a small car there. When I expressed surprise at this to one of her lady friends I got the reply, "Why, she's the Barney Oldfield [a great car racer] of Santa Fe!" She never married because "Mr. Right never came along." But she did not give an impression of suffering from this cause. She taught singing for a while and was a singer who rather early decided against a concert or opera career. It is my experience that music tends to give both men and women a combination of emotional vividness and emotional discipline that somewhat justifies Plato's views on the subject. Almost every girl or woman (other than a relative) I have especially liked has been more musical (in training) than I am, to put it mildly.

Aunt Amy and Lillie Zietz

On the Hartshorne side of the family an important and consistently constructive person was Aunt Amy. She took me in charge for a year when I was less than two years old. She made me memorize: "Charles must *mind* Aunt Amy!" I'm sure I did mind her. She never married and no one expected her to marry. She did no physical work and was, let us say, not slender. I recall the softness of her hands. She was well off financially by inheritance, with no worries about money that were ever heard of. She was sane and fairly worldly wise. Her hobbies seemed to be traveling and reading French novels. She left her French books to us because she liked Dorothy's excellent French accent.

Amy Hartshorne took a great interest in her thirteen nieces and nephews, was always ready to be hostess to any of them, and never failed to send them nice presents at Christmas time. Except when we were quite small, these presents took the form of money. Each of the thirteen, I believe, got the same sum on a given year. When one of us married, Aunt Amy decided that he ought to have an unusually large amount; but as she always treated all alike we all got that amount. So the marrying one, Alfred, could tell the rest of us, and being a punster had to do so—"I've raised the anté!" This was the best of Alfred's puns.

Each year, Aunt Amy or one of Father's other sisters, or his brother's wife Aunt Clementine, gave a huge Christmas party. What a benefit that was! It guaranteed that (after my family had moved to Phoenixville, near where the relatives lived) we all got together at least once a year, and not only the thirteen first cousins but some more distant relatives. Aunt Amy gave the party more often than the others. She had both the servants and the free time to do so. For many years she had as companion and some times chauffeur (she never drove herself) a trained nurse whom she had come to know when she was hospitalized by an illness. Lillie Zietz was her name. Lillie was a strong character, given to memorable ways of expressing herself, and she entered into family affairs with an interest comparable to Aunt Amy's, but with a tarter tongue. She was a mature person, who had early faced life, drawn up a balance of its forces, and made her choices once and for all. She had felt love for a married doctor, decided this was a blind alley, and so gave up marriage. One surmises that when Aunt Amy proposed to share with her a comfortable life, with only a moderate amount of work to do—except when she had nursing duties or arranged travel—and to be a member of a large family group and companion to a person of character and sense, this seemed acceptable to her; and Lillie never complained about her part in it.

From Lillie's perspective, Aunt Amy was a bit naive and self-indulgent. "Amy, for a grown woman . . ." I recall her exclaiming. Once when they came to see us in the Indiana Dunes, Amy came into our cottage with a bag of tomatoes from her garden. "There," she burst out, "Lillie said I couldn't do it."

At a Christmas party (I suppose it was), D. C. H. told Lillie about my having assured her at the time of our engagement, "You're marrying into a good family." (I claim I meant chiefly that they would let us alone and be more likely to help than to need help financially. These expectations were borne out.) Lillie said, "Don't you believe a word of it. They are perfectly respectable, but they'll never set the world on fire." (Just the same, five of us thirteen Hartshorne cousins have appeared in Who's Who.)

Once when Lillie, Amy, and I looked into a Protestant church somewhere in Europe to see what the interior looked like, Lillie (who was Catholic) said scornfully, "There, you see. There is no host, no light. It's so dead it stinks." "Lillie!" was all Amy could say to that.

I was impressed by Lillie's discernment in ethical questions. There was a brother of Amy and of my father—we called him Uncle Ned— who had an undistinguished career in some office or other and was retired pematurely even from that. His wealthy father, Charles Hartshorne, I gathered, had pressured him into an occupation that did not suit him. However, he came to be known as the man you could count on for unselfish help in good causes. Lillie told me, "I have seen that man reach great heights." Like my brother Jim, he was a noble failure (though, because of inherited means, not poverty stricken), but ethically he was a great success.

When in the summer of 1909 we moved from Kittanning to Phoenixville and were therefore only 20 miles from Holmhurst, at Merion, where Aunt Amy and ten other relatives lived, instead of 300 miles as before, Aunt Amy soon had herself driven over to welcome us to the East. "Now that we are living near you," I said to her, "I can ride my bicycle over to see you." "Oh, Charles!" was the reply, "you couldn't possibly ride so far." "Certainly I can," said I. "You couldn't— why I'll give you five dollars if you do that." "I'll be over quite soon."

It may not have been the next day but it was only a few days at most before I turned up on two wheels, entered the parental great stone house (where Amy then still lived) with my hand out for the five dollars, which were quickly forthcoming. In those days it was safe enough to ride a bicycle anywhere, not, as it is now, a hazardous matter. I had ridden about as far near Kittanning some months or a year or two before that, so I saw no special problem in the project. I was used to reading maps. Later, I and a brother or two also walked the distance to Holmhurst. This was more tedious. After we got there, we soon started playing a game of tag with the cousins (the Westons and the E. Y. Hartshornes) and a rather weary ankle of mine gave out when I jumped over a flower bed. So the day ended in less than ideal fashion.

The estate of Charles Hartshorne (my grandfather) in Merion, Pennsylvania, where Amy lived until she bought her own house in Haverford, was also the home (in a separate building) of my Father's only brother, Uncle Ned. His children were all likable. The eldest, Carol, was very spastic, which affected her limbs and her speech, and indirectly of course, much else. But she was sound and good in sense and character and looked after her much younger brother, the only boy, in admirable fashion. Her life was not wretched; she always found some *modus vivendi*, but she died in middle age, and I suppose was not normally happy much of the time. Her ailment did not directly limit her intelligence; but indirectly it certainly handicapped her mental development somewhat. (See letter on pages 172-73)

How many families now live on the many-acred and long ago subdivided Hartshorne estate I cannot say, but no doubt they are numerous. Apart from servants, twelve persons lived there after the death of the grandparents (of whom I have no conscious memory): Aunt Amy, Aunt Mary, who had married the Ethical Culture leader, S. Burns Weston, their three children, Uncle Ned (E. Y. Hartshorne), his wife Aunt Clementine, and finally their four children.

Both Aunt Amy and Lillie, thanks (or not thanks) to modern hospital resources lived until they were no longer fully themselves. But it was not, I heard, Lillie who turned unfriendly to the other. The long association did not have a very happy ending. If the human species survives for another century or two we shall, one must hope, grow up in our attitude toward death enough to realize that enabling people to physically outlive that which makes them worthy of respect is a dubious gift of science. "Respect for life"—all life, including that of insects and bacteria? This has its place and I feel that respect. But particular respect for *human* life presupposes that the humanness is there. In some bodies lying in hospitals it is no longer there. And even short of that extreme, a soured ignoble remnant of humanness is a dismal way of ending a human career.

My parents escaped this fate. Father, in his eighties, went to his office the Friday before the Sunday on which he died. Mother grew somewhat senile—but soured, quarrelsome, unfriendly, never. Her touch of saintliness perdured to the end. As my sister (a good judge), who alone visited her much in her last years and months, said: "If I did not go to see her [a half hour's drive away] for a fairly long time, she never said, 'Why haven't you come more often?' but always, 'It's so nice you've come.'" Mother (as Father had always done) paid her other children's fare when we came to visit, saying with a smile, "My money is for my own pleasure, and I like to see you." This was always my parents' behavior after we reached maturity. They did not act as though it was our obligation, or pleasure, to come to see them as much as it was theirs to enable us to do so. They did not demand attention, they awaited and welcomed it. Dorothy and I have tried to do likewise with our daughter Emily.

Lillie was always cordial enough to me; but she did make a few criticisms. When my brother Henry died after an illness of some weeks, I was writing my Ph.D. dissertation, which I had left to the last few weeks before I was to go abroad for postdoctoral study. Father wrote about Henry, "anything may happen," which I realized meant that death was very possible. Yet for a good many days I did not go home. Lillie was one of those who put family relations high in the list of obligations. She said I should have gone home at once. I have no brief for my conduct on this occasion. I finally got home just after Henry died. What effect my coming earlier would have had on anyone is, of course, speculative. My parents made no comment on my delayed response. But Lillie was certainly entitled to her judgment in this case. As she put it, "I know just what you had been told."

Perhaps the dissertation was less important in inhibiting my response to Father's letter than the sense I had that Henry was a defeated soul and that I had been too little with or in touch with him for several years (really about seven) to have much chance of boosting his morale or giving him pleasure. But I doubt if Lillie would have thought this a sufficient defense. Possibly my presence would have made this, the most tragic time in my parents' lives, more bearable than it was. They were both far sadder than I ever saw them before or after. Doubtless, this implies that, taking the world in general as the norm, they enjoyed rare good luck in their lives as a whole.

After I had had all my college and university training and two years of study abroad, eight years in all, Lillie said to me, "With all the wonderful opportunities you have had, you ought to do good things with your life." I have often thought how right she was. Noblesse oblige is a principle I don't need to have explained to me.

Professor J. Duncan Spaeth

Clearly, the most colorful of our relatives, husband of Mother's favorite sister, Uncle Duncan was the only one Father quarreled with. One reason was perhaps Spaeth's habit of buttonholing a listener and talking into his face from only inches away. He talked wittily, however, and on a wide range of subjects, in and beyond his specialty of English literature (especially in its early period). He had a barrel chest and could fill a large hall with his voice without help from loud speakers. Once when he telephoned from New York City to Princeton where he lived and taught, the man who lifted the phone listened to the booming voice for a minute and then said, "I can't quite hear you Duncan, you'd better telephone." Uncle Duncan had so many functions at Princeton that in retirement he would boast that he had been "replaced by four men." One function was coaching the rowing team. The joke about that was that when his wife had one of their children he was not present for the birth because a race was being rowed miles away from Princeton. Meeting a colleague, he was accosted with hearty congratulations. "Oh," said Uncle Duncan, "the chief credit goes to the boys." "Duncan, you have a son!"

Again about the voice. While Spaeth was teaching King Lear, he recited the "I shall go mad, mad . . ." speech so loudly that another professor down the hall dismissed his class with the remark, "I guess we must give up mathematics and go mad with Dr. Spaeth."

After a lecture on Thoreau, someone asked the usual question, "Then should we all go to live in the woods?" "No," roared Uncle Duncan, "you'd spoil the woods!" (That there can be no Utopia in the woods [See W. H. Hudson's *The Crystal Age*] is what convinced me long ago that there can be no Utopia—period. For if not in the woods, how could it be Utopia?)

When Alfred Noyes taught at Princeton, students could say that they "took Alfred Noyes one semester and Spaeth Noise the next."

Spaeth's contribution to wisdom about Abraham Lincoln was, "He split rails before he split hairs." He poured out lively bits like this in such abundance that I found it almost torture that I could remember so few of them. He made a telling criticism of my Harvard philosophy teacher Ralph Barton Perry, whose *Chief Contemporary Philosophical Tendencies* reminded him of "a man of weak digestion who goes from one restaurant to another complaining about the food in each." And in truth Perry's criticisms were too external to the major systems he attacked. He never really understood what it would be like to be at home in one of these systems. (I do recall, though, that he was able to detect in Whitehead a highly individual creative originality "like that of Bergson, for example.".) Spaeth, who was partly German, was sensitive to anti-German propaganda during World War I. He said of Perry's vigorous contributions to this propaganda, "He spat fire!" He also remarked, "Perry is not as big a gun as he takes himself to be." However, Perry's pretensions diminished as he grew older. In the end he was modest enough.

Uncle Duncan was very sweet to my wife after our daughter's birth. Once when he and Mother's favorite sister, Marie, Duncan's wife, were having a slight disagreement while visiting us, Duncan said, "It's all right Marie, you've made the world safe for marriage." I have always treasured this phrase, which I could as heartily use about my wife.

Duncan had a small son, Johnnie, with a tiny voice compared to his father's, but plenty of spunk. My brother Henry, I recall, could give an amusing imitation of the lion's roar of the father and the squeaky soprano of the son standing up for his rights. In such ways Henry's more artistic nature, compared to James's, would be expressed. Not that James was totally without appreciation for the humorous or picturesque; but he was less creative in this line. James did like to play harmless practical jokes, such as suddenly causing his fishing rod to double with a hypothetical fish after several of us had sat forlornly without a bite. Or, upon meeting him in a public place, one would for a few seconds be given signs that he regarded one as a total stranger. It was Henry, though, that called his twin "a jackass" (with no ill humor). Mother records how Henry when quite small said some rather unkind thing about someone and James replied, "I don't think that's nice." It was of James that Father remarked, "He is refined clear through!" (This refinement caused James to be displeased by a woman my sister invited to visit us. "She looked common and she was common," he said to me.) But it was Henry who, when he felt that he had been given less financial aid than the rest of us, said, "I'm going to take the family pulse," by which he meant, find out if the establishment would acknowledge the justice of his request for money to visit art museums in Europe. Father saw the point and gave Henry the money.

That Henry looked upon Father as the establishment (my phrase; his attitude) went back, he told me, to a strange incident in which Father was not at his best and appeared to the child Henry as somewhat brutal. (I recall nothing like this between myself and Father, even though I once was physically whipped by him. But this was after I had thrown a piece of dry mud at a lady passing along the street, and I felt no injustice at being punished for this gratuitous piece of hooliganism.) "Ever since then," said Henry, "I have been afraid of that man." Calling Father "that man" would not have occurred to any of us but Henry.

The twins had always roomed together at home and so they started college life (at Haverford) in this way; but they soon saw what a mistake this was. In general, identical twins see too much of each other and are too much alike to furnish each other with enough challenge and adventure.

Returning to Uncle Duncan; he was confronted with what he felt was a disaster (not only, Richard says, because of prevailing social attitudes) by his daughter's becoming fond of a black man. It was not, Richard says, his opposition that prevented a marriage, but the Afro-American's misgivings. The daughter married no one and her life was hardly a happy one.

Uncle Duncan argued with Father and others about Woodrow Wilson. He was asked, "Then what would you do in the situation?" "I would do about what Wilson does," he replied. The issue was as to the *how*, not the *what*. A Spaeth epigram I find moderately profound was, "By experience we learn the insides of things, by experiment the outsides of things." This comes close to outlining a major tenet in my philosophy of science. I have no idea, however, how Spaeth put his basic ideas together into anything like a system, or if he did that at all.

Richard has told me about witnessing an argument between

Paul Haughton and his brother-in-law, Duncan Spaeth, in which Spaeth had the better of the argument. Paul then turned to Richard, after Spaeth had left, and said, "Well, he wiped the floor with me in that argument, didn't he?" "Mind you," he added, "that doesn't prove that he was right and I was wrong. It only proves that he was the better arguer, and you knew that beforehand." Uncle Paul was like that. He saw things realistically, but he sometimes lacked the vigor and fortitude to cope with them.

CHAPTER FIVE

Haverford College

(1915-1917)

Choosing a College in 1915

When the time came for me to go to college, I accepted Father's proposal that it be the one he and his father had attended. I do not recall considering any alternative. How different such things are nowadays! This is one of the many ways in which worldly sophistication is now forced upon the young, perhaps without the maturing of character being equally facilitated. During my second year at Haverford, I decided that for my last two years of college Harvard would be preferable. Father made no objection, saying that, for a writer (he had already correctly diagnosed my primary ambition) he could see advantages in Harvard.

Haverford was reached easily from Phoenixville, partly by electric trains from Norristown, connected with Phoenixville by the Schuylkill Valley branch of the Pennsylvania RR. So I could return home for a weekend now and then. The main reason I did not want to do all my undergraduate work at Haverford was that (by statistical probabilities and in fact) the number of fellows in my class with interests congenial to my somewhat specialized ones was small. At Harvard I felt sure there would be many more. Cousin Carl Weston confirmed this expectation. He had gone to Harvard. (As Haverford is today, things would be somewhat different, both because of a student body more than four times as numerous, and because, as I believe, of greater selectivity in admitting students.)

Some Classmates: Frank Morley and Evan Phillips

In my time Haverford had 250 students. Only a few in my class seemed marked for any very astonishing achievements; the rest would become mostly solid, decent citizens. In the first year we elected for president a tall, strikingly handsome, blond young man who seemed at first a charismatic leader. He was intense, and a sentence of his I recall was, "I have to live by inspiration." Unfortunately, the supply of inspiration was intermittent. Our president was temperamental, and under stress he lost patience or confidence. "Fellows, I don't care what you do" is one petulant exclamation that comes to me. (I once was guilty of this remark when forced to be an administrator.)

In the next election a replacement for the president was obviously imperative. We elected Frank Morley, the youngest of three brothers each of whom went to Haverford and became a Rhodes scholar—surely a unique case. The other brothers were Felix and the poet Christopher. Morley was wonderfully different from the previous president (as often happens in second choices for a spouse after a divorce). He was even-tempered, rational, urbane, and discharged his duties with perfect ease. Morley showed his rationalistic slant by saying that he didn't admire Rufus Jones, the Quaker mystic who taught philosophy at Haverford, because "he thinks with his emotions." Rufus influenced me a good deal, however.

Morley has written several books and has been a member of a British publishing house. I came to know him even better later. After my two years stint in the U. S. Army Medical Corps (ending in April 1919) which put an end to my studies at Haverford, Frank, his parents, and I made a trip to California. Young Morley was an admirable, amusing companion. We shared a fondness for poetry and a wide sweep of interests. Some of Frank's expressions at that time were, "How I hate a half-wit" (whispered when someone was being stupid); "Good soup, no bones!" (when he liked the food); and "Pay me!" when he had done something useful for the group. He related a somewhat astonishing tale supposed to show what life was like in a half-starved family, "Why are you crying, child?" Well, Pa puked, and Johnnie got all the big pieces."

Once when we were visiting my family, while Frank and I were still students at Haverford, I proposed to drive Frank, in the car Father had bought for his children, to the big city and the theater. A member of the family (possibly Father) asked Frank if he would mind landing in jail, this being the degree of trust that my relative had in my driving. "On the contrary", said Frank, "I should prefer it!" This was not only his usual tact, it expressed his love of adventure. Two years later, when we were both in California, Frank hired out on a ship going to Alaska, I suppose to see that part of the world and experience life at sea. Later still, he wrote a story of whaling that got at least one good review. It was Frank who called my attention to one of the most perfect and moving poems in the language by reciting it from memory:

> *Ah, what avails the sceptered race*
> *Ah, what the form divine,*
> *What every virtue, every grace*
> *Rose Aylmer, all were thine.*
> *Rose Aylmer, whom these wakeful eyes*
> *May weep but never see,*
> *A night of memories and sighs*
> *I consecrate to thee.*

Morley also liked the same poet's

> *I strove with none, for none was worth my strife,*
> *Nature I loved and next to nature, art;*
> *I warmed both hands before the fire of life,*
> *It sinks, and I am ready to depart.*

(Incidentally, Landor lived many a year after writing this.)

On our California trip in 1919, in a Berkeley boarding house where the waitress memorized the menu, she customarily rattled off the names of four or five dinner desserts. The second time this happened Frank simply said, "Yes, please." She looked at him and he repeated his phrase. She took his point and when she came with the desserts she had all four or five for Frank. He managed to eat them all. As I think back to that time, it seems to me that Frank was the very embodiment of high-spirited youth in a wonderfully sound form.

Frank slightly tried me in one habit of his. When we went hiking in the Canadian Rockies, he insisted once (I probably took pains to see it was only once) on our starting out for an all-day walk with no provisions other than a large bar of chocolate. I once had a birding friend who would start out before breakfast for hours of birding with an empty stomach and no food at all. But in each case this was my sole complaint against either person.

Reading newspapers and watching TV, it is easy to forget how many beautiful persons there are in the world. The birder just mentioned had a Panamanian mother married to an American father living in the Canal Zone. Dorothy and I visited in their house at a time when the father, as it turned out not long afterwards, was dying. The mother was staying in the city to be near her husband's hospital. I did not see the father, but did meet the mother, who said to me, "I'm so glad you have come, and my son has someone to share his love of birds." The son, Jim Ambrose, who knew *all* the local birds, said of his mother, "She's very conservative. But, we're liberalizing her." (*We* were he and his brother.) "And—she has a heart of gold." Obviously he was right. When watching some modern plays, say Tennessee Williams's *The Glass Menagerie*, one may well wonder what experiences would lead a writer to create such hateful and destructive female characters as appear in these plays. Nothing in my childhood or youth would have suggested the possibilities of such characters. So differently can a human being experience human nature!

A word more on this matter of how men see women. In Victorian times it was supposed to be womanly to faint in a crisis. I know by direct experience of men fainting (including myself several times, though not exactly in a crisis), but never once a woman. Men faint at the sight of blood vastly more often than women do, and the whole idea was an expression of male chauvinism that women used to permit to mold their own behavior. The women I have known don't cry much either. It is distressing to note how much male chauvinism there is in television shows, mostly written by men, I presume.

Frank Morley's parents, who had produced three Rhodes scholars, were utterly charming people. Professor Morley, a mathematician at Johns Hopkins, was English (perhaps still a British citizen) He called me Sir Charles, this unofficial knighting being the first of several that I have enjoyed. Mrs. Morley was a violinist who had lost her ability to play through a form of "neuralgia." My guess is that this was psychosomatic. Her wifely and motherly cares put obstacles in her path as a musician, so . . . I repeat, this is my guess. She wrote music for a song, and I still remember the tune. The words were, "She's somewhere in the sunlight strong/She's somewhere in the falling rain." The music also "fell." It was a pretty tune. The words, I think, are by George Sterling, a California poet, who fell deeply in love with a woman who refused him. The man she married, when introduced to her, said "You look as though you need a good rest," or something like that. Sterling had been wooing her in exquisite verse as an angelic being; but she wanted a husband who would see her as earthly and quite human, So she told some one, "There's the man I'm going to marry." Poor poet! This was rather the opposite situation to the one pictured in Shaw's *Candida*.

In 1923 I visited Morley at Oxford and showed him my Harvard dissertation on "The Unity of Being." He made the briefest and perhaps the most appropriate comment on that work: "It's a stout effort." (It was full of energetic arguments for my then system of metaphysics, a kind of qualified spiritual monism. None of it has been published. But writing it gave me a good platform on which to stand while learning more subtle and professionally competent and relevant ways to think about metaphysical problems.

Early in his career in England (which became his country, as it had originally been of his parents) Frank Morley felt the need of money; so he went to the East Anglian Railroad Company and told them: "The scenic beauties your line goes through have not been properly appraised. I know the man who can do this and—I am the man." They accepted his proposal. Morley was not conceited; he simply knew his abilities. When he asked me why I did not seek a Rhodes scholarship, and I said something about not being a suitable candidate for the honor (thinking not about intellectual capacity but about some notion as an "all-round man") of a Rhodes scholar, he said, "You're too modest." Actually, I was bent on going to Harvard, which at that time was more prestigious to me than Oxford. I am glad now that this was so.

Morley finally gave up living in this country, saying that the British culture was "less coarse." Perhaps the real difference is that a much larger proportion of our population has exaggerated pretensions to culture, and power to make its tastes prevail. Our television illustrates what I mean.

When my wife and I visited Morley and his wife in England in 1930, he told us how he had "almost lost a perfectly good wife." Early on (that choice British phrase) in the marriage (or perhaps before it?), Frank told his wife she should do as he did and start the day with a cold shower. So she took many a cold morning shower until finally, one day, she burst out: "I *hate* cold showers!" "Why didn't you tell me so?" asked the startled husband.

Always, in my early life, there seems to have been at least one playmate or companion whose character was for me beyond reproach: Dick Bowers before Yeates; Hayword Smith at Yeates (besides Richard Hartshorne); and Evan Phillips (besides Morley) at Haverford. Of these perhaps only my brother was of outstanding intellect, but as companions they left nothing to be desired.

Evan had a distinctive verbal twist. To express disagreement with a positive statement, he used,, "Oh, but no!" And for a negative statement there was, "Oh, but yes!" In itself this little trick was a slight thing. But with the accompanying smile of quiet humor, imperturbable sanity, and perfect good will, it made an unforgettable and charming pattern.

In later years, I went for some days on a sailing trip with Evan on his sailboat that slept two. As I was not a sailor, I undertook the food preparation. When it was mealtime Evan would say, "Break out the dishes." The first morning I asked Evan how many prunes he wanted to eat. "I eat seven" was his reply, which I felt was characteristic. For me each occasion tends to call for a fresh decision in such matters; but Phillips lived less impulsively. We skirted along near the coast of Maine and had a peaceful if not exciting trip.

Later on my wife and I visited Phillips and his wife at their home in St. Louis. We arrived in the evening. Evan warned me: "Our young son, who is now asleep, is going to ask you a question the first thing tomorrow morning. When we told him you were coming, and that you were a philosopher, he asked, 'What is philosophy?' We told him he would have to ask you about that." I might have felt a bit easier about the next day without the prospect this opened up. To explain "philosophy" to adults is hard enough, but to a child! The prophecy was fulfilled, the boy did put the question right away on greeting me. I struggled through a not very brilliant answer, and it was accepted. So that crisis was over.

The Phillips marriage ultimately became tragic through health decline in the wife. Intelligent people more and more are coming to realize that although death does not hurt the dead (there is no pain in not being) not dying can hurt greatly, and that one can still be, yet not be in the full sense, oneself. Yet I also hold that while there is awareness at all, there is some good in life. It is another question, though, how far this good justifies the cost to others of maintaining it. Let no one expend scarce resources to keep me alive when I no longer contribute to the life around me.

Phillips became a schoolteacher, the right vocation for him. He had the patience, the human understanding, and tact, as well as the academic ability to be valuable in it. It was not surprising that Phillips most precisely formulated my problem as a youth: a struggle to keep my supply of "common sense"—which (I estimate) was neither radically deficient nor with a wide margin—in balance with my "uncommon sense"—which was always rather obvious, as numerous acquaintances and colleagues from all periods of my life have seen.

Some Upper Classmen

The Haverford student who probably most influenced me at the time was William Henry Chamberlin, a senior with whom I roomed as a sophomore, a highly irregular thing to do. It was his idea. He thought it would be interesting to exchange ideas with me. And so it was—for both of us. He had a finely tuned intellect and read widely. He observed human affairs with rather cool detachment, considering his age. One could discuss with him for hours and never have to worry about who was getting the best of the argument. It was discussion rather than argument; for he was scarcely an advocate of anything. If I expressed some sort of social-political idealism, he would say, "You ought to run for office on a socialist ticket," rather than try to reason me out of my folly. I was more religious than he was; but this did not seem to create any tension. He was satisfied with his irreligion, whatever exactly that was, and interested to observe my somewhat different state. He wrote a series of satirical essays for the Haverford literary magazine on the history of the idea of Satan. All that I recall is the phrase "His satanic majesty" and the satirical tone. There is a German "History of the Devil" (*Geschichte des Teufels*) but perhaps this was written later. Chamberlin said that if he were to inherit a sufficient legacy to live on, he would spend his life writing the history of the Hohenstaufens. In fact he became a journalist of distinction (*Christian Science Monitor, Wall Street Journal, The Progressive*) and wrote *Russia's Iron Age* and other books. He acquired a brilliant Russian wife who converted him to communism; but who later became disillusioned and started him on the same path of deconversion from the Russian form of Marxism. He tells the story in his autobiography. When I met his wife, I understood her influence upon him. He was one of the lucky ones in choosing a wife.

Chamberlin was a brainy fellow who suffered fools gladly, even joyfully. There was a man in our dormitory (not in my class) who seemed too stupid to be in college; and one could scarcely imagine him really earning a degree. (Whether he got one or not I do not know.) Chamberlin would tease him good humoredly and in such a way that the victim seemed to enjoy it. "It's out, S— — —, and it's all over town," is the phrase I recall. Overtly, there was nothing seriously offensive in such a formula, as it entirely avoided the real charge to make against the man—that his brains were deficient.

Some Haverford Teachers

The teachers at Haverford included the great scholar F. B. Gummere, whose splendid gusto for the whole of English literature was exhibited in a survey course in which he lectured. I recall him reciting:

> *Take Oh take those lips away*
> *That so sweetly were forsworne,*
> *And those eyes, the break of day*

Lights that do mislead the morn
But my kisses bring again, bring again.

(I tend to forget the sixth and final line: "Seals of love, but sealed in vain.") Gummere was a classic case of being a learned scholar who was quite unpedantic and a magnificent human being. He was invited to a chair at Harvard, which he would have honored, but he turned it down, because, he was quoted as saying, he knew a good place to go fishing near Haverford and feared he would miss it at Harvard. Haverford students had no ground to complain that all the teaching was done only by the undistinguished men.

Our teacher in English composition was Snyder, the editor of a widely used anthology. Under him I wrote an essay "On Taking Things for Granted." It was, I imagine (for I recall almost nothing of it), a one-sided discussion of the method of doubting everything— without benefit of Descartes, whose views I did not then know. But it was practice in thinking and writing, as was an essay I wrote for the *Haverfordian* on "The Seasons and the Life of Man." Chamberlin commented on the poetic style of the essay. It, too, was chiefly practice, as I told my mother when she wondered what I was driving at. I was trying to think rationally about my love of nature, of which the seasonal cycle is one aspect. But I knew too little and had as yet clarified my own values too little to achieve much in either essay. Yet it earned me an invitation to join the editorial board of the *Haverfordian*.

Snyder somehow displeased Frank Morley, who played a trick on his teacher. Because Snyder praised R. L. Stevenson and suggested that we read him to learn how to write well, Morley selected a sentence from Stevenson and (to test Snyder) incorporated it without quotation marks into his essay for the course. The teacher praised the style of Frank's essay in general, but did not think well of the Stevenson sentence, apparently taking it to be Frank's. My own feeling was that Snyder was acceptable without being outstanding as a teacher.

There was a charming mathematics teacher, much beloved, named Wilson. I took his course in advanced plane geometry (in addition to one other mathematics course). It was a fine experience. I regretted later, however, that I had no course in calculus. I failed then to realize the importance of mathematics—and physics—for my future work. In biology I had better luck. There was a young man who taught evolutionary theory: the essential evidences, arguments, and hypotheses, as they stood in 1916. It was an excellent course for a future philosopher. I am grateful to that teacher. His name? I've no idea. He was shy, but he could think.

The other mathematics course referred to was taught by "f of x," and that is the only name I recall for him. He was not one of the better teachers. He was a bit pathetic, for two reasons. One, he stuttered somewhat; and two, he made a little too much effort to please by rather labored jokes. A tradition had grown up through the years that a joke by $f(x)$ was to be greeted with *prolonged* laughter, say 20-30 seconds or more by the entire class. The poor man seemed genuinely flattered by this ribald celebration of his notorious efforts to amuse.

In that year I was reading *Tom Jones*; and its numerous pages interested me enough so that I used sometimes to read in that book instead of listening to $f(x)$. When time for a test drew near, I had to do something to find out what I had missed. It happened that a man in the class named Harold Hubler loved mathematics, was good at it, and thought it a privilege to bring me up to date about the classwork. His father owned a shoe factory that he expected to work in and, I presume, eventually inherit, so that he did not have academic ambitions. But he did like mathematics and certainly could have become a teacher in it. (This is a clear case of how chance and circumstance mold our careers.) He was a most amiable and sound individual. Jewish? Possibly, but in those days I would scarcely have even put the question. Even several years later when I knew a boy named Lippman (not Walter) I was surprised to discover that he was Jewish. "Yes," said he sadly in Shakespearian phrase: "t'is true, t'is pity, and pity t'is t'is true." He was a melancholy person who took life hard, extremely different from Harold Hubler.

Haverford had a history teacher who was a thorough Quaker pacifist. He gave a public lecture about Theodore Roosevelt's behavior concerning the Panama Canal, quoting this president's, "I took Panama." He didn't anticipate Hayakawa's jovial version, "We stole it fair and square," but was severe in judging our nation's or its president's conduct on this occasion. I might have thought better of Professor Kelsey than I have through the years had he not, as I felt, rather insulted me in the following manner. He asked us what we thought of the Declaration of Independence and called upon me. I hesitated, whereupon, in his heavy humorless manner, he said, "Don't be afraid to speak up and say what you think"; thus, accusing me of cowardice without the slightest understanding of the cause of my hesitation, which was simply that I had never encountered the question and needed time to think about it. Fear had nothing to do with it. Kelsey then showed us what could be said in criticism of Jefferson's "glittering generalities," a phrase he may or may not have used. I was too annoyed to store up for later recall much of what he said on this topic; but probably it did start me thinking analytically about Jefferson's doctrines. For all I know, I learned a good deal from him.

There was a required course in physical hygiene, the only one in which I ever encountered the names of all (or was it only most) of the bones in a human body. The teacher was regarded as an intellectual lightweight. I was startled by his statement, "Eating is the greatest pleasure in life." My idealism didn't like this idea. It is the pleasure that occurs all through life and the one that is common to all animals, whereas sex as physical pleasure is confined chiefly to more or less adult phases and (in most animals) a small part of the year. But the most persistent satisfaction is just in feeling or experiencing, perceiving, remembering, thinking, and moving our bodies. The thinking aspect is enormously variable in degree and complexity from infancy to age, and from lower to higher animal forms. But awareness is the basic value. Eating and sexing (to coin a word) are special cases. Simply as such, they do not set human animals apart from the others. Thinking (to an extent that even chimpanzees and whales probably do not) by means of symbols does that. I guess I still do not like what the hygiene teacher said; but at least it was memorable, which is more than I can say for most of his utterances. Yet, the hours spent listening to him were not bad hours; rather they were in part amusing and in part the absorbing of possibly useful information. Alas, though, I still could not name most of the bones.

A considerable part of my education at Haverford came from

not-required reading: Meredith's *The Egoist*, Fielding's *Tom Jones*, Coleridge's *Aids to Reflection* (a rehash of German idealism), H. G. Well's war novel *Mr. Britling Sees It Through*, and Tolstoy's and other authors' essays advocating strict pacifism (which for a time convinced me, but soon led me to put questions to myself to which the pacifist answers seemed unacceptable). Another part came from listening to Rufus Jones speaking in Quaker Meeting and also in morning Collection, as it was called. He was the first teacher of Philosophy I had ever seen, and his personality was forceful. I suspect that he influenced even Frank Morley, who resisted the influence consciously. Like most Quakers Rufus had a nonrigid form of religious belief and was, I think, a constructive influence. His most nearly rigid dogma was his pacifism. For the rest, his was a thoughtful, nondogmatic mind.

Once Rufus (as he told Dorothy and me) had a meal with Herbert Hoover, also a Quaker. The president, known for profanity, began to swear when a certain topic was introduced. Rufus soon stopped him with, "Herbert, I think thee has said enough!" After I left Haverford I kept in touch somewhat with Rufus. I followed at least one piece of advice he gave me, which was to read essays by Creighton, editor of the *Philosophical Review* (one essay for each year, as I recall). In consequence I have always had some understanding of the school of thought of which Creighton was the founder, an American form of idealism that in a certain way relativized "the absolute" and enabled idealism to take time and process more seriously than Royce, Bradley, or even Hegel had unequivocally done. I also liked Creighton's idea that value (Plato's *the Good*) is the supreme principle, and that all experience and thinking is valuational. This was a conviction that I had come to while in the army; but Creighton strengthened it. Plato, Peirce, and Whitehead confirmed it again later.

Rufus said one unforgettable thing: "In every philosophical system there is an *impasse* somewhere." (One may also say: in philosophical skating there are loci where the ice is perilously thin and the options are evasive tactics or a plunge into very cold water.) Whitehead has admitted as much in his own way. Bergson, in some of his writings, by his rejection of logical thought almost makes evasion the whole story; and this has always seemed to me his greatest mistake. For this reason, his *Introduction to Metaphysics* is his worst book. Another point I have retained from Rufus is his relativizing of the distinction between mystics and ordinary people. Being directly aware of God or not aware of God is a matter of degree and clarity, rather than an absolute yes or no. I hold that no other view makes sense, assuming that some do have the awareness. For God is by essence ubiquitous and cannot be absent from anything, including any experience, if he (or she) is present anywhere. The theistic question is partly one of self-knowledge. Either no one is aware of God and the idea is baseless, absurd, or meaningless, or everyone is aware of God; in the first case theists deceive themselves, in the second, nontheists do. We may claim to know what nonabsurd beliefs we do or do not hold; but this belief that we understand our beliefs and their degrees of coherence and clarity—how secure is it? Modern logic has discovered subtle sources of confusion in beliefs held even by great intellects. The real issues of philosophy are related to these sources of confusion. Linguistic analysts and deconstructionists, too, are not mistaken in this contention. But they are more arbitrarily selective or extreme than they seem to realize in their application of the general principle.

Because of three superior teachers and several acceptable ones, also some wonderful fellow students and many acceptable ones, I have always felt grateful for my days at Haverford. In view, too, of the connections to the institution of my father and grandfather, I was gratified, many years later, when the news came from its president that it wished to give me an honorary degree (my first, as it happened). It does not contradict this, I feel, to add that, when my always-understanding daughter Emily wrote me on this occasion, "Daddy, I don't think a degree is what you need," I replied approvingly. I do not recall that any such thing as a postdoctoral degree has ever been my desideratum for happiness. Another relative, whom I generally have found understanding, somewhat astonished me by writing: "Now you must be completely satisfied." I think she was thinking of her husband getting less recognition than she herself had. At the time my real concern was completing, or placing for publication, a manuscript for some book. I have written for readers, not for those in positions of power who might be told by readers to honor me.

As in all things there is an element of luck in such matters. Already at Yeates, I had appreciative readers in a small group in which, for all I now know, I and my brother Richard were the only potentially good writers. Dr. Frederic Gardiner was to be thanked for that opportunity. Haverford was another limited group, and even Harvard was not huge, like the great state universities. The blessed Society of Friends was to thank for Haverford. There was another element of luck at Haverford. By crossing a footbridge over a highway that bounded the college property and walking a few hundred yards farther one reached the home of Uncle Ned, Aunt Clementine, and their children. Every one of these people was a remarkably good human being and just fine for a college freshman or sophomore to talk to.

As Heidegger, in one of his best moments, said to an American friend, the final word is—gratitude.

CHAPTER SIX

Life in an Army Medical Corps

(1917-1919)

Volunteer – or be Conscripted?

As our entry into World War I drew near, young men had to consider their attitude toward taking part in it. My initial response was to decide to take the voluntary military training course given at Platts-burg in the summer of 1916, between my (nearly) two years at Haverford. This was my first exposure to military personalities. Prob-ably it was somewhat untypical. Our commanding officer seemed a fine type of human being, a cavalry officer, who accordingly said, "Forward – ho!" instead of "Forward – march!" This was by habit, for he was not training us for the cavalry. The second in command also seemed, as one of the trainees said, a "fine fellow." No doubt they were picked for these qualities, as they were dealing with men not actually subject to military discipline.

There is a great range of personality types in professional mili-tary men. General Patton said to a former colleague of mine, at the time when Marshall had removed him from office because he slapped a shell-shocked soldier, "Here am I, one of the greatest killers in his-tory, with millions of sons of bitches needing to be killed." Imagine Marshall, George Washington, or Robert E. Lee talking in this way! Sherman also was something of a sadist. But there seems no evi-dence that this is a universal rule.

In my tent at Plattsburg were a squad of men most of whom are now ciphers to me. One discontented soul said plaintively, after we had competed at target shooting and he had not come out first, "Always there's somebody better than I am." Perhaps he eventually became reconciled to this rather common predicament, and learned to accept the proposition that we are obligated only to do our best, and that, if there is usually, or almost always (at least taking the wide world into account), someone better, many may be far worse; and the first prizes are not the only ones worth gaining.

I found the simulated military life interesting. One had only to obey orders and instructions and the days passed easily enough. But somehow I was not fired with ambition to shine as a soldier, and the return to Haverford and a student's life brought me back to my usual form of existence.

Then came our entry into war. I had given up isolationism and a temporary fascination with sheer pacifism and was not surprised or shocked. But how the country's crisis was to affect me was a matter that I do not recall thinking much about until some person or persons came to the college and made an appeal for volunteers to serve in the army medical corps that would take over from the British a base hospital in France. If I had any difficulty making up my mind how to respond to this appeal I have no knowledge of this now. I seem to have seen only one side to the issue.

By volunteering for medical military service a young man insured himself against being conscripted for one of the fighting branches of the service. As Father once remarked to me, this was "not heroic." I did not think of it as heroic. But neither was it a calculated move to escape danger. The situation was complicated.

1. Conscription was surely coming, of that there seemed no doubt. The *New Republic* editorials, which I read in those days, had made as much seem a certainty.
2. Conscription meant, or so I thought, being taken to a training camp somewhere in this country for several months. My training at Plattsburg was an interesting experience, but I had had enough of it.

3. As for getting into a fighting branch, there were two objections, danger aside: (a) I had been an extreme pacifist for some months during part of the previous year and though I had thought myself out of this position before Wilson declared war and before going to Plattsburg, I still did not take easily to the idea of killing people; (b) I had the idea that I might not be a very efficient soldier, not from cowardice but for other reasons.

4. Our country needed volunteers for medical service right away because, whereas we had virtually no fighting units ready to go to France (the regular army personnel being needed to train the huge numbers of new recruits that were expected), there were doctors and nurses who could be put into use with virtually no military training, and these, with volunteers ready to serve as orderlies and the like (i.e., relatively unskilled workers), would enable the country to send help to the Allies immediately. (As I recall, the only other form of immediate help sent to France was a unit of army engineers.)

5. I thought, rightly as it turned out, that I could take some books along (of pocket size; e.g., Everyman Library units) and continue my studies, which were important to me, in my spare time at the hospital.

Putting these considerations together it seemed that, although unheroic, my action was not unpatriotic; and it made sense in terms of my potential career. One strong attraction was the assurance that we would go immediately to France and not be sent to a training camp in this country. I had never been away from the northeastern portion of the United States and the idea of going directly to France had a romantic appeal.

A more mature and more practical person than I was would very likely have thought of the possibility of going through the war in an officer's uniform. If I did not think of that it was partly for much the same reason that has always kept me from wanting to become an administrator, a politician, a businessman, or even a lawyer or doctor of medicine—simply the fact that I am a man of thought and feeling rather than of action; a potential artist, musician, poet, literary person, scientist, or philosopher. A soldier in an actual war is a man of action if anyone is.

Father characteristically listened to my reasons and then said, "But Charles, you may not be able to do what you want to do: there may not be time for study. And – the Germans may win." I replied calmly that I did not think they would. (Until the horrible Vietnam venture came along the outcome of each war that occurred seemed to me a foregone conclusion.)

We volunteers did go right away across the Atlantic (in April 1917), but first to England. I shall never forget the beautiful English countryside in spring. We were sent to the seaside resort of Blackpool, allegedly for training, but no training to speak of took place. The doctors and nurses were sent to London; and what they did there we privates were not told. After a few days we were put on a channel boat to France.

Crossing the Atlantic had been a tremendous experience. The boat was smelly below, but several of us found we could sleep on the deck under the stars. I had, one night, close to a mystical experience thinking about God in a new way I had been working out after reading H. G. Wells's attempt to arrive at a theology on the basis of William James's notion of a finite God. As we approached England a British destroyer met us and convoyed us to the landing. At one point the destroyer began firing at what, at first, looked like a submarine periscope, but turned out to be a floating log. For a few seconds I thought we might be about to be blown up and had an anticipatory sensation of our flying upwards. I do not recall any definite feeling of fear, just an almost neutral sense that something was about to happen.

On the boat to France for some reason I thought I could see a better place to sleep than the one assigned. I was awakened by a man with a horse who told me that he was about to lead the animal over the spot where I was lying. I quickly revised my idea of where to spend that night. In France we were put in a freight car with an open door and watched the exquisite countryside go by.

A Base Hospital and Its Nurses and Patients

Our American medical corps was sent to a British-managed hospital ensemble on the chalk cliffs several hundred feet above the Channel coast near the resort town of Le Tréport. This town is on the bound-

108   LE TRÉPORT. - Les Villas de la Plage. - ND

Fig. 15. Le Tréport, France, site of army hospital during World War I

ary between Normandy and Picardy. The surrounding country was exquisite and unspoiled. There was a Canadian hospital unit, with which we (other) Americans had little to do. Near the edge of the cliff was a large concrete hotel building, not at the time used as an hotel, and I am utterly vague (were the Canadians there?) as to what it was used for. I never saw the inside of it. Our part of the base was all in smallish temporary huts. After the first few weeks I was sent to what was called Isolation, where patients with contagious diseases were sent; and there I stayed for nearly two years.

Oddly enough none of us in Isolation ever caught any of the diseases (aside from a few cases of flu). I say *oddly* because, though we were told to wash our hands with carbolic soap and more or less did so, I cannot believe we were altogether meticulous in such matters. Perhaps our good state of health and youth was the main reason. We had some tuberculosis patients, some with spinal meningitis and erysipelas, and of course quantitities of those suffering from dysentery. But I had little experience with the last group, which were in a hut reserved for them.

The base was many miles behind the front lines at all times, and only during the final desperate German "push" did we hear the artillery. We did occasionally hear German planes (their sound was distinctive in that war) going overhead to bomb the port of Dieppe some miles to the southwest. We also heard the bombs explode. Otherwise, only the patients reminded us that we were at war, and in Isolation even they were usually not wounded, only sick.

Near Isolation was a British outfit. They had some Scotch bagpipes to enliven their drill. Why they were drilling I do not know. We did not drill. But from the music I acquired a lifelong fondness for bagpipe music.

Isolation was at the extreme Southwestern corner of the military area, well back from the cliff edge. Beyond it was pasture, devoid of habitation in the visible foreground. A wire fence, easily stepped or climbed over or under, separated us from the pasture land. One could walk a mile or two through the fields, parallel to the cliff and reach the next little stream bed making a break in the cliffs. Here was a tiny resort with the lovely name of Mesnival and a tavern that a Haverford friend and I visited once. There were a few available girls here that, apart from a kiss or two, we left to others. The women there did not look like the hardened scornful kind I saw in Paris many years later outside a hotel where I was sent when a hotel I had hoped to use was full. One could walk several miles further southwest and reach a larger resort with many summer cottages.

In Mesnival I somehow, at a later time, made the acquaintance of a quite lovely young French matron who invited me to accompany her back to her summer cottage in the larger resort farther along the cliff. Here was her mother (or mother-in-law) and her children, two I think. This was a refined, educated family. I made a second visit to that cottage later and was met at the door by the grandmother. "*Ah, l'Americain*" exclaimed she gaily. I was served tea in glasses with silver holders, my first experience I think with that style. The husband, a bearded soldier, also was there that second time, on leave from the front. He did not seem worried about his wife's acquaintanceship with me, but neither did I sense much interest in me on his part. This was about the extent of my coming to know French society during those two years.

Inland from the coast, the nearest town was Eu. Our enlisted men had a time with the pronunciation of these two letters. One could make it a two-syllabled word, one could say *you*, or *oo*. One could, but this was perhaps rare, pronounce the word as the French did. One is reminded of the joke about "Wipers (Ypres) on the Eyesore (Isère) River." Actually, of course, it is English not French pronunciation (and spelling) that defies logic and threatens sanity.

What impressed me the most about French scenery was what Eleanore Castle Neff writes so eloquently about in her book, the way French villages seem to belong to the landscape, to have grown out of it like the vegetation. This, I thought, is what my country lacks, this exquisite blending of the natural and the human. One can find it in Germany and other European countries, but this I learned about only years later.

The climate of the Normandy coast left an impression of mildness, except that one might go for weeks and not see the sun. It is not a promising area for solar power. Of course this is the case in western Europe generally, including Britain. When the Alfred North Whiteheads left England and came to live in Massachusetts, Mrs. Whitehead was amazed by the "bright light." What would she have thought of Central Texas where I now live? Or, much brighter, Arizona.

Our nurses were all enlisted as second lieutenants, except for one, the Matron, with higher rank. Thus, they outranked most of us who were simply privates. I do not recall saluting them. They were no more used to military etiquette than we were.

The doctors in general (also lieutenants—first, I presume) meant little to me. Our orders came through the nurses. Never since public school days (indeed not even then) had I so much to do with women who were not family relatives. On the whole this was a pleasant feature of those twenty or more months. Three or four of these women were agreeable friends, none caused me more than mild irritation or disgust, and one was ... but I am coming to that.

A result of having experienced hospital life, not from the side of patients but from the side of those attending patients, is that when, luckily rarely and not for long, I have had to be such a patient I have had none of the feeling of strangeness or horror from which many appear to suffer, but quite the contrary. I expect nurses and orderlies to be fellow human beings, a bit better than most people both in intelligence and good will. I know a philosophy teacher, now retired, who swears that he once had a positively sadistic nurse. I believe him, but I also think this must have been a very rare case. I have once, by mistake, been briefly in "intensive care," once in "emergency," and a few times in regular care, and except for some delay in finding out why I could not drink the acid fruit juice offered me when I was scarcely able to explain things after an operation (my throat had been hurt by a device put in my mouth) and hence failed to receive nourishment for a day or two, I have no complaint at all about how I was treated. But then I know what it is like to have to furnish the treatment, not to one but to many. I really agree with Mao on one point: we should all have had some experience of doing menial work for the good of others and at their beck and call. Jesus washing the feet of his disciples is one item in the New Testament that I most completely respond to as symbolic of the highest goodness.

Fig. 16. In the Army Medical Corps,
1917-1919

A slightly troubling memory is of having to use a catheter with a patient who then became infected. Was I sufficiently conscientious in sterilizing the device? I was told about the need but feel a gnawing doubt about how well I followed instructions. Deaths of patients were not very common. These were young people, being given good care. The death I recall best was of a tubercular German soldier. I knew some German, but he said scarcely a word. I do not even know if he knew he was dying. I felt no hatred for him, but only pity as for someone remote from my understanding. He had not become vividly human for me.

A nurse I had respect for was a sharp-witted, thoughtful middle-aged person who looked more like Voltaire in profile than anyone else I have ever seen, judging by the statue in Paris. She, Miss Ralston, was the first nurse who had to teach me my orderly duties. After several weeks I remarked that I had learned a lot about them. Instantly she reduced me to my proper level: "You don't know any more about taking care of this hut than a newborn babe!" So long as I was working in her hut we had no trouble understanding one another. She said two things about me that no one else had ever said. Both were perceptive, in my opinion. One was a remark to another nurse, "This one's masculine enough." I have always been rather mystified when I hear or read of persons who feel a need to demonstrate their masculinity. Such a need never entered my head. The other remark was "There's not a lazy bone in your body." I did not particularly need this remark either, except that my conscientious mother had for a time feared that I was going to turn out lazy. Edmund Husserl put emphasis on how hard he had worked. Well, I could make the same claim. Sometimes I wonder *why* have I worked so hard.

Unfortunately, after Miss Ralston (she had never married and probably has never done so, being middle-aged, independent, and strong-minded) was no longer in charge of my operations, she was quoted to me as saying something about me that I thought untrue, so—the last time I ever saw her, I'm sorry to say—I accused her of this untruth. Too bad. She was a good friend in her way.

I had a comfortable older matronly nurse with whom things were easy. She remarked about how the two of us "never got upset at the same time," and ever since then I have thought this to be one of the first principles of married life. The plays of Noel Coward show what happens if the anger of one fires up the anger of the other. Indulging in temper is for one partner or the other, not both at once.

I had as my boss for some weeks a nurse reputed to be the mistress of a certain nonmedical Army captain in our hospital organization. She was a dour individual. She brought up the mentioned item of gossip about her without any prompting by me and neither exactly denied nor admitted it. Indeed the point of her bringing it up at all seemed unclear. She was hypercritical of my work in an annoying way. I had three stoves to light every morning before going to my breakfast. She would pick out the stove burning least well and complain. The patients sympathized with me about this, so when I finally indulged in an angry and somewhat profane response they told me on the sly they thought it was about time. The nurse asked the sergeant in charge of our division of the hospital to take me out of her hut, which he cheerfully did, to my satisfaction.

One poor nurse, a rather pathetic and not very appealing, serious young person, fell in love with the sergeant just referred to. She expressed her trouble to me by saying that she wondered whether love caused more happiness than unhappiness, or vice versa. The sergeant had only mild pity for her, though he knew her state of mind. He was a handsome enough fellow and could pick and choose in his romances. Many years after the war, the hospital unit had a reunion and the sergeant was there. He had become a lawyer in the town he grew up in, as he had always intended to do. I was surprised that he was thrilled, as master of ceremonies, to introduce me as a Ph.D., a privilege he said he had not had before. I would have expected him to have hobnobbed with Ph.D.s now and then or, even if he had not, to take them as a matter of course. He and I had gone on leave to England together during the war, at least we started together and ended together. What he did in between he affected to tell me, but I had my doubts, especially after he hinted they would be justified, about the accuracy of his account. He was intelligent and amiable and probably reasonably honest as a lawyer. Certainly he did no harm that I could identify in his operations as sergeant.

My favorite nurse was considerably older than I, an intelligent, charming ladylike woman of very high character. She had no intention of having a romance with me or anyone else at that time, and she told me long afterwards that she had resisted a temptation she felt on one occasion to comfort me with an embrace, but decided, "Better not." (Not all the nurses did resist that kind of temptation and at least one—she became pregnant—had reason to bitterly regret it.) I have had few friendships with a woman that equal this one. Alas, soon after her probably happy marriage, perhaps a dozen years after the war, to a medical research man, they were both drowned in a very rare kind of ship-sinking. Carolyn Robelen was like Dick Bowers—a faultless character, indeed a Rose Aylmer. I was not quite in love with her, but she charmed me and warmed my heart from the outset and to the end. Her death not very long after her marriage some years after the war seems too bad.

Miss Robelen said something I have not known any other woman to say. She heard some nurses talking about their sexual experiences (presumably mostly with doctors) and she knew from me that there was much similar talk among the orderlies. She said roughly this: those of us who avoid such indulgences do not entirely miss what the others enjoy. "We have it in our dreams," she said in her gentle voice. I had not previously thought of women having erotic dreams. I did however always take it for granted that women can and mostly do physically enjoy sex. Alas that some unlucky women have been unable to do so! That this is the normal fate of women has never seemed at all plausible to me. Men and women who have thought so must be oddly lacking in biological sense, strangely remote from nature. (Also from much of the world's great literature.) But then that is what some victims of civilization really are, denizens of an unreal half-world created by that ingenious thought-ridden animal *homo sapiens.*

A pleasant feature of our lives as orderlies was association with patients convalescent enough to be permitted to help in the kitchen. Serving (not cooking) three meals a day and washing the dishes was a large part of our job. Once for some days I had a jolly New Zealander, tall and blond, and a short, dark cockney (a comedian in peacetime) helping me at the same time. They called me Sir Charles. The cockney had been on the stage with Charlie Chaplin before his rise to fame. He thought Chaplin had become too much of a snob to admit that he had ever known his former companion. However that may be, my little friend was himself quite funny and clearly worthy to have been Chaplin's associate.

For the first year or so the patients were all British, though from every portion of the Empire—including Jamaica (perhaps my first experience of an educated black man), India, Australasia. (It occurs to me that I recall none from Egypt. After the war in Germany I came to know a nice Coptic student.) Finally, as the American army got into the war, we began to get Americans. The contrast was vivid. Farmers from Kansas stand out in memory. I had never met anyone much like them. They seemed naive and wholesome.

Several patients were British nurses. There was a separate room in which two of them convalesced. They were friendly people. Decades later when I went to Australia to lecture for some months I said to myself: "In that far off country, with ten million people, there must be at least one person that I already know." It turned out that there was such a person, and she was one of the two nurses that had been my patient thirty-four years before. Reading about my visit to Australia in the newspapers, she telephoned or wrote, and my wife and I had some nice times with her and her sister. They had a car, as we did not. They took us to look for birds, among other things. I thought she did well to remember my name. I had forgotten hers, which was Miss Malster. She had not married, but her sister was widowed, and they lived together. They were good fun.

The contrast (as the war became more and more our war) between British and American patients was matched by that between British and American rations. One of the few items that stands out distinctly is that the excellent British orange or lemon marmalade was, at least partly, replaced by blackberry jam. I must have enjoyed this because I was called by one chap "the biggest jam hog in camp." (This was the man to be mentioned later whose angered friend's lip trembled.) My recollection (possibly self-serving) is that I did not deprive others of jam by liberally helping myself because we were not limited in supply. The only limitation was that when a crate of orange marmalade came (or was opened) we ate that for days or weeks, then we started on a crate of lemon marmalade and had that until we were weary of it, and so on. The other definite item in the rations contrast is that we got rid of the British kind of porridge, a food I remember with some distaste. It varied but at its worst was really awful.

The exposure of young men to the close presence, (sometimes on night duty) of nurses, one orderly and one nurse to a hut, resulted in one unwanted pregnancy that I learned about and two marriages that took place after the war. One of these was, I heard, a bad failure; the man being rather cheery and sexually experienced but the woman a very serious humorless seeming member of an evangelical sect. The other involved a good friend of mine, and though it did not end in divorce, still it was not, in my view, the best possible marriage, and it ended in a seemingly needless early death of the man. I have never been convinced that this death would have occurred if he had been truly satisfied with his situation. But this is a guess, and there was a reason, quite apart from the marriage, for his lack of a strong will to live. He inherited enough money to live comfortably without any vocation other than managing his inheritance and being a reliable head of a family. He once told me his design for living, "Nothing is necessary but to enjoy yourself." I thought that way myself once, but not for long. Soon thereafter the realization of our mortality, among other things, taught me that motivation must transcend the self that is perishable and aim at something greater than simply one's own wellbeing. Yet this man was one of the most appealing male friends I have had.

Some Professional Soldiers

After we arrived in France, a regular army sergeant turned up who was a classic specimen of the ostensibly bold and fearless fellow not to be trifled with, but a coward at heart. He began ordering us around in a harsh manner, also pushing a man here and there. But when he did this to the volunteer who later became the sergeant I have described, he was met with a threatening and stern, "Don't you push me!" The incident ended right there. For one thing, the would-be tough hombre (he boasted he was the "toughest guy from Texas," or somewhere West) was obviously of slight build and probably not nearly as strong as the man he had tried to bully. The rest of us were encouraged by the outcome of this encounter. Not much to fear from that mixture of the bull and the mouse.

The army captain I referred to earlier seemed a hardened, rough type, unlike a number of army officers I have known. Years after the war I was told that it was he who had had me taken out of the main cookhouse where (my first job in the army) I washed pots and pans, giving as reason that I was "too *refined* for that job." I had not known that he knew the meaning of the word. How wrong we can be! Actually there was another reason. The cook and I got on nicely—he was Scotch and taught me the few Scotch songs I can still sing—until one day when he cut his hand and went to have it dressed leaving me in charge. I couldn't make up my mind what to do for supper, so when he got back things were in bad shape seeing that the troops were about ready for their meal. The cook (like Queen Victoria) "was not amused" by my dilatory behavior. Ever since, I have been a bit ashamed of my failure to rise to the occasion, even though it got me away from the pots and pans.

The Scottish cook, a British army man, challenged me to tell him what I had gained from attending college or from reading so much. I didn' t very brilliantly meet the challenge. I told him that, for example, I knew why one should not commit suicide. He was not impressed, for he knew the answer to that question: "It wouldn't be fair to my Maker." My answer would have been more elaborate but not necessarily so different or so superior. I then knew nothing of Kant's Categorical Imperative and little of the classic ethical philosophies other than biblical or common prayer doctrines. I was only beginning, at age twenty, to think out my religious beliefs. Royce's *Problem of Christianity* was about the extent of my reading of professional philosophers.

The camp had in succession two British quartermasters. The first looked like a pig in human form. This seems to have been his nature. He was eventually charged with massive theft of supplies for his own illicit use. Learning that retribution was on the way, he managed to have himself shipped out as a patient to a hospital somewhere else before the charge was formally made. However, he did not escape—so I heard after the war from a friend who had worked in the personnel office.

The second quartermaster was an extreme, even ludicrous contrast to the first. He seemed to be an ascetic type, and was said to go through the ashes of the incinerators to see what equipment of value might have been illegally burned by careless orderlies. His punctiliousness apparently made him unpopular for when, after the armistice, a rumor flew about that we were all going to be shipped to Russia instead of being sent home, it was also rumored that the quartermaster was responsible for this unwished for fate. I can't imagine that this had any basis in fact; however, a group of the men gathered around the quartermaster's office in threatening fashion. Someone with sufficient authority arrived in time to prevent serious trouble.

Commanding Officers and Psychosomatic Eye Trouble

The base hospital had several commanding officers (medical people), one after another. The first, as I recall him, was a pompous and, I thought, rather stupid man. One day when we learned he was to make a round of inspections I took pains to absent myself from the hut where I was working, leaving the nurse, Miss Ralston, to take the heat. She told me with some scorn what had happened. He had stepped into the tiny kitchen from which we served the food to the patients, looked at the sink, and pointed to a cake of soap lying in the sink. "Gaze in there," he intoned, "that's how sinks get stopped up." In sixty years of experience with sinks I have yet to see one stopped up in exactly that way.

The next C.O. assembled the troops as he assumed office and gave them a speech in which all was sweetness and light. Its closing words were: "You help me and I'll help you." At once the troops dubbed him "Promising Harry." That any special good or special harm came from this man, I do not recall. After all, the hospital was run largely by the ordinary doctors, nurses, sergeants, corporals, and orderlies doing the work.

A third chief officer was more impressive than the other two. Like the others he was a medical man, but one that gave the impression of being a very able applied scientist, a no-nonsense man concerned with real problems. I came to know him only because he received a letter from my Father, who was worried about my eyes which I wrote him were giving me trouble. (Years afterwards I came to recognize a psychosomatic factor in this ailment. Somehow I had acquired the notion that my eyes were deficient; and this resulted in my tensing the muscles of my eyes, which produced symptoms of strain and even actual soreness in these muscles.) The C.O. summoned me, told me of Father's letter, and talked to me in a way that made me feel that there were more important things for him to think about than any trouble he could see in the condition of my eyes.

The colonel was quite right, whether or not he had fully understood the precise nature of the condition. It was years before I understood it, after consulting several noted experts on vision, the last one a famous German doctor so convincing and kind that he was called "Der Liebe Gott" by some in his city. He told me, "*Sie haben sehr gute Augen.*" Ever since then I have often recalled, to my comfort, his assurance that I have very good eyes. And so I finally stopped wondering what was wrong with my glasses, or my eyes, and changed my habits in reading to relax those muscles. No more eye trouble. This is one of several ways in which I have learned roughly how much of illness is from mind's malfunctioning inducing body's malfunctioning. I have no doubt that this applies (as one factor among others) to cancer and many another ailment. One of the best doctors I or my wife ever had declared: "I will admit no other cause of stomach ulcer than emotional strain." This is well verified in our family experience.

My Life Is Saved; Fellow Orderlies; Alcoholism

My life once beyond any reasonable doubt was saved by a fellow orderly who slept in the same hut with me for many months. Named Jabot (originally French no doubt), he was a biggish man, good natured and more mature than most of us. He had been a hospital orderly in peacetime.

There was an argument going on in the mess hall while we were all eating and I tried to swallow a too large piece of meat in order to say something before the talk had gone past me, so to speak. The meat stuck in my throat. At first I coughed and went to the doorway to do so there rather than at the table. But then the meat stuck so exactly in my gullet that I could not even cough or breathe at all. What came to my mind was simply, "What a stupid way to die." (I feel sure of the exact words.) I then looked toward the others still at the table, I suppose as a mute appeal for help, and instantly Jabot, who must have been watching me, rushed to the doorway, gave me a strong blow on the back (the popular remedy), which proved useless, and then without hesitation did what, sixty years later, I have read in a newspaper account is the approved remedy. Standing behind me, he put his strong arms around my middle, and squeezed rather mightily. (This is not to be done carelessly or without cause, as ribs can be broken by it.) This forced out the residuum of air in my lungs that my own muscles for breathing did not suffice to expel and this bit of air was preceded, and its path thus opened up, by the chunk of meat that I ought to have chewed instead of trying to swallow whole. The newspaper account mentioned told how thousands of people die annually in this way, for lack of a competent person present and ready to act in the limited number of minutes, almost seconds, in which a life must in these situations be saved or lost.

How did I thank my rescuer? No recollection comes about that. But I never ceased afterwards to regard him as the person who had intervened in my behalf to prevent a death otherwise only minutes away. True, he ran no danger to himself by this action, as does the one who tries to swim to the rescue of a drowning person. But my gratitude was and is scarcely less strong on that account. He did not hesitate, he acted, and he applied the perfect method. I recall definitely and confidently only one sentence that this man ever spoke and that was at a different time. He was talking about his wife. "Let me get back to her," he said, "and I will show you a 1917 [or 1918] movement that is right!"

Perhaps it is "logically possible" that without Jabot I might have made a mighty effort and forced out that bit of air still in the lungs. A Physiologist would perhaps know if there would have been any chance of that. But it is a fact that many do die in the way I seemed about to, and that I had no sense of any remaining remedy that I myself could have applied.

A providential incident? I say no, a lucky one! I entirely reject the idea that it can be a function of God to take the role that belongs to the creatures; that is, determine the details of what happens. "The world is not a kindergarten" (Freud). I have no use for the notion that God cares about *me* yet not about the ones for whom there is no

Jabot in the moment of need. We should outgrow this kind of fake theology, egocentric or merely absurd as it is. I believe in the perfection of the divine wisdom and power, but God's functions are not ours. The Unsurpassable does not play the game of life for us. The creatures are the players. In details they are their own and each others' destinies. But all play has to have rules and the rules for cosmic play are not set by the players, but by the Superplayer, service of whom is the final meaning of existence. We need God all right, but not to substitute magic for the orderly patterns of happenings sufficiently reliable to make learning from the past and preparation for the future possible, yet not so rigid that the creatures have no decisions of their own to make. In this regard some philosophers and theologians (Socinus. Berdyaev, Peirce, Bergson, and Whitehead) for all their differences, have agreed, and I honor them for their wisdom. To ask for freedom without risk, or life without freedom, is to ask for one knows not what. To make belief in God depend upon belief in predestination is one of the worst of religious heresies. It gives atheists a fearful weapon; indeed, the best weapon they could have. But theologians forged that weapon.

One of the interesting things about our medical outfit was its mixture of college students and men whose education stopped at an early age. In our "Isolation" sleeping hut, as in the camp generally, the majority of orderlies were not college bred. To the others I was something of a mystery. What made me want to read books rather than get drunk or find women, this and no doubt some other signs of oddness, made them wonder if I was in my right mind.

One fellow, hard to describe, named Bleisingale (spelling?), whose education perhaps, and whose intelligence and knowledge of the world certainly surpassed the majority's, grasped what sort of phenomenon I presented. "Charley is not so crazy as you all think," he remarked. "When he gets out of the army and into the right kind of work, like reviewing books [I have reviewed close to one hundred], he'll do all right." This man's design for living included functioning as the humorist and wit of the assembly. He would come into the hut and address Jack Zerega, a one-time runner of Olympic quality who, I think, was a college student and an amusing rakish fellow: "Well Jack, what do you think of the situation? Think it's pretty bad?" His remarks were studied, and by his standards polished. Thus, "The parade was like a row of piss ants going to a funeral." There seemed no harm in this fellow, he merely wanted to amuse and be thought amusing.

Another chap, one of the college men but not from my college, took pleasure in his special vein of profanity. He would describe some ceremony or gathering he had witnessed thus: "Christ himself (meaning the C.O.) was there and ..." After he had initiated us into his jargon he could simplify, "Himself was there ..."

In one respect at least the army corrupted me. Since then, when suddenly angered, usually by things not people, I am likely to find myself swearing. This happened once when I was playing some tape recordings of bird songs for a group that included an Episcopal minister, who knew me slightly and knew of my writings. I was using the awful kind of tape that stretches into an unholy mess if one is not careful. The minister said, with some emphasis, "Professor Hartshorne's natural theology seems not sufficient to save him" or something of the sort. My profanity, however, has never employed the word I quoted earlier, perhaps because my Christology is tenuous at best.

The British "Strike me pink," or simply, "Strike me!" is one of the mildest of World War I exclamations. I enjoyed it greatly. The favorite "bloody," and its merely obscene sustitute, never much appealed to me except in one employment: a British soldier telling of his long stay at the front would say, "Since nineteen f— — — fourteen." This at least is as funny as it is obscene. A soldier would also say, "Before you come up [to the front] I was out here bleedin fer ya." I used to like the British way of shortening certain words. Thus cookhouse was "cookous" and latrine was "sh—ous."

In Isolation were two very fine young men (one of them named Hammond), both I think college men who were manifestly close friends. Their friendship finally came to a tragic impasse, as it seemed to me. Some misunderstanding arose that caused one of them to show as severe symptoms of really profound and intense disappointment and anger as I have ever seen. His lip trembled. He did not shout or threaten, it was evidently too serious for that. These were disciplined, well-controlled persons of considerable refinement. The unhappy turn in their friendship came very late in our stay in France; and I did not learn whether they finally made up the quarrel. If I had any understanding at the time of what the quarrel was about, it is gone now. But nothing was clearer than that a beautiful relationship was threatened with utter collapse. I do have recollections that seem to exclude the possibility of this being a homosexual relationship. I have vivid mental pictures of both of these men, though for some reason I did not particularly talk to either of them. One of them I saw often because he ate in the small Isolation mess hall and slept in the one hut where Isolation privates (except those on night duty) all slept. The other came to Isolation on some sort of official errands from time to time, if I recall corectly.

Orderlies on night duty slept in the daytime in a special tent where they would not be disturbed by the wideawake majority. I rather enjoyed my spell on night duty. In this tent was an obviously intelligent and educated fellow. I recall him as a lawyer or law student. There was a young rake who was shamelessly sensual well beyond the norm of the easygoing majority and a man who was eventually taken away as a drug addict. I am not entirely sure whether he was the one I have described as intelligent and educated. My guess is he was not. He certainly was not the rake. Anyhow I once explained to the intelligent fellow sleeper my idea that human motivation is in principle neither self-interested nor altruistic in the conventional sense but is in principle the interest of the self as at the given moment in selves as at other moments. I now care for me tomorrow, or I care for you tomorrow, the common element is the interest of life in other life, temporally at least *distinct* from the life taking the interest. Later I learned from Buddhists and certain Western philosophers to emphasize still more the plurality of selves involved even in self-interest. My companion in the night duty tent heard my explanation of this and then said, "That's a perfectly good little doctrine." This was the first time I had communicated and been understood on that topic. I would hope that more philosophers today understood what a good doctrine it is. As for the drug addiction, I was unaware of any such thing going on in that tent. On the whole I believe this was not the intelligent tent companion but a third person who made no distinct impression on me at all.

Discipline was less tight in our outfit than in fighting army units. A former Haverford student, a very sophisticated and internationally experienced fellow whom I shall call Jack, worked for a time as handy man for the chief nurse, the matron. He was accordingly called, the "matron's bitch," unplausible as that now sounds to me. When the pompous C.O. referred to earlier approached to inspect, Jack was scrubbing the walk leading to the Matron's office. He pretended not to see the C.O. and kept on scrubbing. "Get out of the way boy" was the response to this mildly insolent behavior.

Another sophisticated college man and fellow private, a M.A. from Columbia, was learned and subtle but lazy (and later, so far as I know, he never rose above a humble rank of actor in which role I once saw him). He replied to the question put to him by a British officer inspecting the camp, "What did you do in peacetime, my man?"with "I was a cook, sir." Those in the ranks who heard this interchange knew perfectly well he had been nothing of the kind. How straight they kept their faces my memory does not tell me. Another time, asked by a higher authority what he was doing (he was mending a road of the camp), he replied, "I'm making the world safe for democracy, sir." The officer, I gathered, could think of nothing further to say. This fellow private was given the job of emptying toilet buckets around the camp (there were no sewers, though the privates had latrines). This was not a very clean or sensorily attractive job but, because it had short hours, or because he was his own boss, so to speak, he was apparently content with it. He had a fine voice and liked to read plays (was it Shakespeare's or was it Greek plays? one or the other or both) to an audience of nurses. He and Jack were friends, both older and more sophisticated in many ways than I was. They were gifted fellows in their way.

Most tales of war are pretty grim and more or less sordid if realistic. Our outfit was a special case. We were neither killing nor being killed; rather the opposite. Only one orderly died that I know of, and he did so from the terrible influenza racing around the world at that time. I caught it, or at any rate had a rather high fever, but the idea that I was in danger did not occur to me. I was too busy, as it were, dozing off my feverish condition, and I had complete confidence in the medical persons treating me because they were experts and to some extent friends. The worst thing was that in this time out from work I lost the most "cushy" job (to speak in British terms) I have ever had in my life—taking care of the disinfector. This meant polishing the brass of the machine and occasionally firing it up to make steam for a new lot of dirty uniforms or mattresses needing purification. There were many hours of leisure, and the hut housing the machine was at an extreme corner of the camp, outside which were only grazing cattle and (much of the year) overhead-singing skylarks—a perfect place to sit in warm clear weather with back to the hut reading a book. The spot could not be seen by anyone remaining inside the camp. But of course my illness led to someone else being put on that duty, and equally of course he would not think of giving it up again once he found how trouble free a task it was. I recall little about the firing up process except that there "was nothing to it." In a hut an orderly had several fires to make *every* day. The fuel used was coke, in colors the most beautifully burning of all fuels. To get it going we used wood and also (using due care) kerosene.

Jack once used kerosene to avenge himself upon two English officer patients who annoyed him by failing to keep up the fire he had made in their officers' special room at one end of the hut. He had instructed them in the business of refueling from time to time, but they did not carry out his instructions and the fire went out. So before their eyes he put fuel and wood in the stove, poured in plenty of kerosene, took a piece of rope which he soaked in kerosene to make a fuse stretching from the stove to a point near the door. He then lighted the door end of the fuse and left the room. The officers, I suppose, had to choose between jerking away the fuse before it ignited the kerosene in the stove and running the risk of the stove exploding in their faces. Jack soon returned and found the fire going merrily, and everything intact except for some debris blown out through the stove door into the room. Just how the officers felt is not recorded. Another time Jack amused himself by haughtily refusing a tip which a British officer patient, in normal British fashion, offered this low-class fellow from America, a mere private and hospital orderly.

The Germans made their, futile but costly big push in the last spring of the war. This was a wicked waste of lives to save generals—or the Kaiser?—from admitting the defeat staring them in the face; but then even R. E. Lee—or Jeff Davis—did not surrender until well after his ultimate defeat was virtually certain, this being one of several arguments against starting wars, that they almost never end when reason says they should). At that time, our hospital was evacuated of all but a few patients practically dead already, because our railroad junction seemed about to be taken. So at last we (most of us and for a short time only) had no patients. Jack took the unopened bottles of ale and stout (which only officers rated in the hospital) and drank the contents of "all seven" bottles, so he told us an hour or two later. Rather soon we saw from his condition that he had told us the truth, or something much like it. Incidentally I have never consumed anything remotely like that much alcohol at one time not from resisting temptation but from never feeling any such temptation. Hopeless addiction to any dispensable substance has always seemed to me a somewhat strange business, whether to alcohol, tobacco, coffee, tea or some other drug. True I have not tried many drugs. But, though I have never been a teetotaller and for twenty years or so smoked some, nothing was easier than to stop smoking, and alcohol has never been a strong temptation.

My no-longer-living friend of Haverford and army days, also from later times, Nathaniel Hathaway, used to say that the one necessary rule about drinking is, "*Never* drink when you are unhappy." The reason is obvious. You come out of the spell and your troubles are not only still there, they are probably added to by the drinking. So you have all the more reason to drink again. And so on. But if you drink only to celebrate, there is no such vicious circle.

My former colleague, the astute T. V. Smith, remarked once that after his experience in occupied Italy at the close of World War II he gave up hope of understanding the world, meaning the human world. Well, I shall never understand the popularity of alcoholism. I have been beautifully exhilirated by a drink or two, and I was once depressed by two quick cocktails at a time when my career was not going as I wished. That one experience finished me with two quick cocktails. In any case, the joy of being able to really think and put thoughts into clear expression is for me too precious for the prospect of watching my speech grow halting and my ideas fail to take on clear form to pose any temptation. I was pleased to learn about Charlie Chaplin that (except—moderately—after retiring) he did not drink. He knew what it would do to his talent; he appreciated the wonder of being fully conscious and clearheaded. One thinks of many a gifted writer who has lacked this appreciation. So don't ask me to empathize very vividly with the wretches afflicted with alcoholism. With their relatives yes, that I can easily do.

Another thing beyond me to understand is the capacity of many to remain naively unaware that they are alcoholics. The signs are common knowledge, one would think. Yet—one qualification. Individual capacities to absorb alcohol healthily vary widely among individuals, as the chemist Roger Williams has pointed out. This opens the door for some to pride themselves on their capacity, which increases with its exercise. This is a dangerous slope to start down. Mere physical size must be important in this matter of tolerance, which is one additional reason beyond the more obvious ones why women should be especially on guard in their use of intoxicants. In sum alcohol, like automobiles, may be useful but it is also deadly dangerous—and in this statement I exaggerate not at all, with respect to either article. Yet millions act as though they had never heard of, or refuse to admit, the truth about these two matters. Through intoxicated driving the two dangers are closely connected in modern life.

Even if the statement that marijuana is no more risky than alcohol is true; this is no very high praise for marijuana, the risks of which seem greatest for the immature. I am not talking about what the law should be, but about what is wise behavior. Legality is another question. At some point we must be taught, or elect and learn, to be wise.

The camp had a sodden drunkard, a Britisher, in what official capacity I do not now know, but it seems clear he could hardly have been exercising it. He seemed only half alive, a wretched-looking sight. To me a discouraging aspect of our culture is the way our entertainments seem to glorify our vices. The glamorous actors and actresses cannot be on stage or screen long without lighting that cigarette. It used to be that no one really knew how destructive the practice was; now that this is known the glamor is still there and yet free art as well as commercial advertising seems to imply that the knowledge does not exist. Is this not an ugly cultural lag? We have so much knowledge; we use so little of it.

The real problems of "health care" probably are less than half matters of access to doctors and hospitals. They are more than half matters of really wanting to be healthy (and showing this will to health in action) and knowledge of the results of science relevant to how we should treat our bodies. I wonder how many of the rebellious young rebelled against the enslavement to nicotine, a typical part of the established system they scorned, a huge commercialized vested interest.

Our own daughter was not told by her parents whether or not to smoke or drink. She was told, and it is true and too little considered, that smoking starts many fires and causes in that way many deaths, and that it is an economic waste. And her parents drank lightly and on most days not at all. We did not talk about the harm done to the body by nicotine for that was then not well established. Entirely on her own Emily decided not to smoke or drink at all. How often that must have saved her from trouble and added to her resources for other purposes. But if she had been forbidden to smoke or drink, and on no clear rational grounds (as multitudes of children used to be), of course she would have done both partly just to show that she could design her own life-style.

Religious-Philosophical Experiences

A feature of my two years in the army was the way they were pervaded by the sense of religious change. One aspect of this change was somewhat painful. I had ceased several years before to believe explicitly in the basic Christian doctrine (at least as usually interpreted) of the incarnation, but had not been troubling myself much about this loss of faith. Reading H. G. Wells's now forgotten book *The Bishop* (or was it *God the Invisible King*?), his most theological novel, probably caused me to look hard at the Christological issue. Or perhaps it was being in a Catholic country. I remember going about with a slightly morbid question in my mind, as I encountered one or another of my fellow orderlies, "Does he believe in the divinity of Jesus?" Not that I spoke to anyone about the matter.

At much the same time as this inner trouble was an opposite sort of experience. There was a little ledge a few feet below the top of the chalk cliffs of the French coast that bounded our military camp on the west. On an afternoon off I sat on a bench some sensible person had installed there when the concrete building that now formed part of the hospital assets had served as an hotel. One looked west into the sunset and toward the English coast, seeing no human beings, only gulls and crows flying about. There I read William James's *Varieties of Religious Experience*, which was radically different from any book I had read. The combination of mystical convictions in the quoted testimonies and James's attempts to judge these rationally was stimulating and actually thrilling.

It was about this time that I thought out answers to two questions: the relation of mind to matter, and the relation of individuals to one another. The first answer came to me as an intuitive datum, or what I much later came to view as a "phenomenological" insight, that the physical world is directly *given* entirely in emotional terms. (This is implied by many passages in Wordsworth's poetry. (See Chapter 15, 5th Section.) The world is first felt and only afterwards thought. Sensation is through and through emotional, though partly in ways much too subtle to be obvious under ordinary conditions. Later I wrote a book devoted to exploring the evidences bearing on this. Also later I learned about the rather numerous thinkers who reached the same conclusion, Bishop Berkeley being perhaps the first and Whitehead one of the most recent. I argued: if the world is *given* as emotional, then thought, which has to base itself on the given, cannot legitimately claim to have a concept of mere dead matter, neutral to emotional qualities. This argument is to be found in Berkeley (usually not noticed by his commentators) and most explicitly in Croce, also in Whitehead—but I knew nothing of this at the time.

On the question of the relations of individuals, I had begun with a conviction that motivation was essentially a seeking of one's own pleasure, then became skeptical of the argument for this way of simplifying the motivational problem, and finally almost reached the Buddhist-Whiteheadian view I now hold, which is that both self-identity and nonidentity between persons are relative rather than absolute. At that time the only reading I had done on the question was Royce's *Problem of Christianity*, especially the essay on community. Royce sees clearly and even overstates the relativity of *non*identity between persons. He knew that we have personalities chiefly by internalizing each others' feelings, thoughts, memories, perceptions, hopes, fears, and purposes. But Royce sees less clearly the relativity of identity whether within or between persons. He admits no genuine independence or external relatedness among the actualities making up reality.

This suggests a third question, that of deity or the cosmic individuality. My view then was a vague one. We are related to God as ocean waves, dashing on a coast and split by rocks into separate runlets ascending and then descending on the slope of the shore, are related to the ocean. I was not in the least worried about the temporal finitude of the career of an individual as thus pictured. No great horror of death as such has been in all my experience. One of my earliest recollections as a youth, perhaps almost a child, is of thinking how good it would be to reach an advanced age and be able to think that I had discharged my obligations and not failed in whatever vocation life had presented to me, so that I could die in peace. Nor by peace is here meant the absence of the fear of hell. That ignoble fear has also not been mine. No, it was my own shame at not having done the good it was in my power to do that I hoped to avoid. I had a bit of fear that I might have to feel such shame when near the end.

The foregoing is not to be taken as meaning that I have *never* believed in "a future life." Two lines of my first poem remain to disprove such a denial. Writing "The Evening Hymn of the Hermit Thrush," I wrote:

> There's a foretaste of heaven in his lofty strain
> To deserve which from sin may I ever refrain.

These lines are hardly poetic, even by the standards I sometimes reached, but they show my acceptance at the time of the conventional view. An odd, somewhat puzzling recollection is that my pious mother did not like these lines, I believe on religious grounds. Either she felt (rightly) that the motivation suggested was not the most worthy one for avoiding sin, or she felt distrust of me as a too-young theologian, perhaps both. Her father had been scholarly as well as pious, and her husband had a vigorous, well-trained, theological mind.

The Thrill of Youth

Conrad's novel *Youth* expresses, as perhaps no other literary work does, what I often felt in my twentieth and twenty-first years while in the army: the thrill of being alive in a world whose novelty is still vivid and in which, even for the worst things, there seems compensation in the sense of adventure and of rapidly expanding powers. At this time I discovered what a Buddhist I read over fifty years later has called the escape from *the prison of individuality*. It happened like this. The hospital ensemble stood high on a cliff that forms much of the north coast of France. Wherever a stream flows to the sea there, a valley forms, an interruption to the cliff. The valley is narrow or wide depending on the size of the stream. Le Tréport is in a fairly wide such valley. To reach it we either took the funiculaire that descended the cliff or walked down the slope where the cliff gradually diminishes in height toward the bottom of the valley. There was a concrete walk near the edge of the cliff descending into the town, which lay at the bottom of the valley. Thus, glancing to the left and the sea, one looked abruptly down into a part of the town nearly at sea level whereas looking ahead, one saw a gradual slope downward and in the distance the reforming of the majestic cliffs on the far side of the valley. I had two special experiences near the top of this walk. I am about to relate them.

I had been thinking of certain aspects of my life that seemed discouraging. These somewhat gloomy reflections were interrupted by a simultaneous multitude of shrill sounds. Looking to the left almost vertically down to the bottom of the cliff I saw a school playground filled with shouting, laughing French children. I thought. "Suppose my own life is unsatisfactory. So what? I am a tiny fragment of human life. The rest of it is not all unfortunate or wretched. Nothing compels me to think of myself miserable rather than others — those children — happy." Never since then have I allowed myself to identify, unless briefly, the question, Is life good and beautiful? with the question, Is my life now good and beautiful? And I have not wavered in the two convictions that there is some minimal good, beauty, in all life, including my own, and that what finally matters, even to me, is the life of the Whole, the Something that includes me, outlasts me (save as I contribute myself to it), and contains more good than I can distinctly imagine.

The other special experience occurred when I was looking ahead from the concrete walk across and up the valley, at the beautiful wide landscape. I had been thinking about the question of mind and matter and toying with the dualistic hypothesis that these are two ultimately irreducible kinds of reality. The Santayana definition of beauty as "objectified pleasure," a phrase I had read somewhere though I do not believe I had read Santayana, occurred to me as I thought of the beauty I was experiencing. But then I noted that the pleasure was not really "objectified," if this means, first given as one's own feeling and then projected onto the world. No, the colors I was experiencing were themselves feelings, and they were as truly given, experienced as facts, as anything at all. The pleasure did not have to be objectified, it was simply given as objective. It was really there if anything was there. I did not analyze the matter further in France; rather I drew the conclusion I still draw: materialism and dualism misdescribe experience. They verbally posit a world no one can experience. (See Epilogue for further discussion.)

A less profound but vivid experience was my first encounter with French wine. I had not previously drunk wine or alcoholic drinks, other than some hard cider and some communion wine. My family did not drink wine, beer, or hard liquor. The first taste of good French champagne, also good sauterne, seemed unspeakably beautiful. A *very* few glasses one evening put me into a perfect glow of euphoria so that, for perhaps nearly an hour after getting into bed, I had a sequence of all happy and beautiful thoughts. I was scarcely drunk, and had taken only perhaps three glasses. Since then I have sometimes had more moderate effects of a similar kind except that, instead of pervading solitary reflections, the "glow" has suffused social interchange with a friend or friends.

So, with all my horror of alcoholism, I can see some good in the substance. But only as it facilitates a lively flow of thought or speech. And now with the automobile, death is always near if one will drive in such a state. And I for one refuse to become dependent for happiness upon any special substance, even tea, coffee, or chocolate, other than the proteins, carbohydrates, minerals, and vitamins that our organisms require. Giving up coffee to help cure an ulcer taught me that I can do without coffee quite easily. So now I save the money that item costs. *What goes for something needless cannot be spent for something needful.* And I gave up long ago the idea that one can have superfluous resources. If one has nonrich friends (and I pity whoever does not) and is aware of the countless good causes in the world, this cannot be true, though one were a billionaire. Finally always there is scarcity. There is ultimately no economy of abundance, and I reacted against Galbraith's *Affluent Society* title, much as I admire that author. In addition Switzerland and Sweden are much more *pervasively* affluent than my country.

A puzzling army memory is of signing a petition asking to be transferred to a fighting unit. As I have said, I did not set out to be a war hero. Yet, late in my army career for reasons no longer clear, I did sign such a petition. I can say now only that I have no regrets that the petition led to nothing. That killing fellow human beings has so often seemed a duty sheds a lurid light on the nature of this species of thinking animal to which we belong. Once released, as we all are, from the firm instinctive guidance of the other animals and at the mercy of theory for our behavior, fearful consequences may follow. "Sometimes it causes me to tremble, tremble, tremble," to adopt the words of the spiritual.

Not nonhuman nature is ethically horrible—human nature is. The reason is less obscure than some philosophies and theologies have made it seem to be. To think freely, yet be without divine wisdom and self-control and subject to stresses coming from a social environment over which any one of us has but slight control, simply is dangerous. Yet to live by thinking is what we must do. We might do it better if we had more respect for the wisdom embodied in the world of nature that produced us, also more sense that the aims of life transcend the self and even the nation, or the species; more awareness that human egotism takes many forms, including those of national, religious, and ethical intolerance; more realization of the difficulty of arriving at a tolerable degree of consensus when practical problems usually have no obviously right and unique solutions.

That ledge on the cliff where I first read William James had disappeared when I paid a visit in 1924 or 1925 to the site of the military hospital encampment near Le Tréport. The slow erosion of the chalk had caused the ledge to slide down into the sea, probably carrying the bench with it. So no one can ever again have the experience I had with sky, sea, sunset, gulls, and crows alone visible or audible. Incidentally, of the huge encampment, housing thousands of people, few vestiges remained, apart from the concrete building near the cliff (not used by us Americans) and one concrete block that I recalled as having been near the surgical hut equipped for operations. Cows were grazing where all that human activity had gone on. The meadows that had surrounded the encampment now swallowed it up. And now the sky larks could sing over the whole of it. An extraordinary transformation, and a not unpleasing one.

CHAPTER SEVEN

Harvard, Europe, Harvard

(1919-1928)

Some Fellow Students (1919-1923)

In my two years of undergraduate study at Harvard I scarcely knew
most of my classmates (Juniors and then Seniors) and did not quite
come to feel myself in the full sense a "Harvard Man." My social relations were mainly through the Liberal Club, of which I was in a sense
one of the founders. (There had been a liberal club once before at
Harvard, but it had died out. We brought it back to life.) The club had
a president whose mother did us all a wonderful favor by buying or
leasing a small house for our use. We ate lunches there and some
members lived in the building.

The membership included some of the most interesting students then at Harvard, including Walter Gardner, who became my
roommate in my last year as a graduate student. It also included a
genuine case of paranoia (son of a very successful businessman) who
was systematically against whatever was proposed and whoever proposed it. We should have recognized that his behavior indicated a
precarious emotional state but we were too naive in such matters. It
was my first encounter with a clear case of mental illness. Eventually
he disappeared for treatment. Later still he returned to graduate
studies and seemed all right, but then again collapsed. The ultimate
outcome is not known to me.

Another case of mental illness interrupted the career of a Harvard student I knew slightly; however, this illness was not paranoia.
The man was not against anyone in particular, but he had a scheme

Fig. 17. In civilian clothes

for "saving the world" (his expression, I believe) that did not even make sense. He roomed with an undergraduate (son of a famous physicist) who found the experience rather traumatic. I simply could make nothing of the case, having then read no psychiatry—or psychology either.

In two years of graduate study in philosophy at Harvard I must have associated with a number of graduate students that I cannot now recall from those days, though I came to know some of them well later. One of them has told me that I was annoyingly argumentative, though I was "forgiven" for this. An excess of argumentativeness had been my mother's chief complaint about me long before I reached college age. An aunt made a similar charge. I have to plead guilty to some extent on this score. It is perhaps a worse confession that I forget a number of people from those days who recall me. Apparently what happened in the library, or the classroom, remains with me better than those arguments with students. I recall considerable discussion with a nameless individual who, I am rather sure, did not go on to teach philosophy. He was an almost if not quite pathologically skeptical fellow who despaired of philosophy's giving him anything to believe. I don't think he minded my arguments; simply they didn't help him reach any firm conclusion. But he was stimulating. I recall Brand Blanshard from those times, but only as an idealist with whom as such I felt some common ground. I gave him an argument for idealism. "I think that is valid," he said. Our serious disagreements became clear only much later as he developed his own version of Absolute Idealism. (The absoluteness persisted but scarcely the idealism.) I was (and for sixty years have been) a sort of idealist who gives a very important place, in a sense the most important place, to relativity, contingency, and plurality. Thus, we ended up rather far apart.

A smiling, pleasant, intelligent face shines out of that long ago, devoid of a name, the face of a man who, after the others in a little group had been arguing the question, Is metaphysics possible? closed the discussion by saying, "I think metaphysics is inevitable!" This suited me well enough.

Another nameless man, a Canadian, inclined as I was to idealism, agreed with me in wishing that W. E. Hocking (author of *The Meaning of God in Human Experience*) would give us more cogent arguments than those we heard from him in his famous metaphysics class Phil. 9.

I recall Wilbur Long, a convinced personalist, talking in Perry's seminar about the "gentlemen's agreement" between idealists and realists. Agreement as to what? I recall more vividly than almost anyone Harry Helson, who became a psychologist. He was, I am told, enthusiastic about my book on sensation. Also Dorion Cairns, whom I came to know better at Freiburg. But various others whom I ought, it seems, to remember from those times I fixed in my memory only at later times.

Some Professors

I was president of the Philosophy Club one year and recall two speakers I got for the club, Mary Whiton Calkins from Wellesley and Irving Babbit. I found both of them interesting speakers.

It had seemed a sensible thing, while I was an undergraduate, to visit classes of some of the most distinguished professors then at Harvard. Irving Babbit was one of these. So I heard him discourse on romanticism. To hear him recite, in his harsh unpoetic voice, one of Wordsworth's less eloquent verses was unforgettable:

> *Once more the ass, with motion dull*
> *Upon the pivot of his skull*
> *Turns round his long left ear.*

Babbit brought to class some large volumes containing writings of Chinese romantics, Taoists no doubt, to illustrate the intercultural status of the "pantheistic revery," or feeling of oneness with nature. I asked him after class, did he not think there might be some truth in the feeling? "Yes," he said, "some deep principle of unity." I recall him also saying that he was "all for analysis." This saying often recurs to me.

When at boarding school I had experienced the pantheistic revery in a form close enough to Wordsworth's to make his mystical poetry readily intelligible to me. (And I had also experienced the partial fading of that feeling which he describes so well.) Once when I showed Jacques Leclerc, my most sophisticated friend of Haverford and army days, a poem of mine written in that vein, he looked at me and said, "You little Wordsworth!"

Mary Whiton Calkins talked in her vigorous way in favor of idealism. After she finished I proposed a brief statement defending idealism as I understood it. Her comment was, "That's a very impressive statement. Don't you think so?" here turning to a well-known philosopher who was present, but whose identity is unrecoverable. (Second thought: I believe it was the psychologist McDougal.) Unluckily the impressive statement is forever lost.

I visited Kittredge, the great Chaucerian and Shakespearian scholar, who never got a higher degree and whose justification for this neglect was the unanswerable, "Who could have examined me?" He courteously gave me permission to visit. I was interested in the lecture but recall nothing definite. However, when he lectured at Chicago many years later, he said of Chaucer that "His was too healthy a mind to 'thank whatever Gods may be/for his unconquer-able soul'."

I visited a class of Haskins, the great medieval historian. He described how a French peasant might be living on land that had been in his family for centuries, and how the buildings in part might be a thousand years old. This picture of a French farmer and his possessions remains—but nothing else except the rather thick-set figure and quiet strength and dignity of the man.

I visited the great eccentric teacher of writing, Copeland ("Copy"), who berated his class because I was the only one in the room who could answer a question he put to the others and finally to me. The question? Lost, without a trace, in the foggy sea. He also greeted a loud noise made accidentally by a timid youngster (shutting down the folding miniature desk with which Harvard seats were provided) by a reproachful. "How *could* you?" He also took steps, at least as I interpreted them, to get rid of me. Thus the second or third day he suddenly looked at me and asked, "Who are you?" I gave some answer or other, but did not come again to his class.

As at Haverford there was a general survey course in English literature by an eloquent lecturer, Bliss Perry, for many years editor of *The Atlantic Monthly*. I recall only two items from his lecturing. Neither seems now altogether to his credit. One was his rebutting Walter Pater's ideal of having one's life burn "with a pure gem-like flame" by: "The sufficient answer to this is the case of Oscar Wilde." The other was his describing the problem of causality and freedom as "insoluble." I think it has been (in crude outline at least) solved by science and philosophy between them showing that unqualified determinism is not and indeed could not be true even were there no such intensely thinking animals as human beings in the world. Indeed, it is not true even of atoms. And there is no cogent reason for the assumption that the quantum physical limitation of causal reg-ularity is the only such limitation. For quantum physics assumes isolated systems, which organisms emphatically are not. Much more could be said, but this is not the place to say it.

John Livingston Lowes, the great student of Coleridge and author of *The Road to Zanadu*, taught a fine course on Milton. He asked a question on examination that intrigued me: Discuss how far Milton's own poetry exemplifies his dictum, "Poetry should be simple, sensuous, and passionate." I argued that Milton's verse was all three. Lowes commented on my paper: "At its best, Milton's poetry is simple and sensuous, but not passionate." One might settle perhaps for saying that the passion is low keyed.

Lowes was a little man with a certain intensity. He has been quoted as bursting out to a class, "God dammit, don't you fellows know anything?" The thought sometimes crossed my mind that Lowes, a good scholar, like Babbit was very far from a poet himself.

Levy-Bruhl, the famous author of *The Mentality of Primitive Man*, was visiting lecturer at Harvard the year I began my philosophical studies there and I heard him a few times. In his final lecture he begged us to regard him as a friend and to look him up should we come to Paris. So when, as a postgraduate student in Europe, I came to Paris I called upon him. He asked about my work. Learning that it was in metaphysics, he remarked, "I think with Hume that our line is too short to plumb such depths. However," he graciously added, "it is an honor to try." This man always impressed me as a noble spirit. He invited me to a most interesting party, at which I met some French intellectuals, including some of the many intellectual White Russians in Paris.

It was Levy-Bruhl at Harvard who, in a flash, introduced me to philosophical idealism. He was lecturing on Descartes, and he said that this philosopher's *cogito ergo sum* was the origin of modern idealism with its argument, "without subject there can be no object." Instantly I was almost overwhelmed with the to me new argument for a view I already held, that mind is the universal principle of reality. I realized that the subject-object dichotomy is exhaustive, and that the status of object requires that of subject. It was some years before I became clear about the sense in which the argument holds and the sense or senses in which it does not. For one thing, if an entity is to have the status of object there must indeed be some subject or subjects, but no particular instance of subject need be required, just as, for a person to be admired there must be admirers, but any particular admirer, or set of admirers could be dispensed with. Also, it is not necessary to suppose that to be an object is to be a special kind of entity. Even a subject can become object for another subject and must become so if it is to be known or experienced. Indeed, the correct idealism is that which holds that all concrete and singular objects are simply other subjects (they need not be of the human type), and everything else is some sort of abstraction or collective, as Leibniz maintained.

I vividly recall Levy-Bruhl beginning his lecture on Hume by saying that he was "the most deep" of the British Empiricists. Oddly enough this is all I recall of that lecture. Yet, I am sure that I learned a good deal from this wise and humane philosopher.

At Harvard in those days, to earn a doctorate in philosophy passing an examination in psychology was required. How glad I am that this was so. I became an admirer of Leonard Troland, then unsurpassed in this country in scientific psychology. I also heard William McDougal, an impressive lecturer, wise in psychiatric questions and something of a philosopher. With Henry Langfeld also I learned about psychiatric matters.

My warmest friend (besides C. I. Lewis—see Chapter 13) in the philosophy department was a man who, I soon learned, had been named after my maternal grandfather James Haughton. J.H. Woods was a scholar in Sanskrit who had had years of study in India. His father, like my maternal great grandfather, had been a successful businessman. Woods was the man whose wisdom, imagination, tact, energy, and knowledge of the world were principally responsible for turning Whitehead, an English mathematician, logician, and physicist, into what he "had always wanted to be," a teacher of philosophy. Woods also was my advisor as student in philosophy. All his advice was good.

The flavor of Woods can be indicated partly by relating Mrs. Whitehead's remark about him: "He is a saint—but a Yankee saint," and partly by some quotations from his conversation. He was acquainted with a wealthy man interested in philosophy. "By some very careful work," he told me, we got — — —to leave money to the philosophy department." (By this means instructors and professors in that department for one or more years got higher salaries than was then normal at Harvard—until President Lowell abolished the difference by raising salaries generally *except* in the department, arguing that it was not desirable for any department to have special privileges. Woods was not able to prevail in this case.) I recall him saying, about the problem of finding money for good causes: "There's always a victim somewhere." Also his greeting me on campus, some days after telling me I was going to get a scholarship with such and such a stipend, by saying: "Hartshorne, I think we can get another slice." Some time later I was informed that a larger scholarship was to be mine. Woods told me to study logic—"It's the coming thing." How right he was. Lewis gave similar advice. I have followed it, but not enough.

Woods had a tragic first marriage, ending in his wife's death, after much suffering for both spouses. His second marriage was very happy, to a woman deeply interested in philosophy. He was a shrewd, lovely, humorous, and thoroughly good man. Between the two marriages Woods lived in an apartment in a campus dormitory. For some months I sublet that apartment while Woods was away somewhere. When Woods first showed me the rooms they looked extremely crowded with books. There were books not only on shelves and tables but also piled on the floor. Rather thoughtlessly I jumped to a conclusion: "I see you are moving!" Woods roared with laughter and I realized that his rooms were in their normal condition. I much enjoyed living in his bookish quarters, though I have forgotten what books I read there.

Woods was somewhat conservative in philosophy of religion (though he had learned significantly from William James). He believed in personal immortality in a more conventional sense than I have come to believe in it. His experiences in India may have had a bearing on this, though I don't know that he accepted reincarnation in the East Indian sense.

In saying that Woods had learned from James, I mean merely this: he accepted James's basic contention that a theism which takes providence to guarantee the absolute realization of ideal good, excluding any aspects of chance, risk, and dependence upon human choices, is unacceptable. On this point W.E. Hocking would agree. On the other hand, R.B. Perry was a determinist, and this means either no chance or contingency at all, or else no contingency except the overall cosmic, contingency that this world exists rather than some other, or none. Perry was the official Jamesian at Harvard but on this issue he was poles apart from James, who believed in piecemeal contingency. Each moment previously indeterminate aspects of the world get determined. Each moment each of us participates in the creation of new definiteness. Peirce, Whitehead, Bergson, James, and some others held this view. Without it I would not give a nickel for any philosophy of religion. Lewis defended determinism when I was a student, but (as I know from an unpublished talk of his) eventually changed and accepted a degree of indeterminacy.

I do not recall as ordeals either of the two oral examinations I took as a Harvard graduate student. W.E. Hocking, in some ways on my side in philosophical issues, asked the only question I found troublesome. The psychologist Troland asked how I viewed *matter*, the atoms, and so forth. When I gave the panpsychist answer he said, "I guess you and I think alike on that question." Probably none of the philosophers there would have said this, and I had not gotten my view on the question from them—or from Troland either, though I knew a little of how he thought about it.

Years later I ran into a man who told me that he was the one who, at my request, had accompanied me on a walk either the day, or some hours, before the final oral examination. He remembered, though I did not, my telling him that I did not want to study during that time. I suppose I had some idea of not wearing out my mind, so to speak. Or, was I really afraid I would worry somewhat if I were alone, with no one to talk to? I recall nothing of any preexam feelings and extremely little of the occasion itself. In my student days, fear of not succeeding was scarcely a problem.

The minute I began to teach, how different things were! Now I was responsible for learning not by one familiar person but by many, differing widely in interests and abilities in ways one could only very incompletely understand. A student who is bored can think of other things, ostensibly write notes about the lecture but really about something else, or perhaps read surreptitiously. A teacher who is boring cannot but feel humiliated, for it is a teacher's job to interest. The teacher who gives low grades fears he or she is too severe or has failed to communicate. The teacher who gives high grades may be lowering standards.

If taking an examination never seemed to me an ordeal, giving one often did. I recall one case where a question I had thought clear turned out to have two quite different possible interpretations, as the answers showed. I had been unintentionally ambiguous. It was I who had flunked! Oral examinations have similar pitfalls. Besides the room for one's own blunders or clumsiness in putting questions, there was also this: if my teachers had sometimes been boring I found that colleagues putting questions to students could be equally so. Altogether if I know what fear or dissatisfaction with my abilities or associates are, it was not being a student but being a teacher that enabled me to learn this.

On the other hand, in some ways teaching has not been hard. With or without much preparation for a particular class meeting I can always manage to keep talking. One thing leads to another: a student question usually can be elicited if one has run dry, and in answering this, new ideas nearly always come. I recall only one occasion when I had to dismiss a class after half an hour. Probably I had run nearly out of blood sugar, a rare occurrence for me. A puzzling aspect that many teachers have probably had is that there is no very clear correlation between carefully prepared class meetings and especially successful ones. Sometimes extemporization works better than using elaborate notes. Sometimes, it works poorly.

As I think about my total experience as pupil or student and as teacher in educational institutions, the overall impression is that whereas both were satisfying roles, only the former was trouble free. Being a student was simple and easy. One had only one responsibility: to learn and show that one had done so.

The foregoing does not quite mean that when I read, in the 1960s, that students are "an oppressed class" I had no idea of why this was said. It means rather that I could understand the statement only by considering ways in which things have changed since my early years, or ways in which I had special individual luck. (I did not have to "work my way through college.") One of the big changes is in the pervasive sense of uncertainty and mistrust arising from many things, such as the atomic bomb, Vietnam War, exposure to evils and dangers through TV, and high-powered journalism. More precocious sex, earlier incurring of responsibilities for others, with or without marriage, including possible or actual children, a less dynamic economy, are some of the factors. The idea of participatory democracy was in my time less prominent (to put it mildly) among students. There were authorities, there were rules; I understood the rules and was sure I could prosper under them. After I left Harvard in 1928, I had to start over again learning new rules; but now I was among those who had to see that they were enforced, and to consider whether and how they ought to be improved. I have never since been quite so sure that I knew the rules and could profit by them as I was in the days when I had no responsibility for making or enforcing them.

If paying for the education of his six children was any hardship for Father, I at least was not made aware of it. True, Mother reported Father as saying once, "It was rather hard having four children going to college at the same time." To this Mother had replied, "It was rather hard having four children [Frances, Charles, James, and Henry] in diapers at the same time." Remember, there were no commercial diaper services or disposable diapers!

Two Roommates

At Harvard I had a room to myself two of the four student years and a roommate the other two. The first roommate was from my home town and was an even-tempered, well-balanced, reasonably intelligent but not exciting chap. He later became a schoolteacher. Rooming with him was no strain and not much to "write home" about. I recall few moments of that experience. One was when Harry complained that just too many things were going wrong with him at the same time. He listed them; they were all fairly trivial, and only the multitude was impressive. Ever since, at occasional moments when trivial simultaneous misfortunes seem unduly numerous I recall Harry's mild complaint against the operations of the goddess Fortuna.

The other roommate, Walter Gardner, like myself then, was a graduate student; but his subject was economics. He was intellectually and in general a rather strenuous chap. His tennis was on a higher level than mine, and I could not play against him after the first crushing defeat. He was a mental athlete, also. Like his father, he had chosen economics as his subject; but this did not prevent him from taking philosophy quite seriously. And he had a definite and firmly held philosophical position, which was a Bosanquetian monism. For this he was always ready to argue vigorously. With the monism, logically enough, went a strict causal determinism. He was a classic devotee of that doctrine. Without it, he thought, the world would not be intelligible, either scientifically or philosophically. By that time I had already bade a hearty farewell to the doctrine he regarded as indispensable. Only for a short time years earlier had I ever definitely believed it. So we argued away now and then, without rancor or hostility, over two main issues: determinism, and the question of the reality of multiplicity. Is the world simply one Reality, with the many "things" and "persons" of common sense only ways in which the unitary reality appears in experience? Or, is the multiplicity real and not merely apparent? And is there any freedom of indeterminacy, such that, at a given moment, a given individual is physically and psychologically capable of performing *this* action but also capable of performing *that* incompatible action, of feeling or thinking in just this way, or in another way? Do causal conditions uniquely and precisely determine what happens next, or do they merely limit the possibilities more or less narrowly? I held for the latter view. A third issue, connected with the other two, was whether the Supreme Reality (and we both believed there was such a reality) could have anything like personal relations with persons in the ordinary sense. If in reality there are no persons in the plural, then of course there are no personal relations either, whether among the persons or between the Supreme and the lesser realities. I held that the idea of a personal God was not simply an illusion, that personality is our best sample of reality and value and could not be simply set aside in trying to conceive the cosmic, universal, and supreme form of existence.

Walter Gardner well understood the logic, such as it is, of the monistic position. An Advaita Vedantist from India would have found his views congenial. He came to see that I understood the logic of my opposing position. "You are perfectly consistent," he said. Neither of us changed the convictions of the other; but I probably arrived at a sharpened awareness of some of the issues between us. For me now a chief interest in recollecting these discussions is that, although at that time (1923) I had not yet seen Whitehead and I knew little of his views on philosophical questions, I did know definitely and with some precision how and why I must differ from the extremes of monistic and deterministic theories, and also from extreme pluralism. This is one of the ways in which I can claim to have come to be a (more or less qualified) Whiteheadian by a sort of preestablished harmony between my views and Whitehead's. The dissertation I was writing that year argued for a middle position between mere monism and mere pluralism, or between a doctrine of all internal and one of all external relations. Whitehead began, in the following year, when he came to Harvard and I was in Europe, to present such a middle position. It was another year after that before my return to Harvard made me aware of what Whitehead was doing. In some respects his doctrine was much more finely articulated than mine, and immensely beneficial for my further development. The same could be said for the metaphysics of Peirce, which also, more definitely than most other going philosophies, was a similarly median position on the question of the one and the many. With Peirce, too, and without yet knowing it, I already was in considerable agreement. In some ways, Peirce was clearer than Whitehead; in other ways, Whitehead was clearer. Whitehead had a more fully rounded and thought-through system; but Peirce had analytic tools that have great power in clarifying issues.

Many years later, when my wife and I visited him in Washington, D.C., Walter Gardner still was a Bosanquetian, and we renewed our argument a little. But we both knew it was hopeless. My former roommate had rejected an academic career to go into government service and ended up in the monetary fund. Thus, he did not acquire the fame he could probably have had as a professor. But it may be right to say that he was more vigorous than imaginative or creative.

As usual, I am surprised at the small number of sentences I can resurrect from that year of sharing a sitting room between our two small bedrooms. I have quoted one short phrase. Another equally short was spoken when I received word from home regarding brother Henry's illness. Walter asked me what *anything may happen* meant. "Does it mean that he might die?" When a law-trained brainy person like my father says *anything* in such a context he certainly means to include dying. So the question pretty much answered itself.

Any other of Walter's sentences? Yes, talking about an economist in the Harvard department, Walter said, "I have never known anyone to shake him" (in argument or questioning). Why should I remember that particular utterance?

An absurd recollection is that we sometimes improvised our own meals in the sitting room, and that my roommate's habit was to eat an entire head of lettuce at a sitting. I have never felt up to that feat.

I am ashamed of one recollection. Walter offered me an opportunity to meet his fiancée and I refused it. For some reason I felt short of sleep and the proposal meant staying up late. I thought I would be poor company. But still ... Walter merely said later, "You passed up the greatest privilege a man could have." This was always his attitude toward his wife, and later (when I had my wife and had met his) I came to understand it better than I could then.

I owe this much to Walter: he and some of his economist friends taught me something of the content of economics and made me at least less naive than I otherwise would have been in that subject, in which I never had a course. Later at the University of Chicago I came to know Paul Douglas, Henry Simons, Aaron Director, Frank Knight, and several other of the Chicago School of free enterprise economists. They, too, contributed to my education in the "dismal science." My idealism pushes me toward socialism, my respect for the logic of free enterprise pushes me away from socialism. This has been a tension thoughout my career. Simons once said, "Socialism is all right as a description of Heaven." His pamphlet, *A positive Program for Laissez-faire*, was my bible in economic questions for some time. He thought government regulation was a feeble compromise between competition and social ownership. The present state of railroads would not have surprised him. I still bitterly regret his premature death from sleeping pills, one more of the many chemical inventions whose benefits have to be weighed against positively mammoth harm to the human species, harm the advertisers do not advertise nor does the Food and Drug Administration do enough to protect us against. Do they even yet warn against mixing alcohol and some of the other drugs that are potentially dangerous in combination with alcohol?

A Boston friend of those days and later, was John Marshall, an intelligent student of E. S. Brightman at Boston University, who made me more aware of that philosopher's existence and work than I might otherwise have been. When I told Marshall that in my view our existence becomes an objective reality, along with other existents, only by our being content of the divine love that embraces all creatures, Marshall began a discussion of this thesis as follows, "I am lovely ..." This was characteristic of his combination of humor and quick wittedness. It was also true. It is like me, I fear, to forget the point to which this was a preamble.

Some Landladies

Out of my seven years in residence at Harvard, three of them as humble member of the faculty, four were in rooms not owned by the university. So I was dealing with landladies. One of these, Miss Shepherd, was a delightful person. She earned my gratitude by her good humor when once I came home late without a key and had to wake her up. The door opened and her cheerful voice came out of the darkness, "Don't knock over my Kewpie!" I had expected to hear a complaint for my negligence. She was always pleasant and was obviously a very sound sort of person. She did take a dim view of a fellow in the house from Arkansas, who had once disobeyed her strict injunction not to try to operate the hot-water system for bathing but to call upon her when a bath was desired. To me he seemed a stupid chap, unworthy of much notice.

Miss Shepherd had a favorite among the roomers, and I was not it. It was a man from Colorado who was a distinguished amateur boxer but also a student in the law school. He was a person of good quality and I could not fault the landlady's taste in liking him. She invited him, alone among us, to have tea with her. The boxer told me how he was dissuaded from becoming a professional boxer and that he was glad he had listened to the advice. (He also told how an English lord that he knew well also was an amateur boxer.) Years later I saw his name as judge in an Olympic boxing contest (I think it was). This seemed appropriate.

Another landlady proved a trouble. I had then more passion for fresh air than I have now and I used to leave the window open on cool nights. Mrs. Day held that I ought to wake up early and shut the window. I said that I was satisfied with the temperature of the room and that it was my business when I shut the window. To my contention that the temperature of the room suited me she replied, not very relevantly it seemed, "Actions speak louder than words." We both adhered to our positions and I finally gave up and moved. Now that I am more energy-conscious I see some point in the landlady's idea. I was not only cooling my own room, but to some extent the rest of the house.

The only other landlady I recall was no trouble at all. She was the mother of several children, psychically warmhearted but with a physically weak heart. Her son, a dentist who should have known better, took her out to the Colorado Rockies where the altitude nearly finished her. This is not the only case I have known where an overweight person with a heart of limited strength had her life shortened by a visit to Estes Park. It is no place for a person whose heart is barely able to do its job at sea level. This woman had the name of a famous murderous Shakespearean character with an equally murderous wife. One odd thing in the house was the most timid small dog I have ever witnessed. Came anyone not a member of the family into the room, that little animal crept, visibly trembling, under the sofa or into a far corner. It must have been cruelly mistreated early in its life. I don't remember if the family knew any details of its early history. Certainly it was not they who had been cruel. Probably the animal had been a stray, mistreated by strangers, so that it still feared strangers.

Volunteer Work in a Camp for Boys

In a quixotic moment, I volunteered to direct a group of Boston boys in a free summer camp for several weeks. What led me to do such a rash thing I do not quite know. I believe the only material compensation was the board and lodging. It seems now a "rash thing" because, although discipline has scarcely been a problem in my university teaching of philosophy, a group of precollege kids of miscellaneous ages presents a very different challenge from graduates and undergraduates who have elected to study philosophy. But, fantastic luck, the camp had an athletic director for whom discipline was a mere matter of course. He was tough but good, and there was no shadow of doubt about who was boss when his part of the schedule was in operation. He looms in my memory as much like the farm boy Hercules (see Chapter 14, first Section), strong and secure but with a habit of issuing commands.

I tried, among other efforts, to impart a little of my knowledge of birds. But the only effect of that which I recall was the following curious incident. There were two Italian boys, brothers, in the group which otherwise I remember as purely Irish. The Italians were rather at a loss to relate to the others, but they knew how to handle me. The younger—one of the smallest of all the boys—was a little demon for finding ways to be disobedient, and when I tried to rebuke him he was adept at changing the subject. For instance, "What bird is that?" he once asked, pointing at whatever bird, or perhaps mere tree capable of hiding a bird, that was at hand. The older Italian seemed to have a flair for getting himself hurt by the Irish. I remember him flicking a towel at a pair of Irish legs whose stung owner immediately responded with still more painful violence. The Italian seemed to find this method of retaliation astonishing, natural as it looked to me, and cried bitterly.

One procedure worked rather well. This was reading fairy tales in the evening. Most of the boys were glad to listen; but a few of the older fellows got bored and started creating distractions. However, a candid appeal to them to give me and the more interested younger boys a chance got fairly good results. I detected no really bad individuals in that group. My chief feelings about those weeks (was it two?) have always been, "I got through them! Bless the athletic director."

Another quixotic venture while at Harvard (or was it at Haverford?) was conducting a class in speaking English for Italian immigrants. We met too little and at too long intervals to accomplish much. (The way to learn a language, and most other things as well, is to do little else for a time. The Italians were friendly and mildly appreciated my efforts but, I suspect, knew that I was not doing a great deal for them. It was far too much a sideline with all of us for that.

A Traveling Fellowship (1923-1925)

Harvard disposed of an award called the Sheldon Fellowship designed to enable Harvard students to do postdoctoral study in Europe. I was given this fellowship in 1923 and it or something like it a second year, so that I had more than two years in Europe, mostly in Germany, but with productive or at least fascinating visits to England, France, Austria, Italy, and Holland. I met many philosophers in the first three of these countries, made a lot of progress in reading and speaking German and French, and acquired some sense of what European scholarship is (or then was) like.

The longest single stay was in Freiburg, Germany. Husserl was the most famous philosopher there, but I learned a good deal from four or five others, and also came to know slightly the famous mathematician Zermelo, who lived there. He was skeptical of Husserl's thinking—as was I. Heidegger's fame was just getting underway outside of Germany, but already was beginning to rival or surpass Husserl's in Freiburg itself, and before I left Germany, Heidegger was given a position at Marburg, whither a crowd of students followed him, I among them. At Marburg, Natorp was still active, though he died a year or so later. Nicolai Hartmann was another celebrity teaching there. All of these people were of some interest, but none came close to making me their disciple, even as much as my Harvard teachers had—still less, as much as Peirce and Whitehead did later. But altogether Europe gave me a second education in all sorts of ways.

Some Letters and F. C. Hartshorne's Last Public Address

Haverford, Pa.
February 15, 1922

Dear Charles,
    That certainly was a nice letter you wrote me and I was very glad to get it. . . .
    It is so nice to think that Emily [her sister] is really engaged to so nice a man as Stuart Mudd is. I don't think she could have found a finer type and he came along just in time, didn't he? They both have it very badly as you will soon see if you go on the house party with them. I hope you do go and I hope you write and tell me all about it as Emily never has time to write anymore.

*I am much interested in what you said about Bobby
[friend of her cousin (and my sister) Frances]. . . . I wish
he would marry. He needs someone to pet and make a fuss
over him all the time. Just the same I hope he does not
marry Frances.*

*Have you really plans for a trip abroad in the near
future? I hope you have and I hope you carry them out as I
understand that that is what you would like to do best. . . .*

*Between the remarks that Rufus Jones made to you
and some others that someone said to Emily I feel quite
proud to be related to such a clever person and to one who
I am certain is going to be famous some day. We may all
laugh at your absent-mindedness and queer ways of doing
things, but we all would be mighty glad to have the brains
you have. I would give anything if I could be carried away
by my thought from all the petty and sordid details of life
and make my mind think creative thoughts. However I just
wanted you to know that even if I do tease you sometimes,
it is only in fun, for I really have great faith in your abilities.*

*Don't forget to write me all about . . . anything, I am
always interested. Yours affectionately,*

Carol Hartshorne

This cousin, the oldest of four children, was severely handicapped
in muscular control from birth. If she ever had a mean thought in
her life I never heard about it. She was particularly helpful to her
youngest sibling, the one boy, who grew up to be the distinguished
and tragically killed E. Y. Hartshorne, or "Ted!" She delighted in my
promising future, in her sister Emily's romance; she no doubt took
satisfaction in her brother's promise—what about her own prospects?
She had a practical plan for that, a sort of small commune for handicapped persons, but hardly hoped for either fame or romance ("having it badly"—as she put it, possibly with a *soupçon* of envy). She is
my idea of a truly brave and truly good human being, giving as much
to others as she could possible hope they would give to her. True, she
had one advantage many of the handicapped lack; she did not face

poverty. The family and inheritance would take care of her financially. But she had to limit her hopes rather narrowly, and it seemed not in her to complain.

Concerning the absentmindedness Carol referred to, mine in my late teens was sometimes almost as extreme as, years later, it acquired the widespread reputation of being, though by that time it was actually somewhat less so.

Why it was better for Frances not to marry Bobby (as she did not) I have forgotten; but I have no doubt that Carol was right. Her observations were disinterested and intelligent. She was as right as she could be about Stuart Mudd, one of the noblest male friends I ever had. He did a fine thing for me once. I was having trouble making a certain decision in the winter of 1923. In June I was to take a traveling fellowship and go to Europe for further study. I could do one of two things, postpone finishing my dissertation for the doctorate until returning from Europe (or perhaps finish it while in Europe) or finish it in the few weeks left before June. The objection to the latter option was the scant time, considering that I was also taking courses for which I needed credit. Objections to the other choice are obvious enough, though it might mean that in the end I would have a more mature and finished piece of writing. Stuart, Emily's husband by that time, found out I was in a dangerous state of indecision. We were having lunch together at the time and I recall him saying, in his earnest way, "Now Charles, we are going to decide this here and now. You are going to tell me exactly what the pros and cons of the two possibilities are until it becomes clear which is the best one." I did as he bade, and it became clear to both of us that, despite the rush with which the writing would have to be done, it would be foolish not to get the thing out of the way before going to Europe for a new chapter in my education. I regard this as a classic case of how, occasionally, advice can be helpful. Stuart did not tell me which of the two courses to follow, he told me only what to do about my abulia, my tendency, to postpone facing the issue and coming to a decision. And his advice was so sensible and his motivation so obviously right that I knew I must heed it. The dissertation was written in little more than a month, over 300 pages. It was not a mature work, but full of ideas that could be matured later.

Paul Weiss later was helpful in a somewhat similar way when I worked on the Peirce writings. There were so many conceivable ways to arrange the papers. One could follow chronology, though not all the papers were definitely datable, to put it mildly, one could follow a scheme Peirce himself outlined for a major opus, to be called The Principles of Philosophy. I inclined to the latter scheme, but could see arguments for the other. Weiss is a decisive fellow. After he had seen a lot of the essays and we had made many decisions about which essays to publish and which to set aside, he began to press for a final decision on the major question. Why not follow your systematic scheme? He wanted to know. In this way my hesitant inclination became a firm plan of action. I really do not know how long it might have taken me to make up my mind without this extra prod from Paul. I do know that it was well to get the matter decided, and that in any case the job was too much for one person. That the other person was as energetic, hard-working, and ingenious as Weiss was greatly to the good.

It has never seemed to me that, as some have seemed to think, I was quixotically generous in accepting Paul as fellow editor. I needed his help. One good thing about it was that neither of us looked upon being known as editor of Peirce as a major goal in life. We both had far larger ambitions. In any case, had it not been for Paul, neither of us might have received credit for our work; as there was a move in the Harvard Philosophy Department to give the department rather than any individuals the credit for the editing. Paul's energetic re-sistance caused the abandonment of that plan. I was away in Chicago while the controversy was going on; he was in Cambridge.

Finally, Paul always bore in mind that I was senior editor and that, in cases of disagreement, the decision had to be mine. It was a trouble-free relationship for me. I wish I knew which of us first had the idea, adapted from Wittgenstein's *Tractatus*, of the paragraph numbers. I guess it was Paul. (Later he confirmed this, and that settles the matter.)

Freiburg.
1923-24

Dear Tina [Clementina Hartshorne]:
Are you still the luckiest person in the world? [I

guess she had become engaged, or married, to Richard
Jenney.] I hear at last from the new parents (her sister
Emily and husband Stuart Mudd; their first child had been
born). Stuart writes a nice, cordial, and most welcome letter. And promises (rash fellow—nicht?!) one from Emily,
when she is able. Fortunately I shan't think she is incapac-
itated because she doesn't write. I know the lady too well
of old and now she will not be less occupied than before. It
depends upon whether she tries to combine baby and
laboratory, partly—I don't know if any such combination is
planned or not. [Emily had been helping her husband in
his experimental work.]

It was a good long time after your postal announcement that I heard—because after I left Wien I got no mail
until reaching Strassbourg three weeks later. I have often
wondered about how Emily was and was very glad to
have the uncertainty ended.

I am quite comfortably installed here—in the shadow
of a great philosopher, Husserl. There is a Harvard friend, a
phil. stud., and his brother, a med. stud. He revenges himself (the latter) upon us for talking so much phil. by telling
the most gruesome tales from the operating room. But altogether we have an excellent time. Marvin is very clever at
phil. and helps me in learning to understand Husserl,
whom he has been studying under for a number of months.
He is also very aggreable. ... Ditto the brother.

Then there is a famous mathematician, Zermelo (does-
n't he sound like one?) of whom I had heard at Harvard,
as author of "Zermelo's Axiom," who joins us at mealtimes,
or at tea, now and then. He is both witty and comical. He
has lived alone so much that he is constantly forgetting the
company and talking away to himself—particularly when
it comes to paying the bill. For like profs. here in general
now, he has no money to spare—to put it mildly.

Speaking of girls at college, he finally summed up his
view of why girls go there by asserting that he knew girls
who had been to three universities (one changes univ.

much more often here) and still kein Mann gefunden hatten.
He is usually a bit cynical—but amusing.

The two Farber brothers and I were invited to the
Husserls last [New Year's] evening. The old man talked
splendidly at various points in the conversation, especially
as the clocks and bells were announcing the last hour, or
rather moment of the year. He made quite a speech about
the calling of philosophers—to recall people to the "Inner
Life"—the real meaning of existence. Then he wished us
all a happy New Year, and kissed his wife's hand. She is a
funny thing in comparison with the great man. But he
has his funny traits too. And its lucky for him he married
her—for she does all the work of the house practically, and
in these days that helps! But she doesn't know much about
"phenomenology," that's sure. It proves a philosopher need
not marry a wife who can discuss Plato with him, for they
get on fine. I mentioned the fact that the Herr Geheimrat
kissed her hand, because I wanted to add that she looked
so pleased and happy, and also sensible of the humbleness
of her own qualities in comparison with his, that it was
quite touching.

I am to take lessons in German handwriting from a
young girl, and an attractive one at that. Zermelo and the
Farbers call her Salome, since seeing O. Wilde's play (John
the Baptist's head, remember the damsel?), but whether
the actress also had red hair, or for no reason at all, I don't
know. [My memory of this German girl is zero, oddly
enough. I remember several others fairly definitely.]

Zermelo is already jealous (a bachelor of 50) and
wants a tea arranged so he can meet her.

Do write!!
Charles

Frau Husserl's loyal humbleness toward her husband is legend-
ary. She asked Ryle if her husband was as great as Plato. Ryle thought
not. Then "Is he as great as Kant?" I do not know Ryle's answer. But

Ryle's view of Husserl I mention elsewhere. The only American I have known who knew Husserl and thought him one of the very great philosophers was Dorian Cairns. Unlike Farber, he truly was a disciple. Farber was brought up as a Marxist and ended up, from my perspective, a rather crass naturalist or materialist, with a thin, secondary layer of the psychical. However, he was violently critical of Heidegger, seeing his limitations but scarcely his better insights.

Marvin Farber was primarily a good organizer and editor. Sydney Farber became a "brilliant" medical researcher. Sydney and Zermelo made fun of Husserl when we were together. I don't think they were much in awe of him intellectually. Marvin was not either, perhaps, but he had invested time and effort in studying with him and was too practical a person not to make what use he could of what he had learned. I may be wrong but I found Husserl himself and Cairns, in his few essays on Husserl, more to the point than Marvin Farber's book on the subject.

This letter to Tina is one of many that have turned up, to my astonishment. I would have said that I knew her only through conversations with her and had totally forgotten corresponding with her. Her doctor, when she lived in Cambridge, was a German, which is perhaps partly why I felt free to include some bits of German.

A Philosopher Advises a Lady (Dorothy Eleanor Cooper)

Cambridge, Mass.
December 14. 1926.

Dear Dorothy,

It is pleasant to hear that you want to continue the study of philosophy. [She had had some courses in it at Wellesley.] I hope it will prove worthy of this continued interest. I say this because much philosophic writing in recent times has been so out of touch with what is vital in modern thought that it is hardly worthy of the attention of one trained in science, for example [as Dorothy had been]. Modern science has confused phil. thought for over three centuries, partly because, although it [science] got results,

*it was itself [somewhat] confused as to what it was really
doing; partly because philosophers naturally did two things:
one, exaggerated the changes called for by the new situation and too hastily threw certain traditional concepts over-
board; and two, they unconsciously assumed traditional
ways of thinking ... [that] really were antiquated. Today
science is beginning to see that the conception of inert
lumps of matter, for example, is not the fundamental principle, and thus the materialistic trend is less likely to mislead from now on. Moreover, after three centuries of effort to
adjust the traditional metaphysics to modern empirical
science, we have learned about what in that tradition is
really relevant to our task; and the one-sided radicalisms
and conservatisms are alike discredited. Thus all things
point to a new synthesis such as only the Greek, Hindu,
and Medieval classical periods have known — but this time
on a basis of assured and exact science such as no age has
known. That's the excitement just now.*

*There's another thing. Philosophers can address
the entire world. At the philosophic congress [at Harvard]
most parts of the world were represented. The situation
that enabled St. Paul to carry the Faith over the Medi-
teranean world now holds for the entire world (peace and
safety of travel, spread of certain languages, especially
English, etc). I expect the missionaries to do some scarce-
dreamt-of things in the next centuries. They are already
doing much more than is generally known, I gather. I see
that a student of Turkey holds that the adoption of democracy will prove fatal in the end to Mohammedanism, that it
will lead to the adoption of the religion of Democracy,
namely the religion of Christ. Now all this will render
precarious those too extreme Europeanizations in our own
religion that Orientals will see through even more than we
are beginning to. Thus we will get missionized, in certain
ways, too. In philosophy ... our lingering materialisms will
meet with one more foe. A Hindu, in fact two of them, made
such points effectively at the congress, and even my tiny*

knowledge of Oriental thought makes clear to me that most of our traditional problems and solutions have pretty creditable parallels in Hindu thought. That will help some I hope to show what is really universal in our thought. Where we differ from the Orient it's up to us to show that we do so on the basis of some definite source of insight not equally open to the Orientals. This puts an emphasis on our exclusive possession of many sciences. That again shows the importance of Whitehead and Peirce, who, as perhaps no third, have made these sciences basic in their philosophy and yet do some justice to those central ideas that rest primarily on a deeper plane than physics and in harmony with all the peoples who have thought and felt intensely upon these things. The Chinese in Whitehead's course, by the way, did brilliantly in the first reports. It is a good time to study phil., only, as we are just emerging from a period of great confusion, if you read writers who, like the majority, are still half or more unemerged, you make things difficult. That's the difficulty of advice-giving just now. Peirce is rather inaccessible and even Whitehead has yet to give us more than a sketchy introduction to his system. But his new book on religion, if used together with the other [Science and the Modern World], *is some help, though frightfully condensed in many parts. But I suggest getting the only Peirce volume there is if still in print: Love, Chance, and Logic [ed. Morris Cohen]. Kant, I suspect, is chiefly for the professional student unless read in connection with a course. For so much of him is now badly antiquated, in a sense in which Plato, for example, is not. Kant built more narrowly on the state of science of his time, he is more ambitious to say the last word — the surest way to limit oneself to saying at most the first word — and thus tries to be more definite and complete than his arguments warrant. Plato avoids this as no one else has done. Kant is a difficult writer who often buries his idea under his exposition — though this is far from always the case, and finally because of the provisional and overhasty unbal-*

anced character of most modern thoughts as already suggested. Sooner or later one ought to have a fairly prolonged
look at him, but it might be postponed a bit, I rather think.
Try Spencer's First Principles and James's writings in the
Modern Library cheap edition. Try Bergson's Introd. to Metaphysics. Try Dewey's Experience and Nature. And finally I
recommend strongly J. H. Randall's The Making of the Modern Mind. That's a very fascinating thing and a good supplementary history of phil. since the Middle Ages. You likely
have some ordinary history of phil.? I like Weber as a good
brief one; Windelband as a magnificent fuller one; and,
really, Rogers is good as he gives many quotations and is a
sound critic.

    Whitehead already gives you clues to possible
ways of viewing traditional thinkers. Find some thread to
follow out... let me know what it is and what happens. I
shall enjoy it. There is one more book, Science, Religion,
and Reality, edited by Joseph Needham, Macmillan. In this,
two essays are of special philophical interest, the one by
Eddington on Physics, and the conclusion by Dean Ing
[Ing—rhyming with sting not cringe, as someone has said].
I am not personally a very great admirer of the Dean, but
that essay does give a summary of the present situation
that is worth reflecting upon. Eddington is simply magnificent... He may well have written the best brief summary
of the point to which science has advanced in its bearings
upon metaphysics.... Any reading in Plato is pretty sure to
reward you. The Theatetus, Phaedrus, and Timaeus are the
most essential ones, I suppose, unless one wants especially
the ethical side, in which case the Protagoras, Gorgeas,
Philebus, and the Republic are the ones.... I would even
claim that the full significance [of Plato] is reserved for the
future of philosophy to discover. At least one must have
read Peirce to see it (if so it be I am not deluded).

    Well, no doubt that is enough.

    This letter is all philosophy, isn't it? The next
time perhaps a little more general gossip will be a good

*alternative. Anyhow, I am very glad to hear from you
always.*

*My own book (on sensation) is now fully outlined.
It remains only to write it. This isn't really such a joke, as I
feel that deciding the general plan is the hardest thing of
all. ... The little subsidiary decisions that remain get
decided by instinct and habit a good deal, whereas the
main plan ... seems to require an almost violent fiat of the
will. "It shall be this though the heavens fall," and though
any number of other ways might be as good perhaps.*
Thank you for the card, which was a nice one.

Yours cordially.
[no signature]

These lines, yellow with age, were written (as I now type this) more
than 62 years ago. One should bear in mind that Dorothy was more
than six years younger than I was. Also, that she had written asking
for advice on what to read in philosophy. Her father, she now tells me,
had access to the University of Chicago library and got the books I
recommended for her. The odd thing is that neither of us seemed
aware that we might, only two years later, find ourselves husband
and wife. Instead, the assumption was it would all be a matter of
correspondence only.

Apart from a few omissions and bracketed explanations, I have
scarcely edited the letter. It shows the extent to which I was already
(aged 29) something like the prose writer I am now. It also shows, I
think, the immense element of chance or luck in life. I see no strong
evidence that my marriage to the lady was already predestined, though
it was certainly fortunate, and though I am amazed at my stupidity
in not seeing that I should have been already trying to bring it about.

This letter show the influences upon the writer of Peirce and
Whitehead, both influences tending to much the same result. When I
wrote my dissertation three and a half years earlier I had no such
vivid sense of the importance of modern science, or of Oriental ideas
either, for philosophy. And I certainly did not acquire this sense from
my studies in Europe.

The letter also shows, though I did not yet know the significance of the fact, that I was writing to the person to whom I could express my ideas as freely as I felt like doing. I was giving, but myself seemed in need of, advice—but not on the same subject.

F. C. Hartshorne
121 Church St.
Phoenixville, Pa.

Feb. 1st, 1926

My dear Charles,

Very glad to get your letter. I can well understand that the first examination [that I gave as a teacher, not took as a student] would have been a strain. But the greater ease and calmness with which you tackle the second one should make you realize one of the truths of human experience, namely that that which, on the first doing, is 'agony' is far less agonizing on the second doing, and upon the tenth doing becomes almost mechanical. Remember that the next time you have to do something quite new.

That quotation [from Peirce] upon poo-poohing is perfect. Such a history would be wonderfully instructive and interesting. One might start with Noah, whose ark building was universally poo-poohed. Then there was Agrippa, poo-poohing St. Paul, who, he declared, with a little persuasion would fain make him a Christian! Poo-poo! Nothing doing! Columbus, also, came in for many doses of the same medicine. One of the most famous instances in our own history is that of George Westinghouse, inventor of the air brake, and Commodore Vanderbilt, head of the New York Central R.R. Westinghouse, a young man, went to see him and commenced saying that he had a device that would stop a train in its own length, when the Commodore waved him to the door, saying, "Poo-poo! I have no time to waste on damn fools." Some years later, when the device was in use on other roads, the Commo-

dore wrote that he would like to have an interview with Westinghouse, to which the latter replied, "Poo-poo! I have no time, etc."

Dr. [sic] Peirce expresses exactly what I would often like to say to Mr. Reeves here. I have had more suggestions for the good of the Parish simply poo-pooed than I have ever experienced elsewhere. In all my relations with men in Philadelphia, some of them upstanding men in the affairs of the city, I can always get a hearing for suggestions, and often they are adopted, in whole or in part. Human affairs go forward largely by virtue of compromises; you admit and accept one or more of the other man's points, and he, in turn, if he is used to conferring, accepts some of yours, and the compromise result is supported by all, and is generally pretty nearly right. But Mr. Reeves is apt to react at once against an idea, largely because it is new, or different from what has been, and one can get nowhere with argument, because his conclusion, being instinctive, is not influenced by reasons or facts. . . . He has had very limited experience in meeting and conferring with men who are his equals. His knowledge of finance is positively infantile, largely because he hates the idea of money.

By all the ideas and customs of business men he owes me $100 because of a certain transaction, but he has no idea that he did not pay me in full, and of course I cannot tell him! But I wouldn't mind that if it were not also true that one cannot get him to give any real thought to the financial aspects of a parish problem, which is calamitous here because the financial problem is pretty certain to be a very serious one here some day. He would have made a splendid bishop, and I might have made something of a business man, and I suppose it unconsciously annoys him to find in me qualities that he does not look for in a clergyman. The amazing thing is how his very fine character and very unusual bearing, combined with a certain Reeves haughtiness of manner, afflicts all with whom he comes in

*contact with an inferiority complex! It is quite unintentional,
of course, but very real. The picture used in advertising the
Victor machines, the dog listening to his master's voice, is a
perfect representation of our vestry meetings! Or, that
description which Job gives of himself, "The young men
saw me, and hid themselves. Princes refrained from talking,
and laid their hands upon their mouths; the voices of
nobles were hushed, and their tongue cleaved to the roof of
their mouth." Or, the banquet scene in Macbeth, where
Banquo's ghost came to the banquet, but didn't eat anything. Our vestry meetings consist of me, Mr. Reeves, and
the Ghosts! I suggest something; Mr. Reeves says "I think" (I
wish he did think!) and that's that.*

*If it were not for my Philadelphia experiences
and associations I would have a hopeless inferiority complex by now. But I have only to recall Mr. Barba, former
manager of a bigger steel company than the Phoenix, and
now assistant treasurer of the Dioceses, etc., standing in
our church and saying of himself and others in Philadelphia, "When Mr. Hartshorne speaks, we listen for we know
he knows," and that recollection enables me to say, in
mind, to the Poo-poohers, "Poo-pooh to you." There is a solo
and chorus in Patience and we will say "Poo-poo to you,
poo-poo to you." Indeed, patience and a retentive memory
came to the aid of those poo-pooed, as they did to
Westinghouse. Six years ago I said to Mr. Reeves, "I think it
is a mistake to have separate drives in the community;
we should have a Community Welfare Chest, as some
towns have." It was quickly poo-poohed. Well, this spring
Mr. Reeves and others are out for that very thing! But I
am afraid they have missed their chance, and are now
too late.*

*You are quite right in what you write about the
possible mistake of tying up Christian beliefs with Greek
formulations of them. Dr. Foley, of the Phila. Divinity School
is strong on that point; says that the Nicene Creed met
what was in the minds of Greek Christians of those days*

but finds nothing in ours. There was a strong effort at the last meeting of our General Convention to take the Creed out of the Baptismal Service on the ground that multitudes of Christians at the first came into the Church without any such confession. It did not prevail, but such a movement once started, always prevails in the end, because reason and history are for it, and only later custom against it.

Of course the situation as to the New Testament is serious. But the battle is raging all along the line, and one cannot see much for the smoke. I have a feeling that the most radical positions must be wrong, because they prove too much. I mean, one proves too much if he proves that such a thing as Christianity had no substantial foundation. That offends my scientific temperament, for the cause must be adequate to the effect. Tear the New Testament to tatters, if you will, and throw the tatters to the flame, but if you do, I demand that you furnish me with an adequate explanation of the existence and persistence of the Christian Church, the Christian Sacraments, and why this is the year 1926 A.D. Experience shows that in commotions of this kind the destructive critics always have their innings first.

But of course in my articles [some of them about the Old Testament] nothing of the N. T. situation will be even touched upon. I am not at home there. Besides, it is not the psychological moment for a popular treatment of these problems. If you put before the people articles on problems which they themselves have not yet met, they are not helped, and are annoyed. But for you they would not know of the problems, and they do not thank you for your efforts to solve the problems. But the Old Testament problems, and the broad problem of the inspiration of the Bible, are already in the minds of the people. No one wants the doctor to come around unless he feels sick. As yet the N. T. problems affect only the Scholars and those at college, and of course the church news reaches only a few of those.

*Kepler's saying, "I am thinking God's thoughts
after Him," is the fruit of Christian Theism, as you say. The
absurdity of the Fundamentalist position, that God's
thoughts are to be found only in the Bible, is that God
would take the trouble to reveal a few scientific facts and
conceal all the others. That's the hopelessness of their
position and the main reason why it cannot be held
indefinitely. Their declaration of war against Science is an
attempt to set up a prohibition against thinking and learning which will prove infinitely more difficult to enforce
than that against drink. And if prohibition stimulates a
certain amount of drinking in defiance, how much more
will an attempt to prohibit learning the truth about anything? Men may, I believe will, find drinking out of mere
defiance a very poor pasttime, but learning facts will prove
fascinating in itself. And when it is realized that God's
thoughts about man may be found in the Bible, as men,
from time to time, were able to conceive of them, God's
plans and workings in Nature are to be found where He
has left his record, in Nature itself, there will be religious
enthusiasm added. The Fundamentalists, with their fury
and violence, which would wield the sword of persecution
if it could, are but another instance of that mental
standpattism that Christ referred to when He said, "The
time will come when those that kill you will think they are
doing God a service."*

*After reading your letter I read Stratton's [anti-
evolution] article in the Forum. Of course I have no use for
him or his attitude; but I do think that he makes out a case
against the museum authorities and especially against
their words. I would say that the motive for that exhibit
was polemical, rather than sober instruction, and therefore
he is justified in striking back. Each reconstucted man
must be admitted to be a mere hypothesis. It simply is not
truth to speak of anything about the development of man
as something we KNOW. As yet [emphasis added] the data
are lacking. They would have been [well] advised if they*

had confined themselves to illustrating the evolution of the horse, for example, for there the data are more numerous and convincing, and there is no dispute as to their significance. I doubt if any considerable body of scientists would support such an exhibit, especially under its title. It is not science, it is propagandum [sic], and science at least should not lend itself to propagandum, one of the worst curses coming out of the War. Science does not need to descend to any [such] methods in combatting Fundamentalism, and greatly weakens its case by so doing. Science can make an unanswerable case against Genesis by simply pointing out, as I did in my article, that Genesis describes the creation of things which we do not believe exist at all, e.g., the firmament and daylight as separate from the sun. Fundamentalists have not realized that difficulty because they were too ignorant to know what the firmament really was, in the conception of ancient people. I don't believe that anyone who has read my articles will ever again believe that God created the firmament and put waters up above it. As to that they are 'through.' And one such instance breaks down the whole Fundamentalists case. You don't have to fill cases in a museum with doubtful evidence and unproved claims. If the biblical account should be illustrated in the museum they should set up a model of the firmament, with windows in it, etc. And then we would see what they would say when the children would ask, "Is that the way the sky really is, and if not, when did God change the sky?" For they could not represent the firmament by a model of the heavens as we know them, because they would have to put the waters up above it! I stand by the statement in my article that none but the ignorant or disingenuous will attempt to reconcile Genesis with WHAT EVERYONE NOW BELIEVES about such things as rain and daylight.

I am not in position to advise in any way about leaving or staying at Harvard. I would think that, unless something unusually attractive should offer, another year

might be well spent at Harvard. [The next year was
my last.]

> *Your affectionate father,*
> *F. C. Hartshorne*

The examination I felt as a strain was one I was giving, not taking. This confirms my recollection of being more anxious about my role as teacher than as student.

The poo-poohing quotation is Peirce's remark that he thought of writing "a logic of poo-poohing, and perhaps a history of poo-poohing."

The letter gives a remarkably comprehensive account of Father's interests and of a central difficulty in his career, that he had to deal with an individual made powerful by status and who with the best of intentions naively assumed the right to make decisions virtually unilaterally, rather than working rationally toward a consensus. I find it difficult to make as generous allowances for the individual in question as Father did. I recall the man as very solemn and earnest but otherwise not impressive or interesting. I take his behavior and its results to be a paradiomatic instance of how great wealth can distort and misdirect human relations. Reeves was not intentionally my father's enemy, but in effect what else was he? In my longer career I have had only one (partly intentional) enemy, but he was so intelligent and knowledgeable that what I could learn from him probably outweighed any harm he did to my career. Also, he learned something from me. So even in that way I achieved something. My father was less lucky.

Father's articles on Old Testament topics were published in *The Church News.*

Father Takes Leave of His Parishioners

> *Cynwyd, PA*
>
> *April 25th, 1928*

Dear Friends,
   On the eve of the coming of your new Rector,

who will take up the work I laid down some months ago, I want to write you a few words of farewell and of good wishes for the future of the Parish. First, I fear that some may have thought that I resigned because I was tired of working, and wanted to retire and live in lazy ease. Not at all; that would have been setting a very poor example. I would have been glad to have served you some years longer, if I had felt that there was nay prospects of my being able to inspire the members of the Congregation to that increased degree of willingness to work and give which I believed was necessary for the future welfare of the Parish and the spiritual health of its members.

But as there did not seem to be any such prospect, I felt it my duty to hand over the leadership to someone else. That having now been done, whatever excuse defects in me or my working may have furnished any of you for not taking more interest in your Church has been removed, and the responsibility for the future is now upon your new Rector and upon you. For the next few months will be as much a test for you as for him, for his most earnest efforts will accomplish results only in proportion to the response you give to them. So let none stand on the sidelines, watching to see what the new man will do, but let everyone think what he or she can do to help, by attendance at services and meetings, by responding to Vestry appeals, and by praying for him and for the Parish.

And now, in, as it were, handing over to a new shepherd you who, nineteen years ago were committed to my care, and amongst whom I have gone in and out ministering the Sacraments and consolations of our holy Religion, I pray that you may have a pure intention, patient faith, sufficient success upon earth and the blessedness of serving our Lord in heaven and I hope to remain, as in past years I have tried to be,

Your friend,
[*not signed*]

Concluding Portion of F. C. Hartshorne's Probably Last Public Address *(read to the Club of Episcopal Ministers, early 1950, the year he died—in April)*

Anyone who has lived through the last sixty years as an adult, as I have, has seen taking place in men's thinking greater changes than in any other similar period in the world's history. This has been especially true in science and religion. Indeed, the effects of Darwin's work and writings has been more revolutionary in religious thinking than in scientific. For science it just meant accepting a new theory as to the development of the organic world, the kind of change scientific men are always prepared for. But for religion it raised a tremendous and irrepressible conflict. It was at once seen that no one could accept the new theories of the evolution of the universe and the origin of man and of all species and still accept the account in Genesis as true in any sense. But to so regard Genesis involved a disbelief in the verbal inspiration of the Bible, which, while never a Catholic doctrine, was by that time universally accepted in all Protestant bodies except the Church of England and this (Episcopal) church. Consequently, many earnest men felt that the whole future of the Christian religion was at stake, and that the Bible and Genesis in particular must be sustained and all the new ideas of science declared outlawed for all who wished to consider themselves Christians, and many such rushed valiantly to the defense of the faith, doing untold harm in their blind and mistaken zeal, and drove thousands out of the church who would otherwise have remained in it.

Matthew Arnold, speaking of Wordsworth in one of his poems, says,

> *Although his manhood felt the blast,*
> *Of a tremendous time,*
> *All in a tranquil world was spent*
> *His tenderer, youthful prime.*

But for me and thousands of thoughtful young men then in college, say between 1884 and 1888, it was our tender youth that felt the blast of that tremendous time. Then was there war in the gates, Gladstone and Huxley engaging in a great magazine debate over a series of months, the one trying to defend the Genesis account of creation and the other demolishing it. Everyone was reading them. To me, as a young student taking special interest in chemistry and the new and fascinating science of biology, Huxley had all the best of the argument. Up until then I had rather expected to study for the ministry upon leaving college, but I felt that if it meant that I would have to defend Genesis that profession was not for me, so I switched to the study and practice of law. Whatever else Gladstone may have accomplished he certainly kept me five years out of the ministry, and must have driven tens of thousands of other choice young men out of the church, or at least of active work in it. I had two brothers-in-law who I am sure would have been in the ministry of their respective churches, but, being nearly ten years older than I, could not wait to get straightened out, or afterwards change back to the ministry, but became Ethical Culture lecturers.

About the same time there developed in Germany what was called the Higher Criticism of the Bible, which was so-called because it was about the only criticism that had been applied to the Bible at all. The final and most outstanding result of the conflict which then raged between science and religion was the retreat of religion from positions it should never have tried to hold. Except among those of lower level of education or intelligence, Genesis is no longer accepted for more than it is, that is, a record of what the Hebrews believed as to the origin of the world, men and animals. But that involves giving up belief in the VERBAL inspiration of the Bible, and many do not yet realize what that means, no more than they realize what means the new belief that in the New Testament we do not necessarily have the ipsissima verba of Christ but what, some three centuries after His Ascension, Christians generally believed were His words and teachings.

For no theory of inspiration has come to take the place of the discarded one.

And chief among the discarded ideas is that of the Fall and original sin, and inherited guilt. And here, again, few realize the far-reaching results of giving up those ideas. Leaving infant Baptism without theological support is by no means the most important one, which is, perhaps, the necessity of a wholly new thinking of the Atonement. With [the] idea of inherited guilt gone, what do such words as

> There was no other good enough
> > To pay the price of sin;
> He only could unlock the gate
> > Of Heaven, and let us in.

any longer mean? Or what is the reaction of Christian minds today to such descriptions of the Saints in heaven as those "who have washed their robes and made them white in the Blood of the Lamb"? I dare to say, revulsion and puzzlement. And the description of Christ as the Redeemer has largely lost its significance because it really means "Ransomer," and was a favorite term in the days when as the Hymn indicates, we had to be ransomed from some being who held us captive or threatened us with harm unless someone paid him his price. No one is ever ransomed or redeemed any more, but people are being rescued from death and peril and pain all the time. Christ as Saviour, not from God's wrath, but from being the servants of sin, not so much from perishing hereafter but from being less fine and good than we might be with His help, is an idea easily understood and helpful, but speaking of Christ as the Redeemer strikes no responsive word in men's hearts and minds today.

I have called your attention to the changes that have taken place in men's thinking about religious matters for the purpose, if possible, of inducing you in your preaching and teaching to scrupulously avoid using old words, phrases and symbols, however hoary with age and redolent of old time sanctity, and use instead ordinary, present-day words that have some chance of ringing bells in their hearts and minds.

Incidentally, I wonder just what is gained by our addressing Christ as in the Agnus Dei, "O Lamb of God, that takes away the sin of the world, grant us thy peace"? Figurative language is all right and helpful if the people really understand it. But how many do? Is it not likely that it is "all Greek" to many of the listeners, who cannot be expected to have much idea how a lamb could take away world sin or grant peace.

I find that there are certain very real satisfactions in having lived long enough to see some changes working themselves out in one's lifetime, especially if one has long wished that certain things could be changed because they ought to be, and then sees the changes actually coming. For that reason I got great pleasure out of the Bishop in "Lambeth and You" saying "It is OBVIOUS that just baptizing a baby cannot make it a member of the Church." Great! And maybe, though I doubt it, I may live to see that become obvious even to our House of Bishops.

Just before Christmas I got monkeying with some electric wires and got electrified, and I can't recommend it; 30 seconds was just 29½ seconds too long. But in the end I gained something. I had to stay home and I listened to Dr. Salmon preaching and strongly urging his hearers, probably several thousand of them, not to think that the Reason God's Son came into the world was because there was an angry God who needed to be appeased, because there was no such God and no such necessity. Hearing him drive home those blessed truths so electrified me in mind and spirit that it almost made up for the other unpleasant experience. Original sin, Inherited Guilt, an Angry God locking the gate of Heaven and holding open the gate of Hell are on their way out, and I have lived to see it.

A Wise Friend

600 Grant St.
Pittsburgh, Pa.

Dear Carlos,

*... What a real pleasure it was to hear from you.
And what fine big things you are doing. You don't know
how proud I am to know you, my sometime-to-be-famous
Carlos. ... In a few years I shall probably be saying "I
knew him when"—I hope not—I want always to say, "I
know him now."*

*To go back to your letter, you really did for once
tell me about yourself. I don't believe you have changed
much in things that matter—for which I'm glad. To bring
out the little point of difference in our correspondence, I did,
you know, have my address on the card I sent you. Can
you say the same?*

*About girls, Carlos, I see difficulties ahead for
you—perhaps. It has been said that he who walks on the
heights must walk alone—it may be the price that one
must pay for fame but I doubt it. It is rarely given to one
woman to have personal charm and the type of mind that
would appeal to you—but it does happen and unless you
can be satisfied with half-measures, it might be better to
wait and hope. I'm not at all convinced that half measures
aren't better than loneliness. However, I'm not advising
you— some married people are the loneliest folks I know. I
would be happy to know that you had met the right woman
whom you can love with your body-mind-and-soul.*

*Now what news is there of me to tell you? Very
little—a few gray hairs ... [I am] infinitely poorer than a
year ago because of the death of two friends [including]
my brother in law—[and] the one whom you met in
Wilmington—the artist. ... This sounds like a rather dismal*

self-pitying account. I'm truly not pitying myself. I'm still
doing the same work but thirsting for new problems. . . .
*   Thanks again for your nice letter—do it again*
very soon.

Affectionately,
Caroline R. [Robelen]

It seems clear that this letter was written before the writer knew she was going to marry the medical research worker with whom she went to her death not long after in a coast-wise vessel. My meeting the brother-in-law (whom I have totally forgotten) occurred when I visited the lady in Wilmington, about which trip I recall only that we had some friendly talk much as we did in the army. I cannot date even approximately either the letter or the visit. There was a later letter about the engagement or wedding, but no further communication between us, only a newspaper account of the sinking of the ship and names of those drowned.

How precisely the letter outlines the major personal problem of my twenties: half measures or the real thing! With the least bit of ill luck somewhere along the line, how easily I could have settled for half measures. A close friend had predicted: "The first girl that makes a try for you is going to marry you." She nearly did, but the naiveté that got me into the fix got me out of it also; for as I began to realize that I had been imagining myself in love with a person simply not my kind at all, as I was not hers. I tactlessly allowed my misgivings to appear and, as she put it, "succeeded in making me very angry." After that freedom for us both was only a question of time and a rather short time, too. It was one lapse from tact for which I have no regret whatever.

CHAPTER EIGHT

Some Youthful
Experiences With Women

An Old-fashioned Way of Learning about Love

As a man is in love, so is he.

(Balzac?)

The variety of human approaches to sex must be something like the variety of human beings on this planet and throughout history. If we are literate, we learn about this variety through many books as well as through direct observation and spoken gossip or confessions.

A philosopher friend I have known said once that he would not wish a daughter, if he had one, to marry a man without previous sexual experience with women. With one qualification I can see some justice in his contention, but otherwise I regard it as a self-serving rationalization of his own behavior (he was then not yet married). The qualification is: only if the inexperienced man is too ignorant, conceited, or stupid to have and make use of the ability to read in preparing himself for the role of husband — by consulting something at least as good as Van de Velde's classic on the subject — is there reason to accept my friend's attitude. I had a relative refuse such a book before his marriage, saying that he might read it later. The marriage was a dismal failure. Probably it would have been so, considering the woman he chose to marry, if he had consulted the book. Even so, and even if, as may well be, he had in fact had previous experience, I still would not attribute his refusal to wisdom. Rather, it was of a piece with his choice of mate. In our society reasonable initiation into the accumulated wisdom of one's ancestors (such as many tribes transmit orally and ritually) is provided chiefly through the written word. Without it we tend to be less than barbarians!

At the age of fifteen I had learned, twice over and once and for all, the lesson: if you don't know but wish to know about something and have time, access to a book store (and a little money), or a good library, you can probably find out. I learned this once by nearly memorizing two well-written little books on camping (including camp cooking) and "woodcraft" before or while undertaking to plan camping trips for myself and several brothers. I learned it a second time by using a book so small it fits into a hip pocket, and a field glass ($5 postpaid, advertized therein) in order, entirely on my own otherwise, to identify perhaps a hundred species of the small birds in my (three) parts of Pennsylvania. Thus three books and some practice sufficed to make me in my early teens a competent camper and bird watcher. From that time on I have tried to keep always in mind that books are vast resources for accomplishing innumerable ends. I confess I have hesitated to tell students how little they might need my classes if they would only read my books and the books that I have had to read to be able to teach those classes. How many professors might be out of jobs if this were really taught in the grade schools. I cannot believe it is taught there.

As I said earlier the variety of human approaches to sex is virtually infinite. My own history in this matter seems rather different from anything I have read about. About five times before marriage I felt vividly what may be termed the *magic* of heterosexual social relations, quite apart from physical fondling or completed sex acts — or the serious intention to engage in them. In only one of these cases did I so much as kiss the lady, or believe that I was in love and definitely wanted that person for a mate; and even in that case this state of mind persisted only for a short time. It happened at all only because the woman (after our first talk) deceived herself into thinking that she wanted to marry me and, by employing her greater experience (she was also older) and all the feminine wiles she could think of, brought me temporarily to the same state of self-deception. She admitted all this later. The lack of suitability in the match was (luckily for both of us) too great and glaring for us to remain long in the spell and the whole matter came to an end without any great suffering, at least for me. It left me much astonished that such a thing could happen.

In two previous cases, without being in love, but on the theory that probably I was not a person able to fall in love and would have to marry without that luxury, I proposed to the girl. Luckily each rejected me forthrightly, whereupon, comically enough, I felt unmistakable relief and even gratitude. In two other cases, for various reasons, I did not see the girl again after the first time I met her. All that happened was a letter from me which she did not answer or answered perfunctorily. I was not much troubled by this casual treatment.

In another case, the girl was charismatic and for a while enjoyed my company, but was certainly not for me, or I for her. She was too self-concerned to win my commitment, and too much in need of fatherly protection to look to me, who was also fairly self-concerned at the time, as the fulfillment of her dreams. She found what she wanted in a less brilliant (to be blunt) but more unselfish and outgoing divinity student whom we both knew. Because I clearly struck her as clever (as she herself was) but still, she felt, could not give her the stability she wanted, she began to resent my personality and this offended me. She first admired and then poured scorn on my philosophical pronouncements. (It was this alteration, and my reaction of wounded pride, that put me in a state that led my mother to formulate her exquisitely condensed maxim, "Life is big.") After her marriage I visited the girl in her home. The magic, the charm, was still there, but I felt well out of entanglement in her existence. She seemed a little less sure how lucky life had been to her. But then she was probably chronically a little discontented. She was a charming orphan, with a likewise charming brother, both brought up by a good and sensible aunt. I had another orphan girlfriend (to be referred to later, a Radcliffe student) who never quite charmed me at all, but was acceptable company for a while.

The remaining case of being charmed, but not quite in love, was with a nurse (already mentioned) in the army hospital where we both worked for two years in World War I. This was the most beautiful essentially "platonic" friendship that was ever mine. It was beautiful partly because there was never any conflict of purpose or hope between us. Neither wanted from the other anything more or less than the other was glad to give, simply friendship without physical sex. It was something like an ideal mother-son and something like an ideal brother-sister relationship. Only I was to her a younger not an older brother. And this was not what either of us wanted from marriage. In addition Miss Robelen was scarcely close enough to the intensely intellectual kind of life it was natural for me to live. This was less apparent at the time than it might have been later. She was a mature person whereas at that time I was still not too far from childhood.

Would any of the two-person relationships mentioned earlier, or any others that I had before marriage, have been the better for including overt sexual activity? *I do not see it!* They still would have had to terminate, and surely more messily and with more damage to one or both parties. Would I have learned priceless things about women in that way? Or enjoyed great happiness? The literature of our free-wheeling youth does not seem to give much evidence of such treasures. I learned a lot about women as it was: above all, to see women first as people (intensely imaginative and thinking animals) and only secondarily as sex partners complementing oneself in physical anatomy.

The foregoing remarks should not be taken as expressing complete scorn for the new freedom in sexual matters. I feel some scorn for it, but also a good deal of scorn for the Victorian mores that preceded it. The older system at its best produced much beauty; for all I know so does the present system—if there is one. As for the two systems at their worst, this worst is in both social forms so awful that one shrinks from trying to compare them. (Thus, consider the girl who, without being a prostitute, so it was reported, physically had known 100 men. Or consider the many Victorian marriages that brought no fulfillment for at least one of the parties, or the frightful treatment sometimes meted out to women of deviant behavior.) Both Victorian literature and recent literature tell of some dismal happenings, and in both cases prevailing moral ideas could plausibly be given part of the blame. When a psychiatrist that I read recently writes that our society is still repressing sexual desires with great psychical damage to many people I am not prepared to prove him wrong. Something or other surely is grievously damaging multitudes of people. To "know all the answers" in sexual matters one would have to be wise indeed.

I do know that the ideal of faithfulness in love can bear glorious fruit. My luck in this may be rare but it is not unique. We have all known examples. Nor is the logic of that ideal obscure. To commit only one's near future is to commit less than one's entire will. It is to be not quite single-hearted in the most intimate of all personal relationships. Probably not many marriages (if any) or lasting love relationships are entirely free from severe stress at times. Without the steady commitment to give permanence the full benefit of every doubt, perhaps scarcely any marriage would survive such stresses to the end. Yet every year added to the stock of common memories adds new values and possibilities from which to select in achieving mutual entertainment and inspiration.

One more thing. Has it really been proved that "sublimation" is in no sense a reality? That I could have poured out the energy I have in study and writing, besides teaching, and also have enjoyed full Marcusian sexual freedom from puberty on, seems to me wildly unlikely. Yet at no time have I been really miserable. Once in the army I told a refined close friend that I was unhappy. He refused to believe that anyone who smiled as I did was really suffering. He had something.

I have said nothing of autoeroticism. In my teens it did not quite occur. Thereafter it was indeed a factor. Luckily my parents had never told me any of the Victorian lies about the subject, and I had not read any of the most misleading old-fashioned books that tell them. My mother once told me of a ladies' group that discussed the topic rationally from a parent's standpoint. A sophisticated Haverford and army friend said perhaps the most apt thing on this subject: "The trouble is, it's so inartistic." For one who believes, as I do, that aesthetic principles, adequately generalized and seen deeply, are fundamental this is not a trivial comment.

Sex goes deep enough so that there can be no easy panacea. One of the grim ironies about praise of the new freedom (in addition to the upsurge in several diseases) is the massive increase in unwanted pregnancies in the very young. Nothing less was to be predicted in our kind of society. Foolproof methods of birth control other than sterilization are still outstanding. It depends on the degree of folly, ignorance, bad luck, or financial resources, how "proof" the method is. And our society breeds ignorance and folly enough—also poverty for some. Let us hope it will do better in the future.

President Carter has spoken of his wish to find alternatives to abortion as means of avoiding unwanted children. The only alternative that would be a solution of the entire problem is a degree of wisdom and self-discipline imparted to the very young, and to their parents who set them examples and role models, such as few have even dreamt of. Realistic alternatives for all are not presently available. That is the hard truth of the matter. Many of our advertisements favor crude attitudes toward sex and public educational institutions do too little too late to counteract the harm. Sufficiently wise teachers are probably very exceptional. Every new invention (auto, TV, new chemicals with which people drug themselves into incompetence, not to forget the old and ever dangerous invention of alcohol) is employed to exploit more than to ennoble sexuality. Ah well, one must not be an elderly scold. Humanity has great resources to remedy its own faults. It might even rediscover God, not by simply returning to old theologies, for they pretty much all show marks of human blindness, undisciplined imagination, or folly, but by taking advantage of the best thought of recent decades. Yes, you are right, reader, I *am* thinking, among others, of some of my own writings.

Social Relations of a Wandering Student

During the two rather solitary years (1923-1925) of my postdoctoral study abroad, I had not a great deal of female society. One German girl at a boarding house, who was rather handsome and certainly intelligent but not especially attractive, asked me to play tennis with her. She beat me too badly to encourage me to play with her again. It was the second time I had been badly beaten by a girl. (To me this was no worse than being beaten by a man.) She hinted that she was a lesbian. If my game had been even nearly as good as hers I would have liked well enough to repeat the play with her, but it was not. There were two generations of females in the family at Frau Utz's boarding house in Freiburg, who furnished a society of sorts, but even the younger generation was considerably older than I was.

By far the most appealing young woman I saw in all that time in Europe was an Hungarian girl of good family (the family also was there) staying at a boarding house kept by two Scottish sisters in Vienna where I stayed for several weeks. The girl had everything: looks, education, and character, so far as I could see. We talked about *War and Peace*, among other things. Nevertheless I did not fall in love with her. I merely saw that she lacked no quality that a young gentlewoman should have and that the entire family was on that level. Did we converse in German or English? I no longer know. Quite likely she was trilingual, as so many in Europe are. What is sure is that our conversation was not in Magyar.

In the Viennese boarding house just referred to was a young Austrian (but not Viennese) chambermaid named Rosa that I took to have fallen somewhat in love with me. I suppose I could have seduced her, though I did not have the impression that she already had been seduced. She was mildly pretty and had the charm of youth. Indeed she was too young and sensitive for the job. The house was run by one of two Scottish sisters who were remarkably different as persons. The one who acted as boss seemed a hard-hearted person who gave evidence of literally hating that young girl. The other sister was a gentle and likable enough person, but she kept out of the business side of things.

It puzzled me to see the hatred just spoken of. Was it envy of the young girl's attractiveness? Her employer was not only no longer young, but one questioned if she had ever been attractive. I saw no legitimate reason for her feeling toward the girl. And the girl suffered from it. There was a somewhat older chambermaid who appeared to suit the landlady. She was a young Austrian woman with inner security, and she and the other maid seemed good friends. After I had left the flat, I received a sad letter from the unhappy Rosa, who had given up the job and gone back to her family. Her father kept a small inn in a village somewhere in Austria. That's the last I heard from or about her. An elderly boarder at the flat, an impressive German lady, had told me, probably truly, that I had been no real help to the girl.

At a little hotel in Strasbourg was a young chambermaid who did not, I think, fall in love with me; but I did go with her to some sort of fair. She was less naive than the Viennese one. And no one was showering hate upon her. She has probably taken care of herself well enough.

The two somewhat solitary years spoken of were not really unhappy ones, and this for a number of reasons. Two former fellow students at Harvard were at Freiburg with me for all or part of the time and were interesting: Marvin Farber and Dorion Cairns. Farber's brother Sydney, later famous as a researcher in medicine, was a jolly, amusing chap. I recall his saying, "Some day you are going to tickle some girl to death." Probably, it took a medical student to put matters that way. I went with him once to witness an operation, the only one I ever did witness. It was upon a woman, and I disliked the surgeon's male chauvinist attitude, as I felt it to be, as he talked to the medical students about the procedures.

In two ways my lack of female society while studying abroad was qualified. One of the girls who had rejected a proposal from me and had thereby done me a favor, as I quaintly realized at the time, had subsequently become for me an object of poetic platonic love without any ulterior end. Immodestly enough, I felt in this experience an analogy to Dante's relation to Beatrice and Shakespeare's to his lady of the sonnets. (That the sonnet lady was really a man is in the same class with the Bacon-was-Shakespeare foolishness. As for Marlowe he was apparently homosexual, but not Shakespeare.) While in Europe, I wrote a number of imaginative letters to this girl to which she replied in a calm, friendly way. Later she married a considerate businessman, thereby confirming the view that a philosopher was not what she needed. In fact she distrusted philosophy.

The other qualification, or slight interruption, to my rather monastic existence was somewhat ludicrous, but not harmful to anyone. I have mentioned, as an orphan with whom I did not fall in love nor did I imagine that I wanted to marry her, a Radcliffe girl I had known somewhat at Harvard, was studying in France and wrote me that I should join her in Italy for a time when we both had academic vacations. I replied affirmatively, and we did meet in Italy. Not having seen her for a year or more, I could work up somewhat romantic feelings by substituting imagination for precise memories, as one sometimes does in such a case. But the feelings were mild enough, which was well, because there was mighty little romance in what occurred.

My recollections seem to begin on a train to Venice, I think from Florence. I expressed some enthusiasm for our destination. "We're going to Venice," I said, too ecstatically to suit unromantic Genevieve. "Oh," she said, "you're so conventional," or something like that. This set the tone for the rest of the trip. We took different rooms in Venice, and I have no recollection of intending anything else. But I had not intended quite the psychical distance that separated us. What we said to each other in Venice is gone beyond recall. We did see the sights. But what happened then?

Strangely, as in dreams, I recall three different locales but no order among them nor how I or we got from one to another. In some city, there were three of us (two men) all students from the United States, at a theater or opera. The seats were in a box, with only two chairs in front. Of course Genevieve sat in front, but which of us men was to sit beside her? I made room for the other man to take that seat and for a moment he did. Then he thought better of it and insisted that I have the seat beside the girl. It was fairly clear somehow that none of the three of us cared desperately how the matter was arranged. It became manifest before long that the two men were more nearly on the same wavelength than either of them was with the girl. Indeed that chap and I took to each other from the beginning to the end of the time we were together in that city, whatever city it was.

I recall this fellow and me discussing Anatole France. Neither of us shared the rather common admiration for this author, who was once referred to by a prominent American philospher as "a very wise Frenchman." In any such identification of worldly sophistication and disillusionment with wisdom Genevieve's other boyfriend and I saw a lack of discernment. I had been reading a French book called *Anatole France, est-il un grand écrivain?* and had been convinced by the negative answer the author gave to his question. "France has been compared to Voltaire. But Voltaire's laughter rings down the ages, while France merely smiles. Voltaire wrote: 'Leibniz knew what there was to know in metaphysics, that is to say, very little.' France would have written, not 'very little' but 'nothing at all' and thereby spoiled it." As a lifelong metaphysician, I agree exactly with this point. "Is France intelligent? Look about you. Bergson is intelligent. Poincaré is intelligent. But France . . . ?

Besides the stay in Venice and perhaps in another Italian city, I saw Genevieve in Bordeaux where she was studying. She took me to a party on an estate where I met the heir, a young man, and also a woman with some ostensible function in the household, but whose primary value there (I was told by Genevieve or some other American) was to provide the heir with a suitable mistress until he could be provided with a suitable wife who would, one gathered, be of a different social class from the mistress. Genevieve seemed, if I understood her, to have no criticism of the double standard so far as it concerned behavior of men before marriage, but condemned the similar behavior after marriage. In that whole trip I recall nothing that either of us said that gave any special satisfaction to the other. It was not a painful situation, merely somewhat absurd.

Genevieve did marry a professor, but not a philosopher. I think she knew what she wanted—and probably got it.

As I look back upon all the experiences touched upon in this section, I find nothing to seriously regret from a self-interested point of view; and if I did any harm to any woman, I think it was slight compared to what a man easily can do. That this is so, if it is so, I attribute to good luck quite as much as to any good management or virtue on my part. The wrong turning one was able to avoid taking was not as irresistible as it might have been if chance circumstances had been a bit different.

I accept life as a gamble, and I refuse to attribute my own or anyone else's happiness exclusively to my own or anyone else's virtue or divine providence. Always, there is a mixture of (1) providence, (2) good or bad chance, and (3) one's own self-management, good or bad: these three. The first factor is always good and nothing else; but the other two are potentially Janus-faced, good-bad. My process metaphysics shows that this must be so, and in any possible world-state. Providence makes life's gamble possible. It does not play the game for us. There is nothing life could be but a gamble. If one is lucky, one should remember that others may have been less so. If one is unlucky, one should remember that, while morale is maintained, any moment luck may change and give good management its chance to improve matters. If morale is lost, then one is unlucky indeed. Perhaps, someone more fortunate will extend a hand.

What Makes Life Together Endurable?

Before I met my wife, my chief concern about a possible wife was the impression I had of the suitable girls of my age (and this excluded my cousin Emily and the nurse Caroline Robelen) that their conversation was insufficiently interesting. After a short time there seemed little to say or listen to. I had the definite fear that perhaps this was the way it must be. A newspaper account long after those days shows the extreme to which this matter of nothing to say can go. In this case, the man's speech was limited. A woman was granted divorce on the ground that, "Since marriage her husband had spoken to her only twice. The custody of the five children was awarded to the mother."

Though funny, this touches on a serious matter. There are two great evils, conflict and boredom; and it is not worth trying to decide which is worse, for either one at the limit is unbearable. A basic aesthetic law, applicable to many deeper matters than the prettiness of flowers or the ugliness of a face, is that beauty, significant harmony, is a mean between two extremes, one being monotony, or a lifeless order or regularity (undiversified unity) and the other being chaos, or a wholly unintegrated diversity. All that is bearable has to be somewhere between these insufferable opposites. The middle region, nicely balanced as to diversity and unity, is what we tend to call the beautiful. These ideas are relevant not only to works of art or the beauties of nature, but to life itself as the inclusive art. It is an aesthetic imperative, "Be not too predictable, too merely regular in your behavior; but also be not too unpredictable, too irregular in behavior." Otherwise expressed, be creative, treat each day, even each moment, as a fresh occasion, but with reasonable reference to the expectations of others—and of oneself. Life is bound to have some unpleasant surprises; if there are no pleasant ones to compensate for these, it is simply too bad. Security is not enough. One must be faithful, reliable— but not dull, monotonous, too easily anticipated.

Another story, also humorous, bearing on the question of regularity of behavior, is the following. A new member of the philosophy department at Stanford was once asked by Professor Ralph Chapman Brown (no longer living) about his children. The new instructor replied: "I have four: the youngest is four years old, the others are eight, twelve, and sixteen." "Well," said Brown, "I'm glad to see that you are a man of regular habits."

It is easily shown that our main Western theological tradition, like Newtonian physics, profoundly underestimated the positive value of an element of chance, irregularity, and unpredictability in life and reality. It had a rationalistic-moralistic ideal that thought in terms of absolute laws and eternal fixities. The absolute principle is creativity, not order; it is freedom, not necessity. Order, necessity, and fixity are secondary and good only so far as they optimize the opportunities open to creativity. The solutions of the theological problem of evil that try to exclude chance are all sophisms. Not God, not the devil, and not some particularly wicked individual or social system is the ultimate source of suffering and conflict in the world. Rather it is the chance intersections of lines of creative activities that bring creatures into conflict, frustration, suffering. Ultimately, evils simply happen. No one intends them just as they occur, but *countless intentions happening to conflict*, are the final account to be given of them. Life is risk taking or nothing. Sheer security is meaningless. Providence does not exclude chance; it only guarantees a predominance of chances of good over those of evil. That predominance is real. Every organism while it endures is a harmony (essentially beautiful and only secondarily ugly) of various organs and activities. Life is essentially good. Were it not so, creatures would not be able to go on living. Something, consciously or otherwise, motivates them to do so, whatever verbal account some of them give of the matter. Their mere act of living refutes all extreme pessimists. They enjoy their melancholy at least a little. Schopenhauer was not a mere mass of suffering, whatever he wrote about the evils of life. God is not mocked, existence is basically good!

Homo- and Heterosexuality

It seems surprising that, in a life exposed (for instance in the army hospital) to such a variety of social settings as mine has been, I have never learned definitely about a homosexual male acquaintance. None ever propositioned me, none ever talked about it, and indeed I seem to have heard nothing on the subject in the army, at school, or college, until, as a teacher, I had a colleague tell me of being propositioned in a men's room. Graffiti on the subject one sees commonly; but extremely little talk has come my way.

That persons (perhaps not only men) in prison are given to it is what anyone with his wits about him and who knows how things are arranged in our prisons would expect and take for granted. Confinement for long periods away from spouses and others of the opposite sex is "cruel" punishment, whether or not it is "unusual." That our society, which has laws against homosexuality, pretends not to see this is, I fear, one of our worst hypocrisies. I have never had any impulse to practice homosexuality, but to understand why it occurs puzzles me not at all except in the extreme cases where it is the only form of sex the person is capable of. For such persons I feel compassion, and I regard as public nuisances those who either lack such compassion or are under the illusion that homosexual teachers go about trying to make converts among their pupils. More likely is it that heterosexual male teachers will try to seduce girls. The Anita Bryants (but even she finally partly saw the error of her behavior) are people I am tempted to wish did not exist, as well as all the people that pass, or do not repeal, laws trying to tell consenting adults how to behave to each other. This is one of the several subjects on which I find myself in agreement with Nicolas Berdyaev.

Since this chapter was written, the emerqence of the AIDS viral disease horribly complicates the problem of the preceding paragraphs, I still stand by what I said. We desperately need a religion, or philosophy of life that inspires us with the courage, strength, and goodness to be kind to one another in all matters, including sexual ones, in spite of the strong passions or desires that are natural for our species. We have to try to subdue the fears and rages that fuel wars and are now technologically suicidal in implications, also to see for what they are the remnants of male chauvinism absurdly leading many men (followed by some strangely unwitting women) to care more about the rights of relatively mindless fetuses than about the rights of pregnant mothers who are not comparably mindless. And we have a population far too little educated in either science or philosophy, and hence at the mercy of whatever atavistic form of religion or shallow irreligion happens to be appealingly presented to them. It is also a population that, with its political leaders, has scarcely begun to think honestly about the mathematical fact that, as the astronomer Fred Hoyle points out, the entire known universe is not capable of furnishing room for our species if it continues to increase its numbers at recent rates for a few thousand years. Either death rates must rise or birth rates decrease. It is not babies, no matter how poorly cared for and little wanted, that we need, or that will best enrich the divine life, but babies wanted and well cared for so that they will, when grown, help with our many problems, rather than constitute still more and worse problems. Surely to grasp that one needs no giant intellect.

Alas the trouble is that a purely philosophical religion has serious limitations. There have to be symbols, including sacred writings as symbols. And we have to maintain continuity with the past, with tradition, while remaining free to grow. The balance between momentum coming from tradition and openness to growth, especially to the growing edges that are science, philosophy, and art, in their most creative forms, is endlessly difficult. I may have been unbalanced on the rationalistic side. But we have to follow our intuitions, with whatever precautions and attempts at self-criticism. In fact, I do not now believe in God because of the Bible. I should do so if I could forget the Bible. Yet without the biblical religion I was brought up on, who knows what I should have come to believe? So there is the riddle.

Living in the Bible Belt for many years now leads me to wonder how many of those who use the Bible as weapon with which to beat homosexuals, or women who wish to resort to abortion, remember that there was a time when, in the same part of the country, the Bible was freely used to justify slavery.

To end this chapter on sexual relations with an excursion into religion is perhaps not inappropriate. I recall a reviewer of some book or other explaining that the author began with the hero in search of God and ended with the hero finding woman. "One might wish," said the reviewer, "that the sequence had been reversed. Either way, however, there is a connection. Love is the key both to relations to God and to the other sex. For some of us marriage is a sacrament, almost *the* sacrament—provided one means by marriage that which obtains between "true minds" who love as Shakespeare describes in his great sonnet on the subject.

CHAPTER NINE

The University of Chicago

(1928-1955)

"She Was a Phantom of Delight"

Almost the first thing that happened to me in Chicago in October 1928 was my finding a wife. She was Dorothy Eleanore Cooper, whom I had already known while at Harvard but—as I realized on first glancing up to her as she looked down the apartment stairs where she was now living with her family in Chicago—not known well enough! Only a few days were needed to settle the matter. Rarely can two people have been so serenely confident that they wanted each other.

By bad luck Dorothy, near the end of her junior year at Wellesley had been told she should have an operation (now no longer considered sensible) for a tilted womb. She left Wellesley and returned to her home city, Chicago, for the operation. She almost died in the operating room. In connection with this, her father, whose lively sense of fun will be exhibited later told her how, when he was a boy listening to his mother talking to other ladies, it seemed to him that they were always talking about tilted wombs and especially about falling wombs. "I heard so much about falling wombs that"—here for once he hesitated, and for once Dorothy could get ahead of him—"that you made up your mind you would never have one!" Needless to say, her father was delighted with these words put into his mouth. It is no accident that both daughters of this man are witty people. One of the earliest things we learn, if we do learn it, is a sense of fun. Yet the only boast Dr. Cooper ever made about this was that he had taught his girls when little to act like angry kittens in the expressive use of the tongue. He taught them much more than that, but in a similar vein.

Dorothy's recollection of having almost died is of hearing the doctor say, "We've lost her." Apparently, her pulse threatened to stop. One thinks of Robert Frost's characteristically penetrating lines, "The watcher at the wrist took fright. No more to build on there." The incident illustrates how chancy life is. Both Dorothy and I came so close to death at least once, probably several times, before meeting each other that it cannot have been more than a turn of the dice that we were both even alive together in early maturity, not to mention how easily we might never have met. This meeting came about through two married friends living in Cambridge in 1926 who thought we should know each other and took pains to see that this happened. The man, the Plato scholar Ronald Levinson, one of the choice spirits of this age (whose luck was poor in certain ways), took me aside and said, "Charles, this girl is talented. I've watched

Fig. 18. Dorothy Eleanore Cooper at ten months

Fig. 19. Dorothy, small but determined

her." She was and he had. No friendly hint was ever more appropriate. Yet it took me 2½ years, largely because of a geographical
separation, to fully see the point. Once I did see it, I knew the possibilities were for "the long haul." In a few seconds, shortly after
our engagement was settled, I intuited what sixty years have not
contradicted. They did not seem merely probable, those possibilities, they seemed certain. Whether possibilities become actual is always at most only probable but, literally in a few days, almost in
seconds, we achieved definitive communication of what there *could*
be for us two.

One wonders how many weddings involve so little fear on either
side as this one. True, our ages were favorable: twenty-four for her
and thirty-one for me. We knew ourselves reasonably well and had
reasonably compatible purposes. I knew even then that life was loaded
against female talents and I intended to work against this unfairness.

She knew what scholars need in their lives and was determined to promote my scholarly activities. Of course, conflicts have arisen. But we *knew* the positive possibilities and their value. That we managed never for long to lose sight of them is neither simply good management nor simply good fortune, but an inextricable mixture of the two. How common such a mixture is, who can know? But some do know that it is possible; and there clearly are those who have never known this. Their misfortune? Their bad management?

Bertrand Russell has told about the financial difficulties the Alfred North Whiteheads had in their early years. Mrs. Whitehead told me she took over the money matters of the family because they had been going badly. I have sometimes wondered if famous writers who spent their money foolishly (I seem to recall Goldsmith, Mark Twain, Scott) would not have done better had they put more of the

Fig. 20. Dorothy, serious and older

Fig. 21. Emily Hartshorne as a young
child

responsibility for financial decisions upon their wives' shoulders. I
tended to these things for a number of years after marrying, and so
far as I am aware they went passably well. But they have gone better
since Dorothy Cooper Hartshorne took them over. The notion that
only men can understand economic affairs is no sounder than all
the other follies in the male chauvinist list. My favorite humorous
novelist, Peacock, pointed out long ago that if many women seem
silly creatures it is because they have been expected, educated (or
undereducated), trained (or undertrained) to be so. Peacock was one
of the first authors to know the score in this matter.

My wife has been a successful schoolteacher, a professional, and
also locally famous amateur singer and actress, and a professional
book editor with a brilliant record; she is deservedly listed as one of
this country's bibliographers because of her work on my writings,

and she is now (when I first wrote this) a learned writer on some topics in Japanese cultural history. She has significantly edited virtually all my writings. Thanks above all to a gifted and dedicated Wellesley teacher, Howard Pulling, she had a fine introduction to the natural sciences, especially botany.

In Japanese etiquette it is not permitted to boast about one's wife. I understand and partly share this feeling. But it is impossible to give much account of some lives without taking into account the person's spouse. Trollope says of his marriage "it was important only to us." This would hardly be true in my case.

"Love is blind" has only a very limited truth. The wonderful poem of Wordsworth's, the first line of which is the heading of this section, is an expression of knowledge, not illusion. If any reader

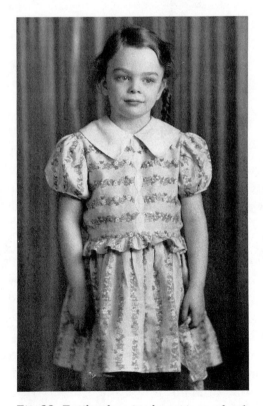

Fig. 22. Emily when in elementary school

doubts it, let him read De Quincey's account of Mrs. Wordsworth. She was a rare person, compatibly married to a rare person, by great good fortune to both.

The pseudo-sophistication that makes some people think that an individual's intelligence is wholly at the mercy of bias in judging a spouse or other close relative I find somewhat annoying. We have only one child, an extremely bright daughter. Do I so describe her because she is my daughter? Not so. If I had a mediocre daughter I would try to make the best of it, but I would know it. At the progressive school where Emily studied for two years, the physics teacher said to me: "If I had your daughter's brains I would be something in physics." When this was quoted to another teacher in that school he said, "We [Emily's teachers] could all say that. Your daughter is the brightest child I have ever taught."

When John Matthews Manly, Chaucer scholar at the University of Chicago, died, a colleague, lamenting his death, exclaimed, "and that mind of his!" When I once discussed with our family doctor in Chicago (a superior general practitioner with a Ph.D. as well as an M.D.), about a physical difficulty of Dorothy's that requires self-discipline to overcome, he said, "She can do it—with that mind of hers!" He was using words as discriminately as Manly's colleague was. I have never known a human being more knowledgable than Dorothy, if both variety of specialties and rare depth in some of them are taken into the reckoning. Mention almost any subject, and she thinks of something relevant and, usually, quite accurate. This, once again, is not just my opinion. In a women's play-reading group to which Dorothy belongs the name William Morris was mentioned. One of Dorothy's friends, either not knowing herself or thinking the group might not, turned to Dorothy and asked, "Who was William Morris?" Dorothy gave a standard, brief summary of that famous Englishman's place in history, whereupon the friend said to the group, "See!".

John Stuart Mill was inspired to write his great essay on "The Subjection of Women" partly because he had married a gifted, knowledgeable woman. Ralph Waldo Emerson, another early feminist, had two marriages to exceptional women and at least one female relative with outstanding qualities.

Scientific and artistic abilities are rarely equally marked in a person. Dorothy could have been at least a competent scientist, but a greater musician and actress. Her daughter is less artistic and more capable in mathematics and science generally, though at present chiefly trained in history. Both mother and daughter are persons of great good will. Of either one it could be said, "She never lets a friend down." And both treat close relatives including spouses as friends. Both have had some trouble in focusing upon one line of endeavor long enough and with enough freedom from competing obligations to make the most of their abilities. In this they are like many others of their sex, except that the unusual number of things they can do at least passably well makes choices especially complicated. This was my father's case, as I have said.

If I add to the foregoing that Dorothy is very brave and considerate of others in emergencies, the reader may think I am trying to describe a faultless and scarcely human person. Here again I can agree with the wise poet, who found his wife "not too good/for human nature's daily food." A combination of poor tact or inconsiderate behavior on my part and anger and hurt feelings on hers have made for some difficult times. But I had such proof, early in our own marriage as well as before it, that Dorothy *could* understand me, that temporary misunderstandings never seemed more than that to me. If this was a little less true of her, if she came closer to real despair about our marriage, it was perhaps because in her childhood experiences there was less emotional security. In the end we experienced a sizable portion of the range of possibilities in marriage, omitting all the uglier ones in which mutual hate, dismal boredom, or indifference, take over, but including the raptures and quiet satisfactions. In fifty (now sixty) years I think I have been intensely angry (I forget about what) only once, and even then very briefly. So how angry was I?

My deciding in 1928 to go to Chicago was because my only job offer for that year came from the philosophy department there. Mead and Tufts were its oldest members. Both were philosophically somewhat close to Dewey, who had been in the department for some years, but had left because of the career needs of his wife. Smith, Ames, and Burtt had been strongly influenced by Dewey and Mead. All six were either definitely atheistic or (Moore, Ames, Burtt) more or less markedly agnostic; all were either materialists or dualists, depending on how these terms are defined. None were, as I was, a metaphysical idealist and theist. Except for Moore, they were not persons I could easily or greatly enjoy. All were able, especially Tufts, Mead, Ames, and Smith. The last I came to admire more and more as a very sagacious and practical fellow, on a good side of political issues, cognizant of his intellectual limitations, and a man whose advice could be counted on for its disinterestedness and relevance. Little as my philosophy was like his, he did not underestimate my abilities. Ames, too, was a grand human being. But the backgrounds of these people were markedly different from mine and their training in philosophy had not a great deal in common with mine at Haverford, Harvard, and in Europe.

To some extent I was a lone wolf in my new position. When Charles Morris and Charner Perry came as they did in a year or two, they were always interesting, friendly, and appreciative of me. But they were under similar influences as the older members of the department. So they did not greatly alter my considerable (though not extreme) intellectual isolation in the department. Hall's idealism helped some, but he soon left the department (and in time left also his idealism).

When in 1930, Robert M. Hutchins came to the university things began to change in the philosophy department. The new direction had no simple relation to the previous one. Hutchins was a very serious, clever, high-minded young man, trained in law and with strongly marked convictions about education. He had come to know a group of young philosophers, above all Mortimer Adler, Richard P. McKeon, and Scott Buchanan whose ability and promise appealed to him. The four talked about what they could do to improve education if they were all in the same university. So Hutchins tried to have all of them accepted by the philosophy department. He began his campaign by informing the chairman, George Herbert Mead, that his opinion of the department was not high (he was presumably relying partly, if not largely, upon the opinions of the three philosophical friends just mentioned) and said that he knew three young men whose addition to the department would greatly improve it. Mead replied that the situation called for the following procedure: Hutchins should send a questionnaire to the principal philosophical departments in the country and ask them to rate the persons in the department, in comparison with the three—or was it four— that he was recommending. This was done with results that are said to have somewhat surprised Hutchins, meaning disappointed him.

Nevertheless Hutchins continued to press the department in behalf of his proteges. I was in Europe while this was going on, (I had promised my wife some travel, of which she had had little up to that time and was taking a quarter off). The department objected, I later gathered, to admitting McKeon, but Hutchins got the Greek department to take him on, because his specialty was medieval philosophy and to understand this it was necessary to master the Greek background. Adler was grudgingly accepted. Buchanan never was, although some way was found to have him given some sort of role for a time on campus. Adler was not made welcome by the philosophers and a place was soon found for him in the School of Law, his dissertation having dealt with the question of legal evidence. The ultimate outcome of the struggle was complex: Adler left the university for significant activities elsewhere, eventually in an institute designed for him to test what teamwork could do in philosophical research; McKeon was taken into the philosophy department; Mead left to take a job elsewhere but was prevented by illness from ever functioning in it; Burtt and Murphy left for positions at Cornell and Brown respectively; Everett Hall left for a position at Stanford.

Even before some of these events the department lost the services of two men by illness or death. Tufts contracted anemia and left Chicago permanently for California. He survived his illness, but because of it I was asked, early in my first quarter, to begin teaching his class in aesthetics, a subject I had never even contemplated undertaking, though it was actually very congenial to me. And Moore, whose health was not good, died prematurely. So now, of the six professors mentioned earlier only Ames and Smith were left. I appreciated them as colleagues, but Moore, Tufts and Hall would have been nice to have too. Mead I somehow never came to enjoy, but then his wife's terminal illness and the squabble with Hutchins meant that I saw little of him.

Ames was a wise man of many jobs and interests, but was not significant for my technical philosophical concerns. And something like this could be said of Smith. McKeon, the new influence, was defi-nitely a learned intellectual historian. One could have a splendid con-versation with him on historical topics. And he communicated his scholarship to students with remarkable effectiveness. They tended to become competent teachers of the history of philosophy. He also communicated something else, a kind of skepticism of definite re-sults as to objective truth, not about human intellectual history but about God or nature, subjects that mattered much to me. McKeon has been heard to say that the present age is a new age of sophism in the original Greek sense and that the most suitable role in philoso-phy today parallels that of the classical Sophists. It seems that he reached this position starting with Aristotle as for a time his model, but with Dewey, whose lectures he heard at Columbia also in mind. He has even confessed a liking for Bridgeman's operationalism. The rumor that McKeon was a neoscholastic or Thomist was always far from the truth.

Hutchins, Adler, McKeon

My twenty-seven years' stay at the University of Chicago included all of President (later Chancellor) Hutchins's stay with more at both ends. In other words I preceded and outlasted him, thus experienc-ing the entire episode, except for being in Europe for the autumn of the year when the big fight over the philosophy department was at its peak. When Hutchins, the boy wonder, arrived to take over a great university at a tender age, he characteristically warned the faculty: "Twenty years of Hutchins [I quote from memory] might be bearable, but what about forty or fifty years of Hutchins?" It seemed to me admirable that Hutchins in fact stayed less than half of the largest of these figures. He left when he was ahead; for his relations to the faculty had never been better. And he was going to a big, adventure-some, constructive position. When some begged him to stay, he said that he could judge better than they could the ability of the univer-sity to do without him.

Because Mortimer Adler, who was so central in the difficulties Hutchins had in the early years of his administration, has now pub-lished an account of his part in the turmoil, it is easier for me to discuss my relation to it. I find Adler's account honest and in essentials accurate. What he says about his philosophical difference from another protégé of Hutchins, Richard P. McKeon, is in some degree coincident with my own difference.

At that time, I was an inconspicuous younger member of the department; my philosophical values were neither those of the "Chicago School" nor those of Hutchins and his group. I knew all along that Hutchins and McKeon were not Thomists or belated medievalists, but I thought (and think) that they were far too little aware of what has happened in speculative philosophy since Kant and Hegel. I had thought more than the Chicago School of Mead and Smith about ancient and medieval metaphysics, but I had drunk deeply from a tradition, going back in some respects to Leibniz, and coming down through Peirce, Bergson, Whitehead, Montague, and others, which constitutes an alternative to what Hutchins and Adler regarded as the great tradition in philosophy. In some respects, it is truly Platonic, as against the ancient disciples of Plato, the greatest of these being Aristotle. But it is in some essentials quite far from Plato. It is also in some respects rather far from Dewey and Mead, and hence from the Chicago School. All in all, I was somewhat detached in the battle of ideas that was going on.

McKeon, when he became dean, wanted me to be "acting secretary" of the department. For the time being there was not to be a chairman. When I demurred, he said that "the unwilling administrators are the best." Later I think he felt that I did not illustrate this principle. This was not because I deliberately failed to do my best at the job. When I wrote my father that I was an unwilling administrator, he replied, don't try to justify your lack of enthusiasm for the job by not doing it well. "There wouldn't be much satisfaction in that." I agreed with him, of course. After somewhat more than a year I was mercifully relieved of administrative duties once and for all by being invited to Stanford for two quarters. This was one of the pieces of good luck in my life.

One chief accomplishment of my year and a quarter in a seat of (not much) power was the acquisition by the department of Rudolf Carnap. The proposal came from Charles Morris and I backed it. Obviously Carnap was hardly my kind of philosopher, but he was lucid and vigorous and I thought I and our students might learn from him. It seems reasonably probable that if I had refused to recommend Carnap, the administration, which strongly opposed the move, could not have been persuaded by the rest of the department to make it. I do not regret having to this extent brought it about. What perhaps was foolish on my part was to have bought Morris's entire package, which included Reichenbach as well as Carnap. This was too much logical positivism for one department, and made it seem that I was a mere yes man for the Chicago School. On the other side (though this is hindsight shrewdness), if only Carnap had been recommended, would not the administration have been able to refuse without seeming excessively negative to the department? As it was, Hutchins and McKeon could compromise and reject the one while grudgingly granting the other proposal. Of the two, I think they chose the right one.

So far as I have heard, it was not the department but only the dean that was dissatisfied by my operations as secretary. I had one conference with Hutchins, which was pleasant enough. Charner Perry was chosen to take over while I was at Stanford, and it was assumed by all hands that my part in the job was finished. I had never pretended to want the position. Since the age of fifteen I had thought of myself as a writer. Teaching came less naturally but fairly naturally. Lecturing here and there, not in standard classes, came between teaching and writing in naturalness.

Hutchins's disappointments with the department perhaps were partly the reason that salary raises or promotions in it were not easy to get. Also, the Depression was under way, with its inevitable effects. For a number of years it depended on McKeon how the money was distributed in the humanities division. If I have any reason to be grateful to him on this score I am not aware of it. He told me that it was unwise of me to put my energies into philosophy of religion, as that was "less exact" than other branches of philosophy.

Possibly I would indeed have been smart to pay less attention to religious questions than I did after my book on sensation came out. But to me it was apparent that the traditional ways of philosophizing about religion (say in Hume or Kant) were not as exact as, with twentieth-century resources, they could be made. And the clearheaded and creative minds in the profession were doing a better job on many other parts of philosophy than on philosophy of religion, if they were not almost entirely neglecting it. So I thought I saw a vacuum that needed to be filled. In the end I think this strategy has worked out moderately well. Religiously interested people, such as once looked to Adler for help, seem now far less sure that medieval theology had the answers. The Episcopal theologian Norman Pittenger, who likes my work, agrees with me that Roman Catholics are now as interested in Whitehead and Hartshorne as are Protestants, Jews, or Universalist-Unitarians.

If Hutchins caused some trouble and perhaps ultimate loss in my career, and I think also in that of the philosophy department, what did he do to or for the university? Here I hesitate. "What is not good for me is not good for anyone," a more or less unconscious but popular, though false, axiom. Probably the university as a whole was fairly lucky to get Hutchins. American education in general was even more lucky to have him as mentor and stimulus. And his work at the Center for the Study of Democratic Institutions and on the *Encyclopaedia Brittanica* and *Great Books of the Western World* programs seems largely admirable. In any case I have yet to think very ill of so very witty a person. There is some connection, I feel rather confident, between wit and detachment from self-serving preoccupations. My last letter from Hutchins, not many years ago when I sent him an essay mentioning him and one of his friends, ended, "I am delighted to see that you are still around and riding high."

Perhaps this is the place to mention "my most embarrassing moment." I forgot until too late about the commuter train necessary to get me to a luncheon engagement with Mortimer Adler and Scott Buchanan, two protégés of Hutchins who were both at the time in Chicago. I had invited them to meet me at International House. (At the time I was living in our country cottage in Indiana.) The next train was an hour later. So I arrived as Adler and Buchanan were eating dessert, having paid for their own luncheons. I invited them for another time. As I rather expected, only I turned up. I met Buchanan on campus and invited him a third time, asking that he tell Adler. Buchanan and I had lunch, Adler sending his regrets. Buchanan remarked, "This is a rather historic occasion!" Presumably word of this affair got to Hutchins. Possibly it was this ghastly blunder that did the most to earn me my reputation for absentmindedness. That it was extremely unusual for me (a once every half-dozen years sort of thing) did not prevent it from being dreadfully conspicuous.

Buchanan and I had, some eight years before, been in a class of Perry's together at Harvard. He then impressed me as a clever young man with remarkable lack of awe for his teachers. I myself never minded disagreeing with teachers, but Buchanan went far beyond mere disagreement. When he presented his seminar paper, Perry (as usual) asked him to explain the meaning of his key terms. Scott simply said that the terms were Kantian and that, "since every student of philosophy knows their meaning, there is no need to explain them." This to me seemed student nerve carried into the stratosphere. It was such boldness, in very bright people to be sure, that seemed to attract Hutchins.

It was not the fault of Hutchins that he was one of the tallest, handsomest, wittiest, and quickest-witted persons on his or any campus. But one cannot doubt, it did, somewhat intimidate many of the professors over whom he had power. Here again is a nonmoral factor that had its effect on personal relations. He needed a wife with very contrasting qualities to balance his home life, and in his second marriage he gained her.

Once, when Hutchins and T. V. Smith, Mrs. Smith, Dorothy, and I happened—a rare occasion—to be together on the campus looking for transportation somewhere or other, T. V. went off to find a taxi, but before he returned the presidential limousine appeared, whereupon Hutchins said to Stuart Smith, "Now if that idiot husband of yours returns, we can go." The reply he got was, "See here young man, don't you talk to me like that!" This was once when the other person had the last word.

Concerning the quarrels the faculty had from time to time with Hutchins, the philosophy chairman in the early 1930s, stout-hearted and wise Edward Scribner Ames remarked, "This is all very colorful!" There was a preacher who did understand the aesthetic side of life!

Several years after Hutchins's departure, he returned to give some lectures on The University of Utopia. A lady professor in one of the language departments, whose professors felt they had been insulted and really damaged, by Hutchins's description of their courses as "tool courses," stood in my presence looking at the announcement posted on the wall advertising these lectures. "The University of Utopia," said she grimly, "that's where he belongs. He ought to go there and leave us alone!"

The importance of words, in relation to people's feelings, was borne in upon me at the time when the "tool course" business burst upon the community. For another novel word usage, not due I imagine to Hutchins, also came into being about that time and produced comparable indignation, at least in one professor in the divinity school. A course that had always been called "Religious Education" was to be relabeled, given a face-lift so to speak, with a more fancy title—Personality Development, or something of the sort. The professor who gave that course was upset and argued bitterly against the change. Hearing him, and remembering the fuss about "tool courses," I thought of the importance of words as well as of what the words stand for. The famous economist Frank Knight liked to say, "This is a verbal question—and therefore very important!"

On the other hand, there can as easily be a false emphasis upon this importance. Karl Popper has said, "If people ask me to define a word I have used, I usually, instead, propose a different word." One of the ways to judge a philosopher is the extent to which he or she is dependent upon a single word for a key idea. Nothing really fundamental has to be said in just one term. I can think of a professor in a philosophy department whose basic idea is indistinguishable from the word he uses to express it because he admits no synonyms or paraphrases. What Whitehead calls *actual entity*, can also be called *unit-event*, or *truly single actuality*, or a *single concrete experience* (human or not human). It can hardly be called a *substance* (which comes closer to what Whitehead calls a *society*), but some functions of substance are performed by actual entities. Whitehead's language here is appropriate and convenient but not indispensable. What Whitehead calls the *Consequent Nature of God* I also call *God's concrete and contingent actuality*, the content of which is perpetually enriched by divine perceptions of the world. The Primordial Nature, as I construe it—and Whitehead is not entirely free from ambiguity here—can be termed the *abstract, eternal, noncontingent essence of God*, as distinguished from the divine accidents. If I thought any belief I hold could be verbalized only in one way, I should cease to hold it. Peirce's *Secondness* is, with an important but easy and clear qualification or two, Whitehead's *Prehension*. And there are other words for the essential idea, which is that of the one-way dependence of experience (both in memory and perception) upon previous actualities. Peirce's *Tychism* refers to an aspect of what Whitehead and Bergson call *Creativity*, for which Plato's *self-movement of soul* is a somewhat dim but recognizable early anticipation.

I have used *idealism*, carefully contrasting my use of the term to some historical usages, also *psychicalism* for Whitehead's doctrine of "reformed subjectivism." I avoid *eternal objects* because I seem to disagree somewhat with Whitehead concerning that doctrine. I never use the expression *finite God* for my view, because the whole point of my natural theology is that God is as literally infinite as finite, and vice versa, the union of these contraries (not as contradictory of each other but as applying to diverse aspects of deity) being the essence of "process theology." I avoid Whitehead's *philosophy of organism* because, though it can be given a reasonable interpretation, it may suggest to some a complete "organicism," as though all relations whatever were internal to their terms, which turns Whitehead into Bradley or Hegel. We would not need Whitehead if that were his doctrine. He is at once highly monistic in some aspects of his thought and highly pluralistic in other aspects, and this is a feature of his philosophy second in importance to none.

The X Club

A great stroke of luck for me at Chicago was my being taken into one of the two scientific clubs there soon after I arrived. This could happen because the club had a policy of having just one philosopher among its members, and E. A. Burtt, who had been the one philosopher, had left with the exodus of several members of the philosophy department because of the quarrel with Hutchins. There may have been other reasons, but luck was surely involved in such a combination of factors. By belonging to this X Club (wives, by an obnoxious pun, being called "XS"), I was guaranteed a considerable education in various sciences. Each month a member read a paper designed to be intelligible to those not specializing in his branch of science. This worked fairly well for me—with the exception of papers on work in chemistry, in which subject my ignorance was particularly dense. Each of us had to serve as president for a year, and I had this chore (more than honor) twice. When the leading chemist of the society spoke and I announced the title of his talk, he mischievously asked me if I knew what the title meant. "You know damn well I don't," was the best I could do with that one.

A glorious result of the association with the X Club people was exposure to the finest scientific mind I have ever known intimately, the geneticist Sewall Wright. The club also included that superior physiologist Ralph Gerard, who wrote a book with the beautiful title *Unresting Cells*, and another fine physiologist, Ralph Lillie, who was almost a philosopher and perhaps too literate in philosophy to do the fullest justice to his science. These were the club members who could understand any of the papers, perhaps even mine.

Alfred Emerson, the great termite expert, was in the club. I had only one really hot argument with him about a quite philosophical topic, I'm not sure now which one—partly because the discussion was in a manner blown up and put an end to by the man on the other side of me away from Emerson saying, "I don't know what the argument is about, but I think Hartshorne must be right, because Emerson's madder." In savoring this unusual remark I failed to store away in my memory what Alfred and I had been debating. The remark stopped Emerson—for once! We both believed in the unity of nature in some sense, but with Wright and Lillie I have always believed that mind is pervasive in nature whereas Emerson was more dualistic.

He was the only scientist I have known who preferred to talk to Wright rather than listen to him. It was a case of a good mind seeming not quite fully aware of another's being more than just good. Talk to Wright about his specialty and he is superb, talk to him about almost anything and he is at least good, penetrating, and usually basically sound. That he is a psychicalist, taking mind in its various forms to be the key to everything, has been an encouragement to me. And he was glad to have my agreement with this belief to which he found few scientists sympathetic. (There are more now than when Wright began his career.) He seems to have thought out the doctrine for himself, rather than derived it from any philosopher. He had read Karl Pearson's criticism of W. K. Clifford's version of the idea, which criticism seems to have had the opposite from the intended effect so far as Wright was concerned. When I left Chicago, Wright had already left and so had Gerard.

Emerson was the catalyst precipitating two lines of thinking in the club. One was the question of the status of a group of animals as closely integrated into a communal whole as a termite colony. Alfred called such a colony a *superorganism*. Several of us objected that the degree of integration in the colony was much lower than that in an individual termite. To this Alfred agreed. But then by this criterion the colony was not superior but inferior to individual termites. The term *epi-organism* was suggested, but I do not recall Alfred's response to this proposal. For me and Wright the question had a definite meaning, which was simply this: an individual termite can be thought of as having its own little feelings, whereas the colony probably no more has feelings literally its own than a human colony or family would have. The colony's "mind" would be a group mind, which only metaphorically is a single mind at all.

Philosophers since Leibniz can be put into two classes, those who do and those who do not see what Leibniz saw so clearly and for the first time in history: that before we ask about a physical whole, Is it sentient? we must decide whether it is most properly regarded as an aggregate of individuals or as a single well-integrated individual. This question arises with so-called inanimate objects. A stone is lifeless and so is a waterfall, but by the very criteria that justify this negation, a molecule is not lifeless, for it has integrity and unceasing self-motion, self-activity, and it acts as one, not as a mere collective. This is the key that Leibniz, Wright, Peirce, Whitehead, and many others have seen to the meaning of the division of entities into the animate and the inanimate. It is a point one gets or misses; the number of those who do not miss it has been slowly increasing since Leibniz.

The other dispute of which Emerson was the center concerned the question of how science is to deal with questions of value. Emerson held, as a formerly popular Harvard economist (Carver, I think) used to, that species survival was the only criterion of value science could recognize. To this Ralph Lillie, showing his philosophical sophistication in a rather extreme way, said flatly, "Value has nothing to do with survival." Probably, he added some qualification to this one-sided statement. My view, like Whitehead's, has long been that intrinsic value is a matter of intensity and harmony of aspects of experience, the intensity varying, according to some obscure aesthetic law, with variety and depth of contrasts. Of course this presupposes the occurrence of experiences and, insofar, survival, if not of the individual, then of the species; and if not the species then of something capable of experiencing. Obviously science can measure survival of individuals or species more easily than degrees of intensity or harmony of feelings or other aspects of experiences. Insofar, Emerson had a point.

Another dispute I recall in the club concerned the question, Is a gene an individual? Wright startled us, especially Lillie, by declaring roundly, but surely somewhat facetiously, "The gene is the only individual!" "What do you mean, Sewall, by that outrageous statement?" asked Lillie. I forget Wright's reply, and my idea of a gene is too vague for me to have a firm view on the question, except that of course genes are not the only individuals, if they even are individuals. The very word *individual* I suppose, was invented primarily to express individuality on the human level, and levels directly apparent to human vision or self-experience.

Membership in the X Club for twenty-five years more than anything else enlarged what little knowledge of science Haverford and Harvard had given me.

Carnap

My hope of learning from Rudolf Carnap was partly realized. One had to make an effort to find common ground, and his requirements for "clarity" could be met only partly without giving up aspects of reality to which Carnap was blind. We argued about 'truth,' for instance, whether it is really as independent of time as many logicians, like many theologians, have held. I did get Carnap to grant that the famous Tarsky definition of truth ("The grass is green" is true if and only if the grass is green) is neutral to the issue. Carnap argued that the notion of *new* truths (as the partly indeterminate or open future becomes definite and past) is against common sense, but he admitted that this is not a conclusive objection. I failed to see that he had a really cogent argument on this point.

We argued about internal and external relations. This is really the question of how far things depend upon other things. Carnap held that even G. E. Moore was unclear on this topic. This I could concede. I worked hard to clarify the matter, and an early result can be seen in my book *The Divine Relativity*. A first version of the discussion of relations in that book Carnap read and gave back to me with "n.c." (not clear) marked in the margin at various points. I tried to clarify further, and he read the second version, replying to my query, "Is it clearer?" with a discouraging "about the same." I concluded that either I lacked the knowledge and ability to make my view clear by his standards, or the standards begged the question in some way so that the requirements could not be met. I was totally unconvinced that there was no genuine distinction between really internal or constitutive relations of events and nonconstitutive ones.

Recently I have stated the reasons for this idea in an essay called "The Neglect of Relative predicates in Modern philosophy." Carnap did say that he saw some point in regarding the relation between a universal and one of its instances as constitutive for the instance but not for the universal. (C. I. Lewis says this somewhere; so does Whitehead.) But Carnap was not persuaded by my contention that effects are in part constituted by their relations to causes, though not vice versa. I think I know why he thought so; but I believe him to have been mistaken.

Carnap liked, or at least found interesting, a paper I wrote for an International Congress of philosophers in which I argued that contingent statements require at least one empirical concept for their formulation. He himself held an analogous view, except that, by nonempirical concepts, he meant logical constants, whereas I regard certain metaphysical terms as also nonempirical. However, we agreed that statements like "something exists" are not contingent. But the question then arises, How about only three things exist.? Here are purely a priori concepts, yet surely the statement is not necessarily true. Is it necessarily false? Carnap's view was that it is indeed necessarily false and that "infinitely many things exist" is necessarily true. But by this he meant only that the infinitely many points of space necessarily exist (in what sense?). "Things" in any further sense might fail to exist. I found and find this very odd. My solution is that one must ask, *When* does a certain finite number of things exhaust reality? If the answer is "always," I would regard this as necessarily false. If the answer includes a definite time, then I deny that dates can be specified except empirically. If the answer is, "At some time or other," this is more puzzling, but I think it can be dealt with. Carnap felt that for once we had rather closely related problems.

In another way he was interested when I told him that I thought I had a rigorous disproof of Thomism. He said it was a significant question how far logic can be used to refute a metaphysical doctrine like the Thomistic idea of God. He helped me formulate the matter in a clear logical way.

The following propositions form, I hold, an inconsistent triad. One of them must be false.

P. God has infallible knowledge that the world exists contingently.
Q. The world exists contingently.
R. There is in God nothing contingent.

1. P entails Q.
2. R entails that either P is necessary or God's knowledge is not in God (which is absurd).
3. Hence, Q is necessary (what a necessary proposition entails is necessary).

The non-thomistic solution is to say, with Socinus, Whitehead, and many others, that R *is false, God has contingent aspects (and* is *not wholly* immutable, impassable, and the other Thomistic attributes).

A Thomist must either admit contingency in God, or deny that what P asserts is anything in God. But then what is it, something outside God?

I am reminded that Adler once wrote me that he had used a quotation from me similar, if I recall correctly, to the preceding on an examination and had been disappointed in his students' comments. I have wondered if I did not have some part in Adler's partial loss of confidence in the Thomistic form of theism.

Students

What made the university for me was at least as much those outside the department as those in it, especially the scientists and theologians. And I had my greatest successes with theological students, especially John Cobb and Schubert Ogden, now well known as theologians; also Eugene Peters, who wrote the most readable of the books on my philosophy; in addition William Christian, who studied with me for only a year, and Huston Smith, who is well known as a writer on religion. Smith at one time read all my writings. Among nontheological former students (for limited periods) who have become important are Richard Rorty; the novelist James T. Farrell; Milton Singer, now a well-known anthropologist; Martin Gardner, who writes on mathematical puzzles and many other things; Abner Shimony (who has doctorates in physics and philosophy); and Tristram Engelhardt, who has them in medicine as well as philosophy. Also Abraham Kaplan, who now lives in Israel. None of these was primarily my student or disciple; but I recall all of them vividly and their success has not surprised me. Eugene Freeman has had a distinguished career, partly as editor of *The Open Court* and *The Monist;* he was my first Ph.D. Bill Earle was a fine student, but he went to France and got entangled there with phenomenologists and existentialists. His papers were always eminently readable. Bob Falter was an excellent Ph.D. winner, the one student who always knew the correct answer, even to questions as abstruse as those about "strains" in Whitehead. He eventually became (for some years) a colleague here in Austin. Richard Schlagel, an undergraduate I had some dealings with, has had a career in physics.

A happy memory has been of Norman Martin, a young logician who took some courses with me. He was primarily a Carnap student. Once I put a formal argument on the board; with a cordial smile Norman showed me a fallacy. Next day I tried again. Again a smiling identification of a mistake. The third time, the argument in its re-revised form was accepted. I am always charmed by students who can correct me without fear or conceit, and with a smile. (I had such a student at Emory, one whose father, I was told, was a drunkard. His mother must have been something of a saint to make up, I would imagine. He cordially disagreed with me about something, and that was fine. Some days later he said, "Since I disagreed with you the other day on a similar issue, have I the right to disagree with you now about this one?" "I think so," I replied.) When we needed a logician at the University of Texas I recalled Martin. It turned out that the department already had a folder on him, thanks to David Miller's work as chairman in the past. So Martin became a valued colleague. He was one of the unforgettable students. He is one of the wisest, most careful and knowledgeable logicians I have encountered.

One of many results of my teaching in Chicago that would not otherwise have been realized was the book William Reese and I did together, *Philosophers Speak of God.* No other book, I believe, in any language would as fully justify the simple title. What learned men have made of the idea of deity, in their own words, during nearly 3000 years, is what this book offers, plus what two products of Harvard or University of Chicago training make of the same subject and of the work of those predecessors. The book, I suppose, is more mine than Bill's but it owes a good deal to him. He has a talent for assimilating philosophical ideas, and also a talent for graceful writing, as is clear from a book he wrote subsequently. In 1980 appeared his admirable *Dictionary of Philosophy and Religion,* a most useful work. As my student, he well understood my ways of thinking and he went through the writings of a number of philosophers and picked out passages he thought would strike me as relevant. I then went through his selections, say from Philo or Plotinus, and decided upon the final selection. I could count on his having not missed a great deal, perhaps nothing at all, that I would have chosen. In this way we covered a much larger literature than either of us could have alone. Bill also wrote considerable portions of the introductory and critical materials preceding or following the individual selections.

The only English review I recall of this book called it "pretentious." I have no quarrel with this adjective, and understand easily how an English reviewer might use it of this book. I think only that some other adjectives would characterize it as suitably and more significantly. Pretentiousness is a matter of etiquette, to a considerable degree, and the English have a fine art of avoiding the crasser forms of it. We did have something to be boastful about, that is all I wish to claim now, twenty-five years later. And the book, like most of mine, continues to sell, though in modest amounts.

Bill did one task that may or may not have helped the book. It is hard to decide. He courageously made the first rough translation of the passages from Fechner, although his German was then quite limited. Indeed he practically taught himself German from Fechner and a dictionary—to overstate the matter somewhat. I then had to make what I could of the resulting translation. Would it have been easier to start from scratch; that is, from Fechner alone? As the final result, was I believe, a good translation, the question is of no practical concern.

Bill also talked me into omitting a poem of Wordsworth's, on the ground that the latter was not a philosopher. Yet, on what ground I forget, he accepted the Jeffers selection. Perhaps, he thought that a single poet was an acceptable deviation from the plan, but two would be too many. Or, more likely, he saw, as I did, an illuminating relation between Royce, who surely was a philosopher, and Jeffers. With Wordsworth, so clear an association with a single philosopher might be hard to find. (See Chapter 15, last section)

Actually Jeffers and Spinoza also could be analogized, and the basic objection to Royce really is that he fails to solve some of the problems confronting a Spinozist. Royce verbally admits the contingency of the world; but then trivializes the concession by saying that the wisdom of the Absolute excludes the other possible worlds, which are only "abstractly," but not really, "possible." If this is not Spinozism then it is Leibnizianism, and what Spinoza and Leibniz have in common in their ultra-rationalism is precisely the weakest side of both of them. They missed the role of genuine creative freedom, not just of God, but of even the least creature. The creatures, some of us think, are only roughly preprogrammed; in details they really decide what no God and no necessity from the past can decide for them. "Becoming" simply is such decision-making, as Peirce and Bergson independently saw, and scarcely another philosopher as clearly saw before them! (Epicurus — of all people — came close to seeing it.) No solution of the theological problem of evil is worth much if it does not include this aspect. Books are still written by those who do not see it. After a hundred years they are still behind Peirce.

Theologians and Metaphysicians

I have not mentioned the fact that for a number of years while in Chicago I was technically half in philosophy and half in theology. The chairman, Charner Perry, regarded this as advantageous because it saved the department half of my salary and yet, as he put it, "everyone knew" that all my courses were purely or essentially philosophical. This was a considerable compliment because Perry is not theological. Indeed,I did not change the content or plan of my courses when the change in classification was made; and the only effect it ever had on my teaching, aside from my getting more and more students from the theological side, was that Daniel Day Williams (a former student of mine, now deceased)and I once gave a joint course on systematic theology. I talked about as usual, but Dan did all the chores and kept the students on their toes with homework. Also he provided historical research on some of the theologians. It was an easy course for me. Dan's book on the *Spirit and Forms of Love* is a classic, full of insight and sane idealism, marred slightly by a too-conscientious completeness in the scholarship. It would have more readers with somewhat less learning. Dan knew what love in the religious as well as ordinary human senses can be.

It was good to encounter among the theologians Wilhelm Pauck, the Americanized bilingual German historian of religion. Pauck was a witty, amusing, and also serious scholar. It was encouraging to me that my break with traditional theism, with its insistence on the immutability of God, was acceptable to Pauck. After reading one of my books, he said, "Author knows what theism is." Pauck has written the biography of Tillich.

When the book by John Neff (versatile historian of economics and French painting) on education, a work in the Hutchins vein, was reviewed by Pauck for a religious journal, he wondered what Neff would make of his review. The review ended, "I cannot praise this book." Bill met Neff on the campus. Both men stopped and stood looking at each other, so Bill told me. Finally, Neff said, "Why don't you strike me?"

Neff made a famous speech at a Quadrangle Club meeting to discuss the question of revising the membership rules that had led to a friend of Hutchins being barred from becoming a member. Neff's speech began, "I am a Thomist. Do you know what a Thomist is? He's a friend of President Hutchins." In view of the loose talk that went about at that time, this definition was not entirely out of order. One of the ironies of that business was that McKeon, for some philosophers about the country a neo-Thomist, was in fact far from it.

The truth is that metaphysicians in the pure sense are a rare breed. Paul Weiss is one, in some of his many books, but I am not sure that they are as good as several of his other books. John Findlay is another, and metaphysics really is his central concern. The *Encyclopedia Britannica* (in one edition and anonymously) has called me "the world's leading metaphysician"; a description with which, now that Whitehead is dead, I cannot quarrel. But who else? Justus Buchler seems to want to be a metaphysician; I cannot see his great importance as such, whether that be my error or not. Then there is Gustav Bergman, ditto. Gustav says that some of his students say his ontology is the "ontology of the desert," others that it is the "ontology of the jungle." I take the former option. Grant that it is all true, how much have you got?

The theologians are doing more than professional philosophers, perhaps, to keep speculative philosophy alive. Tillich was something of a metaphysician; unclear and evasive as he often is, he did have flashes of profundity here and there. Unfortunately, I cannot make much of Father Lonergan's or Karl Rahner's attempts to vivify Thomism with some bits of new life. Thomas at least was sharp and clear; these people seem to lose the clarity and gain little to make up for the loss. Thus, Rahner says that God is strictly immutable but yet he really *becomes* a changeable human being. God puts aside but in no way loses his immutability. I think whatever point is made here is better made by talking as Whitehead does about primordial and consequent natures, the one abstract and the other concrete. As for the *infinity* that Rahner makes so much of, to me this is an ambiguous concept and needs explication. The *plenum* of eternal possibility is in a definite sense absolutely infinite — but it is also abstract, lacking in definite actuality. The totality of already created actualities, if beginningless as it seems it must be, is *numerically* infinite, but yet it does not and never can exhaustively actualize the infinity of possibility The first infinity mentioned characterizes the divine primordial nature; the second, the consequent nature.

Rahner seems to think that God had the option of not creating finite actualities at all. What is gained by asserting this freedom not to create at all has never been made intelligible to me. It is better to create than not to create (otherwise the creatures are worthless); but how does it exalt God to say that he could do the worse instead of the better? It is the particular creation that is optional, not the bare truth of being actually creative — of something or other. No, these writers are not adding much to the tradition of metaphysics.

Lecturing in German (1948-1949)

After WWII Hutchins had the idea that German universities, which had lost valuable personnel through Nazi anti-intellectualism and vicious intolerance, needed help. He proposed an "exchange" between the University of Chicago and The University of Frankfurt. At the beginning the exchange was largely one-sided. President Colwell, in the (in a sense) unkindest action he ever took so far as I was concerned, urgently requested me to be one of those going to teach German students in German. It was scarcely possible to refuse. I would have to go without Dorothy — it was only later that wives of men going for one semester only would be able to go, too—and Colwell said that it was difficult to find enough persons linguistically equipped to fill the quota for the semester 1948-1949. I was "needed now, not later." My reluctance was mainly because of having to leave wife and daughter, but also because I had a vivid idea of the damage that bombing had done to German cities and foresaw the ugly mess I would encounter. I had not read the almost daily accounts of bombing missions without imagining the results. Frankfurt was much as I had pictured it, an ugly, tragic mess.

At first my lecturing in German was somewhat cramped by lack of recent practice in the language. A student reported that another student had said that my attempts to express subtle ideas in the German I knew was "like trying to make mosaics out of cobblestones." I wish I knew how that student has fared in life; his metaphor seemed so wonderfully apt. Well before the end of the five months stay, the language problem seemed largely to vanish, and when I got back to Chicago and began lecturing in English again it scarcely seemed easier. (This was partly because I had spent the summer *before* going to Germany reading German books, philosophical and otherwise.) I recall a long discussion of philosophical issues with a German philosopher at the end of which he remarked that he had not noted a single mistake in my German.

I went to Germany with a German lecture written out for use not in class but as a one-time speaker at various German universities to which I might be invited. Olga Pauck, wife of Wilhelm Pauck, the church historian who had gone to Frankfurt (he was allowed to bring his wife because of spending a whole year in the project) was bilingual like her husband, and she went through the lecture with me and showed me how to perfect the style. She was not philosophically trained but very bright and delighted to find she could do for me what her husband had no need of, improve my German. If a sentence was poor German, she immediately thought of an idiomatic paraphrase. Quite often it was not what I was trying to say. No matter, she quickly thought of another one. By the second or third try the right phrase had been found. If the Paucks had not left the University of Chicago a few years later, I would have asked her help a number of times. The lecture was published in the *Zeitschrift für philosophische Forschung* [3, no. 4 (1949): 566-575] under the title "Das metaphyische System Whiteheads."

Our Frankfurt group was a choice little society. It had three witty people, the Paucks and Ferdinand Schevill, the distinguished historian. At eighty years of age Schevill was the life of any party he came to. (He told me that I was a combination, new to him, of naiveté and sophistication.) The other members of the group were all good company. Roger Oak was the official in charge of technical arrangements. He was a specialist in French literature. He, too, was allowed to bring his wife, because he, too, was there for more than one semester. His wife was named Dora and, as Olga said, was a truly adorable person. They had a daughter perhaps nine years old, an appealing youngster.

The previous semester Roger had had trouble with one of the professors, a rather famous scientist with prima donna characteristics. After our group had been there several weeks and no conflicts had developed, Roger said he could hardly believe it, things had become so much easier. Roger had characteristics that one could see might offend some touchy person; but none of us minded them at all. He did me a great favor. I was asked to prepare a lecture to give to a French audience in Paris. I wrote that lecture in French from the outset; but the French was less idiomatic than my German then was. Roger went through it with me and put it into good French. He was more philosophical than Olga but not quite so quick, so my two helpers were about equally useful. Writing in French was easier than it might have been, because I had with me a smallish dictionary, German-French, French-German, that I used to have in my student years in Europe. As I was lecturing in German, and trying to keep away from English, the dictionary I needed was the one I had. But, thanks to Roger Oak, I ended up with good French that was published in the *Rev. de Métaphysique et de Morale* [55, no.1 (January-March 1950): 16-29], called "Le principe de relativité Philosophique chez Whitehead."

Giving the French lecture to the Sorbonne philosophers—I also gave it to another group—was the hardest two hours work I ever did.

Or at least the part of the time spent fielding questions in French was that. It seemed a matter of sheer will to keep my attention on the questions and grope about in my mind for French words with which to answer them. My reward came several years later. I happened upon a French report of the occasion with the following concluding sentence: "The many questions only served to show the speaker's mastery of the subject." So if I had tried hard, it was not in vain.

To communicate with German graduate students I hit on the idea of starting with Leibniz and then showing how that philosopher's "monadology"' could be transformed into Whitehead's process philosophy. I still think this was good tactic. The final version of the comparison was published much later. The student group became quite friendly, and the party I had for them at the end was a cordial occasion. I remember my elementary class less well. There was one youngster in it whose major was business and who said that he had been pro-Nazi and was still confused on the issue. The group's young German chauffeur, Herr Siebel, said that, *of course*, he had been a Nazi. "Who wasn't?" He was fine as chauffeur, which is all I can say about him.

In Christmas vacation I went to Sweden to talk to Professor Alf Nyman, who had shown interest in my ideas, and the theologian Nygren. I found a curious situation. I was to see Nyman and his associates in philosophy Monday, Wednesday, Friday and see Nygren Tuesday and Thursday. It became clear that the two men, both distinguished, had as little to do with each other as possible. Both were cordial to me, especially Nyman, a wonderful scholar who wrote in at least three languages and wrote well. They were on the same dominant committee controlling appointments, but they were not noticeably friends.

Nygren, albeit a famous writer, is to me the classic example of the bookish person who looks at nothing directly. His book on *Eros and Agape*, or on love in two senses, has little to do with love in real life. Friendship, sympathy, pity, compassion are not in the book; only love as desire and love as well-wishing or good-doing to others without sharing their experiences. Karl Barth, whom I also visited in Basel during this European stay, writes somewhere that when Nygren writes about Christian love one does not feel the thing he is writing about; but when Heinrich Scholz writes about it, one does feel this. Exactly my experience.

When I told Barth that I believed God changes, he said, "I say that, too." And it is there in his systematic work.

By far the best thing for me about that stay in Germany was that it came to an end and I returned to my home in Chicago. It was the only occasion in over sixty years when my wife and I were separated for more than a month's time.

The moment I got home I had to begin working on my presidential address to the American Philosophical Association, Western (now Central) Division, which had to be given a month later. I had refrained from working at it, almost from thinking about it, while preparing for and carrying out my responsibilities in Germany. All I had done was to decide the basic theme. I had also decided what I would not talk about. Charner Perry had said to me, as soon as I was elected to the office: "One thing you must not do, you must not talk about God." I agreed, and kept to that decision.

I was a bit shocked when Eugene Freeman told me that my address on "Chance, Love, and Incompatibility" lasted an hour and five minutes. He added, however, "It was the shortest hour and five minutes I have ever spent." And it certainly was better than the two hours and a half of two other presidents I could name. One of them was an egotist who knew what he was doing and didn't care. The other I simply do not understand. Nothing else about him suggests egotism, yet no one with that man's many years of experience could fail to know how long it takes to make a given speech. So I simply give up on that riddle. The same man did an edition of a famous philosopher and radically revised the author's punctuation and spelling, violating various sane rules in the process. Yet, he is an admired teacher and chairman, though unimportant writer. He was also given an international honor. Some things are just not to be understood, as T. V. once said when he was in charge of education in Italy after WWII.

Another similar puzzle: I know a kindly, well-meaning (or so he mostly seems) philosopher of some reputation whose idea of a group discussion is that he talks half of the total time, or a little more, and all the others in the group divide the remaining half. I know a less kindly philosopher (or one even more convinced that he has found the panacea) who also does this. To me it is unacceptable behavior, of which I do not believe I have ever been guilty. I have written at too great length in several cooperative books; but, in those cases, the other participants were not thereby restricted. If a chairman says the time for discussion is short, I make no long speeches.

Why Leave a Great University?

When I left the University of Chicago after 27 years of enjoying its wonderful resources, I made it clear that I no longer found the philosophy department a good place for me to do my work. While Carnap and T. V. Smith were there, the department had four centers of power, and that was endurable. It was like the Harvard department I had known. But when those two had left there were scarcely more than two groups—and I was one of them. This did not suit me, or my students either. I also made it clear, however, that I was not prepared to put all the blame for the situation on others than myself. I had been too detached from departmental affairs, taken too little hand in them, for my own good or that of the department. In addition, in all cases of personal interaction, it is almost sure to be a violent over-simplification to think in terms of blame at all. At least two other factors are to be taken into account. One is chance, simple chance. It was bad luck for Richard McKeon and Charles Hartshorne to be in the same university, good for neither of us in the long run. If anyone was to blame for our being together it was Robert Hutchins. Yet I find it very understandable that he did what he did about that.

The other factor is aesthetic, not moral, a matter of taste, not ethics. Our culture is too little conscious of this aspect of personal incompatibilities. A philosopher I knew well had a bitter quarrel with a colleague of his (in a university other than my own) and he had a clear enough ground to fault the other ethically. But there was another factor that my friend perhaps did not quite understand. There was reason to suspect that the other man had an aesthetic distaste for my friend—as dull, unimaginative, rather humorless. This kind of nonmoral incongruity takes many forms.

I often wonder how many parents of a troublesome or delin-quent child realize that their child's trouble may go back partly to infancy, before the offspring was of an age to receive moral instruc-tion. When an infant is born, the parents, if in the least conscien-tious, take pains to safeguard the offspring's physical health and safety. And they mean, as soon as possible, to teach it proper behav-ior and mindfulness of the rights of others. But a third factor is temporally prior to moral discipline and not less important than physical health. This is mental health. In an infant this means learn-ing from the outset that life can and should be interesting, happy, friendly, and beautiful. This spells out what is meant by the now accepted axiom: children need to be loved. If the parent or nurse seems gloomy, irritable, bored, unsympathetic, unappealing, dull, and uninteresting, then any attempt to impart moral attitudes has at best a severe handicap to overcome. As Whitehead says, it is more important that a proposition be interesting than that it be true. If it is not interesting, who will care about its truth? And much of the fun in life comes from make-believe and in that sense untruth.

Living itself is in a sense an art and the supreme art. Berdayev was the first, I suppose, to state as the highest categorical impera-tive, "Be creative and foster creativity in others." Nice or delicious humor in conversation is an expression of aesthetic creativity, akin to what Shakespeare did in his comedies, and indeed even in his tragedies. No one should be totally inartistic, least of all a parent.

The reason that, when I left Chicago, I went to Emory was fairly simple. I learned afterward that I probably could have gone to a presti-gious university in the East if it had been known that I was interested in a change. Perhaps I was lacking in practical wisdom here. I did have a yen to go South, however. But the main reasons were that Colwell, who first had been head of the Divinity School and then president of the university under Chancellor Hutchins, was now vice-president of Emory and wanted me, as did Richard Hocking and Leroy Loemker. These were people I knew and understood, and knew that they understood me. So, with little thinking about other possi-bilities I struggled for a time with the decision, yes or no.

I have since wondered, Was my acceptance of the Emory offer a foregone conclusion? Could I really, as things stood, have refused?

For all I know my acceptance was predestined. But—and this some theorists seem to overlook—it does not follow that strict determinism obtained in this case. For the option between yes and no is a highly abstract one. Concretely the options always are much more specific. Thus, *when* do I stop debating with myself and make up my mind? What kinds of reasons pro and con do I take into account *before* deciding? What do I *say* to my wife or friends? How do I *formulate* my decision to those concerned? And so on. I have no objection to anyone supposing that my eventual acceptance had a probability approaching one, but I have every objection to the supposition that the more concrete issues were equally predestined. I am deeply confident they were not. Moreover, if at every instant we have some slight leeway as to just what we concretely do, in a lifetime there may be important abstract issues that are also unpredestined, like that between becoming a hopeless criminal, drunkard, or invalid, or a constructive citizen and friend of those around one.

At the dinner given to mark my leaving the department (in 1955) after twenty-seven years, the chairman, Charner Perry, whom I have always viewed as a friend and who was one of the first to show appreciation of my work, spoke of me as a "great philosopher," adding that he was particularly impressed by my "courage." I do not recall myself or anyone else having previously applied this word to me. But Richard Hartshorne later remarked that experience in faculty meetings had made him aware that, whereas in our family courage was standard behavior, it is not notably possessed by some professors. However, I can imagine having been braver than I actually was in facing the outstanding problem of that department. I could also, at certain junctures, have been more generous.

Perry did not intend the all too monolithic department he finally had by 1955. It was partly bad luck and partly lack of insight into the conditions that would have to be met if this outcome was to be avoided. For example, it would have been necessary to take my preferences concerning who was to be in the department not simply as seriously as those of the others but much more so. For it happened that I did not have or exert the power over colleagues that McKeon already had. That this was so is hardly very creditable to me, and I do not particularly blame anyone for it. It was not that some members of the department were sychophants. They just happened, several of them, to be inclined to do philosophy somewhat as McKeon did.

It was unlucky for me that one man I would have urged for the department, because of his strong independence and courage, was a specialist in McKeon's period of the history of philosophy. In another case there were serious personal weaknesses that I could not deny. It was long before I realized that I was balancing pros and cons rather impartially, without special regard to my own chances in the department, while some of the others were more aware of the way an individual would fit into their way of doing philosophy. It is a difficult matter to decide how far one's judgment as to soundness of doctrine should be allowed to determine one's choice of colleagues.

After Perry's speech, I, too, made one, perhaps to Perry's surprise. I was rather candid about my reasons for leaving. McKeon later said it was "a beautiful speech," a not very usual compliment from him. I made an engagement with him for lunch to make quite clear to myself that I understood his view on one matter. He confirmed my impression that it was his belief that the great philosophers, those with a powerful method for dealing with the chief philosophical problems, knew what they were doing when they stated their own views, but not when they criticized one another. Or, if they did know what they were doing in the second case, they were engaging in a political contest, making propaganda, rather than contributing to knowledge.

My own view is that the great philosophers (G.P.'s) have made as great mistakes when they stated their own views as when they offered refutations of other philosophers. McKeon argues that the G. P.'s do not contradict themselves, "they have good memories, they do not forget on Wednesday what they said on Monday." I agree about the memories, but not about the absence of contradiction. True, the inconsistencies are not crudely obvious; but explicit verbal contradictions are often avoided only by failing to provide really unambiguous and definite meanings for some of the key terms—for example, *modes* in Spinoza.

Why should G. P.'s contradict themselves? Because in any culture certain affirmations or denials are almost obligatory, can scarcely be avoided, and there is no guarantee that all of these requirements are mutually consistent. Thus, for 2000 years it was almost impossible to deny (1) that God must be conceived, if at all, as entirely immutable, immune to influence from the creatures, and without contingent properties. At the same time it was required (2) that one grant to God knowledge of the creatures, and (3) that the latter exist contingently. There is no way to give clear and consistent meaning to all three of these requirements. So nearly everyone accepted them and appealed to the limitations of our understanding to explain the inconsistency. Leibniz and Arnauld came very close to agreeing that the inconsistency is there, but saw no possibility of denying any of the assumptions that produce it. As Adler shows in his book *A Philosopher at Large*, he is bent, as I am, on finding refutations of some views in order to arrive by elimination as near the truth as possible. But Adler also tends to overlook the obstacles to the application of logic to basic beliefs. He says that he has learned everything that is most important to him philosophically from Aristotle, Thomas as commentator on Aristotle, and Maritain, the neo-Thomist. I was really shocked to read this. So Leibniz discovered nothing important in his analysis of extension and matter; Plato nothing important in his doctrine of World Soul (which Aristotle omitted); Democritus and Epicurus nothing important (which Aristotle badly missed) in their doctrine that perception gives only a blurred view of the world, omitting all the fine structure that is its pervasive dynamism; Bergson nothing important in his doctrine of memory as incorporation of the past in the present or of duration as in principle creative (doctrines found also in Peirce and Whitehead); the Buddhists nothing important in their analysis of individuals into sequential groupings of unit-events or instances of "dependent origination," a view more adequately developed, probably independently, by Whitehead? No need for all this; just Aristotle, Thomas, and Maritain! What this means to me is that Adler, though a great man, is not a great metaphysician. He is strongest on ethics and political philosophy, where he admits the moderns have made advances.

Adler points to the ignorance concerning Aristotle in various philosophers, including Leibniz. I grant that Leibniz was not a perfect scholar in the history of philosophy; but he knew more about

Aristotle than Aristotle knew about him! This simple fact is more important than Adler supposes. Overcoming the obstacles to clarity and consistency in metaphysics is harder and takes more centuries than Adler is aware of. True, it is not factual (contingent) information that is essential here. But pure mathematics also is in this sense nonfactual, yet it keeps making progress.

Referring again to the philosophy department at Chicago, it was a misfortune for me that Addison Moore, the member of the group that I felt most at ease with and who was chiefly responsible for my being invited to Chicago, was in poor health and died a year or two later. I got on well with Everett Hall, but he left because of the conflict with Hutchins, as did Arthur Murphy, a man I respected as a brilliant teacher and man of character. Burtt was friendly enough but did not greatly stimulate me, nor did he promote my cause as Moore would have done. Mead's wife was ill, and before long so was Mead. Tufts, too, fell ill and left. Morris and Perry came and were fine, intelligent gentlemen, but were not close to me in philosophical concerns. At no time was the department more than mildly appealing to one with my interests and nature.

The last straw destroying any feeling of belonging in that department came with a sketch its students put on "humorously" depicting the faculty. Warner Wick (deservedly) was depicted as Mr. Candler, a genial and sensible fellow helpful to everyone; McKeon as a person with some eccentricities and some very important ideas; I as a person with eccentricities — period. All that needs to be added is that the writer of the lines had never been a student of mine, and the student who acted the part had merely dropped into class a time or two, not to learn what I thought but to note my mannerisms. They were making fun of a stranger, not of a teacher of theirs. The writer met me afterwards with a beaming smile, obviously pleased with her treatment of me. I told her coldly (a rare thing for me) that I thought poorly of that treatment. Recently she reintroduced herself as the author, and I told her, "I didn't like it then and I don't like it now." "Well," she asked, "can you forgive me?" I then told her that I had learned from the Buddhists that our former selves are not our present selves; so, yes, I could forgive her.

A student (not of mine so far as I recall) who kindly came to help me with packing books when we were getting ready to leave Chicago was unable to grasp why I could not accept as good clean fun being depicted as a man without ideas in a department of people with ideas. Kind he may have been, but to me he seemed not all that bright. Eccentric I may be, make fun of my ideas if you please, but to accuse me of having no ideas. . . . Show me a living philosopher in this country with more.

How easily we fail to grasp what is going on around us was shown by the shock that Warner Wick exhibited when he heard I was leaving. Evidently he had scarcely an idea that things were not quite all right for me.

CHAPTER TEN

Some Friends in Chicago, and Elsewhere

My Admirable Relatives-in-law

Clyde Barnes Cooper was professor of English at the Armour Institute; but in my opinion should have been that in a great university. He was a learned scholar, a man of wit and the most truly puckish humor I have encountered. His wife was a highly educated woman with a career as an editor. I met them first when the Cooper family was entertaining me at dinner a few days before I became engaged to Dorothy Eleanore Cooper, the elder of two very accomplished daughters. At that dinner Mrs. Cooper disapproved of a remark Dr. Cooper made about the presidential campaign of Hoover *vs.* Al Smith, the Catholic candidate for the presidency. Mrs. Cooper was strongly anti-Catholic, her husband at least pretended to see some merit in the case for Smith (or against Hoover), so Mrs. C. rebuked him with some severity. Immediately, he disappeared from sight, almost it seemed by a miracle. He was a slender tall man and had managed somehow to slide completely under the table with amazing speed. This was his reply to his wife's reprimand. After a pause, Mrs. Cooper said quietly, "You may come up now, Clyde." Which he did, though just how he managed either movement, the one up or the one down, remains something of a mystery.

On another occasion, Cooper's response to a wifely rebuke was to slap his left wrist as mock punishment for his imputed naughtiness. Usually, however, his response was more verbal. He sometimes referred to Mrs. Cooper as "the boss," which teased her, I felt, because it had just a bit more truth than was comfortable. She was a rather strong-minded lady toward members of her family—which fortunately did not, in this regard, include me.

Here is a sample exchange between my two parents-in-law.

Dr. Cooper:	*So-and-so (a professor of English who had a chair he could himself have occupied with distinction) is a stupid man.*
Mrs. Cooper:	*Clyde, you ought not to talk like that.*
Dr. C.:	*Well, he's not educated.*
Mrs. C.:	*Clyde!*
Dr. C.:	*Well, he's not a human being.*
Mrs. C.:	(gives up)

It should perhaps be said that the uneducated so-and-so had not earned—nor even received—a Ph.D.

Mrs. Cooper for much of her life, though not in her last years, was a teetotaller. Dr. C. in my experience drank not at all (though I gathered he was not averse to some beer occasionally when with students or male friends), but in this as in other matters he liked to tease his wife. Once he stepped outdoors on a cool day and, as he reentered the apartment, said to us, "You mustn't go out; the air is like wine!"

At the wedding banquet for Dorothy and me, Mrs. C. remarked that things were not as they should be, because some marzipan confections, simulating fruits, were of improper sizes. The "cherries" and "strawberries" should not have been as large as the "peaches."

Dr. C.:	*My dear, you're too meticulous.* (Then, turning to my father) *Have you met the meticulous Mrs. Cooper?*
Mrs. C.:	*Well, I guess there are worse things than being meticulous.*
Dr. C.:	(Instantly but solemnly) *I don't know them. I don't know them.*

My father thought this great fun. However, it gave him the false idea that Dorothy's father was only "a clown."

It was Cooper who told me of the man who, hearing of Matthew Arnold's death, commented, "Poor Matt, he won't like God!" (To fully savor this one needs to have been, as I once was, an attentive reader of Arnold's prose writings.) Cooper also told me about Napoleon's caustic reply to one of his generals who tried to excuse some shady dealings by the traditional, "One has to live." Napoleon: "I don't see the necessity."

Cooper indulged in what he called the art of "insidious variation." For example, "a little widow is a dangerous thing" (cf. Pope's famous line about wisdom). When my wife wrote him that I had eaten snails in France, he commented:

Charles ate a snail;
My cheek grew pale
To hear the tale.

Clyde Cooper was not a man who amused merely by reiterating the same jokes or playing the same tricks. Nearly always it was something fresh and unpredictable. Once in a restaurant, when the waitress was handing around plates with some sort of salad on them, he told her not to give him any. "I daren't eat it," he said to her solemnly; "it's the deadly vitamins." A puzzled young woman went off with the plate. Once, when several of us planned to give him a new leather wallet, we tried to anticipate his comment, knowing that we were bound to fail. Looking at the various compartments of the wallet, he wondered, "Where do I put my false teeth?" As he then had only natural teeth, we of course had not dreamt of this response.

A Cooper whimsicality:

Sancho Panza
A bonanza
Found in Kansa
sss...

Letters written in triplicate to his three children scattered about the country contained many such items.

Cooper was pro-English literature and anti-American literature, at least so far as his contemporaries were concerned. I made a feeble effort to combat this prejudice by saying, "They [contemporary American authors] make use of interesting materials." "Yes," he said, "as a donkey uses hay; he turns it into manure."

It was the Cooper family, largely I think under the father's influence, who taught me to appreciate some of the wittiest writers who ever lived, including Saki (H. H. Munro), W. W. Jacobs, P. G. Wodehouse, and above all Thomas Love Peacock, the Bernard Shaw of the novel. Cooper told me about Wordsworth's sadly replying to expostulations about his most banal failures to achieve poetic effects, for example, in Peter Bell: "I had thought it would please."

It perhaps is rather well established that in every humorist are aspects of frustration and sadness. Cooper's career, relative to his intelligence and imagination, was scarcely a success. Also, though his wife was a fairly highly educated and in some limited ways intelligent woman, there were, as with many Victorians, obstacles to a successful marriage. Mrs. Cooper was called cold-hearted by someone who, except for her husband, knew her best. Some men would have become bitter; some would have sought extramarital adventures; some would have left or divorced her. Cooper took none of these options. He once explained himself to me with his usual economy of words and reserve about private matters: "I have resisted experience." In other words, he achieved a kind of stoic or almost oriental detachment, satisfying himself with harmless social rewards for being the life of any party he came to. Even his wife, perhaps, did not greatly mind being the butt of his jokes, and sometimes seemed to find her pride in his contributions to the general merriment more than enough to balance the implied criticisms of her. Doubtless this was not always true.

Once, at dinner, Mrs. C. opened the conversation thus: Mr. — — — (her employer) told me the funniest joke today. You'll be so amused." "Oh," said her husband, "Tell us the joke." It was an account of how Southerners cook ham, with the most elaborate preparations and wondrous sauces. It ended with the comment, "I don't know about the ham, but I'd sure like to taste the pot liquor." "Yes," said Dr. C. solemnly, "and what happened then?" Mrs. C.: "Well, if you don't

like the way I tell the story, let's hear how you think it should be told."
Dr. C. complied with a consummately artistic formulation, ending
with the comment of the hypothetical listener to the recipe, "Why, a
horse block (a now perhaps nonexistent but once common article of
outdoor furniture) would taste good prepared that way."

Professor Cooper liked to play bridge and would have been a
good player had it not been for his almost ungovernable passion for
bidding, whether or not he had a hand worth bidding on. He would
ask, "Who dealt this smear?" I had the feeling that his propensity for
overbidding was a compensation for his lack of success, his frustrations in life. Though the playing was not for money it seemed to me
that there was in him at such times a strong need to taste success,
and that there might be a remote analogy with the passion for gambling, as in the classic case of Dostoyevsky.

The humor of Clyde Cooper made no use of obscenity, or profanity either. Though he drank scarcely at all, he might suddenly
say, "What I need now is a quart of pure scotch whiskey." He did
smoke a pipe.

There was a rather odd family in the city with a son that Cooper
sometimes referred to as "the spite child." It seems that this son was
supposed to have been conceived only to prevent a distant relative
from inheriting an estate.

When Dorothy and I told Mrs. Cooper that we had that day
become engaged, she replied, "This is so sudden" (sic); falling into a
chair, Dr. Cooper had a less hackneyed response, "My boy," he said to
me, "here's your dowry," handing me a dime. It became clear to me
later that this instantaneous response really meant: "I am fond of my
daughter, I think well of you, and I would dearly love to think that I
could be of financial help to both of you. But in fact that is not in my
power." It was an act of a kindly humorist, who from a worldly point
of view was not in a position to do much materially for those he
loved.

A certain elderly widowed friend of the Cooper family was pre-
sumed to be wealthy, as her husband had certainly been at one time,
and it was Cooper's clearly expressed hope that his children would
inherit from her. This lady was judged to be extraordinarily miserly
because at restaurants she always managed not to be the one to pay.

Pathetically enough, when she died it turned out that she hadn't anything but a few worn clothes to leave to anyone. Retrospectively we realized that she had preferred to appear miserly rather than be known for the very poor person she in fact had become.

The nearest thing I know to Clyde Cooper in literature is Mr. Bennet of *Pride and Prejudice*. Or, to put it the other way, Cooper was the nearest thing I have encountered in real life to Mr. Bennet. One difference is that whereas Mrs. Bennet was a silly woman Mrs. Cooper was bright, educated, and, *in some respects*, eminently sensible. Still the parallel is striking. There was a similar sense of restrained discord and retreat from life into humor, as in Mr. Bennet's remark to Elizabeth, "Your mother will never forgive you if you do not marry Mr. Collins, and I will never forgive you if you do." However, the Coopers had no disagreement about my marriage to Dorothy. Nor did I ever receive an unkind word from either of them.

Cooper's premature death (from cancer) is one of the two or three such deaths of persons intimately known to me that I have most regretted. It is also one of a number of reasons why I incline to take somewhat seriously the remark I have seen quoted from a doctor: "I have never known a happy man who got cancer."

We particularly regretted the timing of my father-in-law's death just before he would have become a grandfather through the birth of our only child, Emily. He had shown a beautiful appreciation of his own two daughters as children. I recall his saying to them, as grown women: "You two were some good when you were about three years old." In a diary containing many sayings of his children, he recorded of Dorothy, the oldest child, that she said, on a certain occasion, "Don't say any words." I submit that a more dignified circumlocution for "shut up" could not be found.

Cooper was fond of quoting Dickens. For example: " 'Let us be merry,' said he, 'taking a ship's biscuit.' " (This is not quite as in Dickens but it is, I think, as my father'in-law cited it.) Or another Dickens quotation: " 'Damn anything that's low.' "

My wife and I have found these sayings, suitably modified in a word or two, wonderfully adapted to a variety of occasions. In this generality of relevance they recall Calvin Coolidge's terse comment on the role of a president, "You've got to be mighty careful." How applicable to marriage!

My father-in-law was a skeptic, fond of the philosopher Schopen-hauer (we have his copy of a book of that writer's containing his essay against belief in God). But he had no interest in converting others to his views. His wife was then a loyal member of a Universal-ist church. Its minister was a halting, uneloquent speaker. Cooper summed it up: "Dr. — — — *can't* preach." Alas, it was too true.

A pleasant memory is of Clyde Cooper coming to visit us in our cottage in a woods back of the Indiana Dunes and immediately throwing himself down upon a simple iron bed provided with cush-ions, which we used as a couch in the corner of our living room, exclaiming, "This is the most comfortable spot in North America!" We once had for a time a secondhand Lincoln (bought for $85) with old-fashioned removable curtains. Cooper quickly characterized the breezy back of this vehicle "the cave of the winds."

From this unusual man his children acquired a sense of the comic, a ready wit, a gift for saying and savoring the un-expected that has enlivened countless occasions. It is one more example of the truth that the basic education is experienced in childhood from the example of parents. Wit and good humor are contagious; so are melancholy and bad humor, and many other traits of heart and mind. This is one reason why the gulf between cultural groups can be so hard to cross, why so many generations may be required.

Cooper read widely and kept elaborate notes of his reading. But the mainspring was somehow broken. No enduring work resulted. Only a single essay from his dissertation and a few shorter pieces were published.

Cooper once wrote how he had gone to an automoblie dealer to see what sort of car his daughter Marjorie, who lived in another city, had recently acquired. She had bought an Oldsmobile. Cooper described his interview with the dealer who showed him the model in question thus, "Snooty said I could have it for $—." We enjoyed the picture thus conjured up of the eager dealer hoping for a sale and Cooper, who had never driven and had no idea in the world of buying a car, solemnly examining the machine. And we had no doubt that the absurdity of the situation added savor to the satisfaction of Marjorie's father in looking over his daughter's acquisition.

From the fact that I see pathos and a tinge of tragedy in my father-in-law's career, the reader is not to infer that this man went about complaining or being audibly sorry for himself. Nothing of the kind. He never said he had been unfortunate, or deserved better things. But I was too close to that family not to see that his situation left much to be desired, and that he knew this. And I believe it was a principal cause of his premature death. It is a false materialism that supposes longevity is a merely physico-chemical phenomenon. It is also a psychological one. An ideally healthy population without essential and pervasive happiness is not possible.

Clyde Cooper's most elaborate joke requires some preliminary explanation. During the Christmas holidays, the family had gone to visit with a family they used to know when Cooper was teaching in West Lafayette, Indiana. But Cooper also wanted to visit his parents in Nebraska. So he left the others in West Lafayette and took trains to Nebraska via Chicago. Returning several days later to West Lafayette, also via Chicago, he rejoined the family and they all took the train back to Chicago. Mrs. C. asked how things were with his parents. "Oh, all right," he replied. "But I should tell you: the young woman who has been in my parents' house came back to Chicago with me, and I left her in our house." "What! What young woman?" asked the astonished wife. "Oh, you remember her, don't you? You must have seen her when you visited my parents that time. "No, there was no young woman there that I remember. What's her name?" "Carrie Waters," said he. That was all Mrs. C. could get from him until the family entered their apartment in Chicago, whereupon Mrs. C. demanded to know where Carrie Waters might be. Her husband took her into the living room and pointed to a painting of a female figure with a water jar on her shoulder. "There," said he, "is Carrie Waters."

My eccentric father-in-law used to express his sense that some person was being too highly regarded (usually by his wife) by ejaculating, "Next to God! Next to God!" The head of the division of the firm for which his wife worked was one individual he so characterized.

Cooper's case illustrates the wide range of potentialities that can be in a single human individual. There must have been few who knew him who would have objected to the suggestion that he might, with some different uses by himself and others of the power of free decision making that we all possess (in spite of what Skinner and some other psychologists say), have been, not simply a professor with a mediocre job and students who valued him, but a famous scholar and perhaps a writer of light pieces on the side. Also who could deny that he might have been a professional comedian. He had the talents of a natural funny man. Perhaps he could have been a novelist. He invented an imaginary law firm, "Pooty, Pooty, Pooty, and Schnitz." There was "Lafayette or Lafe Pooty,— — —Pooty,— — —Pooty, and Hjalmer Schnitz." Cooper and I talked of writing a book to be called, "What children should tell their parents about life." It really should have been written, even though, if we had written it in the 1930s there would have had to be some rewriting in the 1960s and again in the 1970s.

Cooper had two unusual ways of expressing mock grief:

"That story causes tears to run down the back of my neck."

"That story, coupled with the news of the death of a dear friend, comes nigh to make a man weep."

Presumably both are quotations, but from whom?

Although my father-in-law never said an unpleasant word to me, he was quoted as having said, "Charles has no tact." What this was particularly apropos of I can't say, but I have no doubt it had a reasonable basis. My father-in-law was himself certainly tactful and had every right to judge me in this respect. To balance his remark I will say that one of my teachers at Harvard, C. I. Lewis, a much admired man, was quoted as saying that I was "the most tactful man he had ever known." I think I can remember being tactful with him: I admired him and he was close to my ideal as a teacher, even when I disagreed with some of his beliefs. His wife was similar. To be tactful with such people is no great feat. But it does trouble me a little that Clyde Cooper made that remark about me. Whatever the occasion or occasions it did not spoil our relationship.

If C. B. C. felt unwell he might say, when asked how he was, "I'm not a well woman." In this way he adroitly avoided distinguishing his condition at the time from that of any other time. This fitted his habitual reserve. He did not favor his own fortunes or misfortunes as topics of conversation. His view was that, as we used to say at Yeates School, "it's a funny world," but his own part in the comedy he preferred to put aside so far as possible.

Cooper's academic career, in an inferior institution, was prematurely terminated by an administration bent on substituting low paid youngsters for full professors. The heads of five departments were fired. The big element of chance in life is illustrated in the fact that a position in a first-rate department (suitable to my father-in-law's qualities and aware of his work) was open the year *before* he completed his dissertation. The next year no position in that department was open. This was not the only time in his career that contingent circumstances worked against him. There was the fact that his wife had a successful career to which she was devoted in Chicago, when he had an offer of a position in another city.

In my philosophy, chance, or luck (good and bad), is a perfectly real aspect of life, not to be explained away by any idea either of providence or of causal determinism. To the question, To what do you owe your success? the only nonsuperstitious and unconceited answer has to include, "Above all, to good luck." To be born of intelligent and unselfish parents is the first dose of good luck; to stupid or selfish ones, of bad luck. To happen to be acquainted with the right potential and available wife at the time when the need for a mate is strong is another. Although there is no such thing as an unlucky (or lucky) individual if this is taken to mean that *all* the chances have been unfavorable (or all favorable) and will continue to be so, still, the ratio of good and bad turns of fortune can vary significantly. As a mostly lucky individual I do not forget that this has merely happened (and could change at any time) and that many others have been mostly unlucky.

Of course luck is not everything. There is also one's response to fortune, one's *management* of one's life, and this, too, can be good or bad. I once spoke about this to an audience of handicapped persons (deaf, in wheelchairs, etc.) and added, "with bad luck and good management we *may* get by." The audience laughed so pleasantly at this that, as my allotted time was about up anyway, I said, "I think I'll stop while I'm ahead." This produced a second pleasant laugh, which was the conclusion of my contribution to the ceremony, in which there were rather many speakers.

To make an ultimate distinction between luck and management it is necessary to believe in real individual freedom and to so conceive causal conditioning that it stops short of fully determining our decisions. For otherwise the whole of one's conduct simply expresses one's good or bad fortune in being born with a certain heredity and environment. The psychologist Skinner makes this starkly clear. So much the worse for his view of things. But he is right to this extent that luck, that is, inherited and environmental factors strongly influencing and partly shaping one's career, is always to be reckoned with, and that if we want to help people we should try to alter these factors, and not simply expect their free will to do everything.

On the other side, it is worth bearing in mind that what looks like bad luck sometimes works to one's advantage, as when I failed to get a desirable position but then got one in a greater university, and above all in a city where I again encountered the one incomparable woman from whom chance and my slow perception of her matchless qualities had separated me and almost certainly would have continued to do so had I been given the first position. There is also this: if bad luck crushes our wills, shatters our morale, then it is bad indeed, and any later turn of fortune in our favor may do little or no good; whereas if the will, the morale, remains intact, every good chance will be more of a help and every bad chance probably less of a hindrance than if we in effect have given up the struggle.

Professor Cooper retained his morale in some important respects, but not in all. He was an asset to all who knew him by his inventive humor. He taught many students how to use the language better than they otherwise would have done. He lived simply, was conservative in his use of energy (no automobile in days when energy was seen by few as a problem), avoided alcoholism, and with his wife maintained a family life far better than many. He was an ideal father-in-law. If he harmed anyone, it was primarily himself. Death at his age from cancer was in my belief partly a question of morale. (His pipe smoking may have been an important factor.) Ideas and emotions can be lethal. That is one reason why philosophy (with religion) retains importance even, or especially, in this age of science.

For all his scholarliness, Cooper was a man who saw people as human beings, not just as members of social classes. He told gleefully about a local Greek fruit store man who, when asked how business was, replied, "Bad! What we make on the peanuts we lose on the goddam banan."

Cooper's treasuring of amusing remarks, whether by scholars, literary people, or just anybody, is nicely illustrated also by his liking to quote a phrase he overheard in a music store in which he once worked. (His mother was intensely musical, and this was probably the reason he thought of working in a music store.) In the back of the store men were filling orders for music. Evidently some orders were for religious music, because Cooper heard a loud, "Rush them sacreds, Joe!"

The nearest to a serious disagreement I, or Dorothy and I, had with my in-laws was over the trust some members of the Cooper family, not including Dorothy or her father, had in the osteopathic tradition in medicine. The best we could do with that topic was to avoid discussing it. With one or two (no doubt tactless) lapses on my side this silence was adhered to.

A trifling but amusing disagreement was over the Chicago climate. On the basis of weather bureau statistics I held that August was less hot than July. Mrs. Cooper insisted it was hotter. So, I think at her sugession, we made a bet on the coming July and August. Mrs. Cooper won and delightedly collected her $5. *That* summer August was hotter.

Mrs. Cooper and I for some years had slightly complicated but trouble-free financial relations. The Coopers had suffered serious losses from speculative investments that in the Depression became worthless. This caused me to worry a little about the financial prospects of the couple when one or both were retired. There was also an immediate financial problem for Dorothy and me in that my salary in those years was quite small. The first year Dorothy's salary (as editor for a publishing company) was better than mine, but she did not want to continue that work indefinitely. So I proposed to Mrs C. that she lend us money, so much each month, to be repaid eventually at 5 percent compound interest. I had tables for this from Teachers Insurance and Annuity. My ulterior motive was to avoid a situation in which the Coopers' possible retirement needs would be met by us through an act of charity. I wanted it to be by money owing to them. There was no indication that Mrs. C. suspected this motivation. She agreed to the scheme and every month faithfully handed over the specified amount, which I do not now recall. After some years it seemed apparent that the Coopers were no longer indulging in speculative investments and were providing for their retirements in conservative ways. So I began paying back the loan in monthly installments, using the same tables in reverse order, if I recall correctly.

The perfect success of this scheme is a counter-example to the wisdom of Polonius—"Neither a borrower nor a lender be, for a loan oft loses both itself and friends, and borrowing dulls the edge of husbandry." I must add, however, that, of several loans that I made to acquaintances before marrying, all but one turned out as Polonius would have expected. In contrast, a loan to Dorothy's sister Marjorie proved quite safe, as we thought it would be. She was trying to establish her own girls' summer camp, with another woman as partner and full-time manager, while she herself functioned at a near-by Camp Fire Girls' camp, her regular summer occupation. The plan failed because the partner did not function as expected. But the loan was promptly repaid.

To have known the Cooper family has been a glorious bonus on my luck in the mating lottery. One of the girls I once thought, for a time of marrying had a family, with only two members, both of whom would have meant trouble and plenty of it—a mother with no money to speak of but expensive habits she had no idea of changing, and a brother who seemed to me the classic case of the egotistical relative who would borrow money whenever possible with no real intention of paying it back. I shudder to think of that crass, impudent face of his, as I shudder to think of the morally weak mother. In the Cooper family everyone was reliable, considerate, capable, and earned his or her salt. No one was even boring, let alone offensive. One cannot claim to deserve such luck, but one can know it for what it is.

Fig. 23. Charles Hartshorne in Hong Kong, 1966

Kurt Riezler

Once a former Harvard schoolmate asked me for a substantial loan
to set him up in a new business, WWII having ruined his first one. I
told him I did not have that kind of money, which certainly was true.
He apologized, saying that the New York apartment we were then
living in gave him the impression of wealth. I do not wonder. It was
the apartment of Kurt Riezler, whose wife was the daughter of a
famous German painter, and it contained pictures by her father and
other painters of note. The Riezlers and the Hartshornes had exchanged apartments that year, he to teach at The University of Chicago and I to teach at the New School for Social Research. This
exchange was Charner Perry's pleasant idea. Our apartment, as I had
written Riezler beforehand, was mediocre and cheap; his turned out
to be magnificent. But Riezler was not the kind of man (nor his wife
the kind of woman) to make anything out of a difference of that kind.

When I came to arrange for us to reoccupy our Chicago apartment on a hot summer day and was carrying more or less heavy articles from the basement storeroom up flights of stairs to the apartment, Riezler insisted on helping me to carry them.

Riezler's wife was Jewish and, because of the Nazis, they were refugees. He managed to get his pictures out of Germany when he left by telling the officials "they are just Jewish things." He had been ambassador to Russia for some years, and commissioner of education under the Weimar Republic. He was, I felt, a sane and noble spirit. He told me that before leaving Germany he had talked to Heidegger about the Nazis and that the impression he got was of a man with his eye on expediency. Why not, in a philosopher from whom no ethical principles have ever been forthcoming? There have been mystics who talked of a state "beyond good and evil," but they grew up in and assimilated an intensive ethical tradition. Heidegger may have grown up in one such tradition (Roman Catholic), but how far he assimilated it is not especially clear. Granted a streak of genius in him, I cannot particularly admire this person as a person.

Riezler was something of a scholar, though I did not make much out of his thinking as technical philosophy. He liked the phrase the eternal human. I asked him, in a departmental seminar, what this meant. Was it to be taken literally, or was it only a bit of poetry? The "logical positivist" Carnap, who had been patiently listening up to that moment, could restrain himself no longer: "It's all poetry!" he burst out. Be this as it may, I class Riezler and his wife with the noblest of the many scholarly, refined refugees that this country acquired because of the Nazi disease.

The man in New York who wanted to borrow a sizable sum told me a pathetic story about his two marriages, both failures. He was a man of much charm. First he fell in love with a married woman, decided he must give her up and then, when another woman fell in love with him, married her and thought they were making a fairly good marriage until the husband of the first woman died. Now he could no longer focus his affections on the woman he had married; so he divorced her and married the widow. But he was still in trouble; for he found he could not get his previous wife out of his mind. "If I could have married first the woman I had been in love with all along I think it would have been all right," he said. But as it actually was, both marriages were spoiled." I have lost track of this man's career. He was a likable and able person. He was still relatively young and I have no doubt much was still to come in his life. It seems obvious his story could furnish ideas for an interesting short story or play. Some children were involved in at least one marriage.

I have known some other marriages that one of the two parties went into less than enthusiastically. In one case, a most unhappy one, the mother of the reluctant girl insisted that the engagement should not be broken. Such marriages are hardly "made in heaven."

A Neighborhood Institution

Harold Wehrwein was owner and operator of the hardware store on 57th Street near the I. C. railroad station in Chicago. He was a friend as well as a favorite merchant for many. His intelligence was always in evidence. Once when I noticed that something I had just bought from him was cheaper than the corresponding item at Sears Roebuck I told him so. "Let that be a lesson to you," said he. When there was trouble in our house, which something in the store could remedy, Harold would send one of his men (John or Bill) to attend to it. When our small daughter was having a party and wanted to make heart-shaped cookies, Dorothy phoned Wehrwein to ask if he had a heart-shaped cookie cutter, "I'll send one right away," said he. When the bill came for this item, it was five cents. When Dorothy went to buy a dustpan, they had no blue one. "I do wish you had a blue pan," said she. "Do you want us to send you a blue one?" Bill asked. When the pan came she saw that it had been painted blue. She still has it. When lights failed in my study, Dorothy phoned Wehrwein and told him that I needed light to be able to finish an essay I was writing. Bill and John soon arrived full of good spirits. "Harold took us off that job we were on with Mrs.— — —in a hurry," said they. (The lady in question was not a favorite of theirs, it was made clear.) "He said the Professor needed help."

Wehrwein, though not many knew it, was an amateur musician and played in a chamber music group. His wife was cashier in the store. His man Bill had a heart attack, and thereafter Wehrwein took the greatest pains to spare him undue exertion. If there was any moral defect or blind spot in Harold, no one in that neighborhood seemed to have heard of it. When he died abruptly in his prime of a heart attack, Bill sobbed and told us how considerately Harold had treated him after his own attack.

There were a number of stores on that part of 57th Street and there was nothing particularly wrong with any of them. But Wehrwein's was more than just a store, it was an institution. And the spirit of that institution was the remarkable personality of Harold Wehrwein. He was a superlative gentleman.

Why did Wehrwein die in his prime? I cannot help suspecting it was from the great American disease, automobilitis, by which I mean having machines substitute for one's own muscular exertion to such an extent that the heart gets too little vigorous exercise. Nowadays, many take to jogging as a cure. This, too, is artificial and may easily be overdone. And many are still living a too sedentary life and dying early as a result. In a flat city like Chicago ordinary walking is not much help. San Francisco has an advantage in this respect. One-story houses are disadvantageous from the same point of view, especially if there is no basement.

Automobilitis is a common disease in this country. I and my wife and daughter and son-in-law have successfully taken pains to avoid it. We recommend the practice. The country has too many private cars and too few strong hearts. Incidentally, my parents, who lived to a great age, always lived in a house with basement and several stories, and they used stairs a great deal. And my father, though he owned and drove a car, took a train, walking at both ends, up a hill at one end, to go to his office five days a week to the end of his long life.

Father's life-style was threatened when the railroad he used made plans to omit the Cynwyd Station stop near Father's house. So Father wrote one of his characteristically vigorous letters, perhaps telling the company that his father had been a railroad builder and president of one, vice-president of another, RR. He got results and was delighted to hear approximately the following conversation between two railroad workmen. "I thought they were going to quit stopping at this station." "Yes, but the *Sky Pilot kicked*, and they changed their minds."

"Bird Friends Are Good Friends"

When, at the age of fifty-five, I wrote to the University of Michigan Biological Station at Pilgrim that I wished to take the summer course in ornithology (the first introduction in the subject I ever had) taught by the well-known Sewall Pettingill, he, having never heard of this middle-aged philosopher, at least not as one interested in a biological subject, phoned the philosophy department at Ann Arbor and asked what they knew of my interest in birds. Their reply, as reported to me, was, "We did not know that he had this interest, but *if he says he has it, he has it.*" I was pleased with the reputation thus given me of knowing my own mind. Before long I got an admirable letter from Pettingill telling me that there were many lines of research to pursue in my announced specialty of bird song. Sewall is a down-to-earth, factual-minded scientist with comprehensive field and book knowledge of the subject and a gift for clear language. He is not given as I am to daring theories—altogether just the right person to turn me from a mere amateur to something more, a sort of unprofessional expert, acquainted with the professional attitudes.

I went to work under Pettingill for two summers. He read my first paper to be given at a meeting of the Ornithological Union and later published in its journal. He said, "Since you are in this in a big way, I shall be frank in my criticisms." He told me where a trained ornithologist would have misgivings about my theorizing, where I could limit my topic (to "make a neater package"), and other useful hints. All this was luck for me.

Another ornithologist, highly expert though not with an academic position, who helped me to become a contributor to this empirical science was the world-famed Margaret Morse Nice. I found her sharply critical and disciplined scientific mind a notable example of the idiocy of stereotyped notions of the housewife, which was Mrs. Nice's status in Chicago. I would try out ideas on her, and if they clashed with facts reported in the literature, which she knew in at least two languages, or with her own justly acclaimed field work, I would quickly learn about it. An admirable thing to see was the way Mrs. Nice's husband, a teacher of physiology in a Chicago school, was perfectly content to be known locally as competent whereas his wife was so known wherever ornithology is seriously studied.

It happens that I have recently reread George Eliot's account in *The Mill on the Floss* of the man who enjoyed exhibiting in company his wife's intellectual inferiority to himself. One hopes that this disreputable path to masculine self-confidence will more and more be overgrown with weeds. Of course the weakness or vice in question is easier to avoid if husband and wife are not seeking distinction in the same subject, as the Nices were not. In some cases where both have the same subject it may work out if the work, for instance experimentation or observation, is done as a joint affair seeking credit as a team. Thus the leading living authority on the wood warbler family may well be a husband and wife team, the Fickens. More and more does happiness depend on how well individuals bend, reform themselves, and create institutions and customs, so as to make it possible for women and men to share in cultural creativities on adult levels as well as on the parent-child incline.

Fig. 24. Dorothy and I recording bird song at our home, 1961

Now and then, at the station, surrounded by people not one of whom, for all I discovered, knew or cared about philosophy, and most of whom were not even ornithologists but students of parasitology, or limnology, or what have you, I felt my situation as a bit queer. I take Nietzsche's dictum, "It is necessary to live dangerously" to refer to dangers to one's self-confidence and feeling of belonging, as well as to more active and obvious threats, and I think of this when in the company of people (physicists, for example) whose knowledge gives me little or no chance to shine in rivalry with them. I have tried not to miss chances to learn from my real superiors, simply because it is more comfortable to avoid them. And I wonder a little at some philosophers I have known who speak scornfully of philosophizing scientists. If they are good scientists, I find they often do better than half the professional teachers of philosophy in seeing the essential questions.

There are also a few writers in philosophy who are neither scientists nor professional philosophers but who likewise do at least as well as half of those who are called *philosophers*. Particularly I find this true of Rudolf Jordan, a grape grower of South Africa. He has a degree in philosophy but otherwise no academic backing. He has read intensively in philosophy and science, and his work is worth reading. He could be regarded as an empiricist and cautious cosmologist and philosopher of religion, as such better than many well known in my profession, which he is not. Why is he not known? He doesn't have a union card, so to speak; no students who must and colleagues who feel they ought to read him. Scratch my back and I'll scratch yours; don't scratch mine and I'll not scratch yours. I reviewed his first book favorably and still admire it. In this way we became known to each other. Eventually he visited me in Chicago. He asked to speak to a faculty group so I assembled the Chaos Club (no officers, no members, no constitution) and he addressed it—with success. I had no reason to be embarrassed by his performance.

Jordan made at least one valid and important point in his *Homo Sapiens*. This is that individuality is a cosmic fifth dimension (I would say, variable) of nature, additional to the four of space and time. It certainly is. There is a hierarchy of degrees of individuation, from particles or atoms of a given type up through molecules with a given chemical formula, single cells, multicellular animals, vertebrates, Homo sapiens. Not only true, this is important. A basic ethical imperative is to respect individual differences in human beings, and one of the most penetrating criteria of the respect due a species of animal is the extent of individual variety found in it. Also the notion that in atoms there is no individuality at all is suspect. "Our nets are too coarse to catch the differences" may be the right way to put that point. But certainly individual atomic differences are worlds apart from human differences. What is wrong with doctrinaire masculinism and some doctrinaire feminism is the same, the neglect of individual differences.

The only review of Rudolf Jordan I have read, other than mine, was by a now-deceased philosopher with a hobby in evolutionary theory that according to a biology group that listened to him talk, was "90 percent sound biology and 10 percent crazy." The craziness was obvious from a simple logical point of view. This man (why give his name, he convinced almost no one?) wrote scornfully of Jordan who was by far his superior by any reasonable criterion. Professors should be able to appreciate good thinking, with or without a union card to certify it.

My ornithological interest was a principal reason for my extensive traveling. There are two kinds of travel. The tourist kind is an escape from our normal work and preoccupations. It may teach us something of the world. But it tends to be shallow as education and at times a new form of drudgery. A Russian studying in Germany said to me, "Traveling is work." The other kind of travel is that which has connections with our normal work and interests: the travel of a student studying abroad, the teacher teaching abroad, and many other forms. I once read about a person with a keen interest in gem cutting and setting who went to Mexico to see an enthusiast there with the same vocation or avocation. He was received with great cordiality and had a fascinating time. I have been lucky in traveling much, but mostly not as a tourist. First in the army, then as a postdoctoral student, then as a teacher, but also as a bird watcher and ornithologist. In a number of countries, bird watchers have shown me great kindness. Once when I worried about a man's taking, as I feared, too much trouble in this way, someone else said, "Don't give it a thought. He's just like all these enthusiasts, delighted to find another one."

I wrote to a gentleman somewhat knowledgable about birds who lived in the Philippines about my wish to learn about the birds during a few days stay in his country. Here is how his letter began, "First, I want to thank you for your interest in our birds." What more needed to be said? When we arrived at the airport and he met us, I asked where he had made reservations for us (as I had requested him to do). He said we were to stay first in his own home. He had, however, arranged for us then to be guests for some days at a biological station a short way up Mt. McKilling, the best bird place near Manilla. This we did and with great joy. Mr. — — — was exactly the gracious person his letter convinced me he must be.

In Australia I had the name of an engineer who was also a fine bird watcher (now deceased), and quickly we were invited to have dinner with his family. After dinner I said that I was a good dish washer, whereupon to my surprise Mrs. Hugh Wilson said, *not* something like "of course that wouldn't do"—the usual response to my statement—but, "I want to see this professorial dishwashing." Needless to say, she remained a friend for many years thereafter. Her husband did a great deal to acquaint me with Australian birds.

Several others in Australia did likewise, including the famous naturalist and author, Alexander Chisholm. My first encounter with him got off to a slightly awkward start. He had invited me over the phone to have tea with him. I could not recall what he had said about the place of our meeting, so I looked him up in the phone book and went to the address given at the time he had indicated. A lady came to the door and said, "But he is at his office." And then I realized that I was indeed in a British country, where tea is a part of business. I phoned Chisholm at his office and told him what had happened. "How could you do such a rash thing?" was his reply, which struck me as a tactful as well as refreshingly original way to greet a mistake of this kind. So the tea was postponed to the following day, with the same third party, a distinguished ornithologist, again included.

Later Chisholm took me on a birding expedition with lots of interesting birds to see and above all hear, as my specialty is song. He did something else. He told me I must get in touch with Mrs. Curtis of Tambourine Mountain on whose place there were numerous rain forest birds, and who knew not only all the birds but "every nest" and other details of the bird life around her. So I wrote to her. She wrote back inviting me, my wife, and our ten-year-old daughter to stay several nights. This we did. It was as Chisholm said, she knew those birds. She was a woman with great pluck, whose husband was kind, but a born loser, as the unkind phrase goes. He had had to give up the occupation he liked, the growing and sending to market of oranges, because the boxes were too heavy for him to handle. So he was taking care of cows, which he did not like and was no great success at handling. A redeeming feature was that he had never tried to discourage his wife's bird hobby. And he was cordial enough to us. Mrs. Curtis, now no longer living, supplemented the family income by growing flowers to sell to florists. Her son is a forester, who knows birds and has done some recording of songs. Twenty years later, I met him and his wife and saw Hilda Curtis once more, then still very spry and active. Her place is no longer the bird paradise it was, though not through any fault of hers. The whole mountain is much less wild and natural than it was in 1952.

I was told of one bird man in Australia that he was not friendly to women, so I visited his place alone. He was reasonably friendly to me. I was told of another birder who was not friendly to anyone, so I crossed him off my list. Ever since I have wondered, could there really be such a bird man? In fact I have known only one other with any such reputation.

D. C. H. and I visited Myles North in Kenya. He had been commissioner under the British but had retired and still lived in Nairobi. He was an excellent bird observer and a recorder of songs for the Cornell Laboratory of Ornithology. He wrote to us that he expected us to come with some knowledge of Swahili, so my wife bought a grammar in that language and when he greeted us in Swahili at the airport she replied in Swahili. He discovered, too, that she was a trained botanist and not without knowledge of birds. "I have great respect for her," he confided to me. North showed us the birds we wanted to see and hear. If I were only less stupid about the mechanical and electronic details, he would have made me a much better recorder of songs than I have managed to become, for he was a master.

North said, concerning the native government about to take over in Kenya (we had a good look at Kenyatta, the expected head of that government, in a restaurant): "Let them try it; they'll find out how hard it is." He was no die-hard imperialist; but only a realist about the situation. His fear was that Kenyatta too soon would be superseded by some less sensible younger man. So far (written years ago) this has not happened. North had a relative, a safari leader, who was far less tolerant of the passing of British rule. He was a former hunter who said that he had lost all desire to kill animals. He wanted only to see them, and was willing to be paid to give others the opportunity to see or to shoot them. He took us at a cost price on a day's tour in the wild animal preserve near Nairobi. Seeing lions was not especially thrilling; they are now semidomesticated. But a leopard, seldom seen by daylight, that my wife was the first to see in the bushes with his tail showing was more exciting, and a mother warthog with young, all running off with tails held vertically upwards, was a sight to remember. The erect tails must help the group to keep each other in sight in the long grass. And of course the ungulate animals, in Africa, always are superb as spectacles. Always—while they still last.

The quotation used to label this section is from the parting words of a Japanese birder who helped me find the now somewhat rare species, the Japanese robin, a relative of the nightingale, in the Japanese mountains. He was a worker in the Japanese forest service, a job he chose so that he always could be with the birds. This man had done for the crown prince of Japan what he was doing for us. We stayed in the cottage built for that royal person, who thought he ought to know his country's birds.

Kasuke Hoshino (another no-longer-living friend), owner of a resort hotel in Karuizawa, also helped us learn about Japanese birds. In this hotel, rooms are named after song birds whose pictures are on the doors. His parting words to us were: "We shall be friends as long as the birds sing in the spring."

Three Russian Aristocrats

H. L. was from one of the leading aristocratic families in Russia, whose name is known to all who read Russian literature. In this country he changed his name entirely. He became a successful professor at a good university and even won a monetary prize for an essay on ethics, his favorite subject. He was highly educated as well as bright; his wife was bright and not highly educated. She had been a dancer. Perhaps this is why he held a low opinion of female abilities. He actually declared to me, "No woman can be a genius." This is not quite so obviously absurd as the old saying in Japan, "The stupidest man is more intelligent than the brightest woman," but considering the highly trained mind that could bring itself to so speak it is in the same class. I have forgotten whether I made what would normally be part of my response to such statements, "clearly Jane Austen was a genius." As a literary critic has said, "Five (or should one say six) novels, every one a masterpiece, do not happen by accident." If the word *genius* is not to be used in this connection, we had better dismiss the word and start over again.

It is worth thinking about, has Russia ever produced a first-rate feminine writer? (This was written before I had read Ayn Rand's *We, the Living.*) If not, so much the worse for the cultural and social traditions of that country. Japan produced an enlightened empress (sixth century) and the first great novelist in all the world (Lady Murasaki, eleventh century), before the blight of Confucian male chauvinism swept over that country. (I learn all this from D. C. Hartshorne.) If ever a great man had a blind spot it was Confucius in his attitude toward the other sex. A Chinese-American scholar I know says that, bad as Aristotle was on this subject, Confucius was worse still.

H. L. experienced the humiliation of his wife going off for a time with another man. Presumably, this did not improve his image of feminity. To do him justice, however, it should be said that he took a substantial part of the blame upon himself. "From a conventional, superficial point of view," said he, "she is to blame. However, looking more deeply, I am not sure." This was the man at his most discerning and unself-serving best.

H. L. told my wife that she was "the most naturally coquettish woman he had ever met" and made it clear that he approved of her for that reason. That she is one of the superbly intelligent and capable persons in the world perhaps escaped him. That her "coquetry"

Fig. 25. With Adam Blatner, a psychiatrist who finds my
philosophy relevant to his work

never harmed anyone, or deceived anyone into thinking she wanted
to seduce him or have him seduce her, he possibly did understand.
In any case it is the fact.

Maxim Kastyluk was another refugee, but in this case from the
Ukraine. He too was from an aristocratic family with a title,
which—as he said—was irrelevant, and hence to be discarded, in
this country. He was a singer with a fine voice who should have been
a great star. He was eking out a living by singing in night clubs and
injuriously straining his voice to be heard over the chatter of such
places. He was a gentleman through and through, and a nice friend
to my wife, also a singer. He taught her to sing some Russian songs;
only later did she find that her Ukrainian accent was a bit amusing
to non-Ukrainian Russians. But that was hardly M. K.'s fault. Dorothy
had learned to speak (I mean sing) *his* Russian. M. K. was one of the
select few one meets in a lifetime in whose character one detects no

moral flaw, no baseness or egocentricity, a *thoroughly* "nice" person. And one not very lucky in his life history. He was a younger man than H. L. when forced to leave Russia, and he had less powerful friends to help him get out.

My third Russian refugee aristocrat, whose name I forget, I met in Germany (three years before my marriage) while staying at a boarding-house in Marburg. The landlady, an excellent soul, told me about him before he came to visit (no doubt to "sponge" on her). She was fond of him and amused by him. He was very much an oddity. "The Bolscheviks did well to kick us out," he said—though in what language he said it I cannot now say. As the landlady told me, "He speaks all languages equally badly (*gleich schlecht*)" He gave as his two great enthusiasms Goethe and Napoleon. He also admired the English, "They have character." Somehow, I discovered in him another enthusiasm, which was for Dante. I happened to have a French translation of the Inferno. So my Russian friend and I worked our way through a canto of that poem and I committed to memory the great dismal passage about Hell that begins, "Per me ci va nella cita dolente / Per me ci va nel eterno dolore. Dinanci a me non fur cose create / Et yo eterno duro . . . " I still wonder at the combination of genius and moral blindness that I see in this passage. I do not recall employing English with — — —. If we used German, my best foreign language, then with my translation we were working in three languages, one of which I scarcely knew at all.

Why were the Bolscheviks justified in expelling the aristocrats? "We were no good. I never did any work in my life. Oh yes, I did once for a short time. It was some translating, but I soon got tired of it. .. "

Some Excellent Household Helpers

Among the memorable people my wife and I have known are several helpers in household tasks. There was Nannie, the black cleaning woman who had been with the Cooper family for many years. Nannie asked my wife, some years after our marriage, "Miss Dorothy, what is philosophy? I know it's what Mr. Charles teaches, but what is it?" My wife gave a brief explanation and then by way of illustration mentioned Kant's Categorical Imperative. "Oh," said Nannie, "say that again two or three times, Miss Dorothy. I want to stand in the door of professor Cooper's study and say to him, 'Professor Cooper, where do you stand on the Categorical Imperative?' "

Dorothy went on to mention the philosophical issue between (one form of) idealism and realism, whether things are or are not merely ideas in our minds. "Oh, Miss Dorothy," said Nannie, "I's no idealist. I's a realist. Why if I were an idealist, I'd say dirt is only an idea, and I'd not bother to sweep up this real dirt here." When told about this, Charles Morris, in my department, said that Nannie should be given a degree.

As Nannie said, she lacked education, but not "mother wit." She called the old male cat "Mr. Teddy," and once was heard to mutter, "Mr. Teddy, I spizes you." She had to clean after the animal, and endure its smells. Nannie also said, "I had one child by my first husband, one child by my second husband, and in between I had one by myself."

Another occasion when Nannie showed her capacity to go straight to the point was when she asked why, when we went to our country cottage in Indiana, we did not take the cat with us and was told it was because a cat might kill the birds. "Oh," said Nannie, "the birds are alla time makin moe." And the fact is that the nonhuman species for ages can survive predation by nonhuman animals; it is chiefly human predators and human habitat destroyers that make our species the great enemy of species in general on this planet.

We had another dark-skinned cleaning woman of superior quality. Myrtle Bomar was a true expert in housecleaning. "I specializes," is how she put it. No dish washing or cooking. But the vacuum cleaning, sweeping, window washing, or floor washing, she took completely in charge, deciding which week to do what, so that my wife had no need, and was not wanted, to instruct her in such details. She planned and executed it all, and according to high standards. She had not had very good luck with men (her one husband was alcoholic and abusive and died after a long illness) and did not especially favor them. She tolerated me, but without noticeable enthusiasm. But she and my wife had always excellent understanding. We kept in touch with her for many years after leaving Chicago. Unlike Nannie she was not very humorous or especially cheerful, but neither did she complain. When our daughter lived for a time in Chicago, after her marriage, Myrtle, who had given up working for people, made an exception for her, partly because of our long relationship and partly no doubt because she knew that our daughter has the kindness, good sense, and respect for persons of her mother.

A warm-hearted household helper (when we lived in Atlanta), a splendid ironer of clothes, was a religious soul with very strong ethical convictions. Her name was Marie. She had recommended another Afro-American woman who helped us now and then, and this other woman must later have done something radically contrary to Marie's principles. For when, after not hearing about her for some time, Dorothy asked how Annie was getting on Marie said, "I have forgotten Annie. I have forgotten that Annie was ever on this earth!" Never again did we dare ask Marie about Annie. Whatever she had done it must have been indeed wicked by Marie's standards, and the subject was clearly taboo. Annie had become a nonperson.

Marie (who crocheted two wool afghans, one for Dorothy, one for our daughter, with us buying the wool) used to sing religious songs softly to herself in the basement of our house while she ironed. I often think about the many people, of all social classes, too, for whom traditional religion seems to do so much but for whom my rationalized philosophical religion would do so little. Over a century ago R. W. Emerson faced this problem. It gives me pause, as one might say. The best I can do with it is to note the fact that some of the ministers and theologians, a minority no doubt, in various religious groups (that include many simply pious people) from rabbis to Catholic priests, lay theologians or philosophers, Methodist ministers or theologians, even a scholar or two in Seventh Day Adventist institutions, find my writings helpful—and show good understanding of them. Nevertheless the whole matter puzzles me.

My late colleague O. K. Bouwsma, the Wittgensteinian, who combined faithful membership in a Presbyterian church with a total absence of any constructive philosophy of religion, and what seemed a complete skepticism of the possibility of any rational knowledge of God, any rationally defensible religious metaphysics, also puzzles me. He was a kind man, but as a philosopher for me very unsatisfactory.

We once exchanged reminiscences about our early readings in philosophy. We both had read pretty much all the English and American idealists of that time, Bouwsma with the hope of finding a justification of his traditional religious beliefs, I with hope of finding beliefs that would have the religious values that mankind needs but without the errors, the superstitions, that I long ago came to believe are to be found in every religious tradition. Bouwsma reached the conclusion that he would have to be religious without any positive help from philosophy. All it could do would be to remove the barriers to faith erected by the false claims of metaphysics parading as knowledge. In other words (Wittgenstein) philosophy is therapeutic, and what it cures is only its own previous mistakes. In contrast, I reached the conclusion that the idealists of five or more decades ago had some aspects of metaphysical truth but, not surprisingly, had mixed these truths with partial confusions and mistakes such as human weaknesses might lead us to expect. First on my own and then with help from Peirce's and Whitehead's and many other writings, I set myself to overcome these confusions and mistakes within the limits of my own human weaknesses.

The most unhappy seeming person who ever worked for us explained her attitude by the facts that she (her name is lost) was a widow who, until her husband died, had not had to do outside work. (One thinks of the saying, "The saddest thing is recalling happier days." Perhaps one strand of wisdom is in cherishing, rather than mourning, memory of good times.) One day our dour helper arrived for once in a lively frame of mind. Here is her story. I was held up on the way to your house! ("Oh?" said we.) Yes, a young fellow sidled up to me and said, "Have you got any money?" "No, damn it," I said, "have you?" "Oh," he said, "that's all right." "But it's not all right," I said, "now get going!"

We once had a helper (I think it was Myrtle Bomar) who told us what we already knew, that the three persons, named Pratt, living next door in Chicago were crazy. There had been plenty of signs of that. "In [some town in Illinois], there were the white folks, there were the colored folks, and there were the Pratts." There was a domineering older sister, a younger sister, and a brother. They had an income of unknown source, but did nothing constructive except keeping house. Finally their house burned down, leaving only the older sister alive. She explained to a reported inquiry how her two siblings had started to come down the front stairs to escape from the fire and she had told them to come down the back stairs instead. In effect she had sent them to their deaths. The ambiguity was not removed. The survivor used to come and poke in the ruins, but nothing was done with the dismal skeleton of a building until the city declared it a nuisance and tore it down. The one male member of the threesome could use musical notation and once sold me for a small sum a song he had written praising Herbert Hoover, then candidate for the presidency. My wife recognized the music as from *Aida*, the Anvil Chorus.

The most ideal household helpers we have had were two foreigners. One was a Mrs. Katayama in Kyoto and the other a German refugee (not Jewish) in New York City.

Mrs. Katayama was a wife and mother who had worked for Americans under the occupation. She had a husband and children to care for, but she came to help us on three visits to Japan. Her English was good and everything about her was good. Rain or shine she came on her bicycle. Was there some screening to tack on, she did that in no time. She did the shopping and cooked lunch, buying economically and cooking exquisitely. When we left Japan the first time she shed tears. When Dorothy said that people in Japan were suspicious of her because of her grey hair, Mrs. K. said, "They shouldn't think that way about you. You're so charming." She promised that any time Dorothy came to Japan she would come to help her. Several times she has kept that promise. Mrs. K. liked the American country music then being much heard on the Japanese radio. I told her this was our only disagreement. I preferred the Japanese music! Once some American songs were being sung in a nearby house. I said the singers were Japanese; she said they were Americans. She went closer to listen and came back with a sunshiny grin on her face. The people were talking in Japanese.

Lillie Olsen was a bright and very likeable young German widow whose part-Jewish husband had been murdered. She knew little English, but she and Dorothy quickly realized that they would understand each other. And when she saw our one-year-old daughter she *knew* she had to work for us. "When I talk German to Emily she really understands me," she said. Of course Emily understood her, language at that age being peripheral. Like Mrs. Katayama, Mrs. Olsen could and would do anything desired. She had been a gourmet cook for Bavarian nobility. She told us how Hitler regularly used to pass a certain spot visible from a window of the palace where she worked and she tried to persuade a man she knew to assassinate him. He was unwilling to make the attempt.

Mrs. Olsen was in training for a better-paid job, though not necessarily a more skillful one. If people were wiser, household help would have been better paid and better treated all along. Money is not easily better spent than on really good household help. So thinks this curmudgeon of a philosopher. Where wives are the chief household help the principle definitely applies to them.

We have had several other very likeable people help us with household chores, including one in Chicago tragically killed by a motorist. Her daughter also gave us good and friendly service. Unpleasant experiences with people in this role have been rare. One troubled us simply by being so persistently gloomy. We have almost never fired anyone outright. In one case a combination of difficulties, including a husband's attempt to get his hands on some money promised as a loan to his wife, money that, we believed, he wanted for gambling, did bring about that unhappy termination. One ill-tempered young woman we were unable to understand fired herself, or at least left a note claiming she was leaving town.

We had one excellent worker, a white woman who was a preacher in a fundamentalist church, who after the oil embargo could not drive the miles separating her house from ours. One unhappy girl living next door did some work for us to earn pocket money and stole a twenty dollar bill, as she eventually confessed by letter, but we had such a dim view of her mother's treatment of her, and of her brothers and her father as well, that we rather sympathized with the poor girl, who was evidently doing her best to change her ways.

"E. L."—A Southern Gentleman of a New School

For the seven years (1955-1962) we lived in Atlanta, Georgia, we had as neighbor one of the most angelic human beings I have been privileged to know. His energetic wife called him by his first two initials, E. L. He was a retired schoolteacher and school Principal. When he retired from these functions, he was given another responsibility for several years in connection with the Georgia schools that required him to make trips to northern colleges. I believe it had to do with scholarship grants for both whites and nonwhites. When we moved into our house next to the Floyds, E. L. immediately came to offer us any help we could conceivably need. At the time I suffered from lingering bronchitis, but still had to work fairly hard as our furniture was unloaded and we settled ourselves in the new home. After a few days of this activity Floyd called out to me, "Come on over. I want you to help me." I thought, "I can't refuse, considering the friendly cordiality he has been showing." So over I came. He pointed to two chairs sitting in the shade by the side of his house, and said, "I want you to help me hold down these chairs. You're working too hard." So I helped him in the manner requested.

Floyd was elderly and suffered from rather serious deafness, but I have not known another man who came so close to soaring above this handicap. It never seemed to dampen his humor. He was full of gusto. Once when I told him that it often seemed to me that, compared to many people, I had never had any real troubles, he said that he felt the same way about his life. Another time, as we looked into the beautiful, wooded, unbulldozed grounds surrounding both our houses he spoke about the wonderful ways of nature: "Don't you think it is all very well-ordered?" I said I did indeed.

For some time I dared not mention race questions to my thoroughly Southern neighbor, who had spent nearly all his life in Georgia, except for short trips North. One day he introduced the subject in his unique fashion. "Did you read what Faulkner said about desegregation?" he asked: "To object to desegregation in these days is like objecting to snow in Alaska." It was quite evident that he delighted in this remark. Though his own father had owned a hundred slaves, he knew that racism was no longer defensible, if it ever had been. On the other hand, he did think that more had been done in the South for the advancement of Negroes than most Northerners realized.

Floyd was an historian and ideally should have written a history of Georgia politics, which he understood from the inside. He

liked to mimic Herman Talmadge making a speech, first to rural audi-
ences, and then to urban ones, to bring out the different approaches
the wily senator could command. He also told how Talmadge would
hire college boys in the summer before an election to dress and act
like country yokels, dropping into village stores or taverns and
pretending to be naive supporters of the senator. Soon after the
famous Supreme Court decision of 1954, the Georgia legislature
passed some hasty bills designed to save segregation. Floyd wanted
to know if I had read about this. "I've been telling you what sort of
legislators we have in Georgia," he said, "but you would never believe
me. Now perhaps you will."

He told me how, when he was teaching full time, he was asked
also to function as principal. He agreed, but he explained how he
survived the very heavy schedule. He would take a big nap before
dinner and after dinner go to his school office to hear complaints.
He would put his feet up on his desk and relax while holding
these hearings.

The Floyds had a married child in Boston who used to send
tape recordings in lieu of letters, which the parents happily played
on a small recorder. Once, when a liberal Georgia legislator who was
also our lawyer was helping us make a will, we all three went over to
the Floyds to have them witness our signatures. The lawyer then told
us a weird tale about a married woman whose will he was asked to
make, in the presence of the husband. The old lady at first said to the
lawyer, "I want all my money to go to the Lord." "Yes," said the lawyer,
"but the Lord has to work through human agents." The lady repeated
her mysterious statement. Finally she condescended to get down to
earthly particulars. The money was to be divided between a number
of agencies, including a kindness to animals society. The husband
attempted to intervene at this point, but was silenced by his wife's
brusque "Shut up, Fred!" Here Mr. Floyd could no longer contain himself. Turning to me he said gaily, "We know all about that kind of
thing, don't we? 'Shut up Fred!' " This merely meant, of course, that
Mrs. Floyd (like my wife) was a woman who knew her own mind and
was not in helpless awe of her husband.

Floyd told how, when he was quite young, he was offered a promising and probably lucrative career in a law office. He told his wife (or

bride, I'm not sure which) about this and said that they might always be poor if he turned down this offer and became a teacher instead. The response was unambiguous. "Which career do you really want to pursue?" "To teach," he told her. "Then," she said, "that's what you must do."

In case the reader is curious about how the lawyer's will-making story came out, it was as follows. The will was made, ignoring Fred; the woman died, whereupon Fred's lawyer waited upon our lawyer to protest the unfairness of the will. "I' ll tell you what," said the lawyer-legislator, "if you will call upon the five institutions named in the will and get them to agree to give half their share of the money to the husband we can settle this thing out of court." And so it was done. If anyone wants an example of how lawyers can be useful, I offer this as a fair specimen.

CHAPTER ELEVEN

The Move
To the South

(1955-1962)

The Era of Civil Rights Begins

Our change of residence from Chicago to Atlanta followed quickly after the 1954 Supreme Court decision had announced the end of the clear separation between northern and southern states on the issue of racism in education. Other forces also were pushing things in the same direction. Many blacks had moved North and so had many southern whites; in both ways carrying northward elements of the southern situation. From now on the problem was more and more national rather than regional, and even so far as regional, it was less and less a matter of latitude. In this respect one does not think altogether highly of academics who refuse offers from southern universities on the ground of southern racism. Racism is alive and well rather far North—tragically enough. And there have been great changes in the South.

I wrote more than one letter on the issue while in Atlanta and the splendid *Constitution* published them. There were one or two hate phone calls. The economic core of the issue emerges ever more clearly as the essential aspect, the one hardest to remedy. T. V. Smith wrote long ago that the key to effective democracy is the possession of skills, ideally by every citizen. Unskilled persons (whether male or female) are difficult to treat as equals; for in a lot that matters they are not equals. (Only some wives—or husbands—only some mothers—or fathers—are skilled even as such, more's the pity.) And so equality of opportunity to acquire skills becomes the quintessential form of equality. Equality in opportunity to acquire political skills is crucial, and in this the South has made its greatest advances.

The improvements were only beginning while we were in Atlanta; but they were obviously on the way. I attended a meeting at which the father of Martin Luther King spoke, as well as Benjamin Mays, the great educator, whom we had met in Chicago.

A former student of mine in Chicago was an able man and an important leader in the NAACP in Atlanta who skillfully managed the desegregation of the buses there. He also taught philosophy at Morehouse College, of which Mays was president; and in addition he was pastor of a desegregated church in the Morehouse neighborhood. Unfortunately, not being superhuman, he could not do all these things and make much progress in his scholarship. Not only did he not finish his work for the Ph.D. degree but he showed no signs of being in a position to do so. President Mays would have liked to

Fig. 26. James, Charles, and Richard in
middle age, 1962

see him accepted as graduate student at Emory University where I taught, thus desegregating that institution. Many of us there knew that desegregation was soon coming; but one wants to begin with a clear case. And there was no one we knew about in philosophy who could constitute such a case. Desegregation of Emory occurred only after I left Georgia.

Emory: A Small but Good University

The seven years at Emory were, except for some misfortunes my wife suffered there, good years. At last I had the experience of teaching in a smallish but good university, a place where one comes to know the faculty rather generally. I was a biggish frog in a smallish pond. I had no enemies, and I did not have to struggle to influence what went on in the department.

A number of excellent students came for graduate work: Lewis Ford (now editor of *Process Studies*), Lucio Chiaraviglio, John Gilmour, Dickens (good book on Thoreau), and a number of others. John Wilcox was already there, and like Lewis Ford went on to Yale for degrees. Wilcox wrote in some respects the best book on Nietzsche. He was an example of the completely liberated southerner, who achieved his liberalism without leaving the South, though eventually for professional reasons he did go North. Lucio I had as student in Chicago. He was trained in science and engineering, and was intellectually as formidable a student as I have encountered. His mind moves fast and commands much technical knowledge. He is at home in symbolic logic, computer science, evolutionary theory, and has become knowledgeable in ethology. He thinks my *Born to Sing* book on bird song "the best" of my books. He was born in Rome, brought up in Buenos Aires, and married a Kentucky farmer's daughter, an Emory graduate student. He is an aristocrat, if there is one.

My colleagues at Emory were very pleasant. I sometimes recalled a remark of Charner Perry's about my going to Emory. He knew that he could not dissuade me from leaving Chicago, but he did say: "I could be happy with people who were not philosophers, and I can be happy with good philosophers, but I could not be happy with poor philosophers." I well understood the three clauses in this statement, and have but a single critical comment: there are several criteria of good when it comes to philosophers. The Chicago department had some very knowledgeable people. They were also gifted pedagogues. Their skill in oral examinations (which I somewhat dislike) was manifest. But how much creative searching for truth about the cosmos was going on in their operations? How much was their knowledge not high-grade pedantry? How much did they talk in clichés? How often did they approach mathematical clarity in their thinking (as Carnap did when he was there)? There was a certain dullness in the talk. Warner Wick once remarked, "We're a prosy lot in this department." There was a lack of poetry. Nor was wit much in evidence.

At Emory the philosophers were not epoch-making innovators. Their writings were not highly impressive. But they were cultivated, scholarly gentlemen; they did not talk in clichés; they had poetry and wit. And they were not pretentious. So I did not feel that Perry's in itself wise remark furnished any reason to regret that I was at Emory.

Roy Loemker was a splendid teacher, a learned man, and besides, an enjoyable humorous companion. He once accused me of being "a triple threat man," because I could write on ornithological, philosophical, and theological topics. There was perhaps a touch of envy in this, for Roy was not without ambition. His duties as chairman, for a time as dean, and as teacher limited the degree to which his ambition could be realized.

Richard Hocking, according to my speculation, would have shone as an historian had his father's example not caused him to feel an obligation to function as a speculative philosopher. Mention a historical topic, either in the history of philosophy or in general history, not excluding Asiatic history, and Richard would come to life in striking fashion. He knew about the topic. Another noticeable thing was the freshness of his language. His grandfather had been a poet and his mother, the poet's daughter, was highly imaginative. One could count on Richard for a picturesque phrase for situations as they arose. "He needs a map of the area," for a student not knowledgeable in philosophy. The special flavor of each new individual or interpersonal situation seemed to challenge Richard to find a word or phrase for it. Such a man I do not find dull.

There was the additional fact that at Emory philosophy of religion was central, whereas in Chicago only the theological seminaries and the divinity school harbored people interested in that. There also were able scientists at Emory whom one could talk to about nature.

A bonus during my stay on that campus was that I had for the only time in my life, the privilege of teaching ornithology. It was a noncredit course in adult education, and produced one very satisfying result. A young woman attended who had a pet hawk which she brought to show the class. Years later I received a communication from her enclosing a poem that is almost certainly the finest poetic expression in any language of the territorial function of bird song. Here is the most essential stanza:

> *Two robins will not share a bush,*
> *Two in a boundary makes a feud;*
> *There is a wall around the thrush,*
> *And song creates its solitude.*

It is good ornithology and good poetry. I am proud to have helped to make it possible.

Dorothy also had some good experiences in Atlanta. She is a singer, and a graduate student there, Homer Edwards, organized a Collegium Musicum in which she happily sang choral music by Bach and other classical composers she loves. Unluckily, an automobile accident in a friend's car gave her some broken ribs and diminished her capacity to breathe in the fashion singing requires. Dorothy also was a principal in organizing an Arts Council, which put on a musical for children that made quite a lot of money and gave a number of children their first experience on the stage. But there was a misunderstanding about how the money earned was to be used. Our understanding was that it should go to the Collegium Musicum; some others had a different idea. The strain of this conflict was one of the two greatest misfortunes of our Emory stay.

Homer Edwards, student in history at Emory, who later became chairman of a fine arts department at Wayne State University, was and is one of our most delightful friends. Besides his service in founding and conducting the Collegium Musicum, and in this way enriching the life around him, his very being is a benefit to others. When Dorothy complained, as she sometimes did, that, though I had taken her half way around the world, I had always brought her back the same way instead of going on around, Homer said, "I see what it is: Charles doesn't believe that the world is round." Once when we were traveling together in Europe and I had bought some dried bananas and offered him one, telling him what it was, he tasted it and said, "Hm—it tastes like dried bananas." Homer was a Georgian, a wonderfully urbane, modest soul, and an example of the generalization I incline to that it is the unegotistical people who are really humorous. He is learned in the history of the arts.

Lecturing in Seattle and Kyoto

One attractive feature of Atlanta was its nearness to the tropics. A bird trip to Jamaica and one to Mexico, a partly philosophical and partly ornithological trip to Costa Rica and Panama, another to South America, were among the excursions whose cost was thus reduced.

A trip to Japan in 1958 was facilitated in a different fashion. Emory was generous in giving me leave of absence (the University of Chicago had also been good about this) and a stroke of sheer luck was added. Arthur Murphy at the University of Washington was going to Texas and wanted a replacement for a quarter just preceding my planned trip to the Orient. He offered me more money than I had ever encountered for so short a time, explaining to me afterwards that he thought we were on a semester system at Emory and he would have to pay me accordingly. "However, it's no more than you deserve," he added.

That quarter in Seattle changed my life once and for all by changing my wife's once and for all. She had learned in Chicago to admire Japanese prints, taken to see them by her father. In Seattle there were excellent courses on the Far East. Dorothy went back to school after over thirty years. A more enthusiastic student, doing homework more enthusiastically, has not been known. Wellesley and her professorial parents had taught her long ago how to do research.

Fig. 27. Receiving an honorary degree from Jan
Van der Veken, 1978

One student in Washington interested me especially. An agnostic, he yet responded to the eloquence and sublime originality of Whitehead's chapter on God in *Process and Reality* by calling it, quite appropriately I think, "the greatest essay on natural theology since the *Timaeus*." He has been handicapped by eye trouble.

Going to Japan caused me to do some reading on Buddhism. I found T. R. V. Murti's *The Central philosophy of Buddhism* fascinating. It showed so clearly how Bradley's problems about relations had been discovered long before in Asia, and "solved" much as Bradley solved them, by a retreat into mysticism. In my opinion neither the Buddhists nor Bradley gave an accurate analysis of relatedness. Eight years later I went to Banaras and discussed the matter with Murti. We reached no agreement, but the judgment I have just expressed seemed to me confirmed. The relations problem has been best analyzed, I am confident, not by Buddhism, Bradley, or Murti, not by James, Russell, Quine, or Carnap, but by Peirce and Whitehead. There still are some loose ends.

CHAPTER TWELVE

The University of Texas

(1962-   )

John Silber

After seven years at Emory I had, according to the rules, three years more to teach there. I would then, unless the rule was waived in my case, be retired. I was prepared more or less to accept this, and had always said that I wanted to retire early. But several things had happened that made Emory less attractive. They had nothing to do with the professional and institutional aspects of the philosophy department, but something to do with the whole social community so far as it affected Dorothy. A terrible car accident had damaged her health (and might easily have killed her). If an otherwise good friend had had seat belts in his car, as (and I think he knew this) I had written years before all car owners should have, she might have been scarcely injured at all. The residual results of this accident, combined with events connected with the community organization for the arts in which she took part, brought about an ailment that made life seem less attractive in that community. Still, I had no definite thoughts about leaving until I was invited to speak at the University of Texas in Austin—or rather, until I actually was in Austin and had given my speech. Then John Silber, chairman of the department, took me to lunch and surprised me by asking, would I come to Texas? A few years before I had turned down a similar request from Texas by my one-time colleague Murphy, telling him that I held, with Big Bill Tildon the tennis star, to the motto, Never Change a winning game. (At Emory things were then going well.)

For some reason it had not occurred to me that Silber had an ulterior motive in inviting me to speak and taking me to lunch. We first had some discussion of his studies at Yale and I was impressed by his account of these studies. Then, the bombshell: come to Texas! For every objection John had an answer. What about my doctoral candidates? We'll let you go back in spring for some weeks to take care of them. This was in fact done. It turned out that at Texas I could go on half pay and half time at seventy, and teach indefinitely that way, whereas Emory retired completely at sixty-eight. Money? Texas had much more of it than Emory, which was then at a low ebb financially. John is a very persuasive advocate in a private talk. As a public orator he is likely to be somewhat abrasive, but he is sensitive to the person in front of him and knows how to talk to just that person. He half convinced me.

Back at Emory I drew up a numerical balance, giving points on various counts, including obligations to students, and so on, to each option. It added up to fifty-fifty. So I told Dorothy, "The decision will be

Fig. 28. With Donald Viney, a young philosopher who has written a book on my arguments for God's existence

yours. Go to Austin, look for a house, if you like the looks of things we'll go." She went, she did; so we did.

I must say for Silber that he did everything he promised and more. No one has ever treated me better. And, so long as he was chairman, I greatly enjoyed the association with him. His brilliant, unpredictable remarks were a delight. He struck me as something like Hutchins, witty, penetrating, ingenious. And of course he had had much more training in philosophy. But, like Hutchins, he was somewhat remote from science. Like Hutchins he was bold and not always tactful or patient, suffering fools or the slow-witted not too gladly. Still, as chairman I found him outstanding and have very little criticism of his operations in that office. He was humane and fair, except in one case where an initial prejudice prevented him, as I judged, from properly evaluating the abilities and personality of a young man whom we did not retain. Otherwise I can see a case for all his decisions.

The change from chairman to dean I could not on personal grounds welcome for I knew, in spite of his denials, that many things would be different the minute he got into that other, more pretentious office. As chairman he knew everyone he was dealing with, most of them very well. He knew the limits of his power and kept within them, but used the power vigorously and with judgment. As dean he could not know half the people whose destinies he strongly influenced, and the limits of his power were no longer clear and obvious. Also he worried about the department he had so largely created, now no longer under his effective guidance. No chairman could please him by his way of running that department. I finally wrote him the one letter of advice I ever wrote a dean: "you have created a splendid department, why not show some trust in your creation?" He saw the point. But it was not an easy situation for him, nevertheless.

John talked a foundation into donating a quarter of a million dollars to introduce an Oxford-style college system in Austin. Higher authorities made him return the money. Such frustrations could not occur to a mere chairman, who could not attract any such sum. Even had the regents not fired John as dean, it seems to me an open question whether a deanship is the right job for a John Silber. It fires his imagination but does not really give him enough power to act on his dreams.

John told me about his early history in the university. Desegregation was beginning to be discussed. The president was opposed. John, a mere instructor, went to argue the matter with him. The president listened a bit and then said, "You remind me of— — —and — — —," evidently naming some Texas liberals of those days. "Oh," said John, "if I were going to imitate anybody, it would be somebody worthwhile, like Socrates or Jesus, not two Texans I never heard of." As a result, it was years before instructor Silber got a dollar of salary raise. But—the whole university knew he was there. The Hutchinesque quality seems to be unmistakable. I can think of no third person who might have made such a reply to the president's remark.

A Great Naturalist

In going to Austin in 1962 I was not going to an unknown region or group of people. David Miller had been in my first class in Chicago, and he was one student I never forgot. Besides that, I had visited the Millers in 1951 and spent a week in their house. The visit was for the chance to go birding in a new area, but I also met members of the department. Miller further introduced me to Edgar Kincaid, that is, to one of the best field naturalists in the world, who took me out for all-day birding. Long afterwards Bertha Dobie, Edgar's aunt and wife of the famous writer of folk tales, told me that she had said to Edgar, "Perhaps Professor Hartshorne won't want to spend a whole day with birds." It was indeed the first time I had ever known a man who could talk birds all day long. But it would not have occurred to me that this was an excess of a good thing. Philosophy all day long might well be too much, but not wild nature.

We later lived more than twenty years near to Kincaid and saw him almost daily. I never put a question about nature to him without getting an informed and careful answer. He belonged to the Texas landed gentry, an aristocrat somewhat different from but recognizably akin to the British sort.

Kincaid is (was until near the end) a cheerful pessimist about the future of the planet as a nature lover sees it. In the book he officially "edited," but actually more than half wrote, *The Bird Life of Texas*, he says of a species unique to Texas and threatened with ultimate extinction, "Perhaps the Golden-Cheeked Warbler will not make it into the Twenty-First Century—but then, who will?" (This proved in his case only too prophetic.) According to the Kincaid world calendar, the planet began going downhill in 1928. And indeed there was much to be said for the world I experienced in my first thirty-one years. Lots of unspoiled forest and marsh, pollution of air and water not much in evidence, few pesticides raining down on the land. In the book referred to Edgar speaks of the "rat-like breeding" of the human species. As a naturalist he knew that there is a genuine analogy here, taking most mammals into account.

Edgar's friends all receive bird names. His is The Old Cassowry. Reason for the choice of this species: whereas birds have been oppressed for centuries by people, the Cassowary is one bird able to strike back. With its claws it has been known to inflict fatal damage to a person confronting it. This symbolizes, not a wish on Edgar's part to hurt anyone; but his wish that birds could protect themselves from the harm we do to them.

One of Kincaid's many original remarks is this: "The two strongest forces in the universe are the condensation of things you don't want and the evaporation of things you do want." I am confident the reader will recognize the truth of this proposition. Early in my serious work in ornithology I asked Edgar to read an essay of mine on the subject. He returned it in an envelope marked: 'Noble pontifications by Dr. Charles Hartshorne; ignoble comments by Edgar Kincaid." The comments did not mince words and I profited from them. I do not recall having heard the word *pontification* before. It is a Kincaid favorite.

Edgar received an award for his part in the *Bird Life of Texas*. His acceptance speech was, as his friend Victor Emanuel, who leads bird trips and is a first-rate birder, put it, "Kincaidian to the *n*th degree." It was so not only because the people referred to as having helped him all had bird names, including this writer and my wife, but also because he made as much fuss about the work of the least of his helpers as about his own work. And in fact he was not only modest but one of the most generous spirits one could ever know. Alas, that he is no longer among the living.

Fig. 29. With Wayne Viney, a psychologist who has written about my theory of sensation in *The Philosophy of Charles Hartshorne* (The Library of Living Philosophers).

Texas Philosophers

The philosophy department in Austin has been continually interesting. We have had some distinguished visitors, Boyce Gibson of Australia, John Findlay (whom I long ago noticed as one of the few in England with a gift for speculative philosophy or metaphysics), Mario Bunge, and others. Douglas Morgan, our lamented, prematurely dead, and in many ways admirable colleague had as high standards for scholarship and academic behavior as I have encountered. David Miller is (was) the authoritative interpreter of G. H. Mead's philosophy, making it clearer than Mead ever did. He, too, set a high standard of academic behavior, and was a reliable and humorous friend.

With the Millers I shared an amusing memory. There used to be a philosopher here named Mitchell. He had married an English lady, a teacher of mathematics, who frankly thought philosophy a rather foolish subject. She had other openly expressed opinions that were uncomplimentary to various people—to such an extent that, as Mary Miller put it, there was no sense in taking any of these opinions personally because they were distributed so widely. Well, during that week I lived in the Millers' house, I twice invited the Millers out for a meal, as they were doing a lot for me. The second time, we were having a merry time talking in a restaurant when suddenly Mary said, "Gracious, it's almost eight o'clock and we've invited the Mitchells to our house at eight. Reese [to her son], go and phone Mrs. Mitchell." "Not I," replied Reese. He knew Mrs. Mitchell only too well. So I rushed to the cashier, paid the bill, and we motored to the Millers' house. Sure enough, there was the Mitchells' car, with the lights turned out, no sign of life. We got out of the Millers' car, the doors of the other car opened, no word was spoken and we all began walking toward the door of the Millers' house. Mrs. Mitchell's voice broke the silence: "You *would* do a thing like that!" No one replied. As we entered the house I thought, "How will the evening go on if it begins like this?" In fact, it went not too badly. I began talking to the redoubtable lady about England and by good luck made a mistake in British geography, putting Blackpool, a seaside resort, on the east when it is really on the west coast. The lady got so interested in setting me right about the east and west coast resorts that the ice seemed nicely broken. I had the feeling that Mitchell was grateful for my helpful blunder.

In Chicago we had another English (Scottish) wife who specialized in rudeness, and in that case, too, one learned not to take it personally. Jane Austen pictures an aristocratic lady with no pretensions to politeness. These three cases together seem to suggest that systematic rudeness may be a better design for living than capricious or malicious oscillation between considerate and inconsiderate manners.

A very able emeritus member of the Texas department was A. P. Brogan. He has done excellent work in ethics and also in scholarly studies of Greek philosophy. He was dean for a number of years and managed to put through a retirement rule by which he, and I, eventually benefitted. It was that, at age seventy, one must either retire from teaching or go on half pay (if the department agrees to retain one). However, administrators must stop administrating at sixty-eight.

In Texas I learned several things relevant to the ontological argument controversy that has raged for nearly a millennium, things that historians ought to have told us but have not. One of them was that Kant was considerably less original on this topic than has been generally supposed, another that Aristotle anticipated Anselm's point that the eternal cannot be contingent. Oddly enough, Aristotle anticipated both Kant and Anselm, in such a way that he would have partly disagreed with both and for cogent reasons. Brogan told me one of these things and Morgan, the other. And nearly all the learned Europeans apparently missed them. I was not greatly surprised. The learned learn partly what agrees with their prejudices. A Texan may have different prejudices.

On the occasion of Miller's definitive retirement there was a call for poetry to mark the occasion. I had ceased to write poetry fifty-five years before, but I felt it was up to me to see if I could "come up" with something suitable. Here is the result.

> *Born on the Kansas prairie*
> *He married the delightful Mary;*
> *Expert on George Herbert Mead,*
> *He's known round the world, indeed;*
> *Skilled worker in wood,*
> *His teaching also is good;*
> *He writes as a sensible man should;*
> *Yet he holds that we remake the past—*
> *At which doctrine I'm somewhat aghast!*
> *But I welcome his view that conditions*
> *Never fully determine decisions,*
> *That becoming is always creative,*
> *That we have some initiative.*
> *As colleague, David's reliable,*
> *Humorous, shrewd, and amiable.*
> *Long life to David and Mary,*
> *Sagacious both, and she merry!*

This was the second time I had been asked to speak in honor of a Texan. For when T. V. Smith left the University of Chicago to go to the University of Syracuse, I, as his oldest colleague, was told by the chairman Perry to make one of the principal speeches. When my wife heard about this she said, "What will you say, that sometimes you have disagreed with him less than at other times?" This was just the stimulus I needed. I began the speech by quoting my wife's jest anonymously (as by a friend) and then said that, in fact, as philosophers go, I thought T. V. and I disagreed no more than was normal for two philosophers. I then recalled T. V. as having praised my style as follows: "When I have been able to abstract from *what* you were saying sufficiently to pay attention to *how* you said it, I have found your style rather intimately satisfying." Now, said I, my case is the opposite. When I can abstract sufficiently from T. V.'s odd way of saying things (example: "be always on the grow") I have found a good deal of sense in what he is saying. T. V. said later, "Charles, it was nobly done."

Since I joined it, the department in Austin has been reasonably free from a monolithic tendency. Various views could get a hearing. Lieb, Browning, and I have taught metaphysics; Bouwsma, linguistic analysis in a radically antimetaphysical vein (not that Bouwsma— who died in 1978—denied the need for metaphysical beliefs, but that he thought these must be matters of personal faith, not things we can rationally know); several persons have done ethics from various points of view; Mourelotos has ably taught Greek philosophy, which is popular among students here; Allaire has taught his brand of skepticism, which I do not well understand, except that he seems to think no theory of truth by correspondence is much good. I once remarked to him that when he criticizes a view or a paper his criticisms seem unusually penetrating. "Oh, Charles," he replied, "it's always easy to take the negative." He has won an award for his teaching. Three permanent members of our department—Kane, Causey, and Norman Martin—are knowledgeable about natural science. Causey is a reductionist; but the others furnish plenty of balance on that issue.

Robert Kane is a very gifted man who repeatedly has won teaching awards and who has written several fine articles. One is on the principle of sufficient reason. The classical form of this principle, he holds, is too strong, leading to strict determinism, among other dubious implications. But a negative form of the principle shows promise and is being used in science. It says that when a type of event that seems perfectly conceivable is never observed to happen in nature, we should look for a law forbidding it to happen. This is on the analogy of the veto on perpetual motion machines. Such negative laws do not tell us very definitely what will happen, but they tell us much about what will *not* happen. (There is something similar in ethics.) Kant's "definite duties" were all negative. Love your neighbor, or be kind and cooperative to or with others, are positive but indefinite commands; in contrast, do not kill, lie, or break promises are definite.) I believe this is on the right track.

Neither science nor ethics should pretend to program details of the future. They can furnish guidelines and establish vetoes but not prepictures of the particular course of events. Our business is to make the future, step by step, and *expect other creatures to do so*

Fig. 30. Dorothy and I with our grandchildren, Eleanor and Charles

within their limits. Science tries to ascertain the limits of decision making, not to set out the decisions before they are made. And this applies even to atoms, not just to the higher animals. Only the limits within which there are decisions grow narrower as one goes down the scale of creatures. This, I hold, is the significance of the new physics of statistical rather than individually determinative laws. It is not that our freedom is the chance nature of the particles within us, but rather that nature is a hierarchy of freedoms, and all law and order is a *partial* aspect of becoming, the other aspect of which is creative decision, adding to the definiteness not just of knowledge but of reality. Our unpredictability is analogous, on a vastly higher level, to that of particles, not a mere consequence of it. I acquired this view almost simultaneously from Peirce and Whitehead over fifty years ago and have argued for it ever since. The busy world has paid some attention and at least the physicists often see the point. But the message still seems to be badly needed, by both philosophers and the world in general. Denying chance, the impossibility of determining concrete events in advance or eternally, the latter being even more absurd, whether in favor of providence, karma, or blind causal necessity (Skinner), is an ancient superstition that dies hard.

CHAPTER THIRTEEN

Recollections of Famous Philosophers—And Other Important Persons

In the fifty years during which, in a number of countries, I have studied or taught philosophy I have talked with many interesting and gifted representatives of the subject as well as with various other persons of distinction. Some of their remarks, especially witty or amusing ones, stand out in my memory.

A favorite among my Harvard philosophy teachers (none of whom is still living) was Clarence Irving Lewis. His father was a socialist, and he was therefore introduced early in life to economic and political issues. He summed up the effect of this upon himself with his usual incisiveness and droll humor. "I am an intelligent liberal—that is to say, a conservative." Conservative he certainly was, by any usual standard. (The only other socialist's son whom I recall knowing is also in much the same sense an "intelligent liberal.") Once when I told Lewis about my having addressed an audience of radicals who reacted somewhat fiercely, he said: "I learned long ago not to be upset if attacked at a socialist meeting. You only have to wait. Pretty soon someone will attack your attacker." In fact this is what had happened in my case: the argument with me soon turned into one between or among my opponents.

Lewis was a methodological behaviorist in his theory of science; but he held that a behavioristic method is one thing and materialism, or the denial of mind, quite another. As he put it, the behaviorist is all right so long as he stops short of "telling damn lies," by which he meant pretending that there is no such thing as consciousness or feeling. I recall his once saying to me, "The behaviorist is all right. He has an idea." "Only," I replied, "he hasn't any other idea." "Let's leave it at that," was Lewis's comment.

Lewis, like A. N. Whitehead, of whom I shall speak presently, was remarkable for modesty as well as ability. I have heard him speak with amusement of the fact, illustrative he said of his slow-wittedness, that he had to cross the Arizona desert twice before he "got the point and saw that it was beautiful." (Similarly I have heard Whitehead describe his procedure in an early book as "extraordinarily clumsy.") In Lewis's part in the volume devoted to him in Schilpp's "Library of Living Philosophers," he sets a new standard for the series in the generosity, modesty, wit, gentle good humor, and charm with which he surveys his career and replies to his critics. He makes one proud to belong to the same profession, and indeed to the same animal species as this man—that species, greedy, destructive, pollution-spreading, malicious, hypocritical—but we all know the abyss that yawns beneath any goodness and clear-headed wisdom that people can display. In his last years Lewis, like Whitehead, radiated a mellow wisdom. Each had a wife of similar qualities who survived him. Each had sense enough to know how fortunate he was. A Brazilian philosopher, Cannabrava, visited Whitehead in his old age, and was delighted to have him say, "I am an old man, and a very happy one." So, thought the visitor, should a philosopher be in his last days. So, too, was Lewis.

Raphael Demos, another of my fine teachers, was a master of the devastating repartee. After he had read a paper on a topic in the philosophy of religion, Professor Randall of Columbia arose and with characteristic mock gravity assured us that what he was about to say came "from the horse's mouth," as he had acquired it while giving a joint seminar with Paul Tillich. Demos: "Professor Randall tells us that his contribution comes from the horses's mouth. But—Tillich is not my horse." There was a serious intent in this. Demos in fact disapproved of Tillich, as the purveyor of a distorted or "Hegelian" version of Christianity.

For reasons that I can partly understand, Demos found my confidence in my own abilities uncomfortably close to conceit. Indeed, this is probably an understatement or over simplification of his feelings about me. At the beginning of one meeting of the Metaphysical Society he accosted me as follows: "Whatever you say in these meetings, I know it will be about God. Always God." Three times I rose to comment on a paper, and each time avoided any mention of deity. Each time I called his attention to this. The third time he said, laughing, his better nature coming uppermost, "I take it back."

My memories of still another teacher, Ralph Barton Perry, cover a wide range, including some valuable suggestions. Perry was helpful to students primarily as counterbalance to W. E. Hocking's eloquently presented version of Idealism. Perry's sharp attacks on this type of philosophy made it nearly impossible to accept it uncritically. But at times his extreme anti-idealistic bias seemed almost ludicrously evident. He was also extremely opposed to the doctrine, often closely associated with idealism, of monism. "A monist is a man who thinks that there is some sort of *juice* which is in everything." He managed to express strong dislike in the way he enunciated the word *juice*. Only inability to empathize intellectually made such a grotesque caricature possible. A fairer analogy would be that, just as the human soul, or consciousness or feeling, seems to pervade the human body, so something still more exalted and powerful pervades the entire cosmos. We shall return presently to the issue between monism and pluralism, either of which, in its extreme form, in my opinion is as false as the other.

Perry used to put elaborate but neat outlines on a huge blackboard at the beginning of a lecture. Once a student raised his hand, when the double blackboard had been completely covered, and asked, "Professor Perry, in which of these views do you believe?" Perry, who tended to be rather detached and noncommittal, at least in classes for beginners, replied, "Well now, that's quite a question. Suppose I were to answer it. Suppose I were to write my name after one of these positions"—pointing to the blackboard—"what difference would it make?" While the student was puzzling over this, Perry could get on with his lecture.

When I was in my terminal year as graduate student, I was introduced to the distinguished theologian Kirsopp Lake. Being told that I had a doctoral thesis in philosophy to write, he said, "That's easy: invent a new term." (So far as I recall I did not follow this suggestion.) Lake as theologian was perhaps scarcely orthodox in his beliefs. What he believed seemed to be something like the metaphysics of Plotinus. The following incident is reported. There was a death in a neighboring house. The maid was sent over with a gift of food for the bereaved family. The maid returned in some excitement. "So and so must have had a terrible disease. He's only been dead twenty-four hours and fornication has already set in." On this the theologian commented, "You imply a more cheerful view of the hereafter than is customarily taken."

Another theologian of somewhat similar characteristics was Shirley Jackson Case, whom I knew slightly at the University of Chicago. As we lunched one day, he remarked that, so far as he could make out, "metaphysics was an attempt to unscrew the inscrutable." It was told of him that in a course he gave, I do not recall under what title, after a number of class meetings had come and gone without mention of the Founder of Christianity, a student ventured to inquire, "Professor Case, aren't you going to say something about Jesus?" "Oh," said the famous scholar, "I think we must do that, if only as a matter of courtesy."

A Harvard professor of English literature, whose name I think was Winter, when I told him that I was going abroad for postdoctoral study, replied in the deep and almost sepulchral voice which he had, "Well, in your subject [metaphysics] you're abroad most of the time anyway, aren't you?" A metaphysician gets used to such gibes. One of my favorite novelists, Thomas Love Peacock, was a master of them.

Although I was already deep in metaphysics, largely without benefit of the classics in the subject, when I entered W. E. Hocking's famous course in it, he did intensify and illuminate my interest. He was very encouraging to me, but less so to one student whom I recall. This man went through a period of radical uncertainty as to the direction his philosophizing ought to take, between Hocking's idealism and Perry's and Lewis' sharp criticisms of idealism. One day, however, I found him a man with his mind made up. He was busily engaged in writing his doctoral thesis, which was to expound the version of idealism that he had just come to believe in. A little later I called on him again. "I've had a terrible thought," he said. "Suppose I should change my mind, and have to start my thesis all over again." "Don't worry," I said, "I can see that you're stuck with this," meaning this philosophy. (Sure enough he never, so far as I know, departed from the kind of doctrine he then defended.) Still later I found him once more unhappy. He pointed to the comment that Hocking had written upon the thesis: "I have been trying to decipher the language in which you have chosen to conceal your thought." Ruefully the student confessed: "If there was anything I prided myself on, it was my style." Such are the tribulations of a graduate student in philosophy. Later this student acquired some fame as a teacher. Many others besides Hocking have found him obscure.

In spite of considerable time spent with A. N. Whitehead (in 1925-1928, when I was instructor and research scholar at Harvard), I am not sure whether any of the wittiest remarks I seem to remember his having uttered were said in my presence or not. I knew him well enough to be able to imagine them as he would have said them, and this simulates actual recollection to the extent that it is sometimes difficult to make the distinction. But I think the following is not a firsthand account.

Bertrand Russell came to Harvard while Whitehead was professor of philosophy there and lectured on theory of value. Whitehead introduced him as follows: "Bertie says that I am muddle-headed. But I think that he is simple minded." Here, in unsurpassably succinct form, is one of the great contrasts between philosophers. There are those who would be clear (and even neat and witty) at almost any cost, including that of vastly oversimplifying things. There are those who above all would be adequate to the richness and many-sidedness of reality, even if they cannot always be neat and clear in their account of it. It is hardly surprising if the former more often make the best-seller lists. At the close of Russell's talk, in which he suggested, no doubt among many other things, that the key to value is the conditioned reflex, Whitehead rose and said:—"There is a lost Platonic dialogue on The Good, and I have often wondered what was in that dialogue. Now I know. When one of Pavlov's dogs' mouth waters, that is the good!"

Whitehead told me that he considered Russell "the most gifted Englishman alive." He added two criticisms: "He does not appreciate the importance of tradition, and he won't qualify." Here again is the charge of oversimplification.

At the University of Chicago we saw Russell on various occasions while he was a visiting professor. At one of these he was to address social scientists. He began as follows: "My function at this university seems to be to talk about a number of subjects that I know nothing whatever about." He then proceeded to inform us that he had discovered "a sociological law." It was that "in any community, the respect for intellectuals is inversely proportional to the intelligence of the community." The proof of the law was this: in the most primitive community, presumably the least intelligent, the intellectual is the medicine man. Obviously he is viewed with great respect. In our civilized, highly intelligent society, nobody cares about the intellectuals.

I had a number of brief but usually significant philosophical discussions with Russell. Of him one could perhaps say what Royce said of C. J. Ducasse (who told this story himself): "Mr. Ducasse, what you see you see very clearly. But what you do not see, you do not see at all." To my half-hearted suggestion that there may be a kind of truth as well as beauty in art, Russell replied: "Ah yes, 'Drink to me only with thine eyes.'" It was certainly a telling example on one side of the debate. In a more serious dialogue Russell said to me (a similar remark will be found in his *Autobiography*, apropos of his difference from Whitehead): "A philosopher can be a thoroughgoing monist or a thoroughgoing pluralist, and I don't see the slightest possibility of deciding, on rational grounds, between these alternatives." It had apparently never occurred to Russell that what reason might recommend (and Whitehead came closer than most to achieving) is the avoidance of both the contrary extremes.

On one side is the doctrine, which Russell confronted in the Oxford philosopher F. H. Bradley, that all plurality is an illusion or mere appearance, that reality is a seamless whole or ineffable unity in which the least item, say the "flower in the crannied wall" of the poet, implicates everything else and there is no loose-jointedness, free play, contingency, or chance in the cosmos. On the other side is the exactly opposite view, held by Russell himself, that each item, say each momentary experience that one of us has, or each state of any individual thing, is logically independent of any other state or event, and might conceivably occur by itself without antecedent conditions or subsequent effects. Thus it would be conceivable, though Russell knew as well as anyone else that it would be far from common sense to believe, that all our memories of the past are illusions, because the world only began a few seconds ago. More technically put, on the one hand, all relations of things or events to other things or events are external, not necessary for the occurrence of the thing. (We have to believe, Russell concedes, in causal dependence, but there is only a practical, not a rational basis for the belief.) On the other hand is the doctrine that all relations of a thing to other things are internal, constitutive of the very being of the thing. With only trivial qualifications Russell (like Hume) has gambled philosophically upon the first of these two extremes.

Yet Russell the logician can hardly be unaware that "either all relations are external or all are internal" fails to exhaust the possibilities, for there is a third option: "Some relations are internal, some are external." There may be aspects of unity, dependence, necessity, in the cosmos, and also aspects of plurality, independence, contingency, or chance. Russell's refusal to take this intermediate doctrine seriously is the key to his confessed lack of understanding of Whitehead's philosophy. He takes Whitehead to be a monist, but though there is a monistic aspect to Whitehead's philosophy, which the great Anglo-American thinker somewhat overstressed, there also is a pronounced pluralistic aspect. This philosophy is about as far from a "thoroughgoing monism" as it is from a thoroughgoing pluralism.

Whitehead was first Russell's teacher and then his collaborator on the great work of symbolic logic, *Principia Mathematica*. But when that was completed, their intellectual association came to an end. Various factors, including strong political disagreements, played a part in this, but basically it was a difference between a temperamental extremist or simplifier and a man dedicated to the search for a balanced position, avoiding one-sided extremes. Whitehead may not have entirely succeeded in this (I think that he did not), but Russell did not seriously aim at it. The wonder is not that they drifted apart, but that they held together long enough to finish their great joint work.

If anyone finds the foregoing account biased, I shall not quarrel with him. But I am perfectly convinced that the truth does not lie on either side of the arbitrary alternative that Russell, for rea-

sons more emotional than intellectual I suspect, sets up as *the* philosophical issue.

On one topic Whitehead and Russell agree: their common rejection of a certain monistic element in our philosophical and religious
tradition. This is the notion of "substance," that the world consists
of things and persons that though changing, are yet absolutely identical through these changes. Thus the man sick and the man well
are but one entity, only with some properties dropped out and others
added. Whitehead and Russell agree that this is a confused view.
Events are the concrete unit realities. "I'm a new man" can be taken
as literally as "I'm the same man," indeed more so, for it is the novelty that is concrete and the sameness is an abstraction. The wise
man is much more than the foolish infant; how can the less and
the more be but one entity? We are new creations every moment,
strictly speaking. True, the new has intimate relations with the old,
the man with the child, but it is the man that relates to the child,
not the other way. The child was innocent of the later man's sophistication, but in the recesses of memory the child lives on in the man.
Whitehead does justice to this retrospective or cumulative unity in
an individual's life as the more extreme pluralist Russell cannot do.
But they agree that the strictly singular unit of reality is the event
or state, not the thing or person. In this they are in agreement with
the Buddhist tradition.

Sadly enough, Russell seems not to have seen what Whitehead
and Buddhists did see, that rejecting or better relativizing, substantial or personal identity has ethical significance. He Is He, I am I is
the motto of selfishness. One is felt to be simply and totally identical
with oneself and simply and totally non-identical with anyone else.
How then can the religions, nearly all of them in some fashion, tell us
to "love the other as oneself"? Royce shows in superb fashion in some
of his writings how our very personalities are made up of shared
memories of the past and shared hopes, fears, and purposes for the
future. For relativity physics all links with the past are causal; but it
is quite as true that other people's past actions influence me now as
that my own past actions influence me now. Substance theories
mostly fail to assimilate this truth. But how strange that Russell should
have failed to see — or at least to emphasize — that this Buddhist-
Whiteheadian view is an ethically as well as scientifically enlightening

view! All genuine interests and purposes transcend the mere self. Egoism rests on a superstitious absolutizing of self-identity and consequent absolutizing of nonidentity with other persons. The concrete units of reality are not you and I, but you now, or you then, or I now, or I then. If "I now" cares about me later on, it can care also about you later on, and much the same act of imaginative sympathy is involved. Calculating self-interest is one arbitrarily limited strand of concern for life beyond the present self. Whitehead once humorously summed up the ethical objection to substance theories by remarking, "I sometimes think that all modern immorality is produced by the Aristotelian theory of substance." A Buddhist would understand this. Russell should too but said nothing of the kind, so far as I recall. Nor did Hume, with a similar ontology.

Some recollections in this chapter come chiefly under two heads that have in common only that both are amusing: wit and oddity. The next item comes under either head, depending upon which participant one thinks of. It happened a few years ago that an English philosopher, less famous than the two just mentioned but still of some standing in the profession — I shall arbitrarily call him Banks — was a visiting speaker at the University of Chicago at the same time as I was, though under different auspices. It happened also that I had a breakfast engagement with Markus Barth to discuss a point in his father's famous writings (which, however, he wisely declined to interpret). This left my wife, Dorothy C. Hartshorne, facing solitary breakfast at the Quadrangle Club. Presently Banks appeared in the dining room and, seeing my wife, whom he had once met in England, he invited himself to breakfast with her. The entire conversation, so far as I have learned was as follows:

B.:	*"Did you know that Aristotle was opposed to adultery?"*
D.C.H.:	*"On what ground? — Expediency?"*
B.:	*"No, on moral grounds. Homer also was opposed to adultery."* (Hereupon he quoted in English what seemed to my wife to be literally pages of Homer.)
D.C.H.:	(sweetly and with seeming innocence): *"Do you really consider that the best translation?"*

A long pause followed. Then Banks, glancing at his watch, said, "I have a nine o'clock appointment. Goodbye."

It did not appear that there was any attempt at humor on B.'s part. On the other hand, my wife failed to see why she should be called upon to discuss adultery the first thing in the morning with a man she barely knew.

During my several years studying, and for a time teaching, in Europe, I collected various impressions of European philosophers.

Jean Wahl, who taught in this country for some years but spent most of his life in Paris, is a so-called Existentialist, as well as a learned and witty man. The following is characteristic:

> **I:**   *"There is a rumor that you have joined the [Roman Catholic] church."*
>
> **J.W.:**   *"No, I have not joined the church—and the church has not joined me."*

Max Scheler, a rather heretical exponent of the Husserl school of Phenomenology, is famous on a number of counts, ranging from his rapid succession of marriages and conversions to and from Roman Catholicism to original and interesting philosophical speculations. His enthusiasm for his own accomplishments seemed to me so candid and innocent that no one could take offence. In a lecture that I heard he spoke of having anticipated Einstein in the theory of relativity. In private conversation he favored me with an account of the book he was writing. "It will be different from my previous works. Hitherto I have always taken pains to find a place for God in my philosophy. From now on God must look out for himself."

At the beginning of a course in 1924 the then not so famous Martin Heidegger, a profoundly original disciple of Husserl, declared, with as I thought a touch of defiance, "In this course there will be no *Wesens-schau* [intuition of essence]." I took this to be a declaration of independence from Husserl, the great exponent of *Wesenserschauung,* to use a longer but perhaps more correct term. He also said (I suspected, with the same former teacher in mind), "I do not claim to speak for eternity." Husserl, professing to make philosophy a sort of superscience, seemed to think that in capturing a timeless essence in an intuition we could arrive at absolute and immutable truth. This claim, as he presented it, was unconvincing to me, as it was to Heidegger.

Oddly enough, however, Husserl, at about the same time and also in my hearing, made or implied the same disclaimer as Heidegger, though perhaps with a rather different meaning. It was after midnight, New Year's Eve, at a small party given by the great man for a few students. German and American. About midnight the founder of phenomenology made a short speech about the future of philosophy. Surprisingly there was no mention in this speech of Phenomenology. Frau Husserl, always loyal to her husband's cause, noticed the omission. "What about Phenomenology?" she asked. "Well," replied Husserl, "in this future progress of philosophy we hope that Phenomenology will play a part. But—who can speak for eternity?" I need scarcely say that Husserl was not always so modest about his own mode of philosophizing.

Julius Ebbinghaus, a close and almost rigid follower of Immanuel Kant (a century and a half later) was accosted by someone as follows: "Professor Ebbinghaus, you must be the last Kantian." His response showed his customary wit: "I am the first Kantian." He has in fact been trying to show, all through his career, how little the alleged Kantians have understood the master.

Ebbinghaus, from whom I learned a good deal about the history of philosophy, but whose Kantianism has always been rather alien to me, told me amusingly how he managed to acquire a degree under Husserl. Mrs. Husserl asked her husband if candidate Ebbinghaus was really, after all, a Phenomenologist. The *Hochgeheimrat* (a title given very distinguished persons) discussed the matter with Julius, and they reached a satisfactory agreement: Ebbinghaus could be regarded as "a peripheral Phenomenologist."

I have been so fortunate as to know Ebbinghaus for over forty-five years. He is almost the only man I recall knowing well who, having had an angelic first wife and lost her by death, married a second equally admirable one, and who had the sense to appreciate his good fortune. The Ebbinghauses entertained me overnight in Marburg in 1948. The Occupation was still in force. I left at night by train, taking it at a suburban station that was officially reserved for American use. As we came to the little station, Ebbinghaus hesitated to enter, but yielded to my insistence that he do so. The little waiting room was well heated, unlike German buildings at that time. Two small Ebbinghaus sons had come along, pulling a little play wagon in which they had put my suitcase. They got the wagon and baggage through the door but failed to close the latter. "Close the door," said their father! "You're letting the American warmth out into the German darkness." For me, and I suspect for him, the remark was charged with symbolic significance. Germany indeed had gone through a dark period, perhaps above all for a Kantian. And in some respects the Allied victory had brought warmth as well as humiliation.

Ebbinghaus came to Frankfurt, where I taught for some months in 1948-49, to deliver a lecture. I happened to be away at the time and so missed the talk. But Hans-Georg Gadamer, well known as teacher and writer in the Heideggerian vein, and hence far from Ebbinghaus in philosophical doctrine, summarized the lecture for me. "Ebbinghaus's remedy for the current difficulties was — we must go back to the eighteenth century."

Another remark of Gadamer's that I like to remember came as he was seeing me off from my stay at Frankfurt. The train was in the station, but the doors had not yet been opened. Many people were standing about wondering how we were to board. Gadamer summed it up nicely, "*Alles scheint in der schönsten Unordnung zu sein*" (everything seems to be in the most beautiful disorder). I felt much better, and soon the doors were opened.

Professor Ebbinghaus was a social favorite during his visit at Emory University when I was there. He usually avoided talking philosophy on social occasions and was always interesting and often amusing. Asked how he felt about the thick ugly ankle socks then being worn by girl students, he replied, "It makes the temptation not unbearable." His manner in class was very different. His technique suggested a drill sergeant. Students were to learn exactly what he thought that he (or Kant) knew. A quite able but decidedly independent student ventured to object to a remark which der *Herr-Doktor-Professor* happened to make about Thomas Aquinas. The rash student was quickly suppressed, but to the next meeting of the class he brought a volume of Thomas's *Summa Theologica.* "I want to show you what I mean," he began. But he was stopped short. "I am the professor, you are the student. I show you, you do not show me."

The foregoing episode is about Ebbinghaus at an advanced age. According to my recollections of him as a young instructor at Freiburg, he was then more urbane. In a seminar in which we studied a Latin text of Wolff I happened, scarcely consciously and I do not now know why, to utter a deep sigh. "*Ach, Herr* Hartshorne," said Ebbinghaus, "that came from the heart." Again, when I, with my rather poor grasp of Latin, had managed to understand the passage to which we had come and found it rather silly, he said, "You may well smile, Mr. Hartshorne. Wolff is not very penetrating. He is not subtle like the Scholastics."

Whereas Heidegger's philosophy permitted him for a time to take office as Rektor of the University of Freiburg under the Nazis, by contrast, Ebbinghaus's Kantianism required him, in his own eyes, to be anti-Nazi. Consequently when my cousin E. Y. Hartshorne came to Marburg as educational administrator under the Occupation, he summoned Ebbinghaus for an interview as possible Rektor of the university there, his record not being *belastet* (burdened) with Nazi ties. Ebbinghaus has told me how apprehensive he felt as he entered the official building and identified himself to soldiers and officers of the occupying army. Then Colonel Hartshorne appeared and directed him into his private office. When he had shut the door, the colonel's manner changed, as he told the little professor that he knew a good deal about him and his record. Things rapidly took on a kindlier aspect as the conversation progressed. My cousin spoke German easily and he began one of his remarks with the phrase "As my old German professor used to say." "Who was that German professor?" Ebbinghaus finally ventured to ask. "Oh," said Ted, "a magnificent person, unhappily killed in his prime, I invented him." The tact of this little fiction moved Ebbinghaus deeply. He was appointed Rektor, not entirely to his own benefit, since denazification proceedings had to be carried out that were hardly a privilege to administer. It was not Ted's fault. The policy was partly determined in Washington and partly, I gather, in Teachers' College.

The career of my former colleague at the University of Chicago, T. V. Smith, has always seemed to me a superb example of the American success story. As his autobiography, *The Nonexistent Man*, shows, he began with close to zero advantages in early upbringing, but by his early thirties he was a professor in a leading university and well on the way to a distinguished career as writer, speaker, and legislator. Another case typical of American success is that of Harry Wolfson of Harvard. Coming to this country from Russia in his early teens, equipped with brains and a strong Yiddish accent and not much else, so far as I know, he became one of the two most powerful writers in the history of ideas—the other being Lovejoy—that this country has produced, his competence covering in masterly fashion the whole history of philosophy down to Spinoza. He also became a success as lecturer to undergraduates. The only funny remark of his that I recall was not intended to be so. Discussing a problematic marital engagement of a young acquaintance he said, "Any two people of the same social background can get along together." Wolfson was a bachelor, and a great devotee of the cinema, but hardly, on these accounts, one would think, an authority on marriage. When I was about to go abroad for one, or as it turned out two, years of postdoctoral study, I asked Wolfson for his advice. He did advise me, but exclusively as to the location of good restaurants in certain European cities.

One story, not first hand, has to be told about Lovejoy, just mentioned. He was proposed for some community responsibility, and a political committee, interviewing him to assess his fitness for the office, asked him if he believed in God. One must know Lovejoy to take his reply in the right way. It was to the effect that, so far as he knew, a number (I think nine) of different meanings had been assigned to the word *God*. He proceeded to explicate these meanings. I don't know if he ever got to the point of endorsing one of the conceptions, or rejecting them all, or declaring his inability to decide. He was given the responsibility. With some persons there might have been evasiveness or cynicism in such a procedure. But to a Lovejoy nothing is more true than that terms of philosophical and religious dispute are full of ambiguities, so that it is idle to take a position for or against without the most particular examination of the way in which key words are used. He was famous for his article, "The Thirteen Pragmatisms," so many were the meanings he found connoted by the term invented by Peirce and popularized by William James.

I cannot refrain from mentioning one more aspect of Lovejoy's great career as a scholar of high order. In a little book, *Reflections on Human Nature* dealing with the sources of the conception of man assumed by the founders of the American Constitution, Lovejoy, after an initial historical chapter inserts one giving his own analysis of human motives. Except perhaps in Buddhist writings I have yet to see a discussion of this topic to compare with this one in depth and freedom from traditional confusions. So far as I know, the publication of this book has caused scarcely a ripple in the scholarly world. This does not greatly surprise me. What scholars take note of depends upon many factors and reveals human weakness much as do all human activities. Be that as it may, Lovejoy charmingly opens Chapter Three by remarking that the historical writers he is about to deal with will turn out to be somewhat confused, as they have not read Chapter Two. I take this, on the whole, seriously. In the Western tradition there are certain pervasive confusions about motivation from which Lovejoy shows himself in this chapter almost entirely free. Whitehead, is if possible, even freer, but he never set the thing out systematically, as Lovejoy does. Rather he provides a metaphysical basis (in terms of categories applicable to all creatures) for what Lovejoy sees in the nature of man.

But I began to tell about T. V. Smith. He had a carefully thought-out theory of political action. Legislators, he held, are there to harmonize, if necessary through compromise, the interests of constituents who otherwise would have to settle their differences by violence. There is, he insisted, no reason why legislators who take opposite sides should not respect one another and even be good friends. Smith told me that when he went to the state legislature, he made up his mind that he would be friends with everyone. However, it turned out that one member was such a rascal that he felt that he could not with self-respect be friendly to him. "But all the rest I was determined to like. I got some of them so mixed up that they didn't know whether they hated me or not." One fruit of this procedure was the following incident. The backer of a bill that T. V. disapproved of asked him to please vote for it; Smith said that he was sorry. In some other case, perhaps, he could be more obliging, but his principles were too strongly opposed to this particular bill. "Well, Smith," said the other, "you've earned the right to be independent. But these other fellows haven't, and by God they're going to toe the line."

On another occasion Smith was particularly prominent in opposition to a bill that was unsuccessfully supported by a farmer-legislator who had set his heart on its passage. Smith felt sorry for the legislator whom he had defeated. Taking a graduate student with him, he drove to the man's farm. His fellow legislator welcomed him and showed him around. Smith, a farmer's son, was quite able to appreciate what he was seeing. The man eventually took the student (from whom I have the story) aside and said, "Why, it's an honor to be beaten by a man like that."

Smith had the corresponding responsibility in Italy to the one that E. Y. Hartshorne had in Germany, but he was given a freer hand. He was quite clear in his mind about what could and could not sensibly be attempted in rooting out fascists or militarists from the educational system. You can't incriminate everybody, he said, or anything like a majority or even very substantial minority. Yet you must eliminate some egregious offenders. So you pick out the worst and clearest cases, and let the rest go. Some of us wish this had been done in Germany. When millions of persons, and their relatives and close friends, are treated as presumptive criminals, the meaning of *criminal* becomes dubious. By definition almost, a criminal is in a small minority. But in Germany it was made to seem otherwise, until the inevitable counterforces got into play. While I was at Frankfurt, an illustration of the confusion that accompanied this process was the following incident. In a meeting of the *Philosophische Facultät* the dean told us about a colleague who was *belastet* with Nazi associations, and who, according to written instructions from the minister of education, was forbidden to teach, but according to telephone instructions from the same office had been bidden to do so. In fact, he had been and was teaching. The dean summed it up: "*Also er darf, er darf nicht, und er tut es.*" (He may, he may not, and he does it.) I cannot recall what we decided at this meeting. The dean's wit alone survives the torrent of forgetting that (except in the unconscious) far far more than remembering relates us to our past.

While Smith was in the Illinois legislature, a bill was introduced to require teachers to take an oath of loyalty to the Constitution. Smith told the legislators: there are three kinds of patriotism, the fighting kind, the sweating kind, and the swearing kind. The least valuable is the swearing kind.

The bill was defeated.

It was on this occasion that Robert Maynard Hutchins fielded queries about communism on the faculty with his customary adroitness. "What about Maude Sly, Dr. Hutchins?" This lady, a distinguished researcher seeking the causes of cancer but not teaching, was rumored to be pro-communist. Hutchins: "Miss Sly associates exclusively with mice." Incidentally, the only communists I was aware of in the city during my twenty-seven years on the faculty of the University of Chicago, covering all of Hutchins's stay there, had no connection with the university, and the only faculty member who seemed even a fellow traveler remained but a short time. Yet I heard a passenger on the I. C. train say, as we came to the station serving the university: "They ought to call it 'the University of Moscow.'" The *Chicago Tribune* perhaps produced this state of mind by clever insinuations. For example, the day Roosevelt ended a speech with a prayer of his own composition, the *Tribune* printed the speech and the prayer, but in the next column, in a conspicuous little box, was a quotation from the writings of the leading Communist Party member of the time. It was headed, "Browder on Religion," and gave the standard communist doctrine about religion as illusion and "opium of the people." Nothing false was said by the *Tribune*, no connection was stated between Roosevelt's prayer and communist doctrines. But a hint to the faithful readers was quite enough. They could put two and two together.

Hutchins would not claim to be a philosopher. "Just an academic politician," he has been known to say. But be that as it may, his wit is beyond question. Once in a men's room I was asked by a fellow member of the scientific club that I had the luck to belong to for over twenty-five years, and who knew that my writings made considerable mention of deity, "Hartshorne, are you still working on God?" Instantly the voice of Hutchins was heard to reply, "He ought to let God work on him." Theologians might well feel that this was better than any reply I could possibly have given.

Many persons must remember Hutchins's crushing retort to the Harvard football coach who, at the time Hutchins abolished intercollegiate football at the University of Chicago (with at least my hearty approval), was quoted as saying, "It is all very well for President Hutchins, who has the physique of a Sir Galahad, to regard football as unnecessary, but the rest of us need athletics." Hutchins: "It is not recorded of Sir Galahad that his physique was exceptional, but only that 'his strength was as the strength of ten because his heart was pure.'"

Another famous university administrator made a remark in my presence that though hardly witty and not intended to be humorous, was unforgettable. It was when a group of Harvard and Radcliffe students were setting up a Liberal Club, about 1920. Charles W. Eliot was president emeritus and it occurred to us that it would be well to have his blessing on our activities. So we called upon him at his house. He was impressive, though far from handsome. One of the boys in the delegation explained our project. Eliot then gravely said, "And now I should like to hear from the ladies." A Radcliffe girl met the challenge. "Well" said Eliot, "I think it's a good idea to have a Liberal Club. But there's one thing. You mustn't have anything to do with socialism. That's pure mischief." We wisely said nothing at this point. The interview was over. But, as Granville Hicks makes clear in his *Autobiography*, we had quite a little to do with socialism; or at least, we had some socialist speakers.

The only other occasion on which I saw Eliot was when he was called upon to deal with an emergency. Cox, Democratic candidate for president running against Calvin Coolidge, was to address an overflow audience at the Harvard Union. The crowd was assembled, the hour assigned had come and gone, but no Cox. Restlessness of course was increasing, and the situation threatened to get out of hand. Then Eliot appeared. I recall nothing that he said. But his presence sufficed, in any case. He was somehow in all his being an effective personality. He could not be ignored. Finally, the man who, for all I know, should have been elected instead of Coolidge, appeared, and the rest of the evening went as planned.

Of Coolidge himself my favorite saying is his reply to the query, "What's it like to be president?" "You've got to be mighty careful," said the master of taciturnity. I have adopted this as a motto of married life.

Another story about Eliot. In the course of some inquiries about Charles Peirce, the philosophic genius whose works have been edited posthumously by me, Paul Weiss, and Arthur Burks, I was told the following. Benjamin Peirce, Charles' famous mathematician father, was speaking at a small faculty meeting chaired by Eliot. There was a dispute between Professor Peirce and a colleague that went thus. Peirce made a statement, his opponent retorted, "No, Mr. Peirce, 'tain't so." Peirce repeated his statement, whereupon the same colleague said again, "No, Mr. Peirce, 'tain't so." Peirce then reached in front of Eliot, who sat between the two disputants around a small table, and shaking his fist at the other, said, "If you say that again I'll pull your old nose for you." "Gentlemen," said Eliot with all his accustomed gravity, "the question before us is . . ."

A third president demands mention: Ike Sharpless of Haverford College. This amazing man resembled Eliot at least in being as impressive as he was unhandsome. His bald head was lopsided in a fashion I have not seen in anyone else. There was a student, nick-named "Zeke," at Haverford who was known to all his classmates for his humorous speeches. He was one of a little group of admirers of Nietzsche in the mostly pious college community in 1916, and it bothered him greatly that weekly attendance at Quaker meetings (with some allowance for cuts) was required. He complained to fellow students that it was inconsistent of Friends, who believed in infor-mality and freedom in religious matters, to make meetings compul-sory. Finally a student suggested that the thing to do was to get up in meeting and present the argument against required attendance. After all, he said, in Quaker meeting anyone who is "moved by the spirit" may speak. The opponent of compulsion expressed misgiv-ings as to the wisdom of this procedure. Finally a group of students offered Zeke the sum of twenty-five dollars if he would do as sug-gested. He agreed. Word got about and this was the one meeting when scarcely anyone took a cut. There was the usual silence for a time, and then Zeke got up and began his prepared speech. In the middle of the first sentence Sharpless rose and said, " — I think thee had bet-ter sit down." Zeke reflected a second or two — and sat down. Later

Zeke argued with Sharpless that he should not have been silenced, because speaking in meeting was supposed to be according to movements of the spirit. "Yes," said Sharpless, "but, if the spirit has to be supplemented by the inducement of twenty-five dollars the principle hardly applies." Zeke then had one final complaint: the president should not put spies in the student body. There was some fuss about whether such a brash and irreverent man should be allowed to remain on campus. For some reason the teacher of Greek was particularly energetic in Zeke's defense, and possibly this was what saved him. Anyhow he stayed. Very recently, about fifty years later, compulsion was dropped.

The Greek teacher referred to once wandered from his subject of teaching Greek to discourse to the class on the unfairness of professorial salaries, urging that a professor could make much more money in nonacademic employment. A student, more like the present generation perhaps than his own, spoke up. "Just how, Professor – – –, could you make more money than you are doing now?" My memory records no definite answer, but yields a definite impression that the professor was not pleased. This experience is perhaps one reason why I have never made such a declaration. (If I were a chemist, say, and not a philosopher, I might feel differently.) To my mind the question of academic salaries is not basically one of fairness or sacred rights. Who knows his own real value to the social whole? It is rather a question of results: if people want their offspring to have good instruction, they will have to pay what it takes to get it. I have always been amused at colleagues who think they know what society has a duty to pay them compared to plumbers and garbage collectors. I am sure I could never know this. But it is clear that a society cannot show contempt for a profession and get the best results from it.

One of the most eccentric of American philosophers was Elijah Jordan. When he began to give his presidential address (I was there), some colleagues far in the back of the room, which was narrow but deep, called out, "Louder, we can't hear you." "Oh," said Jordan, "It's not worth hearing. Go on out." Some of them did. A student told me that Jordan showed him a manuscript not yet accepted by a publisher and said, "I don't know if I'll get it published or not. If I do, I'll think less of it."

Two other stories about Jordan are these. He used to speak harshly of businessmen in class and some student told papa, a businessman, who complained to the president, who remonstrated with Jordan. The latter's response was to resign and write a book called *Business Be Damned*. Once when he was programmed (in the pre-computer sense) to be third participant in a symposium his entire contribution was the following: "In view of what has been said so far, I see nothing to discuss." Obviously he should have been asked to speak first.

Jordan reviewed my *Man's Vision of God*. He said some highly critical things, and then began a new paragraph as follows: "It's a good sound book." I of course looked in the rest of the review for an explanation of what was good or sound in a book of which he clearly disapproved so much, but in vain. There was only further disapproval. Eventually I had a chance to ask him about this. My memory here is vague, but I think his answer was something like, "You said what you really believed, and argued for it vigorously." Or perhaps: "You were consistent."

In a book on aesthetics Jordan used a phrase one might like to plagiarize. Some writers, he said, gave him "logical seasickness." Reading Jordan's own reputedly profound books is less an experience of being tossed about than of drifting through a fog between rocky shoals. In an official obituary it was said of him that, although he rewrote one of his books many times, "this labor was not undertaken in the interest of the reader." Perhaps it was a case of "the reader be damned."

I resist the temptation to relate experiences with Paul Weiss, founder of the Metaphysical Society and my collaborator in editing the writings of Peirce. Only an entire essay would do in his case. However, I will tell here about the one and only time I managed to make a joke at his expense before he had time to make one at mine. Someone had written somewhere that Weiss and I were "two brilliant and loyal disciples of A. N. Whitehead." Knowing that Weiss prided himself, with considerable justification, on his originality, I could hardly wait for our next meeting. Quoting— — — —I added, "I admit that I am brilliant and that you are loyal." Weiss: "That is an interesting division of labor. The only trouble is that it's the reverse of the truth." So I had gotten ahead of him—for a second or two.

About William James, who died before my college days, my father-in-law told me a characteristic item. In a lecture in Chicago James startled his audience by beginning a sentence with, "Suppose a man were to fall out of the universe ..." Professor James Hayden Tufts, of the University of Chicago, a rather solemn man, upon hearing this threw back his great statuesque head, unforgettable by anyone who knew him, and roared with laughter. So far as I know, this highly Jamesian suggestion was not included in any of James's published works. Like many funny remarks it readily suggests serious philosophical puzzles.

Relativity theory, unknown to James, casts a new light on questions concerning the universe as a whole. I have heard Shapley, the superb popularizer of astronomy, tell a story about this. He had explained that the universe might be "finite and yet unbounded." In the question period a lady persisted in attacking this idea as absurd. "Look here, Professor Shapley, you say that even if the universe is finite, it has no boundary. Well, suppose I were to go all the way out there, 9 billion light years—is that how large you say the universe may be?— suppose I were to go all the way out there and stick my finger out?" "Madame," Shapley said he had replied, "I wish you would."

Shapley told a revealing story about Einstein. "I once asked Einstein whether the universe was finite or infinite. His reply was" —here Shapley silently shrugged his shoulders. This is in the authentic Einstein manner. Why waste words if the answer is simply "I don't know"? Well known is Einstein's comment on the question whether the uncertainty principle of Heisenberg represented our human ignorance or the truth about the world: "I can't believe in a dice-throwing God." In other words, the order of the universe, which Einstein regarded with religious awe, must be absolute and exclude any element of chance or randomness. Thanks to Einstein's blunt candor, some of us can state our own opposed conviction by using his very words. For, as a distinguished inventor, Arthur Young has remarked, "A God whose creatures have freedom is indeed a dice-throwing God. He is taking chances on what his creatures decide to do." Furthermore, what would a God be whose creatures were mere puppets? According to my philosophy, in this respect the same as Young's, or

Whitehead's, or that of Charles Peirce, it is not only human individuals who have some degree of freedom; the very atoms do. To exist as an individual is to act as an individual, and this means at every moment to face more than one possibility for action. I call this doctrine *creationism*. There are as many creators as there are creatures, plus the supreme Creator. The world broth has countless cooks, not just a supreme cook. Hence the tragic side of existence. Einstein, great as he was, had no conception of this way of thinking. I was present at a meeting of philosophers at which he made this quite clear. I even said something for the opposing view.

A lovely story about Einstein is this. The mother of a little girl who lived near Einstein's home in Princeton was puzzled to have the child frequently go off of an afternoon saying, "I am going to see Professor Einstein." When the mother called upon Einstein to inquire into the matter, the scientist said: "It is very simple; I help her with her lessons, and she gives me cookies."

The phrase "It is very simple" has for me a deeply comforting ring. I was acutely ill in Spain once, and when my wife had managed to convey to a local doctor that it was not she herself but her *marido* who was ill, and the man had come and looked me over, he began his diagnosis with the same four English words. I felt better instantly. The simplicity lay in this: I had been drinking the city water, which was contaminated. What I had to do was to stop this rash practice.

To return to James, a lady for whom I have high regard tells ruefully of an incident that occurred when she was very small and James was staying in her family's home in California. Apparently she was disturbing the flow of his ideas, for he said, "Can't that child be taken away?" Probably we have all felt what James felt at that moment, though perhaps without believing ourselves entitled to express our feelings.

My many agreeable and interesting experiences with Japanese students and professors do not lend themselves readily to effective illustration. It is not that there is any lack of humor in the Japanese people. (While I was at the Universities of Kyoto and Doshisha an American philosopher, a rather solemn man, wrote to ask me what it was like teaching in Japan. One of his queries was, "Have the Japanese a sense of humor?" It would not quite have done, but would, I felt, have been in accord with the facts, to reply, "More than you have, my friend." Instead I contented myself with an "Emphatically yes!") However, first there is the vast gap between the Japanese and the English languages, across which puns and other linguistically dependent forms of wit can scarcely pass. And second there is the exquisite tact and politeness in which no people can surpass the Japanese. I think of one illustration. I had been disputing philosophically with Nishitani, a thinker influenced by German philosophy as well as by the neo-buddhist speculations of the late Nishida and Tanabe. My wife had warned me not to argue too fiercely with Nishitani, on the grounds that the Japanese are accustomed to more politeness than we are. So after a very lively interchange I said to Nishitani, "I'm afraid that I have been too argumentative." "Oh," he said, "in philosophy that's impossible." What more disarming thing could he have said? The Buddhist culture helps some Japanese to attain and maintain an admirable serenity in disagreement. According to this tradition, the deep truths transcend literal expression; besides, the goal is to soar above egoistic pride in one's own opinion, and hence there is no occasion to be upset, no matter what the other may say.

The modern novel, well-translated into English, *I Am a Cat* by Natsume Soseki, is to me as deliciously humorous as anything that I have read. The narrator is a cat, but a cat whose chief occupation is observing the follies of human beings, observing them usually with more than a touch of feline scorn.

My favorite Japanese philosopher, Matao Noda, is exquisitely humorous. But his humor is extremely subtle and expressed chiefly in hints and gestures. I cannot reproduce it in cold print. I know only that he never fails to detect the ludicrous side of any situation, including those that occur in philosophical meetings.

I must report the following bit, involving Professor Tetsutaro Ariga, who until his retirement from Kyoto (when I wrote this)—he is now president of Kobe Women's College—held a chair in Christian philosophy at the University of Kyoto (Kyodai). My wife, for many months before the beginning of our first visit to Japan, spent most of her time studying Japanese history, culture, and language. Soon after we arrived in Kyoto, Professor Ariga said to Dorothy, "How is it that you know so much about my country?" "I read 150 books about it before I came to Japan," explained Dorothy. Ariga: "I wish I had read 150 books about it before I came to Japan. But I was born here." In the Ariga home someone, learning that Dorothy was a singer, asked her to sing, which she did. As she ended her song, it appeared that she was in the next room, beginning to sing it over again. When this second rendition came to an end, the young Ariga boy appeared in the doorway, and we gathered that he had employed an invisible tape recorder to surprise us in this way. "That's his treek [trick]," said his father.

A stay in India is very different indeed from a stay in Japan. Some of the differences are of course highly favorable to Japan. But not all. One or two percent of the people of India are quite at home in English, some of them employing it brilliantly.

T. R. V. Murti, noted exponent of Advaita Vedanta Hinduism and scholar in the history of Buddhism, delighted me by the following display of wit and temperament. We were in Madras, about to hear from a highly placed official who was to be opening speaker at a philosophical conference there.

Murti, to me: *"These are the new gods."*
I: *"I detect a certain impudence in your remark."*
Murti: *"No, not impudence. Just respect, tempered by reason.*

My last reminiscence is purely American.

J. W. Hudson, in his presidential address to the American Philosophical Association, took as his topic textbooks on ethics in this country from early days to the present. He told us that in the earliest books the stress was on the virtues, long lists of them — courage, temperance, honesty, and all the rest. But through the years the number of virtues steadily decreased until it was down to three, then two, then only one — the virtue of promoting the general welfare — and finally, and here he shouted (he was a little man with a big voice), "NO VIRTUES!" His conclusion was that, after all, we do need at least a few virtues. I could not agree more.

CHAPTER FOURTEEN

Some Other Philosophers

Heinrich Rickert

When, in the mid-1920s, I talked to the neo-Kantian Heinrich Rickert, he told me that he was writing a systematic treatise that would "in at least two volumes *erscheinen*." As he said this, he looked at me with what I felt was a touch of defiance, as if to say, "Don't think that I won't live to finish it." Alas, no second volume of his *System* ever appeared, and as for the first volume (which I bought and read), who cares about it now? I felt that Rickert was, or had been, a man for his time, not for the ages. He wrote elegantly, and his thought had neat outlines, but on one side, it was too close to a Kantian agnostic phenomenalism, and on the other side, too close to what some regard as the platonic theory of eternal forms, to be a great advance.

Rickert spoke of Scheler's philosophy as "built on sand," in which he was not far wrong, except that now and then a brilliant flicker of light illuminates the mostly confused or weakly based thought constructions of that perpetual prodigy of a thinker.

Rickert held seminars at home and was said to have agoraphobia. He sat at one end of a long table (my seat was at the opposite end) made by two tables put end to end in two rooms opened up to make one long room, and as he spoke he stroked his magnificent long beard. In no one else have I ever seen quite such effective beard stroking. I confess that this is all I can recall of the session of the seminar I attended. I rather think he mostly read from his *System*. He was a dignified figure, one of the worthies in his day. One thing I liked about Volume I, was that it is one of the writings, along with Berkeley's *Dialogues* and *Commonplace Book*; also Croce's *Aesthe-*

tica, Whitehead's *Adventures of Ideas*, and some others, that show an awareness of a truth I have been convinced of for so many years, which is that concrete experience is through and through evaluative and emotional, rather than a mixture of two simply different things: value-free cognition (including sensation) on the one hand; and emotions or feelings, on the other. To the contrary, sensations are simply a special class of feelings, more objectified, less obvious in their emotional content, more narrowly determined by the sensory organs and pathways. And Rickert would agree, I think, with other idealists that this alone is an objection to *any* materialism, or any dualism of mind and *mere* matter. The dualism Rickert proposed was only that of ever-changing phenomena and timeless forms. In that respect he resembled Whitehead (who in this is all too Platonic — but how platonic is it? — for my taste), except that Whitehead, with all the neo-Platonists, regarded the forms as abstractions from the *nous*, or divine intelligence. Rickert, with Kant, was too agnostic to indulge in such speculations, at least so far as Volume I takes the reader, if I recall correctly.

Of course, Rickert's distinction between natural science and the "spiritual" disciplines is still more or less an issue, but how many go back to him for help in the matter? To be dispensable it is not necessary to be without great ability; it suffices if the ability, though great, is not great enough. Libraries are full of examples. There is nothing more competitive than writing for the ages. Rickert did not quite make it. I will give one other example. John Boodin in California wrote well and thought well, up to a point. He paid (I understand) to have his works reprinted on extra durable paper. The paper doubtless survives; but the thoughts, although sensible and, in my opinion, vaguely right, are not sharp enough, original enough, or logically coherent enough to last as long as the paper. Peirce, who did not even take enough pains to get most of his writings published, still is much discussed and will continue to be. For he was of the caliber that appears only a few times per century.

Kallen, Feigl, Langford

At the New School for Social Research, where I taught in 1941-1942, I came to know Horace Kallen, one of the wits of our century, and at the same time a very kind man. He took me to lunch soon after I met him, and before long took me again, insisting on paying both times. I saw that something had to be done, and invited him to lunch. On the way to the meeting place I thought to look in my wallet. No money! In my pockets were some forty cents. So I said to Horace, "My only objection to paying for this lunch is, I haven't got the money." Replied he, "You're the perfect idealist. Nothing stops you but reality!" I went home and told Dorothy, "We've got to invite the Kallens right away." We did. It was a good evening.

Another philosopher with whom I have had no close philosophical agreement, but for whom I have had every liking was the positivist Hervert Feigl. With him I could freely exchange ideas. The last time I saw him, he said, "Don't tell anybody, but I'm becoming more metaphysical." Once I read a piece of his on religion that seemed to me to take extremely inadequate account of the present state of theological theorizing: so I dashed off a somewhat indignant letter. After mailing it I thought, "Why did I do that? I like Herbert, and he might possibly be offended." Upon glancing at the opening words of his reply, I relaxed. They were: "I have never thought of you as an angry young man." My age was then well up in the sixties. Curiously, I had been called an angry young man shortly before that by Raphael Demos. The occasion of that escapes me entirely; but I took the remark in both cases as a compliment.

Once, when Feigl had not been long in this country, he was holding forth to a small group of admirers, "A philosophy," he said, "is like a blanket that is too short. You pull it over your shoulders and expose your feet." (Sam) Langford, that admirable logician whose life later turned from promise to tragedy, whispered to me: "He must be a centipede!"

Langford was a high-strung person (to use old-fashioned language). C. I. Lewis, who knew him best, said about him: "You or I may think we have nerves; but we don't know anything about it. He really has them." The dismal illness and death of Sam's first wife was something he never could quite recover from. This is not the only, but it is the most tragic, case of this kind I have known about in the profession. I felt it as a personal loss; for Langford was independent and penetrating and did not jump on bandwagons controlled by others. He would have been a valuable influence had he kept up his zest for work.

Langford never forgave Harvard's President Lowell for his role in the Sacco-Vanzetti case. He looked into this matter with care and, saw no justification for the decision Lowell reached. Yet in Lowell's own account of the matter I find fairly convincing evidence at least of his effort to reach the truth.

Bag Fuller and E. S. Brightman

B. A. G. Fuller was an instructor at Harvard when I was there, and I once dropped in to hear him conduct a class. I recall his comment on oriental art, "compared to which all Christian art seems rather tawdry." As he said this, he looked the perfect specimen of naughty boy. Fuller, in his lively student's account of the history of philosophy (very good indeed on Schopenhauer) deeply offended E. S. Brightman by suggesting that "Personalism" was a movement of interest only to Methodists. Brightman, reviewing the book, not only protested this unkind judgment but objected to Fuller's history on the ground of its use of slang. Fuller replied in the periodical in question that he had looked in the *Oxford Dictionary* for the words Brightman cited as slang and found them all there; but he mentioned certain words that Brightman had used which were not there. The moral, I think, is that it is not worthwhile for very serious persons to engage in public debate with those for whom witty and not necessarily very merciful interchanges are meat and drink. This holds, I think, even though in fact the *Oxford Dictionary* deliberately includes a good deal of slang. My only other recollections of Fuller are two. First, before the beginning of the one lecture in the elementary history of philosophy class that Fuller was to give, a student behind me said to another student, "He doesn't look to me like a profound philosopher." Second, speaking of Socrates, Fuller described him as "unshockable." I am not aware that this particular adjective has been so applied by anyone else.

Norman Malcolm

My defense of Anselm's supposedly wholly fallacious ontological argument came before, and in some crucial points resembled, Malcolm's famous one; but it was his that made people take notice. My defense was also more qualified, with more reservations, and at the same time backed with much more supplementary argumentation. In the long run, I believe, my approach will have to be reckoned with rather than Malcolm's. My partial defense of the ontological argument is consistent with my general stance in metaphysics. An early version is in my Harvard dissertation. It is one of the issues that distinguish me somewhat sharply from Whitehead and also from the great majority of modern philosophers since Leibniz. I have little doubt that it is not the majority who are basically right on the point, *provided* it be clearly understood that I do agree with the majority in two respects: Anselm's commonly cited version of the argument (following *Proslogium II*) is indeed fallacious; and even the correct version or versions that I have given in several places are insufficient by themselves to justify theism. However, they are sufficient to establish the *extremely important* methodological principle that the existence of God is not subject to empirical disproof. The rational justification for atheism—if there can be one—must be a priori, arguing from the logic of concepts, including the concept of deity. No conceivable experiences could imply the divine nonexistence without also implying that belief in God is not simply false but is without coherent sense and could not be true. Here, I side with positivism. It is the meaning of belief that is to be challenged, not its factual truth. If theism makes sense, it is true necessarily. But the antinomies so often deduced from that doctrine, the way it often seems to be a case of wanting to have things both ways, wanting to digest contradictions, warns us that Anselm's Principle is a justification of theism only for those who can meet the positivist challenge, which is over 2000 years old. Not "Is 'God exists' true?" but "Does it make sense?" is the question.

An important and here relevant difference between me and most philosophers is that I reject as hopelessly crude the dichotomy: essence-existence. Even to talk about ordinary forms of existence, we need a triadic classification: *essence, existence,* and *actuality.* To carry this out in philosophy of religion we have to break definitively with the idea of God as the wholly unmoved mover, as simply the immutable cause of all things. We have to allow God an aspect of change and contingency, as well as an aspect of eternal and necessary essence and existence. I call the contingent aspect *actuality*. Only if my position is discussed with at least the foregoing distinctions in mind, can its significance be evaluated fairly.

Malcolm and I have less in common when it comes to his little book on *Dreaming*. I have had an advantage over him here in that I had long ago, and he had not (as he told me) read Bergson's masterly essay on the subject. There is no other to compare with it. As Bergson was the first philosopher to deal carefully and profoundly with memory, so he seems to have been no less clearly the first to do the same with dreaming. Since reading Malcolm's essay, I have been noting features of my dreams that fit Bergson's account but not Malcolm's. The *sensory content* of dreams is explicable in terms of the bodily situation and condition of the dreamer. The dreamer's interpretation of the content, its *meaning*, is another matter. But interpretation, meaning, is vastly more than sensation. When we lie in bed with eyes closed and in a dim light, our optical apparatus receives at most slight and diffuse stimulation from the environment. Hence, dreams usually lack vivid color and sharp outlines. Occasionally distinct color patterns may appear. But then I in my youth could enjoy such patterns with my eyes closed while still awake. I have lost this capacity. The patterns were *given*, really there, not to be sure in the external environment, but in my optical system. An experiment supports this. Stimulate the eyes for some time with intense, sharply focused light, as by an unfrosted bulb, and then extinguish all light. For a minute or more one will experience unstable but definite color patterns. What is going on? Neural activity is the rational answer. The overstimulated nerves continue to "fire" for a time. It appears that these nerves also, under certain conditions, can be stimulated by internal means, as by electrodes in the brain.

When dreaming, one usually is not moving one's limbs. In my dreams my limbs do not seem to move, even when I dream of good reasons to run away. I do not dream that the limbs move because *in fact* the kinesthetic sensations this would involve are lacking. In dreams one hears more normally than one sees. This is because eyes but not ears are closed, and because sounds continue in the dark. I've dreamt a sound interpreted as of an electric fan, but really an aeroplane passing overhead, as I learned on awakening. The sound quality was the same; only the assigned meanings differed. Always sounds are present in sleep; if nothing else, one's own breathing.

In bed, awake or dreaming, odors are scarcely sensed, for obvious physical reasons. (Any body odors, being constantly there, tend not to be noticed even when awake.) Even more obviously taste sensations are lacking. For one reclining in a soft bed, sensations of touch are nearly as they might be if we rested on air. Hence we often dream of flying —but not really flying, simply floating in air. In dreaming I do not find myself seated in an upright chair or standing up. The bodily sensations are usually not right for that—naturally.

We dream of cold and awake to find our covers insufficient; we dream of needing to urinate and awake to find that is the situation; we dream of sexual excitement and awake to find the corresponding physical condition. I have dreamt of an itchy place and awakened to find an insect bite in that place. The realistic deliverances of dreams are astonishing, if one attends to the facts, and then compares them with the standard idea that in dreaming nothing physical is given. Malcolm admits there are such realistic dreams but then neatly begs the question by saying that in such cases we are not (absolutely) asleep and so it is not *really* dreaming that goes on. But the question then becomes. When we are, *by his criterion*, absolutely asleep, do we ever dream at all? I think not.

Malcolm's motivation in his denial that dreaming is at all like waking experience is to refute the skeptical argument: (1) in dreams we experience no physical realities; (2) waking experience is much like dreaming; therefore, (3) in waking experience there need be no physical realities either, but only more orderly, but otherwise dreamlike, experiences. Malcolm rejects (2) and hence the conclusion (3). With Bergson I reject (1) and hence also the conclusion. So I get the main result he wants, but from the facts about dreams, rather than from a baseless dogma about them. My acceptance of (2) is with qualifications that further weaken the already poor case for (3). The sensory patterns are much vaguer in dreams and not nearly as sharply controlled by stimuli from extrabodily objects. In sum, Malcolm's problem is real; but he has chosen the poorest of two possible solutions without even looking carefully at the other.

Morris Cohen

When I first met Morris Cohen, he said to me, "The trouble with you is that you are too much on the side of the angels." (When Julius Weinberg heard about this he said, "You're not on the side of the angels, you're on the side of the archangels.") At the moment I took this as a compliment, but ever since I've been wondering. What is clear is that it was like Julius to put whatever he was putting so wittily. (Alas, he no longer is able to put anything.) The very last remark I heard Morris Cohen make was as we were parting at the Faculty Exchange in the University of Chicago. I asked him where he was going, to which he replied, "You ought to know that I will walk in the paths of righteousness": whereupon he stalked off with great solemnity.

Cohen was a strange combination. He was a capable philosopher and teacher, a good writer, and in his published works there was always a sense of the dignity of the scholarly role. But in oral exchanges he could be extraordinarily polemical. He once savagely attacked a modest young reader of a philosophical paper that was too ineffective and unpretentious to be seriously harmful to anyone. Or again, in a group of colleagues, including scientists, one of whom challenged a statement Cohen had made about science, the fury with which Cohen replied was surprising, to say the least. He took some disagreement of mine as though it had been a vicious personal attack. One could only suppose that early struggles to surmount initial handicaps in life, and disappointments that his success was perhaps not in proportion to his gifts, had embittered the man.

Once at a meeting I attended, Cohen read a paper (since published) entitled "In Dispraise of Life, Experience, and Reality." Bowman, chairing the meeting, expressed what we all felt when he said that he was eager to find out what this title could possibly mean. The explanation was clear enough. Cohen was attacking the cruder kinds of pragmatism, empiricism, or realism, and advocating more discriminating perspectives. It is, he said, the good life, true experience, and beautiful reality that we should seek, not simply life, any life, experience, any experience, and reality, any reality.

Cohen took a position on a perennial dilemma—a position that I for one can neither endorse nor condemn. At a meeting to discuss the status of Jews in our society he was asked, "Don't you believe that Jews have important contributions to make?" He replied, "Yes—but not as Jews."

Cohen's strength was in history and philosophy of law. Otherwise, he added little (with one qualifiction to be given presently) to what others, especially Peirce, had already written. And, in my opinion, he was far indeed from adequately evaluating the riches of systems such as those of Peirce or Whitehead. However, we are indebted to him for his edition of Peirce's essays (prior to the publication of the largely posthumous *Collected Papers*), which he aptly entitled *Chance, Love and Logic*. I heard A. O. Lovejoy tell Cohen bluntly that his introduction to this work was "uncritical." Cohen's reply was gentle, but then Lovejoy was not a vulnerable man, nor one any sane person could think less than highly of.

Cohen, justly famous as teacher, was an agnostic who, unlike some agnostics, had not quite succeeded in appropriating the ethical idealism and wisdom of his tradition, or at least had not fully embodied it in his character. Yet he was a distinguished figure and a lucid writer. And I found one of his ideas helpful, especially in a subject to which he would not have applied it, philosophical theology. This was his "principle of polarity." The ultimate contraries, such as particular and universal, actual and possible, concrete and abstract, belong together and cannot exist simply apart. There can be no realm of essence, having reality simply on its own, and no realm of mere particulars, devoid of universal aspects, nor a world of actualities with no irreducible aspects of potentiality. (All this, to be sure, is Peircean.) Applied to theology, this means that there can be no God whose entire reality is necessary rather than contingent, or vice versa, or actual rather than potential, or vice versa. In my system this is called the *principle of dual transcendence*. In Whitehead's system it was the principle of dipolarity. God is Eminent in potentiality as well as in actuality, in passivity as well as in activity, in becoming as well as in being. Deity is not mere universality in contrast to mere particularity, but rather the *individual with uniquely universal functions*, whose particularity includes all particularity so far as already actualized and stands ready to embrace whatever further particularity may become actual.

Max Otto

For this ex-Lutheran, the devil was real, if not God. The devil, it seemed, was belief in God. An extremely popular undergraduate lecturer, he was defensive about the fact that his peers tended to ignore him. The reason was succinctly summed up by Father Ward's metaphor, "a thin carbon copy of John Dewey." True, this is not in itself, a condemnation. There may be a place for copies, especially if some (especially undergraduates) find the copy more readable and digestible than the original. But the defensiveness was annoying, and still more so the insinuation that Otto was in a position to look down upon anyone who saw more truth in the religious traditions than he himself acknowledged. Once, in an elevator somewhere, when I mentioned to Otto my sympathetic interest in a certain capable philosopher of religion in his department, his response was "That places you," the words and tone implying, "places you (and that other philosopher) well beneath where I stand."

Upon his retirement, Otto was given a banquet at which the climax of his speech was his reminiscing about the early years of his career at the University of Wisconsin. Repeatedly, he intoned the nostalgic "There were giants in those days." The implication that this was no longer the situation was left, I was told, entirely open. The following year, upon a similar occasion honoring the retirement of another Wisconsin professor, the latter again looked back with admiration upon former colleagues. "Yes," he said, "there were giants in those days—*and there are giants now.*" The applause, I need scarcely say, was deafening. This reminds me of a friend in a university I shall not identify—too good a friend to mention by name—who in an unguarded moment in a faculty meeting termed a colleague who was under discussion "the only creative mind in this institution." Rather different is the following case: a certain Harvard psychologist once declared, "There is only one competent psychologist west of the Mississippi River." Thanks to the anonymity no one needed to take offense.

Eustace Hayden

Still another famous agnostic, A. Eustace Hayden, at his retirement banquet at the University of Chicago, informed us that, although some took his views to be rather eccentric, they were really only what we would all eventually come to think. This reminds me of an incident involving my friend Tom Altizer when we both were at Emory. Tom had been telling us about Nietzsche's "God is dead" passage, and he remarked that what Nietzsche said was only "what we have all come to think." Gregor Sebba asked him how he knew this. "We have your word for it, but how do you know it is true?"

Tom: *"I know it simply by looking into myself"*
Sebba: *"When I look into myself I do not see what you see when you look into yourself."*

Hayden, a very poetic speaker, was once described by a critic as "incorrigibly optimistic." He was indeed! Once I remarked to him how every scientific invention produces new troubles and dangers, giving the airplane as an example. "But," said Hayden, "the mind of man will find remedies for those dangers." He forgot to ask what new dangers the remedies would involve or how human beings could be persuaded to apply the remedies when they exist. As I heard someone at a world's fair remark when various safety devices connected with an appliance were being exhibited: "I don't care how safe the thing is, some fool will find a way to make it dangerous."

CHAPTER FIFTEEN

Odds and Ends

Violence and Some Nonacademic Jobs

When violence erupts on TV, I usually change the station. No doubt my attitude is influenced strongly by the sheltered life I have led. Even my two years in the army base hospital did not greatly alter that. For my fellow orderlies, as I saw them, were not combative. Not a single case of violence occurred in two years, so far as I know. No one hit anyone, or even threatened anyone.

I take it back! One blow was struck, and I received it—on my cheek. It happened in this way. There was a rather grim taciturn man of middle-age among us to whom we were all indebted because every chilly morning without fail he got up before most of the rest of us managed to stir (after the corporal had come to waken us) to make a fire in the stove our sleeping hut boasted. This man, who was called John, was perhaps old enough to be my father and had been only beneficial to all of us. He was an unrefined, little-educated chap; but I had nothing against him. Well, once talking to him—which I rarely did—I said something which evidently struck him as offensive, I have no idea why, whereupon he slapped me sharply. I took this as a way of saying, "Don't be so fresh." It did not occur to me to get angry or to feel badly treated. I understood this man enough to know that he was no bully, and that the incident would not lead to any further aggression on his part. To me it was a closed, if rather puzzling incident. Later some fellow soldier (if we were soldiers) asked me, "Why didn't you hit back?" This was a new thought to me, and I don't recall my comment on it. But later still I asked another chap in the hut what he thought. He was a quite young fellow, rather crass by my standards; but his view was much like mine. "You did the only thing you could have done. John is a little [a good deal, but I am sure he said a little] older than you."

A year or two later, when out of the army and working for a few days in a lumber camp (for the experience and to get a few dollars to pay my way back home from California, whither I had gone with my friend Frank Morley), an old man, down on his luck and disgruntled, was paired with me on the stupid job of lifting boards as they came to us on the rollers and stacking them on a small horse-drawn cart. Well, this job was to me simple to understand and hence not interesting to perform. So I was taking my part of the operation lightly and doing it somewhat carelessly. My partner was in a different state of mind. Stupid or not—and he had had better jobs in his prime—it was his job now, and it was to be taken seriously. So he became angry and threw a board at me. Dodging was easy, and I thought nothing of the occurrence. After all, I had been teasing him with my carelessness. Later, the Scottish engineer who managed the steam engine of the mill asked me the very question put to me in the army, "Why didn't you hit back?" In this case I didn't try to find anyone to agree with me; it was just too plain that nothing would have been sillier than to attack that poor old man. He had done me no harm, and I had annoyed him. There was no score to settle at all, unless one against me.

The same man and I were later put on a task piling brush together and he told me the story of his come-down in status, with no sign of any further resentment because of my behavior. There are bullies that may have to be met with crude force sometimes; but momentary and not wholly unjustified anger needs the opposite treatment.

The disgruntled old man focused his discontent on one feature of the camp, the fact that coffee was served at only two meals a day, and he wanted it for all three meals. Before I left for more interesting activities, he departed, saying that he could not stand it any longer not to have his coffee at that third meal. How pathetically clear it was that the coffee was the least of his real troubles! Any reader of letters to Ann Landers (and her replies) will have noted similar cases.

A high-school boy worked in the saw mill. My boredom with a too-easy job was not his case at all. He liked the life. He also had an immense appetite. Dessert one day was canned pears. He ate his first helping, gave himself another large helping from what was left of the common supply on the table, ate that, asked the Chinese cook for more, which he was given, ate that, and asked the cook for still more. The cook demurred; but, as it chanced, the boss happened along just then, too late to have seen what had happened before the cook's refusal. Evidently feeling fatherly toward the boy, the boss told the cook, "give the boy what he wants." The cook did so, with evident lack of enthusiasm. I wondered how close the boy came that day to eating food worth his entire day's pay, which was five dollars (this was 1919), one dollar being deducted for board and lodging.

We worked ten hours, five before and five after lunch, 7-12, 1-6. One of the men said, not bitterly but reflectively and as though philosophically, "I don't think we were meant to work so hard." We did not work every minute, because sometimes the mill ran out of logs and we sat in the shade until the sight of dust from the horses drawing the wagon with a new set of logs warned us that our rest was about over. The men with the saws, axes, and wagon seemed the real lumberjacks, the real toughies. Yet the engineer and the "sawyer" who set the machine-saw that split the logs into boards were the men who got the highest pay, I gathered. They were the skilled labor.

One of Mao's ideas I tend to sympathize with is that everyone should have done some unskilled labor, preferably for corresponding pay, just to learn what it is like. It is never hard for me to imagine how things look to those who do these things. I have hired myself out, and also my army experience was partly similar.

During the summer between school and college I worked on farms, less for the money than to see aspects of life that a mere student may miss. I began with a farm owned by my maternal uncles Richard and Paul, who however were not themselves farmers. After the hay was in on that farm, I went to neighboring farms. The work was somewhat varied, much more so than in the sawmill job. It was more truly skilled, also. At one farm the most interesting thing was a handicapped boy (spastic) who had to have a frame on wheels to support him as he moved about. It was pleasant to see the good *rapport* between that boy and his father, who was evidently quite fond of him. The boy gave no impression of unhappiness, and was quite cheerful. They had jokes together. What happened in his later life may be another story. There was then no law that the handicapped must be attended to in the schools, a law that humane as it is, will, one fears, take not a little from what is done for the not physically handicapped.

On another farm the striking feature was sad in a different way. Here was a man, against whom those who worked for him seemed to have no complaint, as I had none on my own account. But this man had been in a business that failed and had taken to farming as a last resort. He didn't like farming and obviously took his unhappiness out on his horse. There was no doubt about what was going on, the only question would have to be, Did the man have any inkling of what he was doing? The horse was intensely afraid of the man and trembled when he approached. The man professed to believe that the horse was vicious and deliberately misbehaving. No normal bystander, even one with less empathy for animals than I have had since my early teens, could have failed to see that the horse was acting from sheer fear, the memory and anticipation of the pain that was being daily inflicted upon him by the man who accused him of vicious intentions and beat him for them. Such an experience makes it easier to believe that, as I have heard, there are some (I hope few) surgeons who like to inflict pain.

Here is a third and much happier picture of farm life. There was a lionlike young fellow, a veritable Hercules, but as gentle and good natured as you please. We were put together in a hay mow to distribute the hay in the mow as it came up on a trolley pulled by a horse. The man in charge of the horse would sing out, "Let her ride," and the horse would move. To distribute the hay was a dusty, hot, hard job. I confess that I took it easy and let the other chap do most of the work. This seemed to suit him perfectly. I shall never forget the impression of strength, combined with inner security, that made this fellow, able to pick me up and break me in two if he wished, seem so completely harmless—like a Saint Bernard dog. I don't know that he was stupid. I think not. Stupidity is not all that safe. But muscular strength and emotional soundness were the predominant traits. He was stronger than almost everybody. He knew it; but this only meant that he had little to fear from the strength of others. (In those days handguns had not, except in the West, such a vicious grip on American minds as they have now, *miserabile dictu!*) What that Hercules and I talked about I forget; but we had a friendly time of it.

My farming summer paid me far more than money. It came fully up to my expectations as a valuable change from school, and an instructive interlude between that and college.

The Deaths of Dear Ones

For many people the loss of friends or beloved relatives by death is close to, or simply is, the most painful thing in life. Until now, I have been most fortunate in this regard. My parents lived to a fine old age, were ready to die, and had done about all they could have done for their children. The one brother that died in his twenties I had seen little of for years. I have lost no wife or sweetheart. The nearest to that was Nurse Robelen (Chapter 6), and I felt that more as a loss to the world than to me. The cousin I know best still lives and so does the brother whose interests are closest to mine. Such elements of good fortune are not earned, they happen. My lot in this regard has been easy.

Probably every teacher I ever studied under is dead; but (except for one teacher of Greek whom I vaguely recall) they did not die while I still needed them. At the University of Chicago my favorite colleague died not long after my entering the department. This was indeed unfortunate for me. The dearest of past colleagues no longer living was Douglas Morgan of the University of Texas, who died a few seconds after seeming to be fully himself at the end of the oral examination of a student whose work had been under his direction. "Thank you, gentlemen," said he, and walked a few steps to a completely sudden death that resisted every effort to revive him. This man, fifty years old, was the ideal colleague. He could go into a class by a young new member and, without offending, suggest feasible improvements in the teaching—something few of us would dare to attempt, or if we dared, succeed in. In policy decisions, Morgan's part was always transparently generous as well as sane and judicious. He was a good scholar, a wit, and a beautiful human being.

Morgan had a not very strong heart, and he had one trait that was not simply physical and hardly favorable to his health. He was very competitive, not for promotion or salary raises over his colleagues, but in quite a different way. He became the coach of the student team that took part in quiz contests, and he threw himself into this work with a strong will to win, and his team kept winning. This, and one other thing, was a strain on his health. That was dealing with a tough case of hyperactivism in a young nontenured member of the department whose utter brashness split the department. Morgan tried to take the activist's side but finally decided the department could not stand the perpetual conflict that this promised to bring about and changed his vote. It was for him a painful decision. The pain was not caused by self-interest but by the ambiguity of the situation in terms of the departmental good and the activist's claims for freedom of expression. It was very unfortunate for Morgan that he was faced with so excruciating a dilemma. It was excruciating for me also and I too wavered; but then I had no dangerous weakness of a vital organ.

Mentally Disturbed Students

Among a few students I have had in philosophy who had emotional troubles preventing them from any academic achievement, one at the University of Chicago showed clear signs of paranoia. This time I did spot enough of the reality to treat that student with all the tact I could muster. This was partly because, as I knew, about then Schlick, the great positivist whom I had met in Vienna, had been killed by a disgruntled student. The Chicago student seemed to have ability; but what he wrote never made quite enough sense to be definitely acceptable. He was an enthusiast for Nicolas of Cusa and sought to show in that writer a tremendous break-through into the basic principles of modern science. Others than he have held more moderate versions of this idea about Cusa. But this fellow never got it down in black and white in a reasonably clear form. Finally, he gave up and left us—without shooting anybody. Years later he was in the news as a distributor of a pamphlet praising Hitler. This was after the country had been catapulted into the war against Hitler. He was jailed, poor fellow, until the Supreme Court courageously declared that distributing a pro-Hitler pamphlet was not illegal, even in wartime. This was the last we heard of that former student.

Another former student of mine whose studies in philosophy came to a dismal end for emotional reasons was also a man whose writings did not make sense, and who (after he had been accepted as a student) turned out to be paranoid. In this case, I definitely blame myself. I should have told the department to reject this man's application. For, before applying for admission as a student, he had written to me a long letter expressing interest in my ideas, an interest to which of course I had no objection; but the letter might have been the subject of the famous jibe in English literature:

> Others to some faint meaning make pretence
> But Shadwell never deviates into sense.

He was a miserable failure, who pleased none of his teachers.

I have had two students write me angry letters accusing me of unfair or unkind treatment. In one case all details have left me except that I telephoned the man and invited him to have lunch with me; and that in the luncheon conversation his anger was overcome. He did not seem a very promising student, and I know nothing as to his further career. The other student I recall in some detail. He accused me of interrupting him and other students, of not letting him and them have their say. I wrote as disarming a reply as imagination suggested to me; and we have been friends ever since. I still hear from him. He has written two books, the second of which (by him and another student of mine) I expect to have considerable success. I may perhaps have told him in my reply that I had once been visited by a delegation from a class complaining bitterly that I allowed one member of that class to talk too much. "We don't pay tuition to hear what she says," was their point, which took me by surprise and influenced my subsequent limited tolerance of too-free participation by any one member of a class.

Another student was made very angry, though he wrote me no letter and indeed said nothing to me. Simply, he ignored my existence thereafter. He had tried to support an argument by making his own translation of some key passages in Latin. I suspected the translations and submitted them to a Latin expert who found them quite illegitimate. The reasoning also was unclear, quite apart from the translations. In an unguarded moment I wrote rather harsh criticisms of the paper, not realizing that this was one more case of a student whose intellectual confusion was interwoven with emotional difficulties tending in a paranoid direction. I left that institution before this man's career terminated there and never learned what happened to him. I wish I had seen in time the need for diplomacy in that case.

Finally, I think of a happier case of an angry student, angry not at me but at the department for what had happened before I joined it. My introduction to the student was at a meeting of the committee in authority over his case. The student spoke for some time about his grievance in a manner that I felt must be diagnosed as genuine paranoia. I even felt some fear of that man. Douglas Morgan was chairman of the committee. He wrote a characteristically diplomatic masterpiece informing the student, with no unkind words whatever, that he had three weeks to revise his Master's thesis in the effort to make it acceptable.

I was put on the committee; so I asked the student to come to see me. He came bringing the preface. It made fair sense; so I asked to see the rest of the thesis. He brought it, and a few glances made clear why the committee had turned it down. It was merely a string of acknowledged and properly documented quotations, with only extremely scant and unimpressive connecting tissue. Not all the quotations seemed relevant to the theme stated in the preface. I told myself that this time I was going to be courageous and tell the student the blunt truth, but in an unhostile and mild manner. I reached him by phone and began the conversation as follows: "I think you have been wasting your time. You have taken a whole year to complain [he had carried his case to the dean] instead of rewriting your thesis to make it acceptable." Never in my life have I been more pleasantly surprised than I was by his immediate reply: "You know, I think you're right." "Well," said I, "we must talk about this. Come and see me at my office."

This he did, and he virtually told me the story of his life. In telling it he showed scarcely a trace of paranoia. He was part (one-fourth) Indian, and his people, that is, a minority of his ancestors, had been grievously mistreated by whites. With one part of his mind, which he could assume or put off, it seemed, almost at will, he hated everybody because of what "they" had done to that segment of his forebears. Otherwise, he was a reasonable person. He felt that the manner in which the deficiency of his writing was communicated to him was unduly harsh. So the chip-on-the-shoulder personality had taken over. But, he did not need a master's degree and had a job he liked. He summed it all up as he left my office: "I can take anything from a gentleman!" So I freed the department of that incubus.

Would that more often I had done so much the right thing with a difficult student. But it does illustrate the important role for diplomacy, tact, and gentleness, in dealing with students. Many students respond healthily to rough criticism, but some do not, and they are not all worthless or unworthy of respect.

Opportunity, Genius, and Ambition

Unlike Richard Hartshorne I have taken but slight part in academic decision making. This is a confession. I may have done less than my duty, whereas my brother is known as one who has realized the highest ideals in this respect. In a teaching career of over fifty years I made only two speeches, both brief, in faculty meetings. In one I joined, with some hesitation as to which course was right, those at Emory University who thought that a certain political resolution, with which in itself I was strongly in sympathy, was not an appropriate action for an academic body. Some of my friends congratulated me, others thought I was giving aid to the enemy. And one, a wise historian and admirable person, said, "You never know what good or harm such an action will do."

The other speech concerned a motion that the University of Chicago should adopt a two-week reading period during which students and professors would not go to classrooms, and instead both could study, do research, or write term papers, articles, or books. This was advocated as a help to students and professors alike. With all this I agreed. Some stuffed shirt, however, argued that there was no need for such a period so far as professorial research was in question, because "Those that are born to do research will do it, no matter what." For once I had an issue to which there was really only one side. (So often, in questions of policy, I can see two sides almost equally easily.) What I said was, "Yes, those born to do research may do it, almost no matter what; but they may do it by sacrificing other obligations. They may come to class ill-prepared, or otherwise neglect their students. I know something about this by experience." The motion passed, but I forget what signs if any there were that my speech was needed.

The reason for my scorn of the view that inborn ability, talent, or genius will come to fruition regardless is that it is unintelligent. Not even a genius can work more than a part of 24 hours per day and 365 days in a year. The part of this part that is spent in class will not be spent looking up references in a library. And so on. The more that is demanded in fulfillment of one obligation the less (as a matter of probability at least) will be available for other obligations that differ significantly from the first one. Moreover, there also are human motivations and weaknesses to consider. Taking everything into account I believe with the poet Gray that many a born genius never achieves fame because circumstances are too unfavorable. Any other view is to me sheer superstition about genius as a kind of absolute magic that nothing can stop or baffle.

Consider Darwin and the voyage of the Beagle. His father would have prevented him from making that voyage, but an uncle insisted that his father give permission. Who can know what Darwin would have done otherwise? The voyage was clearly crucial to his mental development. Wallace, the only other discoverer of natural selection, also went to the tropics for a long voyage of exploration. And suppose Darwin had been born of poor parents, or an orphan, with younger sisters, brothers, or aged parents to support. Innate ability may be half the battle, but it can hardly be more than that.

I recall a dispute between French military authorities in World War I. General Nivelle, I think it was, proposed a great advance against the German lines, through the network of trenches, barbed wire, and machine gun emplacements, facing heavy artillery fire. One general spoke about how courage can do seemingly impossible things. Another general went straight to the rock bottom truth: "A man with a bullet in his head cannot be brave." (The advance was made—for a few yards, with casualties of 150,000.) It is only less crudely obvious that those with sufficiently great other burdens cannot be great writers, scientists, or philosophers. Imagine Balzac writing all his novels and also teaching several courses each semester for much of his life! Those who value the achievements of biology in the last dozen decades should think with great respect of that admirable uncle of Charles Darwin. He is on my list of heroes. He saw an emergency where few would have seen one, he acted decisively, he was successful, and he was right!

I am personally exceedingly grateful for the fact that I have never been asked to spend as much of my time and energy teaching as a majority of professors in this country are expected to do. Legislators who think they know how many hours university instructors should

Fig. 31. Emily Hartshorne Goodman and family: (Left to right) Eleanor Amy Goodman, Emily, Nicholas D. Goodman, and Charles Andrew Goodman

spend in class are in danger of exceeding their competence. Neither teaching nor research is just like business, farming, politics, or practicing medicine or law, and each of these has its special conditions. Of course there may well be lazy teachers. But some of us work hard, with or without classes, year in and year out.

This leads me to discuss the question of ambition. My brother Richard once surprised me a bit by saying, "I am not ambitious." After a moment's thought I said, "I believe that is true. I am ambitious, you are not, although you are famous." Richard did an important job in his subject, a job that no one else had done, and it made him famous. He did it because he saw it needed to be done and the doing of it was work he liked. Like all good jobs well done it elicited criticisms by those who in fact were ambitious, but not necessarily comparably gifted and well trained. So Richard was forced to defend the positions he had taken. But he did not early in life decide that he wanted to shine indefinitely brightly, as I did. I have often wondered what determines such a difference. I imagine it goes back rather far into childhood.

I was shocked long ago by a revelation of lack of ambition in a colleague. He had been working hard on a projected book until he obtained a desirable position at another university where he had a good friend. He told me that he would stop working on the book at least for the time being. It had not occurred to me that his ambition aimed so low as to involve merely a certain official university status. I have written for the entire profession, for my peers, or for a still larger group, and for later generations. What a few administrative officers of the moment thought of my work was never of more than minor utilitarian significance in my eyes. I knew that they could hardly estimate my work.

Ambition is a vague term. The basic stimulus, apart from a feeling of abilities and training constituting an obligation to serve humanity, has in my case been the perception, or apparent perception, that most philosophers are partly unaware of the relevant resources in dealing with their problems. They have forgotten or never learned what Plato or Leibniz already had seen, or they have never looked carefully and with fresh eyes at certain aspects of human experience, or in some other way they are badly missing important truth.

Every time I have read a philosophical journal I have been tempted to write an essay setting things straight. Every time I had to plan a course, and I never merely repeated one already given, I found myself thinking things that, so far as I knew, had not been seen by others. There is the further point that the harder one works the more the world expects one to work. Editors think of essays one should write for a book they plan, or a journal they edit. "To him that hath shall be given" applies also to work.

Taking all these circumstances into account, perhaps it is partly intelligible that I have written so much and worked at each item as hard as I have. I can think of at least one contemporary in philosophy who has written as much or more, but how hard has he worked to perfect each item? Milton called ambition ("fame") "that last infirmity of noble mind." An infirmity it is; for it is inseparable from some measure of jealousy, and it means a danger of never being quite satisfied with the recognition one has received. Always, one could have become more widely recognized.

One comfort for an ambitious person whose fame is no greater than mine is that there are obvious penalties for greater recognition. One then becomes a public figure, with less and less privacy. I like being rather well-known to philosophers, and quite a few ornithologists and theologians—but not to Tom, Dick, and Mary, wherever I go. To be lost in most crowds does not offend me at all.

What's Wrong with Everybody?

An amusing English writer on economic problems (I met him, but forget his name) wrote a book of which one chapter was called, "What's Wrong with Everything?" My title is adapted from his. To think that everyone else is insane is to be insane oneself. But the awareness of this abstract truth does not entirely do away with the temptation, in specific circumstances, to question the reasonableness of what appear to be nearly universal views or practices.

Here is a trivial example of nearly everybody being doubtfully right. The fact that ice is now plentiful even in the hottest weather seems to be taken by everyone except me as a compelling reason to chill and in the process dilute with melting frozen water every sort of drink, whether it be whiskey, orange juice, ginger ale, tomato juice, Seven Up, plain water, sometimes even milk, and all this no matter what the temperature may be in the room, plane, or restaurant! To me this is less than insanity only because it is rather unimportant. It does waste energy. Good fruit-juice, ginger ale, or other soft drink juice is just right as it is (in air-conditioned interiors) without being diluted. Moreover, to confront a poor motel or hotel guest with ice water on a winter morning.... Oh, well....

Another perhaps trivial example is the way furniture is made in many styles but, with rare exceptions, in only one size. If it fits a person six feet three, it will certainly not fit one five feet three. If it fits the average height of men it will not fit that of women. Children's chairs are indeed made, but age is not the point. Size is the point and it has only an extremely variable connection with age. It has considerable connection with sex. I actually had a woman selling furniture say, when I pressed this matter, "Oh, furniture is not made for women." Correct, but that means: for half or a little more than half of the human species, furniture is somewhat ill-designed. Clothes are sold in many sizes, because people are of many sizes, and because ill-fitting clothes are more obviously ill-fitting than ill-fitting furniture. Even a stupid customer knows when he or she is getting garments too large or too small. Apparently, to recognize this ill-fit with furniture is more difficult. So chairs are not sold by size, but only by styles.

Not only chairs or sofas are offered *as though we were all alike.* The vastly more important items called "meals" in restaurants and many homes as well, are offered in only one size. Are we any more alike in the quantity of food we need than in the size of clothes we need? I have yet to see any hard evidence that this is the case. And so, in restaurants, one either orders a standard meal or has to make do with a sandwich, and, in many restaurants, even the sandwich is too much for some of us to consume without overeating.

How many calories are required to keep us at a proper weight depends crucially on at least two factors: (1) our lean weight (fat above a healthy minimum not counted), which depends on our height, bone size, and muscular development, and (2) our degree of physical activity. The calorie need may depend significantly on a third factor, our metabolism; that is, the efficiency of our digestive system (and lungs, perhaps). But on this point evidence seems hard to come by. It is time experts did some research here and informed us of the results. It is reasonable to think that a tall man whose lean nude weight is 200 pounds and who is physically quite active needs nearly double the calories that would suffice to sustain a short man whose lean weight (like mine) is 125 pounds, especially if the short man is somewhat less active than the other. And then consider a short, slender woman whose lean weight may be 110 pounds and who also is rather inactive. Add the factor of metabolism and there could be still larger differences. What do restaurants care about this? Mighty little. (What do private hostesses or hosts care about it? Not much more, in my observation.)

Restaurants sometimes offer special meals for weight watchers. But one weight watcher may need half as much food as another weight watcher. Then there are "children's plates." But again, and quite obviously, age is not the point. A large growing child of a certain lean weight needs somewhat more than a small adult of the same lean weight and degree of activity. And the child is, in our culture, more likely to be active. So, I submit, nearly everybody seems not to be in his or her right mind on this matter. It is not only the *restaurateurs* that are at fault, it is the customers who put up with such treatment.

The results of the foregoing mass madness are apparent. One overeats, wastes food, or asks for a doggy bag. Is that the best we can do? And why is it that, with all the countless discussions of obesity, no one mentions the way food is served as "part of the problem, not of the solution?"

There is another neglected factor in the discussion of obesity. There are digestive systems that rebel when heavily loaded and those that do not. People of the former kind are relatively safe from obesity (as I am), because they get warnings when they overeat, or part of the food just isn't digested. People of the other kind are always in danger of obesity; for only deliberate restraint and self-discipline can save them. Their bodies will be apparently quite happy with a huge meal; and only in the longrun does anything go wrong.

It is known that some people have intestines twice as long as others! Such differences do not go for nothing. They affect life-styles and their consequences. But, as my former colleague, the late Professor Roger J. Williams, the chemist, kept pointing out, our culture tends to imply that we are all so much alike that we can all or nearly all safely live in the same style.

The problem of alcoholism has similar aspects. Any idea that we should all keep up with one another in the number of drinks is stupid or cruel, for the number that is ruinous for one will be safe enough for another (though he had better not assume so too lightly). In certain abstract essentials, we are all alike as human; but there are enormous specific differences.

Consider "women's place is in the home as wives and mothers." Some female persons are not suited to these roles, and, with the new life expectancy, most women are going to find their children flown the roost when half their own lives are still to be lived; and they may be widowed for many years also. And some women are born with a precious and rare talent, as Jane Austen and many another woman has been, a talent that cannot be made much use of by one who fills the traditional role of mother of a large family and obedient wife of some male chauvinist.

There are many ways to contrast the human species to others. One of them is this. In all species there are individual differences. But individuation is a matter of degree; and it is there for all but the half-blind to see that individual differences in a species of bird are almost negligible compared to those in chimpanzees, and individual differences in chimpanzees are still minute compared to those of human beings. We are incomparably the *most highly individuated of all species.* The crucial contradiction in racism or sexism arises not from the perception of racial or sexual differences, but from stopping there and not going on to the by orders of magnitude greater and more important individual differences within any group identified merely by race or sex. What all black or blackish persons or all white or whitish persons, or all female persons, have in common are almost metaphysical abstractions compared to what distinguishes, in both groups, the stupid from the intelligent, the lazy from the industrious, the ignorant from the informed, the weak, vicious, or cruel from the strong, right-principled, or kindly, or the ordinary person (not to mention the genuine idiot) from the genius.

When we lived in Atlanta, an Emory colleague who was traveling with the singing group he trained encountered an unreconstructed Southerner. This man told him, "I have found the answer to the race question. It's in a book by − − − [a Northerner who had, as all too many other Northerners have, managed to almost outdo the Old South in racism]. He proves the inferiority of negroes to whites by showing how little civilization negroes produced in Africa through the centuries." My colleague (he was a New Yorker) responded by pointing out that the same sort of argument shows the inferiority of women to men. Women, also, through the centuries have not been the great artists, scientists, composers, philosophers, politicians, and so on. This debate was in the presence of the man's wife. I have always thought the tactic entirely fair and to the point. It stopped the debate; for southern male chauvinism did not like to parade itself crudely. And if Afro-Americans have had to face difficulties in achieving high cultural levels, even more obviously in some respects women have had to face them. Historical arguments are notoriously tricky.

On the race or sex question one can no longer say that nearly everybody is wrong. But enough are wrong, and they have enough influence, and enough of the rest of us are lazy or ineffective in counteracting that influence, so that much is still wrong with our society in that regard, also.

On the energy question: it does seem that nearly everybody has been wrong in this country and this century. When our family first had air conditioning (in 1956) we aimed to keep the thermostat a little under 80° in summer and not above 70° in winter. But the prevailing idea was to keep buildings about the same all year around, *well above* 70° in winter and *much below* 80° in summer. This was wasteful; and besides it made dressing for outdoors much more difficult. It seemed absurd to me. But the air-conditioning engineers did not consult those of us who thought in that way. They consulted some theory of the ideal temperature—as though there were any such ideal, regardless of context, regardless of expense, regardless of energy supplies, regardless of outdoor temperatures! I never liked it, and I cannot be asked to like it now. And it still goes on.

In technical doctrines my philosophy is mostly a minority position. Few accept my view that the existence of God is either logically impossible or logically necessary, so that empirical evidence could no more count against theism than it could count against "2 plus 3 equals 5." Perhaps few Philosophers agree with me that being (in a significant sense) is reducible to becoming or to unit-events or momentary actualities as dependent on many other actualities, and that substantial "identity" is a special case of causality. Few agree with me that the concept of matter is explicable in terms of mind, fully generalized; so that both materialism and dualism (taken as ultimate or absolute) are illogical. Few agree with me that factual or empirical truths are time bound (as William James said): they become true at a given time (and remain true thereafter). (It follows that the truth about the existence of God, which must be eternal, is not empirical or contingent (recall the second sentence of this paragraph). Few agree with me that strict or classic causal determinism is not only untrue but illogical — it could not have been true of any world state. Few agree with me that sensation is simply one species of feeling and always valuational, the achievement of intrinsic value.

I am not in a minority in holding a realistic view of experience, in asserting that in experience something independently real is given. Here I am a common-sense philosopher. However, I may be in a minority (but with Bergson and Hocking) in generalizing this realistic view of experience to cover even dreams. In them, too, an independently real is given. I am also not in a minority in rejecting reductive materialism, but only in rejecting dualism.

That so many disagree with me philosophically I find somewhat irritating and troublesome, but not so very surprising; and not strongly indicative of my being radically mistaken. I see good reasons for thinking that in judging philosophical evidence we are also being judged. There is no clear ground for supposing that metaphysical truth, which is the core of philosophic truth, is likely to be obvious even to all well-trained minds. Moreover, I have some ideas about how most philosophers have been trained. I think that first, my parents, then, Yeates School, then, Haverford, Harvard, and Freiburg and Marburg in Germany, did handsomely by me while I was growing up. In philosophy I simply am an elitist. I do not expect the majority to be right on technical metaphysical issues; nor on religious issues, unless in a very broad and vague sense. If in all this I am arrogant, make the most of it.

There is a sense in which my minority positions are much less so than was just implied. If, in counting heads, not only living philosophers but those of the past, and not only philosophers but scientists of our time, are consulted, then my positions receive somewhat more support. I agree in part with Anselm, Leibniz, Spinoza, Peirce, and some others on the nonempirical status of belief in God; with a host of idealists, occidental and oriental, and including Peirce, Bergson, and Whitehead, about the reducibility (really the enhancement) of the idea of matter to that of mind; with Berkeley, Croce, and Whitehead about sensation as essentially feeling; and with all the Buddhists as well as Hume, Russell, Whitehead, Carnap, and many contemporary physicists about the reducibility of substance to events as intimately related to other events, or the reducibility of substance to a special case of causal dependence. As for the logical impossibility of classic determinism, I claim support here from Peirce, Bergson, Whitehead, W. P. Montague, Meyerson, and some physicists. So, if one distinguishes between fashion, or agreement with contemporaries, and agreement through time; also, between agreement with other philosophers, and agreement with thoughtful and instructed people generally, then my eccentricity and arrogant confidence in my own judgment is somewhat less extreme.

Another matter, concerning which sanity seems the exception not the rule, is the way college and university curricula are arranged. A number of years before my official retirement I reached the conviction that the right way to learn is to concentrate, and that our curricular systems discourage this way, the best way, of learning. Fifty minutes of this, then fifty minutes of that, then some hours or days of some socializing or athletics, then fifty more minutes of this, that, and the other thing—it's a system that may serve the interests of professors fairly well, though I question even that, but not of students. I say this even though I had only this system as a student. But I provided my own concentration more than most students can; also, in the days before coeducation and TV, this was probably more easily accomplished then now.

I have twice taught at the only institution in this country where concentration is built into the curriculum, Colorado College at Colorado Springs. Each course lasts 3½ weeks, then several days without class and a new course. "The Block System," each course falling within a single month, forbids a student taking, or an instructor teaching, more than one course at a time. It meets normally for two or more hours, five days a week. I believed in this system before I taught in it, and still do. What brought me to the conviction was experience in Japan with what was called a "summer seminar," where *summer* meant a time when universities were not in session and where students and teacher had no other course on their minds. We met all morning five days a week for two (or was it three?) weeks. When the plan of this course was communicated to me, I said to myself, "That will be good. That makes sense." It was and it did.

Of the few things we know about intellectual creativity or growth, none is better established than this: it requires concentration. Yet we do not apply this truth to our educational practices. When a great mathematician, I think Poincaré, was asked, "How did you make your discovery?" he replied, "By always thinking about it." During those weeks in Japan, I had the second greatest rush of ideas in my life. (The first was while writing my dissertation.) The chief topic was the ontological argument, in connection with which my name is rather widely known. This suggests that even professors may gain from a system that favors concentration.

These are some of the things that seem wrong with (nearly) everybody.

What is There to Regret?

A famous orchestra conductor was asked if there were things about his life that he regretted. His reply was disarming: "I am a very stupid man and have made some terrible mistakes." If I cannot be so disarming it is because I have been luckier than the maestro. My mistakes have been less severely punished. I asked two women in succession to marry me who would not have suited me very well nor I them; but they were perfectly clear about this and so saved me from any further trouble involving them. I made an engagement to marry a person that would not have liked the marriage any more than I would have. But we both realized this within a few weeks and had begun to suspect it after not many days.

My most vivid regret is not about what I or anyone has done or not done for my reputation, but that my wife's Japanese research, always in competition with her successful efforts to further my work, did not come to fruition before some ailments of age and some other pieces of bad luck reduced and finally ended her will to persevere. Partly it was, as with my father, too many abilities for one person to do justice to.

In relations to students I have not always acted wisely or even always kindly.

In relations to colleagues I have made a few fairly serious mistakes. It is a doctrine of mine that conflicts between two individuals are scarcely ever exclusively the fault of one of the two, and that an element of bad luck is always to be reckoned with. I could have related myself to the department in which I taught for much the longest time more wisely, courageously, and unegoistically than I did.

In marriage I have certainly made mistakes. All I can claim is that I *never* gave up hope, *never* regretted that I had married the woman I did marry, and *never* stopped wanting the marriage to succeed. Which it did, no matter what storm or stress arose. On one point I wish to endorse what a number of experts have said. It is not by having children that a badly going marriage is to be saved or made good. A child can be a cause of conflict as easily as a cause of harmony, and only a good marriage is fit for a child to be born into.

Not long before becoming emeritus at the University of Texas, I was asked to speak in a colleague's class. At the end of the fifty minutes, a student made an objection that anyone with my views must have encountered over and over, with which I felt bored, and which I felt I had in principle already just answered. So I was rather scornful and authoritarian in my reply. I much regretted this afterwards and still do. That is not the way to treat sincere objections.

It is noticeable how fatigue tends to increase irritability in discussions. Rational argument requires that one's nervous system be in good shape. This is one more reason for following rules of good hygiene.

"Publish or perish" has never had application to my case. I was publishing years before I thought of teaching, and ten years before I began to teach, and I would have published almost no matter what. "Teach or perish" does fit my case. I was brought up by realistic parents and did not trust to writing as a means of making a living. Many of the greatest writers have, at least for part of their mature lives, had other ways of earning a living. Chaucer, Shakespeare, Fielding, Trollope, are among these. Jacques Rivière, the French writer, when consulted by a would-be writer whether he should accept a teaching position replied in the affirmative. "Believe me," he wrote, "there is no worse trade than art." So I do not regret that I was not reckless enough to rely on publication as chief source of a livelihood, but became a professor as the only acceptable alternative. But it is as a writer that I have felt most myself and would most wish to be remembered.

Of course being a professor is not merely a way of financing a writing career and not merely that plus mutual communication with students. It is also communication with colleagues, not merely in one's own subject but also in related subjects. And to what is philosophy not related? So in four ways my career has been what I needed: financial support, considerable leisure for writing, stimulating exchange with students, stimulating exchange with colleagues. Even this is not enough to express my debt to universities. To have a job, any job, in the sense in which writing is hardly a job (though it is hard work), is to be protected against certain weaknesses of human nature. Complete freedom as to how one spends one's time is not an unmixed blessing. To have to do a certain thing at a certain time is annoying to those who wish to live by inspiration. The inspiration, however, may not come and laziness, alcoholism, or philandering take its place.

The golden age of the professor has perhaps been the period of my adult life. To start out now as a young instructor in the present job market, with institutions callously and casually dismissing those without tenure on the grounds that plenty more are ready to take their places and just might be better is a much more frightening situation than my generation had to face. I object to the callousness referred to and think it may frequently damage, more than help a department. But it seems likely to continue for quite a time in many places.

Perhaps the best remedy is to explore ways in which academic training can be used in a variety of nonacademic vocations, or in academic ones other than those of one's specialty. Perhaps more highly trained people should be going into high-school teaching. There is no reason why logic and some aspects of philosophy might not be taught in precollege classes.

As for how I have managed my studying and writing I have only rather moderate regrets. I might have done better to publish less, to set a higher standard of clarity and readability, especially during the first decade or two of my professional publishing. I might have done better to write fewer articles, so that more of my energy could have gone into planning and working out well-organized and integrated books. As it is, hundreds of well-written articles seem to clamor for republication; and yet it is very difficult to make a book by "pitch-forking articles into a volume" (Peirce). The abundance of articles came about partly by the fact that, perhaps a hundred times over, I was asked to write an essay for a *Festschrift* or other cooperative volume, or asked to give a lecture somewhere, or to review a book or contribute to a journal. And I am not good at saying no to such requests. I did so once in the case of a *Festschrift*, and still wonder if this was not "churlish," (Asked a second time to contribute to the Library of Living Philosophers, Whitehead thought refusing a second time would be "rather churlish.")

I might better have kept up more with symbolic logic, in which I had a start with Lewis and Sheffer, and which I once taught at the University of Chicago. I might have gone on farther in mathematics, the universal language of exact thought. All in all, though, considering the chances of going wrong in life, I seem to have been lucky in being able to come as close as I have to meeting the injunction, "Avoid sowing the seeds of regret." (Who was it wrote this? Was it Maeterlinck?)

One thing I cannot regret is taking as much time and energy from philosophy as was required to make my ornithological book *Born to Sing* possible. I have written nothing I am more sure is well written than that book. Also, though it teems with factual statements, no reviewer of it has accused me of a single definite mistate-

ment of fact. There are a few factual errors; but a professional ornithologist, surveying a similar range of phenomena, would expect to
make as many. As for the theoretical opinions, they are controversial,
but a number of competent ornithologists are to a substantial extent
basically on my side. I put several fundamental questions not previously considered at all in the literature and assembled enough relevant evidence for my answers to retain significance for a good while
to come. And I gave massive evidence that when I speak of "empirical" inquiry in contrast with nonempirical, or with metaphysics, I
am talking about a kind of practice in which I have intensively
engaged. Finally, I also showed how metaphysics, though not empirical, can be helpful in empirical inquiry and lead to factual discoveries otherwise not likely to be made.

Writing an essentially nonphilosophical book undoubtedly took
something from my philosophical work. One of the metaphysical
principles relevant to empirical matters is that of incompossible values (to use the Leibnizian term). I could in some ways have done
better in philosophy had I simply given up ornithology, and vice
versa. It is in an ultimate sense true that everything has its price. No
truth is more absolute than this: you cannot have *all possible* good
things. This truth applies even to God (who has only *all actual* good
things), though for 2000 years many theologians refused to admit
this restriction, or failed to realize its implications.

It is also reasonable, however, to suppose that my philosophy
would have lost something had I known no other subject intensively.
The "other choice" would have had a price not only for my ornithological potentialities but even for my philosophical ones. So I have
little ground for regret on that head.

It is part of the "delusion" that Buddhists rightly see in egocentricity that we tend to feel unhappy because of a lost personal opportunity. Someone else made that discovery I would have liked to make,
acquired that knowledge or skill I would like to have acquired ("desiring this man's art and that man's scope," as the bard has it). So
what? We are each but a fragment anyway. The Whole of things has
those other good things, not all possible but yet all actual ones. Live
for the Whole and what is the point of envy of the others? Celebrate
Life, not my life, or merely your life, and you can transcend regret—at

least if you can forgive yourself your moments of selfishness or cruelty toward others. Moreover, punishing ourselves as we are now for what our past selves have done will not, by itself, do the victims of our misdeeds one iota of good, There should be a statute of limitation even on this most generous form of regret.

The foregoing is my answer to those (for example, Paul Weiss) who argue that the process view of self-identity as essentially abstract, in contrast to the self now as a new concrete reality every moment, tends to weaken responsibility by making remorse an absurdity. It is an absurdity unless it can motivate us to do better, beginning now, or unless it leads us to reform ourselves and make amends to others where this is possible. And whoever is a celebrant of the Whole and of Life will want to do all this anyway. It is the self now that is responsible, and what it is responsible to is the Whole. (Indeed this seems to be Weiss's view.) To discharge this responsibility one must take into account what one's past selves have done, so far as these past deeds are still relevant.

Always, too, there is the grave question; If my *numerically* distinct past selves have done ill, how different *qualitatively* is my present self? Have I repented and been "born anew?" If so, remorse is not to the point and is merely masochistic. But, have I *really* repented and *really* been born anew? That question the present self does face and no metaphysics can answer it. All a sane metaphysics does is distinguish the two possibilities: I have or I haven't. Both cases occur. The religious tradition that speaks of the "forgiveness of sins" refers to the possibility of being born anew. Any theory of infinite responsibility for past deeds that makes nonsense of this possibility is unacceptable, in my religious view. Merely being unhappy discharges no responsibility whatever.

To contribute to the Whole from the point where you now stand is your whole present responsibility. To do that neither too much nor too little concern with past deeds will help. If another needs signs of regret in you, empathy for that need should motivate you to do the fullest critical justice you can to the nature of your past actions. If the other needs your making amends, if a better situation would result from such amends, then, of course, make them if you can. Dedication to the Whole is no basis for simply dismissing any claim merely on the ground that one's present concrete self was not the one that injured the other. The operative question always is, "Who is in the best position optimally to create such and such values here and now?" This is the relevant question, no matter what theory of self-identity one holds. We exist to create value, not finally, for ourselves but for the Whole, or—if you can rise to so august an idea—the divine Life that includes all lives in its consciousness.

"Life is Unfair"

This remark of President Carter's has obvious truth. The laws of nature do not take personal deserts into account. Good people with good luck will be happy; but mere goodness guarantees only a part of happiness, and scarcely even that if lightning strikes one in the moment of being good, or kills one's wife and children.

Of course it is verbally possible to postulate heavens and hells in which rewards fully match good deeds and punishments fully "fit the crime," to adapt Gilbert. But nothing we know of life suggests any such exactitude between desert and reward. And even this is not the ultimate objection. Nothing we know of life, carefully regarded, suggests that such exactitude is logically possible. Its possibility conflicts with the idea that creatures make their own decisions, rather than simply reenacting divine decisions. For, if I decide to do X, and you decide to do Y, who decides that the combination XY should occur? I do not decide it and you do not. Can God decide it? Not if our decisions are really ours and not God's over again. All this holds, even apart from the objection that making God decide all the XY's makes him the perpetrator of every evil or unhappy occurrence in all history, human or cosmic.

I hold with Stephen Crane (in his poem beginning "A man said to the universe") that the universe is not obligated to give each of us our deserts. And there is still another reason why I take this view. To demand that you or I get precisely what is owing to you or me is to make too much of my ego or your ego, our self-identity from birth to death or even beyond (if heaven and hell are admitted). I have rejected for seventy years (with Buddhists of all sects) the dogma that self-interest (here I am happy to agree with Quine—see his Quiditas) is the basis of all motivation. Concern for one's own future is a very prominent and powerful—often destructive—strand of motivation, but there are other strands at least equally rational. We do not have to help our neighbor merely because doing so is likely to help us in the eventual future. In this context the importance of accepting our temporal as well as our spatial finitude becomes apparent. What will my "future advantage" be when I have died?

I refuse to grant for one minute that if I have a genuine interest in my grandson's welfare after my death (probably in the next five years) this makes sense only on the assumption that I shall somehow still be there benefiting from that future of his. This is just not what I am thinking about in hoping that he will have a good future for decades after my death. And there are the good fortunes of my academic children and grandchildren, and ultimately the good fortunes of this terrestrial species of ours. In desiring these future good fortunes for decades or centuries I am desiring *them*, not my own good fortunes for decades or centuries. I have accepted as the reasonable total span of my life less than 100 years.

With regard to Jimmy Carter's remark, in its context, which was the unfairness of making abortions possible for the well-to-do, but unavailable for the poor (or ignorant), I would incline to question or qualify its relevance to that context. The business of government is to consult deserts, or at any rate needs, in distributing the benefits of taxation. This is a very special matter, quite different from how the universe is run. Taxation is a deliberate action, not a mere chance conjunction of actions. It remains correct that no government actions, and no divine actions, can reduce justice to an exact science. Nor is this impossibility the absolute goal of government, human or divine.

There is a rough justice in life. Goodness is to a considerable extent rewarding, both in itself as an inner harmony of will, and in its effects. There is a probability that others will reciprocate, just as there is a probability that they will punish bad conduct. "The good" need not envy "the wicked," and well may feel some pity for them. But a life whose goal is maximal reward and minimal punishment for the self is an enslaved life. There are greater things, more interesting or magnificent things, than any one ego, especially one focused on its own preservation and aggrandizement. The universe, or the universal and everlasting Self or Reality, is *the* interesting thing, not the mortal (or allegedly immortal) human self. On this the religions come close to agreeing. But they nearly all tend to cloud the picture by dreams of survival of death.

There is a kind of survival, sometimes called *social immortality*. What my process theology does is to include in "posterity" the one truly imperishable Life of God who survives all creatures and cherishes their having been, as primarily interesting, beautiful realities, despite secondary blemishes. This is the form of optimism of which Whitehead beyond all others, is the spokesman. He should be honored for it for many a century, if our species manages to maintain its sanity and survive that long.

To preserve our own sanity and foster it in others needs to be made a part of the goal of every human being. The altruism that people have often shown in war needs to be shown from now on in trying to prevent war, to curb our human destructiveness.

The spectacle of young people living chiefly to indulge in chemically induced flights from reality is a sad and ugly one. It reflects their elders doing something more or less similar, with tobacco or alcohol used more and other drugs perhaps less.

Wordsworth's Vision

More than any other poet, perhaps, Wordsworth anticipated one aspect of the kind of religious metaphysics I believe in. I say *anticipated*, because, although some philosophers (e.g., Leibniz) had an approximation to this view before Wordsworth, only about 100 years ago did the view begin to receive a reasonably defensible formulation in technical philosophy.

The most succinct statement of a principal element of the idea is Whitehead's speaking of reality as "an ocean of feelings." Wordsworth describes nature in similar terms.

> *The moon doth with delight*
> *Look round her when the heavens are bare.*

The budding twigs spread out their fan
To catch the breezy air
And I must think, do all I can
That there was pleasure there.

Of the birds,

The least motion that they made
It seemed a thrill of pleasure.

In the poem from which the title of this book is taken, we read of

Winds, thwarting winds, bewildered and forlorn
. . .
Black drizzling crags that spake by the wayside
As if a voice were in them; the sick sight
And giddy prospect of the raving stream
The unfettered clouds and region of the heavens,
Tumult and peace, the darkness and the light—
Were all like workings of one mind, the features
Of the same face, blossoms upon one tree,
Characters of the great Apocalypse,
The types and symbols of Eternity,
Of first, and last, and midst, and without end.

No further quotations are needed to sum up the entire vision. For many, including the philosopher C. I. Lewis, the objection is that we have no way of knowing that there is here anything more than an instance of "the pathetic fallacy," attributing our human feelings to non-human things. Yet a half dozen or more outstanding philosophers — Leibniz, Peirce, Bergson, and Whitehead, to name four — think that there is much more than that. The fallacy, they hold, concerns details and specifics, not the basic general idea that *feeling is the stuff of nature.* Of course, the moon is not an individual enjoying the spectacle of the world it illuminates. Of course winds do not feel "forlorn." But then science tells us that these things are not individuals, not single entities, at all. They are masses, crowds, of invisibly small entities: molecules, atoms, particles. These truly single, though elementary, invisible realities lack precisely the deficiencies that cause us to deny feeling to moons, winds, or mountains. Air, for instance, moves only if something pushes it, sometimes colder, heavier air, or if gravity attracts it to the earth, or the earth's rotation leaves it behind, and such ways of moving are common to dead things and live ones. The moon similarly moves only in ways common to the living and the dead, as our artifical satellites show. But atoms and molecules move otherwise and in ways distantly analogous to those of living things, though on a much simpler level. *Quantum mechanics* is really a misnomer, if *mechanical* means, behaving in merely routine and or, in detail predictable, manner. This is just what current theory fails to support. Some of us in philosophy believe that the thesis of materialism, or of dualism (that the world consists partly of mere dead, unfeeling matter), is an antiquated doctrine. Some physicists and biologists agree with this.

Wordsworth, who did not have our science, was trying to express direct human experience of nature. We do in sheer fact (in some circumstances) hear winds *as* forlorn or sad, as we similarly hear automobile brakes sharply applied. Phenomenologically this is the *truth* of the matter. It is only theory, *not direct experience,* that inanimate nature consists of wholly insentient entities. Colors and sounds express feelings not solely for Wordsworth but, so far as scientific inquiry has yet shown, for everyone. Various experiments support this. But people differ greatly in their ability to detect their experienced feelings as such, where these are subtle or lacking in intensity. I am convinced, and my first book (on sensation) elaborated arguments on this head (arguments still not refuted) that sensations and certain kinds of feeling are essentially one. To sense the world as colored, sounding, hard, soft, hot, cold, painful, or pleasurable is to feel the world. Feeling is the given stuff of nature; anything simply different from feeling is no direct datum of experience. This was also Whitehead's view, and it has been held by a distinguished group of philosophers. But the average philosopher, like the average practical person is a poor "Phenomenologist." Husserl, the German introducer of this label, was in this respect like the average person. I argued with him about this. Peirce, the first American protagonist of Phenomenology, was somewhat better on this and some other points than Husserl. So were Whitehead and Bergson.

As for the "same tree" or "one mind" — the cosmic unity affirmed by Wordsworth in this poem, as in several others, this is the religious aspect. The ocean of feelings, as which nature is actually given, Wordsworth believed, cannot be a mere aggregate of feelings. There must I hold (with many others), be some highest level of feeling from which all the other forms receive directives by which their conflicts are kept within limits, also by which the others can add up to a significant totality. Otherwise, the world would be an unthinkable and meaningless chaos. This is one way to put the argument for belief in God.

In vague forms all these ideas came to me (see Chapter 6, sixth section) as a private in the U.S. Army Medical Corps at the age of twenty or twenty-one. They were based on direct human experience in the same sense as Wordworth's faith was, plus some beginnings of analysis of the kind that philosophy exists to further.

It is partly because of this faith that I have never felt so desperately dependent upon my momentary relations to other people for a sense of identity, or for ideals, as I gather many persons do. Every animal is a fellow creature, the very atoms are not entirely different, and the Unity of the Whole is a vaguely given reality. My life contributes to that Whole; thus life always has at least a minimal sense.

There are several complications that I did not see at the age of twenty. Experience of nature is not most directly experience of what is outside the body. (This form of "naive realism" is indeed naive — in the bad sense.) For ordinary practical purposes we indeed can say that we experience moons, winds, and rivers. They are the things we see and hear. But what is it to see or hear? It is to feel, and intuit the meaning of, what certain stimuli from outside the body are doing to our sensory apparatus. (Spinoza says this.) In infancy we began learning to *interpret* these feelings of processes inside the body as indications of extrabodily events.

The processes in our bodies are not merely in our minds; they are physical events in our nervous systems. The forlornness of the wind, the agony of the automobile brakes, as directly given, are not feelings in these external realities, but they may be feelings in our own bodily cells, as these feelings are refelt by us. All experiencing is thus "feeling of feeling," a duality in which I vaguely believed before I acquired this phrase for it from Whitehead, and before I had thought much about the mind-body relation. Certain nerve cells may not enjoy some stimuli coming into the ears, or the eyes, in the same way or as well as they enjoy some other stimuli. This helps to explain the expressiveness of music and the visual arts. The "pathetic fallacy" may be much less fallacious if the most immediately felt part of physical nature is taken to be inside rather than outside the body. Our bodies are societies of cells, each cell a well-integrated individual organism. There seems to be no scientific fact that conflicts with the assumption that these cells have their own feelings. Neither Wordsworth, perhaps, nor I in my youth, thought about this aspect of the matter. But it is manifestly relevant.

When Wordsworth said that there is pleasure in budding twigs he was not necessarily saying that twigs feel, or are sentient individuals. There is pleasure in a human body but a human hand is not an individual, whether sentient or insentient, but an organized group of cells. Moreover, there is another distinction to consider. The human nervous system is a special group of cells whose function clearly is to restore on a multicellular level the *dynamic unity of action and reaction* that a single cell already possesses on a more primitive level, and a molecule on a still more primitive one. Because a tree (or multicellular plant) has no such special system of cells and does not react to the world with any integrity comparable to that either of single cells or of vertebrate animals, there is no strong reason to suppose that what feeling there is in trees is anything more than cellular feeling. What acts as one feels as one, what acts as a crowd or colony (which is what a tree seems to do) only feels in that collective sense. Similar remarks apply to termite colonies. Individual termites act adaptively, not the colonies; even though colonial adaptation is a result. Wordsworth's concern is not with special questions of this kind, but with the way things are experienced by human beings, and beyond that with the general truth about nature as a system of participation in feelings on many levels besides the merely human level. Wordsworth was a poetic Phenomenologist. To go more intricately into "the life of things" requires science of a more advanced kind than then existed. It requires knowledge of cells, molecules, atoms, particles, and statistical probabilities governing these last three forms of individuality. Mere talk about the pathetic fallacy is doubtfully relevant.

Wordsworth's kind of poetry is scarcely written now. But this is partly because what Wordsworth did he did so definitively well. It is also partly because we have not yet overcome our somewhat childish absorption in the gadgets applied science keeps producing, so that our sense for the natural in general is weakened. And it is partly because going essentially beyond Wordsworth requires more science and philosophy than most poets and literary people find it possible to acquire. If we can keep up our sanity and courage sufficiently to avoid planetary catastrophe through pollution or war, our descendants may return to the attack on the basic question, What is Nature? Avoiding this question may be fashionable, but is it not a "cop-out?"

A former colleague of mine, now deceased, a very sober and sensible but not highly imaginative chap, known for his writings on the philosophy of science, after coming to understand something of my philosophy said that it must make the world very "exciting." Indeed he thought the excitement would scarcely be bearable. "I don't see how you exist!" he exclaimed with some amazement. Yes, life (seen without blinders) is exciting. But the excitement is bearable. Life need not be dull. To live is to care about, enjoy, and contribute to, the great ocean of feelings that is reality. As the song Paul Robeson so movingly sang has it, there are various rivers, distinct from one another, but "they all flow together to the sea." That sea, considered in its unity, or as embraced in "one mind," is divine. Such, according to Wordsworth, is "nature's holy plan." Current science does not contradict this faith. What does contradict it is antiquated science and alleged common sense that seems essentially that same antiquated science posing as axiomatic.

The true common sense is the sense for that without implicitly acknowledging which thinking animals cannot live. Wordsworth could and did live by his faith and I have lived by mine.

It is true that we cannot live without treating plants and many animals as means to our ends, as though they had no feelings or intrinsic values that we need to take into account for ordinary purposes. But then we treat other people partly in this way and cannot avoid doing so. None of this logically implies that there are no feelings or intrinsic values in these things or persons, but only that our feelings and values have for us a certain priority. All animals must have such priorities. But human purposes are uniquely varied and subtle. For the purpose of grasping the meaning of nonhuman things as belonging to a significant cosmos to which we also in our more complex way contribute, it is helpful rather than otherwise to see nature as the pervasively animate and sentient affair Wordsworth (also Shelley) and prescientific peoples saw it as being. That science no longer stands in the way of so doing is a cultural fact the learned world has scarcely begun to take in. A view that reconciles primitive person's naive intuitions, the most up-to-date science, and a mainstream of the poetic tradition must be more than merely an oddity. Could it not be close to the very truth? Of course there are still puzzles: see the French physicist Bernard d'Espagnat's *In Search of Reality* (Springer Verlag, 1983), especially pp. 115-120. The religious value of the belief that all things are included in "the workings of one mind" is that it enables all life and experience to contribute to an imperishable Life and thus acquire permanent significance. Whatever good we achieve in our own enjoyment, or that of other creatures influenced by us, whatever harmony and intensity of feeling, becomes thereby constituent of the all-embracing harmony of the divine participant in our feelings. The minor American poet Richard Hovey, who died in the first year of this century, wrote the following lines:

> *God has said, Ye shall fail and perish*
> *But the thrill ye have felt tonight*
> *I shall keep in my heart and cherish*
> *When the worlds have passed in night.*

> *Give a cheer!*
> *For our hearts shall not give way.*
> *Here's to a dark tomorrow*
> *And here's to a bright today!*

I associate this with some lines of Blake:

> *He who bends to himself each joy*
> *Doth the winged life destroy,*
> *But he who kisses each joy as it flies*
> *Lives in eternity's sunrise.*

This is my religion of contributionism. We contribute our feelings to others, and above all to the Universal Recipient of feeling, the One "to Whom all hearts are open."

Epilogue

Because most of this book was written ten or more years ago, I wish to end with some reflections on how I see philosophy today and how I try to account for its coming to be as it is. I distinguish three classes of philosophers, call them *ordinary*, *brilliant* (ingenious, clever), and *great*. All may be useful, but the last are for me decisive in the long run. And, I believe there is genuine progress in their succession. The asymmetry in the fact that the later may know the earlier, whereas knowledge in the reverse direction in this case is scarcely possible, must count for something. We human beings are not that stupid!

Consider Russell, whom I knew somewhat personally and read extensively; Was he a great philosopher? Carnap thought "perhaps the greatest." Russell was certainly brilliant, an excellent mathematical logician, a clear and versatile writer, perhaps a great man, all things considered, but in my view not quite a great philosopher. As Passmore, a reasonably unbiassed judge, said, Russell's philosophy was essentially that of David Hume, with some modern technical refinements. Nothing like this can sensibly be said of Plato, Aristotle, even of Epicurus (his revisions of Democritus were substantial), Anselm, Descartes, Leibniz, Hume, Kant, Hegel (no favorite of mine), Peirce, Bergson, Whitehead, in relation to a predecessor. Quine is somewhat similar. He is perhaps the most influential living American philosopher, but how many vital human concerns that philosophy deals with does he leave dangling? His most original contributions include a blurring of the distinction between necessary and contingent truths, a distinction that even Carnap wanted to preserve, and that he defended once in Chicago against Quine—some of us thought, successfully. William James had already, tried valiantly to arrive at an almost holistic empiricism and contingentism, and where Quine went farther he seems not to have convinced even himself.

The best claim among the living to philosophical greatness that I see is Sir Karl Popper's. He has shed a flood of light on many subjects. He was the first to make sharply the most useful distinction between empirical or contingent and metaphysical or necessary truths: that the former would be contradicted by *some conceivable observations* whereas the latter are compatible with *any conceivable observations*. I make a few revisions in this but am largely in agreement with it and regard it as epoch making.

My example, and it is close to Popper's, of a metaphysical truth is, "something exists." Any experience whatever would support this, no experience could contradict it. That "nothing exists" could not conceivably be observed. It is mere talk. But that I have lived to this moment is a contingent truth because there is no absurdity in the idea of my dying or having died being observed long ago. I came close indeed to dying, there were witnesses, and only ignorant or superstitious persons could doubt that death was very possible. (God also was there, but even God could not observe total non existence.) Interestingly, Bergson is in agreement with the proposition that "there might have been nothing" is nonsense. Popper avoids many intellectual traps, as I view them: for example, unqualified determinism, or positivism, or reductive materialism. Admirable also is Popper's contention that what refutes a *positive* empirical assertion is not a negative, but another positive, assertion. Thus, "the earth is observably spherical" contradicts "the earth is flat." *Mere* absences or privations are unobservable. To say, there is no feeling in a stone is to say, there is something in the stone that could not be there if feeling were in it. Descartes said that this something was extension. This is open to serious objection. That mind is not extended cannot be shown; Descartes merely stated it. I do not see what positive trait can exclude feeling from an entire portion of nature. Of course stones do not feel, but they are too static, too identical through change. Atoms and molecules are very different from the stones they constitute. What feels acts, and it is a category mistake to say a stone acts. It can be made to move but this is a modification in the movements of its molecules. Its action is a crowd action not the action of a single agent.

To say, "God does not exist" is partly analogous to the denial of feeling in stones, and partly quite different. We all know what the word *feeling* means, for we have ourselves felt and known that we have, but the word *God* is not so easily and directly explicated. Carnap refused to call himself an atheist. He thought theism could not even be false, rather it lacks any consistent cognitive meaning. As many use the word, I agree with him. More of this later.

Whitehead, in thinking about modern thought, used the phrase, "one long misunderstanding of [ancient] Greek philosophy." This misunderstanding originated in medieval philosophy, or even earlier. Plato and Aristotle were inadequately known, and some of the best in each was missed. (Even Whitehead underestimated both.) In addition, the improvements that Epicurus made in Greek materialism were not appreciated, especially the rejection of strict mechanism, or the imputation of an aspect of free play or randomness on the atomic level. All three of the Greek philosophers just named agreed that events have necessary but not strictly "sufficient" causal conditions, and that there is some disorder as well as order in the cosmos. Plato's criterion of the presence of mind or soul, namely "self-motion" in the broad sense of self-change, which I hold is an anticipation of Bergson's, Berdyaev's, or Whitehead's creativity, or Peirce's "spontaneity," was close to the greatest of Plato's discoveries. It has been fantastically underappreciated. I agree with Burnet's statement that Plato's great discovery was not the eternal forms but mind or soul, the central theme of the *Republic, Phaedrus, Timaeus,* and the *Laws,* Book 10. Plato would have liked to interpret all change as simply the self-change, or creativity, of souls seeking the good. He did say that soul change was the source of all change. But he could not get rid of the idea of mere matter as moved only either by other matter or by soul, and so he was a dualist, not a psychicalist. Aristotle's dualism had much the same source, less sharply formulated.

The materialists tried to muddle through by terming soul a special sort of moving atoms. However, all atoms were for them self-moving, and nature consisted only of these. Hence, by Plato's definition of soul, and Epicurus's cosmology, there is no mere matter. Somehow Epicurus failed to see this. Aristotle did not help here. He even rejected the statement that mind is self-moved. Nor did the Stoics, including Spinoza, help. They had no self-motion in any significant sense. For them each thing did what its causal antecedents, no matter how remotely past, determined it to do. Teleology was simply mechanism with a fancy name. God's decisions are the only ones; or rather, there are no decisions, no freedom, and no contingency. It always is too late for creative additions to the definiteness of reality, transforming mere abstract, not fully definite, possibilities into definite or concrete actualities.

There is also the question of substantial identity through change. For Plato (*Timaeus*) change consists in the vague cosmic "receptacle" acquiring or losing qualities. Aristotle — I here follow Hung Hwan Chen's partly only orally communicated scholarship, at Emory — pluralized the receptacle. Each substance (and this was a regression from Plato) is radically separate from, wholly nonidentical with, every other, contradicting any equivalent of the cell theory of organisms. However, unlike Leibniz later, Aristotle did qualify self-identity to allow for qualitative changes not necessary to the identity; and here Leibniz regressed to an absurdly radical denial of genuine contingency. On the other hand, the qualified identity view raises problems about the extent of the identity, the persisting individual uniqueness and unity. Leibniz rightly saw problems here and took heroic measures to solve them — without resounding success. Ditto Spinoza, in wholly denying the separateness and contingency.

In our time the problems are considerably transformed. Grains of sand are indeed not self-moving , but their molecules are; however, the basic final units of reality are events, not things or persons. Physics has at last come to the view of Heracleitus or Buddhism. In addition, the unity of the world, according to both relativity and quantum physics, makes Aristotle's form of pluralism irrelevant. It never was an entirely good metaphysics. Whitehead's actual entities, his unit-events, prehensively embracing their predecessors and forming enduring, sequential societies, do much of what substances were supposed to do, but the unit realities, the new monads, do have "windows" through which they experience, and thus are influenced by, other monads, and so are their societies by other societies. No windows meant that there were no perceptual prehensions, or at most only mnemonic ones, and because of the lack of quanta, no definite ones even of them because no definite subjects to have them. Peirce was in trouble here, compared to Whitehead; his synechism, or continuitism, was the reason. He lacked the stimulus of quantum physics.

Because Whitehead is free from extreme versions of the dogma of sufficient reason, he can formulate a genuine doctrine of universal freedom as the secret of contingency and of an open future. The problem of evil in its worst form does not arise; there is no need to find a precise *why* for concrete misfortunes, they come from partly chance intersections of multiple creaturely, as well as divine, cases of freedom. Only the *risk* of evil needs explaining theologically, not the actual forms. The risks are justified by the opportunities inseparable from them. Freedom, divine and creaturely, is the prerequisite of both good and evil, and of any possible state of affairs. In short, freedom must be, and be everywhere and always. What is contingent is the special forms of the (not wholly determining but approximate or statistical) natural laws without which freedom entails an impossible chaos or confusion of decisions.

The discovery of microorganisms, which led Leibniz, with a stroke of genius to anticipate the cell theory (the discovery that large organisms are composed of smaller organisms), lends support to psychicalism and was one of the features the Greeks lacked. It is not a detail but a basic principle. Without it the difference between animals and vegetables is bound to be misunderstood and it was so. A vegetable is not an active singular, an animal is. Aristotle's vegetable soul is a myth, but a plant's indeed self-changing cells are primitive souls, psyches, comparable in this to the cells of an animal. With cells, statistical gas laws, molecules, atoms, and so forth, Whitehead could carry the scheme further. Particles, perhaps vibrating "strings," are its present edge.

I submit that where the Greeks were largely in the dark, blindly guessing, about matter, we have an enormously extended grasp of the real physical situation. Notions of the merely inactive, or of merely mechanical activity, can be given up, now that we know where much of the action is in the animal, subanimal, and subvegetable portions of nature. Physical or material need no longer mean nonpsychical, but only the most widely distributed, primordial, and, in unit-cases trivial, forms of the psychical.

I make a distinction between the ability of my fellows in intellectual work to judge ideas and their ability to judge individual intellectual capacities. Both ordinary scientists and great scientists have known that Einstein's views in physics were to be taken seriously. Similarly Sewall Wright, who with his wife were among our closest friends, was widely recognized as a biologist scarcely surpassed since Darwin. Like me he was quite confident that materialism and a mind-matter dualism are both mistaken, indeed logically could not be true, and that nondualistic psychicalism, envisaging a vast variety of entities *all at least sentient*, is the truth about nature. Once when I said to Wright that something or other was obvious, he replied, "anything is obvious, once you see it." I suppose there is a catch in this simple sounding statement, but I also think that unless one has some trust in really definite intuition's of sense, in contrast to nonsense, one is not going to make discoveries of importance.

To me it is fantastically obvious that from Aristotle to Kant Western theology confused a group of at best half-truths with whole truths, so far as the concepts employed were concerned. Of course there is some truth in the contention that the idea of the supreme Reality, supreme power, supreme individual, supreme form of knowledge or love—in short, the idea of God—refers to something that is *not*, like a human or other animal, born or destined to die; does *not* change from weak to strong, wise to foolish, ignorant to knowledgeable, bad to good. So, "I am the Lord, I change *not*." God must have the supreme form of stability. This is one of the half-truths. Was it seen as such? Yes (to some extent) by Plato; Scarcely at all by Aristotle. And which of the two was followed on this point by nearly all later theologians for more than twenty centuries? Clearly it was Aristotle. This holds, with minor deviations, of Jews, Mohammedans, Christians, of Catholics and Protestants—until Fausto Socinus in the sixteenth and seventeenth centuries (and even he was virtually ignored on *this* issue). The deviations were in some of the mystics in all three groups.

Why is the divine changelessness a half-truth? Because the idea of supreme stability, taken as a value justifying worship (and otherwise it is not relevant to the religious meaning of God) logically raises the following question—by an important and I think valid principle sometimes called the *principle of contrast* (among disciples of Wittgenstein) and sometimes the *principle of polarity* (Morris Cohen)—Is there not, must there not be, a supreme kind of change that also is a value, and indeed one without which supreme stability is no value at all? An atom has a much more strict stability than a human person, does it equally deserve admiration, respect, or love? The moon is remarkably stable except for its easily *predictable* motions. How stable is mind compared to matter? Who has told us that *all* change is bad or regrettable? Did Aristotle and his followers for millennia face this question? I think I know the answer. But, the mature Plato did face it.

One argument used to support the Aristotelian view was the following. Change, to be important, must be for the better or for the worse. Because God, to justify our unqualified trust, love, or worship must be "perfect," either kind of change it was thought, must be excluded from the divine reality. (Thus Plato, in the *Republic*, Book 2.) The unnoticed assumption here is that value (what is admirable, desirable, or good) is *in every aspect* and by every relevant criterion, capable logically of an absolute maximum. For if not, then either theism *could not* be true or God can and must be defined as, in some respect, capable of increase in value. I believe, after thinking about this for sixty five years, that this dilemma is a valid one. Where in the Middle Ages did theologians face this problem?

Mathematics discloses no definite greatest possible multiplicity; how do we prove that multiplicity has no relation to value? Do we not have reason to affirm the contrary? Aesthetic value depends on multiplicity, for it depends on contrast and variety. "Variety is the spice of life." Could actuality, divine or not, exhaust possible variety? Leibniz struggled with this. Did he succeed? Let those who think he did stand up to be counted. I say that "most beautiful possible world" for God to enjoy contemplating (do you say God contemplates without enjoyment? Then I say, poor God) is meaningless or contradictory. Ergo, either atheism or the giving up of the doctrine of no divine change in the way of increase, is the right conclusion.

Another apparent justification for denying divine change is the dogma that a cause must at least equal its effect, because it must have what it "gives" to the effect. Granted, *if* causing is simply giving? Wide experience of causation does not support this. On the contrary, causes tend to be surpassed by effects. Adulthood is more than childhood. And if causation does not increase total value, what good is it? A futile effort of running to stand still? Remember Lewis Carroll. I think the dogma of at least equal causes should be given up. Granted that our old age may be inferior to our childhood, still God, as retaining full awareness of our childhood and acquiring also our elderly present, has been enriched. Ultimate effects are not simply in the world but in God as enjoying the world. (This is my version of Niebuhr's "The end of history is beyond history.") Perhaps Fechner was the first to think clearly about the divine increase. And how very clearly he expressed it! A fair number have seen it since.

Socinus, Fechner, and Jules Lequier, who all believed in divine change, saw also that there is no contradiction in saying that God acquires new content of knowledge and love and yet is all-knowing. Not to know X when there is no X to know is not ignorance in the proper or privative sense. "Future events" are not already there ready to be known before they occur. This *would be* contradictory. And that is why logicians (e.g., Quine) who declare all truth to be timeless are claiming implicitly to settle many of the basic metaphysical questions, they are almost running their own ontological argument and deducing existence from a mere definition. I say *almost*, because Quine does argue briefly for his view. One has to know that the definition of God (or truth) makes sense. This applies definitely to Anselm's ontological argument for theism. Mere words about God are not enough; coherent meanings are required. Hence, other than the ontological arguments are always necessary, with theism or any other metaphysical "ism." Peirce, who defended the ontological argument, knew this. In all issues he had more than one line of argument.

Other half-truths not seen as such by the Aristotelians were the contentions that the supreme reality must be cause not effect, active not passive or receptive, independent not made to be, in any part or aspect, what it is by relations to others. Above all, it must be necessary not contingent. Taken all together, these half-truths are the "negative theology." Note, however, as Plato perhaps would have noted, that cause and knowledge are not merely negative, nor are purpose or love, and that to know or care about others cannot leave the knower or lover simply as it would be were the things known or cared about not there to care about. Aristotle, the great founder of logic, saw this implication and, with admirable consistency, denied that contingent aspects of the world, including himself and all individual animals, are known to God. (Plato, on the contrary, said we are divinely known and valued.) Spinoza saw Aristotle's point and tried to solve the problem by the desperate remedy of denying contingency even of the world in its particular "modes." The scholastics simply left the glaring inconsistency intact. Leibniz and Arnauld virtually concede this, but fail to offer anything to mitigate it. As Russell pointed out, Leibniz's "sufficient reason" is really a denial of contingency and puts Spinoza and Leibniz in the same trap.

I have shown elsewhere that two concepts paired as are active and passive (or necessary and contingent, fixed and changeable) applied to two subjects, God and Cosmos, yield *sixteen possible combinations* (permutations not counted) for each pair (allowing for zero cases of no application). In the most complete combination, for instance, *NC.cn* with capital letters standing for divine and lower case ones for worldly necessity and contingency, I argue, we have the whole truth, so far as these concepts go. I attribute this view to Plato, with minor qualifications explicable by the state of science of his time, and then, with similar qualifications, to Socinus, and finally, with lesser qualifications, to Whitehead and a few others, including this writer. The time was at last ripe for seeing the obvious.

Aristotle was not mistaken in emphasizing the modal pair, necessary and contingent, and he was beautifully right in some of the logical requirements. (In general he was right (for his time) in topics close to formal logic. He saw that contingency means chance (no "sufficient" reason) and that volitional freedom entails contingency. He therefore imputed no free acts to deity and no knowledge of such acts. Here, too, he was logically superior to his medieval successors.)

The great intellectual superstition of Western, and to some extent of Eastern, traditions has been necessitarianism, including the deterministic definition, "necessary and sufficient" causal conditions. Until about twelve decades ago this bias was apparent in nearly all modern Western philosophy, except for the explicit and insightful recognition of at least human freedom by Descartes. Crusius also was an exception, but not Kant or Hume. Maxwell and Peirce began the change that made my kind of metaphysics of *universal* freedom for all genuine active singulars, including deity, less difficult to defend. Whitehead independently came to this universality, but I got it from Peirce.

In this volume I omit further discussion of the sixteen logical possibilities and their historical exemplifications, important as these are, and turn to a more general methodological problem, that of deciding among the possibilities, no two of which can be true and, (taking into account the zero possibilities) one of which must be true. The only hope of a decision on rational grounds depends on finding rational rules for relating concepts to concepts and other rules for relating concepts to perceived phenomena.

In 1916, as I learned only during the ninetieth year of my life, Arthur O. Lovejoy, the great historian of philosophical ideas, gave a presidential address in which he was as severe a judge of philosophers of the then-recent past as I am, if not more so. (See the *Philosophical Review*, 1917.) He thinks philosophers have dealt much too carelessly with their problems. They have rushed into conclusions, or adopted whole systems of ideas, without first making a list of the "pertinent considerations" relevant to the topics concerned in the conclusions or systems. Lovejoy urges that philosophers make an exhaustive list of these considerations. Instead they have taken into account such considerations as they happen to have thought of, or encountered in others, not inquiring what other ones might be thought of that would be no less relevant, and perhaps even more so. As I have emphasized exhaustiveness in searching the possible answers to a philosophical question, he stresses the exhaustiveness of pertinent considerations. Perhaps both maxims come to much the same, I am not yet sure of this.

How does one find the pertinent or relevant considerations to a philosophical question or issue? How does one know that one's list is exhaustive? My answer is, by the mathematics of combinations of concepts, either ignoring permutations, or definitely including them. Otherwise I see no way. Lovejoy barely mentions mathematics in the article. I take an example from Lovejoy. He rejects Bradley's extreme monism and Bradley's vicious regress argument against external relations; and he seems to opt for the extreme view that relations are universally external — not mentioning Bradley's argument against that. Mathematically, there are three possible combinations: relations universally external, universally internal, or some the one and some the other. In addition, because a relation has at least two terms (I am not forgetting identity) the nonuniversal possibility has the two possible forms: ARB internal to B and not to A, or vice versa; whereas, with either of the universal forms, the internality or externality of ARB and BRA must be indistinguishable. Bradley ignored the nonsymmetrical case and this viciates all his argumentation. Why this was not seen by the disputants is a mystery. Almost tragically—or is it comically? Russell did the same? Hence, neither exhausted the obviously pertinent third and fourth cases. How many have followed them! So much the worse for many philosophers of this century!

Lovejoy is largely right, however, in the address, and in his historical writings, in *some* of his maxims and procedures. He is right that our choices should not be among systems, for there are large elements of chance in the formation of systems, and by no means complete mutual requirements, or complete consistency, in the way they are combined. Hence his historical writings deal with doctrines, not entire systems. The question is not, are you a Platonist, Aristotelian, Kantian, or Humean? On some issues, each of these will be admirable enough, but on some others perhaps seriously mistaken. Richard McKeon, another learned man, took almost the contrary position. The great philosophers, he held, are consistent enough, and all of them in their way understood reality. Selecting one of them is a personal or political action, not demonstrably uniquely right. I hold with Lovejoy that we must deal with issues, not systems tied to historical names. I have been called a "semi-Whiteheadian," also, in effect, a semi-Peircean, also a Platonist. I quarrel with none of these. I am also a semi-Popperian, something of a Bergsonian, Socinian, Epicurean, and Fechnerian.

Lovejoy was right in opposing extreme monism, but unguarded in seeming to accept extreme pluralism or extreme dualism. He was unguarded in praising the piecemeal method, but well advised in opposing the Hegelian extreme opposite to this, according to which one has *either* everything right *or* everything wrong, and the proof is only the perfect whole. Human beings cannot do things that way. Lovejoy is also right to warn us against claims to self-evidence, but less adequate to the necessity that not all truths are of the contingent kind that could with equal logicality have been false. He admits this, but does nothing with the problem. How do we know? That two plus three make five is self-evident, but not all important cases are nearly that easy to see. But "counter-intuitive" is a significant charge.

Lovejoy is again correct in pointing out that the only way to overcome bias is not for each philosopher to transcend human limitations by becoming entirely disinterested and without bias, but rather by free and reasonably fair discussion with others whose bias is, as it usually will be, to some extent different. But he perhaps goes too far in wanting us to give up all aggressiveness in arguing for our own view. The motivational problem tends to strain human capacities at that point. Part of the fun is in the excitement of argument with eager promoters of partly personal causes. Some delicate balance seems the best we can do.

The principle of plenitude which, the Reese *Encyclopedia of Philosophy and Theology* says, Lovejoy attributed to Plato (my recollection of *The Great Chain of Being* is vague on this) seems to me far from Platonic, though it may be Neo-Platonic and is certainly Stoic and Spinozist. But Lovejoy is profoundly and largely right that there were ambiguities in the great philosophico-theological tradition and that these, for two millennia and more, troubled philosophers without receiving much of a solution. What he failed to see was how the twentieth century offers a new opportunity to refind in Plato an outline of the solution that would be better than the ancient Greeks were in a position to grasp clearly, but the way to which had been or was being prepared by Schelling, Fechner, Lequier, Peirce, Bergson, Dewey, Courneau, Varisco, Whitehead, and others. (I met Lovejoy by accident before beginning my studies at Harvard and later a few times. I also read his books and a few articles with keen interest. He really wrestled with the history of ideas.)

Considering the difficulties faced by philosophers, as distinct from scientists, I find it ludicrous to suppose, as some now do, that what has happened since the pre-Socratics can have shown that philosophy, or at least metaphysics, is a vain enterprise; that all the possibilities have been adequately explored, and we can turn to more fruitful endeavors. I hold with Peirce that we now are in a much better position to see the meaning of the intellectual history since Plato than anyone in previous centuries has been. Peirce's way of putting it was, "In the Twentieth Century metaphysics will become a science." We know at last and at least that some strands of the tradition were definitely mistaken, and that some others are still worth exploring further.

One way to test the insights and biasses of an age is to inspect its encyclopedias. The generally useful *Columbia* is clearly biassed in philosophy of religion toward positivism (or is it atheism?). The many-volumed *Encyclopedia of Philosophy*, edited by Paul Edwards, also may be useful in general, but its editor, when he writes his own opinions, is astonishingly biassed. An essay he wrote for the new *Encyclopedia of Unbelief* was found disappointing by a generally sympathetic reviewer of the work. He quotes Edwards as declaring his wish "to rid the human species of religion in all its forms." My reaction to this is to ask bluntly, "How far is hatred of religion as such separable from hatred of the human mind itself?" Even the Greek atomists had religious beliefs (in immortal deities); Hindus, Chinese, Japanese, whether Buddhists or not, were and are pervasively religious. Let us not forget, either, Bergson's to my knowledge unrefuted arguments for the view that a species of animal as highly thoughtful as the human could not efficiently meet its needs without religion, and this for three basic reasons, given in masterly fashion in *The Two Sources of Religion and Ethics*. None of the three is done away with by advances of science or technology. Indeed, they are intensified. In saying all this I am not denying that there are hateful, as well as superstitious, and no longer reasonably believable, forms of religion. This is only too true. But there is also no great scarcity of hateful and not reasonably believable forms of atheism and quasi-deifications of the planetary species to which we belong.

In his own encyclopedia, Edward's article on "Panpsychism," a topic of special concern to me, seems only trivially informative. He mentions but gives no careful exposition of the views of the leading contributors to the doctrine, which are Leibniz, its founder and first clear formulator in all the world, also Bergson (in his mature period), S. Alexander (ditto), Peirce, Whitehead, and Hartshorne, and the considerable groups of disciples of the last three. The excuse for the virtual elimination of these is that he proposes to ignore the doctrine so far as it is metaphysical and consider it only as an empirical or contingent truth or falsity. He thus begs by far the primary question at issue; Does the idea of mere, insentient, mind*less* matter make any *positive* coherent sense? I say that it does not, and take the panpsychists of importance, Peirce particularly, as agreeing with this. If the issue is really empirical then observations can be conceived at least to show that in large parts of nature there is *nothing* mental or psychological. Long ago I challenged materialists and dualists to explain a non-question-begging criterion for the *total absence* of mind (at least feeling) from an entire region of space-time. Only Descartes and Popper have given answers that I can see as clear or definite, and I have argued that they were mistaken. It has been shown that Descartes admitted his mistake. Kant's argument against psychicalism (partly in a footnote to *Träume eines Gestessehers*, partly in the first Critique) owed their plausability to aspects of the physics, metaphysics, and theology of Kant's time that do not fit the present states of these subjects. Hegel at best is ambiguous on the issue and made little or no use of Leibniz's central insight that matter has no positive property that mind could not have. In close discussions with several Hegelians on this topic, all I get is dogmatic pronouncements or vague rhetoric. Dewey, who set out (as the Germans like to say) from Hegel, is extraordinarily cloudy concerning his reasons for rejecting Whitehead's reformed subjectivism. I corresponded with him about this and his argument remained very vague or unclear. Nor have his followers clarified it. William James, as Marcus Ford has shown, either never attained a clear position as to mind and matter or was a psychicalist. None of the pragmatists did justice to Peirce's definitely psychicalistic "idealism." On no issue, perhaps, is current philosophy less definite and cogent than on this one. It relies on common sense just where common sense should be replaced by science. Subtle discussions of realism are beside the point. Psychicalism *is* a realism, and rejects extreme Berkeleyanism, phenomenalism, and positivism no less sharply than materialism does, indeed more so.

Without nervous systems, nothing in size between the entire cosmos and microorganisms indicates sentient individuality. The signs of sentience are three. Two of these are movement and integrity

—or, putting them together, *acting as one.* A tree is like a termite colony, both of these act, but neither acts strictly as one. Growth is cell activity, and what a termite colony "does" is shorthand for what termites do. To say that without a nervous system there can be no feeling is not cogent logic; what is logical is that without a nervous system there is nothing *closely* similar to *animal* feeling. Equally without a stomach there is no digestion closely similar to animal digestion. But it is a leap in the dark to say there is no feeling or digestion of any kind. Amoeba do digest. To say they don't feel is at best a blind guess.

Why, however, is the earth not, as Fechner thought, a sentient individual? It does move as one. This brings us to the third sign of sentience or mind. Action motivated by a single subject involves freedom and is not strictly predictable. The earth's motion is extremely predictable. Volcanic action (like tropical storms) is not very predictable in our present knowledge, but we understand easily enough why this is so, nor does anything we know support the idea that the earth feels or intends the activities in a volcano. The primitive psychic life in the microconstituents seems in principle capable of explaining the eruptions.

Edwards sets aside metaphysical proponents of psychicalism and focuses on those who regard it as a contingent truth that happens to obtain in this actual world. But I, like Leibniz, Peirce, and Whitehead, regard the matter otherwise. We think *any* genuinely conceivable world would be psychical. "Mind," said Peirce, "is the sole self-intelligible thing . . . and the fountain of existence." If you ask, Does not a mind need a body? Our answer is, "Yes, but a body [as Leibniz said] consists of sentient subjects in certain subordination to a dominant subject." Our experiences feel the feelings of at least some of our subordinate subjects (in the central nervous system). To God all subjects are subordinate, so the Cosmic body is the incarnation of deity. Even particles have neighboring ones as their body. I know too little to spell this out, but it makes sense to me in principle.

The essential question is, Does the idea of mere, wholly mindless matter make sense? If it does, then there should be some criterion of the total absence of feeling in large portions of space-time. Descartes had a criterion, extension. Even he finally saw that this won't do, because pain is *extended and yet psychical.* Popper has a criterion, absence of memory. He does not claim absolute cogency for his view here. The mind is perceiving as well as remembering, perhaps mere perceiving can occur. Moreover, even perceiving gives us the past not the absolute present, according to Whitehead (and some Buddhists) and, because *causality* means the influence upon, at least partial determination of, the present by the past, how could science establish the total absence of memory in every possible sense and form? I like to call perception *impersonal memory.* What we normally call *memory* is awareness of our own past; perception is awareness of our neighbors' past, including that of our cells, our intimate subordinates.

Now that physics has given up trying to find wholly inactive singulars, or singulars acting wholly predictably, why retain the idea of mere matter as a positive alternative to mind (which by its very meaning is activity, and partly unpredictable activity), also why not give up the idea that we must either add physics to psychology or else reduce psychology to physics. The former procedure implies a dualism opaque to any possible knowledge, the latter seems fairly obviously absurd. Instead we can suppose that a completely generalized comparative psychology or sociology would ideally include the active singulars dealt with in physics, chemistry, and evolutionary biology. That we cannot imagine vividly and distinctly the feelings of atoms or molecules is not very surprising. Even other human beings are puzzling enough, or we ourselves at times. With all our science we are not very much like God, beyond what we already were before science in having language with its symbolic capacity to refer to universals as well as particulars, to other kinds of animals, to animality as such, or birth and death as such, and to formulate ideas like those of the universe, and the soul or mind of the universe. We are not the universe, or the mind of the universe. What is it like to be a whale? Mystery will remain, regardless of scientific progress. Such is our human condition.

A basic problem for science not dealt with in the Edwards article is to relate qualities (sweet-sour, pleasure-pain, red-yellow-green-blue-black and white—a long list) to structures (vibration rates, wave-lengths, mass). Only the structures appear in the world as described by physicists, unless talking about human experiences of the world. Psychology is the science that cannot decently refuse to discuss quality. Neither physics nor psychology has as yet any official solution of the relation between the two ways of depicting the world. To speak of the "emergence" of new forms of behavior-structures, as one passes from physics to chemi stry to biology, and then also use *emergence* for the relation between qualitiless matter and qualitied matter is a category mistake, for there is a logical type difference between structure and quality. This is why Wright, biologist, Whitehead, physicist and logician, Troland, engineer and psychologist, and several other American and English psychologists not mentioned by Edwards, were psychicalists. I hold that quality in a molecule is neither rationally deniable nor definitely knowable in its particularity by us. Nor, for practical use of molecules, do we need to know it. For that use molecular behavior-structures suffice. But theoretical purposes transcend such direct uses. For logical, aesthetic, and religious reasons our view of the general cosmic status of quality (and value) influences our behavior, and in this sense its consideration is pragmatically significant. Qualitiless physical objects have no legitimate role in a livable world-view. We experience the world only as qualited. Qualiti*less* matter is a fiction, not a given actuality. Whitehead told me that this was his reason for rejecting materialism (and dualism). Independently, it had long been mine. I had also learned that it was a reason for Leibniz's and Berkeley's idealisms, as well as Croce's, Bosanquet's, and Bradley's. My book on sensation spells out the argument. R. B. Perry tried to refute such arguments; many anti-idealists adopt what I term the method of convenient ignorance. Perhaps, we all use it. But we can with luck correct each other.

My personal religious view has been stated in many writings and in various ways. I offer here one more. There is a short lyric (twelve lines) by Edward Möricke on "New Love" that, in brilliant verbal music, to my mind sums up the mystical aspect of belief in God. It concludes with an only clumsily translateable pun:

Ich wundert das es mir ein Wunder wollte setn
Gott selbst zu eigen haben auf der Erde.

(I marveled that to me a marvel it had seemed
God's very self to have upon the earth.)

In other words, God (unlike any human lover) loves us adequately, is above jealously, envy, or malice, will not *misunderstand us in any way.* And God will *always be there* with undiminished wisdom and appreciation. No human person, no earthly species, can be known to provide this ideal spiritual support. Indeed we reasonably know that only God could do this.

In another poem, a sonnet on "the beloved," the poet first considers his wonderful good fortune in having the human companion he completely loves, but then he considers the precarious aspects of our existence and realizes that his possession of her is not unqualified. He thinks of the divine or cosmic background and looks up toward the heavens (it is night): "There smile all the stars, he listens to their song of lights." Möricke was a humanist in the good sense, but he did not pretend that our species on or in this minute bit of rock, gas, and liquid is the locus of all value. We cannot be absolutely superior to all else, or in any sense central to the whole, and it is our privilege to know this.

I now add another German poet, Goethe. His final word or bottom line seems to be the magically musical chorus in Faust:

Alles vergängliche	*(All that is perishable)*
Ist nur ein Gleichness	*(Is only a likeness)*
Das Unzulängliche	*(The insufficient)*
Hier hat es Ereigness	*(Here it takes place)*
Das Unbeschreibliche	*(The indescribable)*
Hier wird es getan	*(Here it is done)*
Das Ewig Weibliche	*(The eternal feminine)*
Zieht uns hinan.	*(Draws us along.)*

Those who feel the glory of heterosexual love at its best, I suppose, more readily respond to the last two lines than those who do not feel this. I incline to see a kind of feminism in the poem, and there are other expressions of this in Goethe.

As a male feminist of conviction I cannot entirely refuse to see in the chorus and its ending an indication that Goethe really, or almost, grasped the point that femininity is closer than masculinity to the truly eternal and fundamental, or to the divine. The Taoists also seem to see the point. Much Western theology (and some Chinese) I dare to say, has been, viciously over-masculine. I agree here with Allan Watts. Goethe, in *Die Wahlverwandschaften*, pays eloquent tribute to marriage. There are, the title implies, relationships that are thrust upon us, but in marriage we to some extent choose our relativities. In this way the great poet makes amends for his sometimes questionable behavior to women. He also did marry.

When Goethe speaks of likenesses (allegories?), or of insufficiency and indescribability, as universal to the perishable or transitory, I see a partial recognition of the truth that the qualities of beauty (found in contrast as well as similarity) in human (and all nondivine) living, which is always imperfect and (like everything concrete) only abstractly and deficiently describable, yet achieves its final meaning in the contribution it makes to the experiences and memories of others, and inclusively to the universal Other, the everlasting Thou. In other words, contributionism and objective immortality in God as consequent.

In one respect Goethe and Whitehead were alike: they did not accept the idea that the other creatures are there merely for their use to the one human species. I personally would not attribute this view to Jesus. As a medieval mystic had it, "all the forms of being are dear to the infinite being." None are loved merely for their use to some other form. Any reasonable theistic psychicalism or idealism should agree with this. On the other hand, neither Goethe nor Whitehead would agree with those radical equalitarians who talk as though an earthworm were as important as a human person, or anything like that.

With the great poet I pair another German, Beethoven, with whom he was acquainted and with whom he was, it is said, once walking when they met a member of the nobility. To the latter Goethe bowed deeply and said a few words, whereas the composer simply walked on, until, (as Goethe caught up with him), he said—"There are two of us; there are a thousand of them." Like Shakespeare (see the sonnets) these two persons knew that *they*, unlike the kings and dukes, were for the ages not just for their own time. Recall, too, that the brave man who composed great music even when he was too deaf to hear it and who, although for whatever reason he never married, yet paid to marriage and valiant womanhood the glorious tribute of *Fidelio*. In addition he passed judgment on Napoleon—when that sinister genius had himself made emperor—by remarking, as he erased the name of the great slaughterer from the manuscript of the *Eroica* symphony, "Just another one who wants power!" A similar man was Mozart, whose capacious soul needed both the Christianity of his time and Masonism at its best (as in his *Magic Flute*), and in addition, in *Ideomeneo*, voiced with wonderful eloquence the highest political ideals of his time and place. Verdi in *Don Carlos* also comes to mind.

Returning to Napoleon, two novelists, Leon Tolstoy and H.G. Wells, saved some of us, if we needed to be thus saved, from undue admiration for the military adventurer and his half-mad career (ominous precedent for the more than half-mad egoist Hitler). Another novelist, Henry Fielding, in his *Jonathan Wilde, Great Man*, satirically stated his opinion of the outstanding killers and robbers of history, the Alexanders and the rest. The world gave little heed to this, as it did to Peacock's warning about the eventually suicidal character of technological warfare. Now we begin to see—as Kant thought he saw—that war itself has become the enemy. Note, however, that George Washington was not mad and the English king of the time was the presumptuous one.

One more German composer (who, however, lived much of his adult life in England) seems to belong here. Not many years ago a musical play was given called *The Great Mr. Handel*. This simple designation illustrates how much can be done with a few words. "Mr." gives the sex and age (no longer a child or youth); "the great" betokens uniqueness and furnishes a beautifully adequate title—no need for Doctor, Professor, President, or what have you— simply a greatness like no other then in England. Alas, the beautiful musical play *Amadeus*, about Mozart, was somewhat tarnished by its belittling of this marvelous human being. To be fair, one must acknowledge that neither Mozart nor his wife, Constance, had the fortitude and practical wisdom to deal well with their society's underestimation of art and of the abilities and needs of women. Two women writers, Marcia Davenport and Brigid Brophy tell the story.

Another musical play, *South Pacific*, has in it a truly superb song of which Americans can be proud, even though it illustrates one of their greatest national shames—racism. A young American woman in the play is beginning to fall in love with a Frenchman who lives on a tropical island. She is shocked when she learns that he is a widowed husband of a native wife and father of her children. To the American's explanation of how this discovery troubles her, that it is "an inborn feeling," he replies with a sharp denial: "You have to be taught to hate the people your relatives hate." What bitter irony! The producer asked Rogers and Hammerstein, who were making the play from a book by James A. Michener, to omit the song as too controversial. They appealed to Michener, who told them that without this song the main point would be lost. They kept it in, and of course it was a peak moment in the performance. In these two creators of musical drama, the country enjoyed something, I suppose, not equal to the British pair Gilbert and Sullivan, but nearer to it than most such dramatist-composer collaborations, and truly American.

One aim of this book has been to illustrate the proposition that some people simply are good to know, quite apart from anything they do for others additional to their being as they are and showing their friends in daily life that they are so. One of these was our neighbor in Atlanta E.L. Floyd, others were my cousins Tina and Carol Hartshorne, my nurse friend Caroline Robelen, my boyhood friend Dick Bowers, my mother and all my brothers, who learned from her. There are two young women among the interviewers of the television station C-Span, especially one of them, that give me a similar impression of transparent goodness and inner beauty. (In saying this I am not to be supposed to have disparaged any of the other interviewers in this remarkable organization.)

To return to technical philosophy. Among the points that I take seriously in Peirce's doctrines are two. One is that all definite systematic knowledge is best stated as a brand of pure or applied mathematics. All my books illustrate this principle, however inadequately. The mathematics may be childishly simple— as in the sixteen possi-

ble combinations, apart from permutations, of two theological concepts as applied to two subject matters, allowing for zero cases of
nonapplication. The other point is that the most fundamental branch
of applied mathematics is what Peirce (as well as Husserl) called
Phenomenology — or, at first, *Phaneroscopy*. In this I find him superior to Husserl , though I think Husserl — and Heidegger — must have
given me (and many others) some help. They force one to find one's
own focus in this matter. I achieved this by somewhat revising Peirce's
neo-Pythagorean categories, utilizing also Whitehead's epoch-making
concept of prehension and employing both great philosophers' ideas
to clarify and strengthen my own intuitive Phenomenology, begun
when I was a medical army private in a beautiful French landscape,
reflecting upon the relations of sensation and feeling. Fourteen years
later, in my first book, I took also into account the results empirical
psychology had then reached about sensation. Here, too, Peirce and
Whitehead were relevant, as was Troland of Harvard.

It has been said (by Edith Wharton, I think) that there are those
who light new candles and those who are mirrors reflecting candles
lighted by others. Whitehead did both, especially the former. The
same with Peirce. I try to do both and dare to hope with some success. With my seventy years of mentally alert adult experience in
knowing and reading philosophers and scientists, I have at least
reflected a great many and some very bright candles. Like Newton, we
should try to stand on the shoulders of giants. They are not all in
one's own generation, or even one's own milennium. We can also learn
from simply good and sensible people.

I think my final word must be to acknowledge the debt I feel to
the human and cosmic context from which I have received so much
more than some others have, and my wish that even at this late time
in my life I could do more to repay this debt. The disadvantaged are
there, in this country and without; the rich-poor dichotomy is not
being reduced, anything like equality of opportunity is still eluding
us. Marx has not shown the way here, but neither has free enterprise
as so far instituted. Mortimer Adler, among professional philosophers, has courageously and I think helpfully tried, in his *Common
Sense of Potitics*, to deal with this problem, as have Liberation Theologians, and some recent German and French writers, I honor them,

and some other American contemporaries, also the English scientist-novelist C.P. Snow, for emphasizing the aspects of oppression and dismal poverty in the Third World and to some extent in all the world. We scold the Germans for not feeling shame because of their country's shocking behavior in WWII and before it. What about our shocking behavior in Vietnam, and (I cannot but feel) in Latin America. Also the ignorance of our population is shocking. Geographically, racially, in terms of comparative religion what did our leaders, what did our soldiers, really understand of the problems they faced in that Asian war?

Over and over we hear stories about failures of our international intelligence service's covert operations. I have yet to hear of a convincing case in which such an operation had clearly good results. Before the Bay of Pigs a student of mine who had been to Cuba knew how hopeless that project was.

Life is hope, or nothing much. So let us hope and struggle, admitting that for a powerful country we need to try extra hard to avoid collective conceit or our power may be our undoing, and perhaps our allies' undoing as well. The essential tasks more and more clearly are global. Our president seems to know this. Gorbachev seems to know it. So there are grounds for hope.

"It was the best of times. It was the worst of times"—so Dickens begins his book on the French Revolution. Perhaps this fits our time even better. At least, it is not a dull time. Dramatic things are happening. Some of them are better than most of us had hoped for.

Name Index

Topic Index